Male and Female

No-man's land
MANNEd Space shuttz

Male
and
Female

A Study of the Sexes in a Changing World, by

MARGARET MEAD

Morrow Quill Paperbacks   New York

Library of Congress Cataloging in Publication Data

Mead, Margaret, 1901–1978
    Male and female.

    "Morrow quill paperbacks."

    Bibliography: p.
Includes index.
    1. Sex.   2. Women.   3. Man.   I. Title.
[HQ21.M464   1980]   305.3   80-10592
ISBN 0-688-07028-0

Printed in the United States of America

1   2   3   4   5   6   7   8   9   10

The substance of this book

was given as

THE JACOB GIMBEL LECTURES

IN SEX PSYCHOLOGY

under the auspices of

Stanford University and the University of California

San Francisco, California

November, 1946

INTRODUCTION FOR THE

APOLLO EDITION, 1967

ONE OF THE PRIVILEGES OF THE MODERN PUBLISHING WORLD, if one lives long enough, is the opportunity to comment on the continuing relevance or irrelevance of one's work as successive editions appear. Anthropological descriptions of primitive and exotic peoples have a special position, because the conditions they describe usually have altered irreversibly, even a few years afterwards. But these descriptions cannot be revised; originally faithful to the recorded events, they stand. And if this work contained only descriptive ethnography, there would be no reason to write a new introduction.

However, in this book I attempted to place the descriptive materials on the South Sea cultures, which I had studied between 1925 and 1939, within a contemporary context. By the time that the first paperback edition was published in 1955, the American scene had already changed so much that a new introduction—with special apologies to the birds and the bees—was in order. I had expected, when I completed this book in 1947, that American life would readjust itself to a pattern more like that of the pre-World War II era. The Korean War changed all that, and instead we moved into the 1950's—a period in which the flight to suburbia, togetherness, the increasing involvement of young fathers in domesticity, and a general lack of involvement with wider ethical or political issues was the rule. So, in 1955 I wrote my first new introduction.

But by 1962, when a new Pelican edition was to be issued in England and I was again given an opportunity for second thoughts, a still different phase was under way. When I wrote my second new introduction, I confidently hoped it might stand for the next few years. Now, however, five years later, it is necessary to comment on many new things that are happening.

Our marriage forms are altering again, as young people treat sexual freedom—which ranges all the way from freedom to use four-letter words to the freedom to engage in premarital intercourse—as part of their new bill of rights. This unformulated bill also includes a whole new series of other demands: the abolition of the military draft (which often includes the complete rejection of the Vietnamese war), the right to determine the content and conduct of the educational institutions which they attend, and the right to vote at eighteen. A demand for contraceptive information for the unmarried, as well as for the right to use psychedelic drugs, now parallels demands for boys to wear long hair and girls to wear slacks or nothing at all on their legs.

The hope of the early 1960's that the fear of nuclear warfare would be a really effective deterrent to war has been dimmed by the sobering picture of the conflict between India and Pakistan, the continuing upheavals in Africa and the Middle East, and the war in Vietnam. It is now better recognized that warfare is a quite different kind of threat to humanity than it has ever been before, and that each generation of mankind carries a tremendous burden of responsibility for the whole human race. The rejection of any form of killing is becoming more widespread, but the hopes that young men might be reared to know they must never kill are, at least temporarily, fading. The demand for new forms of self-expression and self-validation is growing, together with an increasing interest in comparative animal behavior. And indeed, the aggressive assertiveness toward rivals and the aggressive protection of territory, as demonstrated by innate behavior of animals, are worth thinking about. At the same time, we are becoming more acutely aware that new forms of physical expression must be found for boys and young men. Some form of guaranteed annual income, to cope with the effects of automation, is also becoming a possibility. At the same time, educated married women are being pressured to go back into the labor market, as a major source of relatively skilled and competent manpower. The anti-poverty drive and the increased emphasis on the horrors of the ghetto, the deterioration of the inner city, the segregation of the suburbs, have combined with the civil rights movement to shift interest back toward improved city living. This shift of interest opens the way to many possible changes—different age groups living closer together, young families better able to cooperate, more community service careers, and less approval of the isolation of the aged.

Recent developments in biology, combined with worldwide recognition of the population explosion, are being reflected in our falling birthrate, and in the demand for smaller families and more careful rearing of children. The past need for an expanding population is being replaced by a demand for a balanced population, both in the United States and abroad. With this demand, a new willingness to back research on contraception, to challenge abortion legislation, to prevent the continued breeding of illegitimate children, all are mingling together, as forward- and backward-looking sex

ethics battle with each other. Increasing use of the contraceptive pill opens up the possibility of young marriages without children, to replace the present style in which pregnancy
or the fear of pregnancy is used as a club to make girls' parents agree to premature, economically nonviable marriages.
Clergy, parents, and educators are all questioning the controls on premarital sexual freedom. In response to increased
preoccupation with sex at every level, the mass media have
all become more outspoken as more publications sold openly
on newsstands became frankly pornographic. Members of a
public who in childhood received sex education on the
streets, in the barroom, or in whispers over backyard fences,
are now avidly uncritical toward the treatment of sex in the
mass media and in books.

Where ecumenicism was just emerging in 1962, it is now
spreading, and new controversies have broken out over the
significance of the claim that God is dead, and on the validity of religious experience triggered by psychedelic drugs.
The young are expressing themselves bodily, in forms designed to be viewed on TV rather than read about in magazines. Demonstrations characterized by strange and conspicuous body positions—sit-in, lie-in, sleep-in, bleed-in, be-
in, love-in (in ice-cold ponds on the edge of Spring)—have
replaced the poster and the handout. Clothes and hairdos
have become vitally important indications of ethical and political attitudes. We have moved to a more visual period,
where 'what is seen is more important than what is read, and
what is experienced directly is valued over what is learned
secondhand.

All this has repercussions in the relationships between
men and women. Men are being pulled more and more into
domestic roles, and it is possible that their new hairdos and
clothes may be an expression of a rebellion—against domesticity (or against war). Women are being drawn into the
world of work, and into an increasingly aggressive competi-

tion for mates. The fact that so many children of divorced parents have four parents to contend with may be one condition for shifting and promiscuous sex relationships among the married. It is possible that among all these changes individuality may again have a chance to appear, and young men and women may again think of themselves first as persons, and second as members of a sex. Perhaps friendship and marriage, as relationships that are ends in themselves and not purely utilitarian ways of validating status, may again emerge. Beneath the tumult and the shouting, a new way of life is being born—suited to a balanced population, to warfare that is controlled although not yet abolished, to leisure born of machines, and to freedom from many of life's later ills and fears. But it is unlikely that the basic dynamic provided by two sexes will disappear, even though it may take new and unforeseen forms.

Margaret Mead

American Museum of Natural History
May 8, 1967

INTRODUCTION FOR THE

PELICAN EDITION, 1962

ONE OF THE PLEASANT BY-PRODUCTS OF PUBLICATION IN PAPER-
backs is the opportunity it provides for second thoughts.
I am not, it is true, one of those authors who responds cheerfully to reviewers who insist that one should have written a
different book or at least one without so much about "those
natives." In fact, anthropology is a field in which the original
statements describing primitive peoples can stand forever;
for the peoples we have described will have changed so
much that no restudy of their lives can introduce very many
corrections into the record of what they once were. Had I
not been induced in 1927 by my imaginative first publisher
—William Morrow—to include comparative chapters on the
ways of American adolescents in that period in *Coming of
Age in Samoa*—and found on the whole that this practice
seemed a useful one, I would have still less to say. But today
the section of this book that deals with American behavior
is extraordinarily out of date, far more out of date in fact
than are the closing chapters of *Coming of Age in Samoa*,

written twenty years earlier. The Korean War marked a turning point in American attitudes towards marriage and the family and established as a permanent trend what we had regarded as a Second World War adjustment. So here, in my comparative descriptive account of American manners, very drastic additions are needed. Some of these I indicated in the preface to the original American paperback edition, the New American Library Mentor edition, published in 1955. But in the necessarily final descriptions of primitive peoples' former ways of life, or the lives of people like the Balinese, whose isolated exotic culture is now being absorbed by modern Indonesia and influenced by its social struggles, a sentence written in ignorance of later vicissitudes will have a different ring from one written before these events occurred. This inevitable hindsight must of course at all costs be kept out of the original descriptions or they lose their validity. But the fact that since this book was written I have made a complete restudy of the Manus—who had skipped some 2000 years of possible slow change during the twenty-five years between my visits to them—and that I made a brief reconnaissance visit to Bali in 1957, just at the point when the Dutch were finally being forced out of Indonesia, and found the children born within the previous twenty years since I studied Bajeung Gede village studying geometry, introduces new overtones into my previous evaluative statements, which must also be recorded.

Also, there have been many developments in anthropological theory since this book was completed. Fifteen years have elapsed within which the vivid interaction between cultural theory and observations and experiments on other living creatures, primates, ungulates, and birds, have given us new insights into biologically given behavior and possible types of more specifically instinctive behavior in man. New material has accumulated on early forms of man, extending our horizons retrospectively. The renewed interest in evolution which surrounded the Darwin centennial has combined with experimental work by psychiatrists to provide new concepts for the reinterpretation of Freud's original findings.

In the wider climate of opinion of which this book was both intentionally and inevitably a part, there have been enormous changes. While a few of us were aware of the tremendous alterations in man's relationship to man that had been set in motion by the new forms of communication, the discovery and use of nuclear weapons, the growing strength of communist evangelism, and the growth of population all over the world, public opinion had not yet reckoned with these problems. Other changes that would accompany the exploration of space were still treated as science fiction. The battle between science and religion, which had been such a prominent part of nineteenth-century thought, had not been abandoned to the point that Sir Julian Huxley would be writing a preface to a book by a devout Jesuit, or that Roman Catholic American school children would be learning with devotion about the contributions of Galileo and Darwin. The full implication of the population problem had not been realized. No oral contraceptive was in sight. The whole question of population had not yet been faced with the determination of the peoples of both overdeveloped and underdeveloped countries to increase the size of their families—although for quite different reasons. In brief, we lived in a very different world in 1947; the danger that the human race might be totally destroyed was less vivid and our freedom to wax indignant over small matters was the greater. Those matters over which I did fulminate have proved quite as disastrous as I feared, however. We are still handling the question of breast feeding very badly; on the one hand, failing to support the possibility that all mothers should have a chance to try to breast feed, and, on the other, forcing definitions of being rejecting mothers on mothers whose infants do not thrive on their breast milk. In the field of sex relations themselves we have had fifteen years of over-glorification of simple copulation under the unequal but effective aegis of the Kinsey Report and *Lady Chatterley's Lover*. These works of the statistician and the day-dreaming novelist have contributed neither to the growth of any sense of individuality—within which sex becomes one facet of human development—nor to responsibility, as the sex act itself is willfully split off from its part in the whole biologically given chain of maturation, reproduction, and parenthood. Our tolerance of any form of psychosexual life except serial togetherness, in which pairs form and reform without responsibility for the effect their mating may have on themselves, on their contributions to society, and on their children, has decreased; the castigation of the single, the fear of the invert, the practice of twentieth-century forms of shotgun marriages, and the insistence upon a continuous sex life throughout life as something as necessary as digestion—and indeed very like it—have increased.

All these trends have gone further in the United States than in other English-speaking countries, I believe, but are also found wherever the effect of mass media and the treatment of studies like the Kinsey Report, or the works of D. H. Lawrence, as if they were mass media prescriptions for real life, are the issue; what happens in the United States today may well happen in Canada and the United Kingdom tomorrow, and is a legitimate cause for continuing concern. This is especially so now that our models must do for the whole technologically underdeveloped world as well as for ourselves.

In the immediate post-Second World War period, a new style was set on college campuses by married veterans with government allowances for continuing their education. Cramped quarters and small incomes brought student fathers and young infants close together, and a new style in fatherhood developed. But in 1947, there seemed every reason to believe that student marriages, young wives working to sup-

port husband and children, and fathers' active participation
in the care of young infants would taper off, and we would
experience a return to the earlier conditions of individual
responsibility and small families, with young fathers principally involved in making a living and mothers involved
with the care of a home and one or two children. But the
Korean War introduced a new note of pessimism into American life, reviving the insecurities of the depression years and
the *carpe diem* philosophy of wartime. Parents and educational institutions acceded to the demand for student marriage, young fathers continued to take care of infants, the
demand for early marriage, as well as early parenthood, accelerated. Instead of the dating behavior of the 1930's and
1940's, earlier and earlier actual mate selection became the
rule, with the parents and the community supporting and
insisting upon routines of courtship among younger and
younger pre-adolescents. With these new conditions, parents
obtained a control over their children's courtship choices
which they had not had in the whole of American history,
where wide opportunities and free land made it possible for
sons to defy their parents and women to marry without
dowries. But today parents who must first provide the setting
for courtship for boys and girls too young to drive cars, and
who later must contribute financially to marriages while the
young husbands are still studying, are able to influence their
children's choices substantially. The result is marriage within
narrower limits of class and religious groupings, and instead
of the former expectation of incompatibility among the two
sets of grandparents, co-grandparents today expect to be
congenial allies in the support of their dependent married
children. The complexities of pre-marital sex behavior have
altered; in addition to the onus placed on girls to maintain
their virginity in unchaperoned situations, there is now a
second phase, the attempt of boys who have selected a girl
to resist the girl's relaxation of controls once she feels she has

found a suitable mate. With the whole society attuned to early marriage and immediate parenthood, with young men substituting marriage and parenthood for maturity once based on work and financial responsibility, and with young families competing with each other in the production of children, there is a general connivance in pre-marital pregnancies in appropriate pairs of young people, a form of behavior which is reminiscent of the courtship patterns of peasants in parts of Europe, where pre-marital sex relations occurred in a setting of parental watchfulness and control.

These complex conditions have now resulted in a style of courtship and marriage which places heavy burdens on adolescent boys as well as on adolescent girls. Marriage before the development of earning power sufficient to support a family has become a regular expectation in the educated classes. The girl leaves school or college to work at some menial but remunerative task so as to make her future motherhood possible, or to have a succession of babies which results in the boy's adding to his studying heavy extra work and heavy domestic responsibilities. The continued sense that it is necessary to seize life now and experience all of it at once means that young couples go heavily into debt in order to provide their children with the kind of home for which an earlier generation would have saved for years. An increasingly high standard of living overburdens husband and wife both inside, and often outside, the home. On the other hand, the standards of companionship and communication between husband and wife, between parents and children, are high, have perhaps never been higher. The breach between adolescent children and parents, so characteristic of middle-class American culture a generation ago, has narrowed, although it is still found in new ethnic immigrant groups or new migrants into the middle class.

Ideals of romantic love have decreased in importance and been replaced by a hope of marrying the *right kind* of girl

or boy, and attaining the ideal marriage. But standards for
this ideal marriage are still extremely high, and marriages
break up easily when the actuality does not conform to the
romanticized view of married togetherness and suburban living. There is a sharp discrepancy between the views of the
middle-aged, who see the demand for early marriage as a
demand for continuous easily accessible sex satisfaction by
adolescents, and the behavior of young people themselves,
who are collectively following a style rather than making individual bids for romantic love or legalized sex opportunities.

Several other trends which may be accentuated by this
present style or early dependent parenthood are being recognized: the plight of the half-educated woman whose children
are already grown, the high male death rate in middle age,
the aimless lives of older women, with neither husbands nor
children to care for, the isolation of the divorced or widowed
mothers of young children. In summary, it may be said that
the distribution of roles between the sexes and the generations in the United States has undergone a profound transformation, with a focus upon very young marriage, early
parenthood, large families, and emotional self-sufficiency of
each such unit, isolated in suburbia, strenuously seeking a
romantic realization of a dream in a glamorized actuality
rather than a distant future. This turning in upon the home
for all satisfaction, with a decrease in friendship, in community responsibility, in work and creativeness, seems to be
a function of the uncertainty about the future which is characteristic of this generation. The care of very young infants
by their fathers is something that no former civilization has
encouraged among their educated and responsible men. Delight in motherhood has been recognized as a principal barrier to women's creativeness in work, but there is now added
the danger that delight in parenthood may prove equally
seductive to young men.

It seems apparent, in spite of the efforts of some self-conscious nations—Japan, the Soviet Union, India—to limit births, that a central problem of the century—second only to the prevention of catastrophic war—is the question of whether individual self-realization, by both men and women, is to be seen in biological or in social terms. We face a period when the individual contribution of both men and women, as initiating, innovating, inventing, creating beings, was never more needed, but where this individual contribution is being smothered by a competing style of immoderate biological self-replication.

In the theoretical background, as opposed to the descriptive and normative content of this book, I would, if I were writing it today, lay more emphasis on man's specific biological inheritance from earlier human forms and also on parallels between *Homo sapiens* and other than mammalian species. I believe I underestimated the fruitfulness of comparisons between human beings and birds, for example, where the importance of vision, the requirements of shelter, and two parents for the care of the young provide more than a pretty figure of speech for explaining the facts of life to children.

In 1947, I stressed the need for social devices that would modulate competition between the individuals who made up the human family, a need met by the universal incest taboo. Clinical materials collected during the last fifteen years have underlined the fragility of such taboos and the danger that they may break down where the social sanctions are inappropriate. Present evidence suggests that there are no reliable innate defenses against primary incest, and that each society must build its own taboos and must overhaul and redesign them when they become ineffective.

As a counterpoint to our present over-emphasis on the biological function of the incest taboo as a protection against mental defects has gone an under-emphasis upon the continuing relationship of spouses to whose marriage a child has

been born. It is a curious anomaly of our historically oriented
view of life that a tie through a common parent makes the
relationship between siblings final and irrevocable, but that
a tie through a common child can at present be totally dis-
solved by divorce. As we need new ways of orienting ourselves towards a future in which our children will be the
natives and we the immigrants from another age, the assertion of ties to each other through the future rather than
through the past, through a contributed combination of
genes rather than a passive participation in past combina-
tions may provide useful realignments of our cultural phrasing of our biological inheritance based, as it is, on a relationship between two individuals of opposite sex.

I discussed somewhat fully the current situation of the
young male child who must discipline his impulses towards
a very much larger, stronger, male parent and learn to wait
many years for his own maturity. Today I would include the
hypothesis that this behavior was developed as a biologically
given pattern in earlier human forms, when men matured
much earlier, before the establishment of the learning period
which separates childhood from adulthood today. The crisis
which we call the Oedipus crisis would then be seen to be
the point at which societies of *Homo sapiens* have to deal
with the knitting together of an impulse structure appropriate to a much earlier human form and a culture which is now
postulated on a long period of learning and postponed sexual
maturity. This phrasing is closer to the conventional English
view that strong and potentially dangerous impulses in the
child must be curbed, than to the American insistence that
any defects in children's control of impulsive behavior are to
be laid at the door of faulty parental functioning. It raises
several new questions about the extent to which intractibili-
ties of instinctive endowment may—especially in such large
and heterogeneous societies as our own—affect maturation,
ability to mate, and ability to maintain a biologically nurtur-

ing relationship to offspring. Our view of the possibilities that a benign child-rearing and educational system may eliminate much of the disturbance and malfunctioning found in our modern world may have to be tempered with much more stringent demands for culturally adaptive methods of reconciling or providing for biological discrepancies.

This possibility may be illustrated by the position of breast feeding in a modern population. In a society wholly dependent upon breast feeding, those infants who were unable to thrive on nourishment from their mother's milk died, and mothers with a low capacity for breast feeding were less likely to leave very many offspring. The mother with no alternative means of nourishing her child responded appropriately to an infant who failed to thrive by an increase in anxiety and a reduction in milk. Her biologically adequate behavior resulted in the death of an infant hard to rear and the possibility of bearing another infant who would be easier to rear. With the invention of artificial substitutes for breast feeding, the possibility arose of many infants living who formerly would have died. The probability of any given mother-child pair being a good fit decreases with each generation of such artificially induced survival. To the extent that later individual functioning may be highly dependent upon the infant's experiences during the first year of life, we may expect future populations, artificially preserved by synthetic foods and increasingly effective medical care, to present an increasing number of structural and acquired anomalies of behavior.

Socially we have several possible choices. We may insist on simulating the simpler situation in societies where most breast-fed infants died, by trying to make all mothers breast feed; we may give up breast feeding altogether and produce adequate artificial feeding in all cases; or we may develop ways of choosing between the two methods which will reveal whether or not each nursing couple is in fact a viable unit of nurturing. The decisions we make here will be reflected in, and will reflect, decisions in the fields of sex typing, acceptance of individual differences, of sex roles and of patterns of relationship between the sexes. A recognition of the extraordinary degree to which we are able to keep alive the children of biologically unsuitable matings and biologically mismatched mother-child pairs might lead us to recognize also that we should expect ever increasing diversity of biologically given responses in adult men and women. It should also result in an increasing temperamental discrepancy between mothers and children, and this indicates the need for more (rather than less) freedom of choice in the children.

Experience has shown that the introduction of artificial feeding reduces the infant death rate and that if, after artificial feeding is available, a *selective* amount of breast feeding is also practiced, the infant death rate is reduced still further. We have gone a long way in keeping alive infants who would once have died, in giving glasses to those with poor eyesight, hearing devices to the hard of hearing, prostheses to the crippled. We have gone a long way in insisting on a common style of marriage regardless of temperament or idiosyncratic preference. We have rebelled against any economic order in which men could not afford to marry or to have children. We have been committed to an egalitarianism which attempts to iron out the most gross discrepancies among human beings and between the sexes, and which, in the process, disallows individuality. In trying to give each young couple a full biological life from puberty on, we necessarily neglect individual differences in courtship and in mating. The more young people we succeed in marrying off and keeping married—to someone—the more alike all marriages become. It may well be that a necessary next step may be the exploration of difference and provision for many different styles of self-realization and sex behavior. All over the world, with the spread of modern middle-class standards of medical care, education, and personal relationships, the groups who fall below this standard are being subjected to increasing pressure to conform. While more homes observe hygienic standards, more children learn to read, and more husbands talk to their wives more and beat them less, we should already be considering whether a step beyond this insistent demand that every couple conform to solid parental standards may not be necessary. It is possible that the diffusion of oral contraceptives—especially if they can be cast in a form where it is the choice to have children (that is, the choice that must be made consciously and responsibly)—may provide a new world-wide situation in which individualized forms of sex behavior may begin to develop.

Instead of forcing, as we do now, all boys and all girls into a strait jacket of future expectation of identical types of marriage, with the accompanying need for a multitude of neurotic adjustments, we might diversify our expectations and our styles of life. Thus, from one point of view, the present demand that everyone marry, if necessary again and again and again, and our intolerance of the celibate, the unmarried, the invert, may be seen as an attempt on the part of society to compensate for an increasing actual diversity of endowment and predisposition between parents and children.

In the theoretical discussion of the rhythm of women's lives, I would, writing today, stress some new points. Attention to differences among species highlights two distinctively human female attributes, the hymen and the menopause. Recent clinical work has suggested that the function of the hymen is to decrease young females' erotic awareness of themselves and to give tenderness and the capacity for complex maternal behavior time to mature. If this should prove to be so, the hymen would be an instance of specific evolutionary adjustment comparable to the prolongation of the learning period and the postponement of reproductive potency in both sexes.

I would also stress another aspect of the menopause—its possible evolutionary function in prolonging the lives of women, so making their experience available to the group. Among very early primitive types, females seem to have died earlier than males. So with the menopause cutting down on the period of child bearing, some older women could be preserved to be an important resource to communities whose men died early from the dangers of war and the hunt. If all three of these human traits, the hymen, the prolongation of immaturity, and the menopause, are considered together, these can be seen to provide a rationale for the survival value to early groups of the progressive shrinking of the length of the period of reproduction in proportion to the length of life.

In modern terms, an additional survival factor for women has been introduced in modern medical care for women in pregnancy and childbirth at a period when there is no comparable protection for men. Women's lives have been saved by a decrease in the hazards of childbirth; men's lives await a comparable extension from a reduction of the hazards of their social burdens. If only by analogy, we may ask to what evolutionary use we can put this great body of healthy post-menopausal women, free from a narrowing and engrossing attention to young children. In the present-day world there is increasing talk of the appropriateness of women devoting themselves to the establishment of conditions of world peace. There are even those who have argued that women are inherently more peaceful than men, devoted to life rather than to destruction, and that civilizations which are less even-handed towards the participation of both sexes are likely, lacking a feminine component, to be disproportionately oriented towards power and destructiveness.

On further examination, it would seem that there is little evolutionary basis for this argument. Female animals defending their young are notoriously ferocious and lack the playful delight in combat which characterizes the mock combats of males of the same species. There seems very little ground for claiming that the mother of young children is more peaceful, more responsible, and more thoughtful for the welfare of the human race than is her husband or brother. However, a somewhat better case can be made for the post-menopausal woman, freed from the exacting and self-centered demands of young children, grown wise with many years of care for other human beings, the young, the grieving, the sick, the old. Faced, as her ancient predecessors may have been, with a period of survival beyond her mate, she may find a special role and special usefulness in working for a larger body of mankind. A few preliminary case studies suggest that the knowledge that she will have no children, or no more children, also releases in a woman a kind of wholehearted commitment to art or science or religion, which was previously bound, unavailable, waiting for the specific motherhood that did not come. Focus on a genuine social function for these older women might reduce the present male resentment at laboring at a harvest which will be reaped by women long after they themselves are dead, and increase the possibility of developing a way of life with the cultural protections necessary to prolong men's lives also.

In the light of the urgent necessity for social inventions that will preclude the possibility of world wars that endanger the whole human race, it is also necessary to examine further the various propositions that have been made about the essential nature of the human male, who, with carnivore precursors and a long hunting and war-making past, is often claimed to be inherently combative and destructive. Comparative work on other species has illuminated the great importance of the aggressive behavior with which male birds and beasts protect their females and their young. It seems more fruitful to consider man's behavior towards members of his own species, as in warfare, rather than his behavior as a predator towards members of other species on which he relied and relies for food. To be sure, the long centuries it has taken man to learn that *all* other men, whatever their color or state of technology or religious beliefs, were actually members of his species, have been accompanied by the development both of larger groups, treated as own group, and the relegation of enemy groups to a subhuman or legitimate prey category. An examination of the history of warfare suggests that the kind of warfare which invokes the individual male's protectiveness—protectiveness towards women, children, land, and ideals—calls forth the most sustained fighting. In a world in which warfare was ruled out, it would therefore not be as necessary as many commentators have thought to deal with men's destructiveness and their primary protectiveness could have other uses.

It may be remembered that in the 1920's an attempt to change the position of women was accompanied by an insistence on women's need for sexual climaxes comparable to men's, and the demand that women respond to men became a burdensome demand on them to behave like musical instruments rather than full human beings. The present emphasis on rather simple and unelaborate male phallicism and copulation, devoid of a full context of individuality, may be one accompaniment of the need to re-evaluate the ways in which demands for full maleness are met by the culture. Retreat to phallic athleticism may be an alternative to acceptance of unending domesticity—neither of which is representative of full male potentialities.

It is probable, however, that the young male has a biologically given need to prove himself as a physical individual, and that in the past the hunt and warfare have provided the most common means of such validation. This will be the first time in human history when young men everywhere will have to learn that they may neither kill any member of their own group, for this is murder, nor any member of any group anywhere, for this will endanger all mankind. The promise or threat that someday a boy might be called upon to give his life for his country has provided a historical setting for aspirations to heroism. At this moment in history, young males are in a particularly difficult spot, threatened with a world-wide catastrophe which no individual heroism can prevent and without new means to exercise their biologically given aggressive protectiveness or desire for individual bravery. The necessary virtues of the present age are essentially domestic virtues, virtues that have long been regarded as more appropriate for women—patience, endurance, steadfastness. It is essential that the tasks of the future should be so organized that as dying for one's country becomes unfeasible, taking risks for that which is loved may still be possible. Athletics provide only a partial answer. Possibly the exploration of space, the depths of the sea, and the center of the earth, will provide a more complete answer.

New York   MARGARET MEAD
15 April 1962

REFERENCES

Mead, Margaret, *New Lives for Old: Cultural Transformation, Manus 1928-1953* (New York: William Morrow and Company, 1956); reprinted with a new preface, Apollo A124 (New York: William Morrow and Company, 1966).

———, "Changing Patterns of Parent-Child Relations in an Urban Culture," *International Journal of Psycho-Analysis*, Vol. 38, 1957, pp. 369-78.

———, Participant in *Discussions on Child Development: A Consideration of the Biological, Psychological, and Cultural Approaches to the Understanding of Human Development and Behavior. Proceedings of the Third Meeting of the World Health Organization Study Group on the Psychobiological Development of the Child, Geneva, 1955,* Vol. 3, J. M. Tanner and Bärbel Inhelder, eds. (London: Tavistock; New York: International Universities Press, 1958).

————, "Cultural Contexts of Puberty and Adolescence," *Bulletin of the Philadelphia Association for Psychoanalysis*, Vol. 9, No. 3, 1959, pp. 59-79.

————, "Cultural Determinants of Sexual Behavior," in *Sex and Internal Secretions*, Vol. 2, 3rd ed., ed. William C. Young (Baltimore: Williams and Wilkins, 1961), pp. 1433-79.

————, "The Psychology of Warless Man," in *A Warless World*, ed. Arthur Larson (New York: McGraw-Hill, 1963), pp. 131-42.

————, "Totem and Taboo Reconsidered with Respect," *Bulletin of the Menninger Clinic*, Vol. 27, 1963, pp. 185-99.

————, "Epilogue," in *American Women*, Margaret Mead and Frances B. Kaplan, eds. (New York: Scribner's, 1965), pp. 181-204.

Mead, Margaret, and Ken Heyman, *Family* (New York: Macmillan, 1965).

ACKNOWLEDGMENTS

THE FIELD-WORK ON WHICH THIS BOOK IS BASED COVERS A
span of fourteen years, 1925-1939; the thinking covers the
whole of my professional life, 1923-1948. The field-work
and the research work have been done under several generous auspices: the American Museum of Natural History,
which has sheltered and encouraged me since 1926, and
supported my field-work from the Voss Fund; the National
Research Council; the Committee for Research in Dementia
Praecox supported by the Thirty-third Degree Scottish Rite,
Northern Masonic Jurisdiction; the United States Naval
Government in Samoa; the Social Science Research Council; the Department of Home and Territories of Australia;
the Administration of the Mandated Territory of New
Guinea; the Government of the Netherlands East Indies;
and various agencies of the Government of the United
States. During my long intervals of residence in out-of-
the-way places I have received help from many people,
among whom I specially thank His Honour Judge J. M.

Phillips, C.B.E., Mr. E. P. W. Chinnery, Mr. Edward R. Holt and Mrs. Holt, and the great artist, the late Walter Spies. For collaboration in the field, I am indebted beyond the possibility of adequate acknowledgment to Gregory Bateson, Jane Belo, and Reo Fortune, and our Balinese assistant, I Made Kaler. It is impossible to make articulate to them, or to the world, the debt I owe to those hundreds of people of the Pacific Islands whose patience, tolerance of differences, faith in my goodwill, and eager curiosity made these studies possible. Many of the children whom I held in my arms, and from whose tense or relaxed behaviour I learned lessons that could have been learned in no other way, are now grown men and women; the life they live in the records of an anthropologist must always have about it a quality of wonder both to the anthropologist and to themselves. Out of the main stream of civilization, they preserved the delicate fabric of their cultures, and through this fidelity made a contribution to our contemporary understanding of the potentialities of mankind.

Chronologically, this book represents the developments in my thinking about this particular problem since I published SEX AND TEMPERAMENT in 1935. But it also represents one thread that I have followed throughout my professional life, and expresses my indebtedness for insights gained along the way, particularly from Franz Boas, Ruth Benedict, Luther Cressman, William Fielding Ogburn, Edward Sapir, Reo Fortune, A. R. Radcliffe-Brown, Philip Mosely, Earl T. Engle, Robert and Helen Lynd, Lawrence and Mary Frank, Gregory Bateson, John Dollard, W. Lloyd Warner, Erik Homburger Erikson, Gardiner and Lois Murphy, Kingsley Noble, Geoffrey Gorer, Kurt Lewin, Robert Lamb, Harold Wolff, Gotthard C. Booth, Marie Jahoda, Erwin Schuller, Evelyn Hutchinson, Frances Ilg, Rhoda Metraux, Nathan Leites, Martha Wolfenstein, and Edith Cobb. For help in the preparation of the manuscript I am indebted to my godmother,

Isabel Ely Lord, and to Marie Eichelberger, Marion Marco-vitz, Carol Kaye, Judith Calver, and Catherine Schneider. To my grandmother, Martha Ramsay Mead, to my father, Edward Sherwood Mead, and my mother, Emily Fogg Mead, I owe a belief that knowledge is worth searching for, that observation and analysis can be carried on with an affection constructive both for those who study and for those who are studied, and finally that sense of membership in my own sex which has directed my research work to the study of children.

Margaret Mead

Cobb Web
Falls Village, Connecticut
October 19, 1948

CONTENTS

THE PROBLEMS OF SOCIETY

VIII   Rhythm of Work and Play   163
  IX   Human Fatherhood Is a Social Invention   183
   X   Potency and Receptivity   201
  XI   Human Reproductivity   223

PART FOUR

THE TWO SEXES IN CONTEMPORARY AMERICA

 XII   Our Complex American Culture   245
XIII   Expected Childhood Experience   265
 XIV   Pre-courtship Behaviour and Adult Sex
       Demands   281
  XV   Sex and Achievement   296
 XVI   Each Family in a Home of Its Own   325
XVII   Can Marriage Be for Life?   342
XVIII To Both Their Own   367

       Notes to Chapters   387
       Appendix I. Background and Bibliographical
       Material on the Seven Pacific Island Cul-
       tures: Samoa; Manus; Arapesh; Mundugumor;
       Iatmul; Tchambuli; Bali   403
       Appendix II. The Ethics of Insight-giving   431
       Appendix III. Sources and Experience in Our
       American Culture   451
       Index of Personal Names   465
       Index of Subjects   467

PART ONE

INTRODUCTORY

I

THE SIGNIFICANCE OF THE

QUESTIONS WE ASK

How ARE MEN AND WOMEN TO THINK ABOUT THEIR MALENESS
and their femaleness in this twentieth century, in which so
many of our old ideas must be made new? Have we over-
domesticated men, denied their natural adventurousness,
tied them down to machines that are after all only glorified
spindles and looms, mortars and pestles and digging sticks,
all of which were once women's work? Have we cut women
off from their natural closeness to their children, taught them
to look for a job instead of the touch of a child's hand, for
status in a competitive world rather than a unique place by
a glowing hearth? In educating women like men, have we
done something disastrous to both men and women alike,
or have we only taken one further step in the recurrent task
of building more and better on our original human nature?

These are questions which are being asked in a hundred
different ways in contemporary America. Polls and tracts and
magazine-articles speculate and fulminate and worry about
the relationship between the sexes. In the moving pictures

beautiful girls in tortoise-shell spectacles and flat-heeled
shoes are first humiliated for competing with men, then they
are forgiven, loved, and allowed to be glamorous only when
they admit their error. In the advertisements on the bill-
boards, men are now told how they, if they wear the right
hat, may be the chosen one, the loved one—a rôle that used
to be reserved for women. The old certainties of the past are
gone, and everywhere there are signs of an attempt to build
a new tradition, which like the old traditions that have been
cast aside will again safely enfold growing boys and girls,
so that they may grow up to choose each other, marry, and
have children. The fashions bear the imprint of this uncertainty; the "new look" of 1947 partly captured the fleeting
image of the mothers of a generation ago, the boys could
again find the girls marriageable—as their mothers were—
while those same girls gained a new femininity by suiting
their swinging gait to the remembered feeling of ruffled
skirts like those their mothers once wore. In every pair of
lovers the two are likely to find themselves wondering what
the next steps are in a ballet between the sexes that no
longer follows traditional lines, a ballet in which each couple
must make up their steps as they go along. When he is insistent, should she yield, and how much? When she is demanding, should he resist, and how firmly? Who takes the
next step forward or the next step back? What is it to be a
man? What is it to be a woman?

No single book can hope to do more than touch a question
that is so basic to human life. I have tried, in this book, to
do three things. I try first to bring a greater awareness of the
way in which the differences and the similarities in the
bodies of human beings are the basis on which all our learnings about our sex, and our relationship to the other sex, are
built. Talking about our bodies is a complex and difficult
matter. We are so used to covering them up, to referring to
them obliquely with slang terms or in a borrowed language,

to hiding even infants' sex membership under blue and pink ribbons. It is difficult to become aware of those things about us which have been, and will always be, patterned by our own particular modesties and reticences. We reject, and very rightly, catalogues of caresses arranged in frequency tables, or accounts of childhood that read like a hospital chart. So to make it possible to think vividly, and yet at a comfortable distance, of the way in which our bodies have learned, throughout their lives, how to be male, how to be female, I draw—in the first part of this book—upon the seven South Sea cultures I have studied during the last quarter of a century. Their basic learnings are the same as our basic learnings; each human baby at its mother's breast must learn that it is either of the same sex, or of the opposite sex, from the mother who has borne it, from the father who fathered it. The boy may grow up to carry spears and bows and arrows instead of brief-cases and fountain-pens, but also he must woo and win and keep a woman. The women may wear the scantiest clothing, and spend their days in the simplest tasks, but in their acceptance of their husbands, and in their child-bearing on some green mountain-side, sometimes not even sheltered from the rain, they face their essential woman-hood as surely as the woman who bears her baby in a modern hospital. In following the steps by which their children learn about their sex membership, we can get some sense of the process of learning to be male, learning to be female, some recognition of how we ourselves arrived at our own sense of our own sex; so I have called this section, Part Two, "The Ways of the Body."

In the next section, "The Problems of Society," I draw not merely on the seven South Sea cultures I have studied myself, but on some of the knowledge we have of all human societies, as each has attempted to develop a myth of work, to bind men to women and children, to get the children fed and reared, and to settle the problems that arise whenever

individual sex impulses must be disciplined into social
forms. We can design forms of the family that fit our modern life better if we know what designs have been used in
the past, what are the common elements that no society has
yet found ways of ignoring, how rules about incest have
made it possible to develop family life as we know it. What
does the family do, how does it function, and what is the
relationship between family life, with its strains and its prohibitions, its sacrifices and its rewards, and the natural springing potency of men and the spontaneous slower-flowering
responsiveness of women? Each known human society has
tried to come to grips with these problems, with the incompatibility between man's spontaneity and the monotony of
the domestic hearth, with the over-compatibility between
women's docility and the perpetuation of some tight, outworn tradition. In this age when millions of women are un-
mated and childless, or left alone to bring up their children,
when so many men, restless and unsettled, wander again
over the face of the earth, this old problem is as pressing as
it ever has been, and as inescapable. No people who fail to
meet it survive, as whole human beings.

In Part Four, "The Two Sexes in Contemporary America,"
I come back to the known, the familiar, and the concretely
pressing, to the relationship between the sexes in America
to-day, to childhood and courtship and marriage in these
United States as it looks when seen comparatively—contrasted with the ways of other societies.

And finally, I try to suggest ways in which we, as a civilization, may make as full use of woman's special gifts as we
have of men's, and in so doing develop forms of civilization
that can make fuller use of all human gifts. Each of these
main parts of the book stands by itself. The reader may begin
with human childhood in the South Seas, or with the problems of sex in society, or with sex in the United States to-day
—according to temperament and taste. All three parts stem

from the same method, from the discipline of anthropology, the science of custom, in which we have learned to look at the patterned ways in which men have built upon their common biological inheritance different and challenging human cultures.

THE DIFFERENCES BETWEEN THE TWO SEXES IS ONE OF THE important conditions upon which we have built the many varieties of human culture that give human beings dignity and stature. In every known society, mankind has elaborated the biological division of labour into forms often very remotely related to the original biological differences that provided the original clues. Upon the contrast in bodily form and function, men have built analogies between sun and moon, night and day, goodness and evil, strength and tenderness, steadfastness and fickleness, endurance and vulnerability. Sometimes one quality has been assigned to one sex, sometimes to the other. Now it is boys who are thought of as infinitely vulnerable and in need of special cherishing care, now it is girls. In some societies it is girls for whom parents must collect a dowry or make husband-catching magic, in others the parental worry is over the difficulty of marrying off the boys. Some peoples think of women as too weak to work out of doors, others regard women as the appropriate bearers of heavy burdens, "because their heads are stronger than men's." The periodicities of female reproductive functions have appealed to some peoples as making women the natural sources of magical or religious power, to others as directly antithetical to those powers; some religions, including our European traditional religions, have assigned women an inferior rôle in the religious hierarchy, others have built their whole symbolic relationship with the supernatural world upon male imitations of the natural functions of women. In some cultures women are regarded as sieves through whom the best-guarded secrets will sift; in

others it is the men who are the gossips. Whether we deal
with small matters or with large, with the frivolities of
ornament and cosmetics or the sanctities of man's place in
the universe, we find this great variety of ways, often flatly
contradictory one to the other, in which the rôles of the two
sexes have been patterned.

But we always find the patterning. We know of no culture
that has said, articulately, that there is no difference between men and women except in the way they contribute to
the creation of the next generation; that otherwise in all
respects they are simply human beings with varying gifts,
no one of which can be exclusively assigned to either sex.
We find no culture in which it has been thought that all
identified traits—stupidity and brilliance, beauty and ugliness, friendliness and hostility, initiative and responsiveness,
courage and patience and industry—are merely human traits.
However differently the traits have been assigned, some to
one sex, some to the other, and some to both, however arbitrary the assignment must be seen to be (for surely it cannot be true that women's heads are both absolutely weaker
—for carrying loads—and absolutely stronger—for carrying
loads—than men's), although the division has been arbitrary,
it has always been there in every society of which we have
any knowledge.

So in the twentieth century, as we try to re-assess our
human resources, and by taking thought to add even a jot
or a tittle to the stature of our fuller humanity, we are faced
with a most bewildering and confusing array of apparently
contradictory evidence about sex differences. We may well
ask: Are they important? Do real differences exist, in addition to the obvious anatomical and physical ones—but just
as biologically based—that may be masked by the learnings
appropriate to any given society, but which will nevertheless be there? Will such differences run through all of men's
and all of women's behaviour? Must we expect, for instance,

that a brave girl may be very brave but will never have the same kind of courage as a brave boy, and that the man who works all day at a monotonous task may learn to produce far more than any woman in his society, but he will do it at a higher price to himself? Are such differences real, and *must* we take them into account? Because men and women have always in all societies built a great superstructure of socially defined sex differences that obviously cannot be true for all humanity—or the people just over the mountain would not be able to do it all in the exactly opposite fashion—must *some* such superstructures be built? We have here two different questions: Are we dealing not with a *must* that we dare not flout because it is rooted so deep in our biological mammalian nature that to flout it means individual and social disease? Or with a *must* that, although not so deeply rooted, still is so very socially convenient and so well tried that it would be uneconomical to flout it—a *must* which says, for example, that it is easier to get children born and bred if we stylize the behaviour of the sexes very differently, teaching them to walk and dress and act in contrasting ways and to specialize in different kinds of work? But there is still the third possibility. Are not sex differences exceedingly valuable, one of the resources of our human nature that every society has used but no society has as yet begun to use to the full?

We live in an age when every inquiry must be judged in terms of urgency. Are such questions about the rôles and the possible rôles of the sexes academic, peripheral to the central problems of our times? Are such discussions querulous fiddling while Rome burns? I think they are not. Upon the growing accuracy with which we are able to judge our limitations and our potentialities, as human beings and in particular as human societies, will depend the survival of our civilization, which we now have the means to destroy. Never before in history has mankind had such momentous

choices placed in its hands. True, in the past a small group
of savages could elect to wander too far north and freeze as
the winter came; an angry little band of South Sea Islanders
could bundle themselves into a canoe and sail away into the
sunset never to return; neighbouring tribes could fight a
war that destroyed the culture of both groups and left only
a few battered human remnants who wandered away and
learned the language and followed the ways of some other
social group. Men could sell whole peoples into slavery,
towns and cities could be razed to the ground, colonists
could destroy the very soul-stuff of a people and leave them,
with nothing but their meagre daily bread, to a way of life
far less human than that of the simplest savage; military
machines could regiment whole groups into a strict and impaired social existence and render them unfit for a whole
human life. None of these powers—to kill individuals, to destroy the social integration of groups, and to unravel the
fine mesh of human culture and leave those naked and
ashamed who should have worn it proudly—none of these
powers are new. They are powers man has had in his hands
ever since he began to build a social tradition that contained
the knowledge of how to make weapons as well as tools, of
how to organize armies and practise diplomatic offensives
as well as how to knit together hunting-parties and harvesting groups, a tradition that included the desire to convince
other men that their customs were inferior and their gods
false. But as long as men were scattered over the face of
an earth that it took millennia to populate, and most of those
who started on long journeys did not reach their journey's
end, as long as fifty canoes sank for one that reached another coral atoll, then, though men lived in jeopardy, societies lived in jeopardy, and human cultures were balanced
precariously in the keeping of men who did not know how
to preserve them, nevertheless the great, various, uneven
tradition of human culture itself was safe. True, languages

might vanish altogether, hard as it is to believe that any human invention as complex and perfect as a language—once made, once spoken lovingly by the tongues of old people and growing children—could vanish. Yet languages have vanished, and there are many American Indian languages that we know only in a few texts taken down from the lips of the last human being to speak that language. Our antiquarians pore over the hints of dead languages they find engraved in stone. But the power to have language at all, the assurance that all men who lived in groups would have nouns and verbs, of some phonetic pattern, with which to communicate with each other—that was safe. Because no matter how many languages died, others grew up in other places, among other peoples who were safe from the particular disaster of plague or earthquake or war that had engulfed some other part of mankind and wiped out all record of the language that people spoke.

When those of us who are now middle-aged or old were children, we read in the history books romantic tales of lost arts, and our imaginations were caught first by tales of lost methods of tempering steel or making stained glass, later by the realization that there were whole civilizations which were lost, in that to-day no single man or woman can carry in his gait and bearing, in his speech and way of living, the intricate pattern that had been Greece or Persia, Egypt or ancient Peru. The loss of a useful art—as with the South Sea Islanders who no longer knew how to build canoes and so were forever prisoners on the tiny islands to which they had once come as bold mariners—could give the imaginative a horrid chill. If simple men on islands forgot how to build canoes, might not more complex people also forget something equally essential to their lives? Was it possible that modern man might forget his relationship with the rest of the natural world to such a degree that he separated himself from his own pulse-beat, wrote poetry only in tune with

machines, and was irrevocably cut off from his own heart?
In their new-found preoccupation with power over the
natural world might men so forget God that they would
build a barrier against the wisdom of the past that no one
could penetrate? People asked such questions; poets and
philosophers of an earlier day sensed that mankind might
some day hold too much power in its hands. But however
imaginative we were, however much we wept for the glories
that were Greece or Elizabethan England or Quattrocento
Florence and wondered if human culture would ever be cast
again in such a perfect mould, we were still only taking
spiritual exercises, practising our minds and hearts for
greater sensitivity to our whole human tradition—not dealing with a real and pressing problem.

To-day we live in another world, a world so closely knit
that no smallest group can go down to disaster—by plague
or revolution or by foreign aggression or famine—without
shaking the structure of the whole world. No matter how
much they may wish to do so, it is no longer possible for a
people to keep inventions like gunpowder to use in fire-
crackers rather than in cannon. We are approaching the
place where every step we take not only *may* be important
for the whole world and for the whole of future history, but
where we can almost say it *will* be important for the whole
world. As the culture of each small human society in the
past grew, changed, blossomed or decayed, vanished or was
transformed into some other culture, and no act within that
structure was wholly insignificant for the whole, so to-day
the culture of the world is becoming *one*—one in its interdependence, though far from one in the contrasts and discrepancies within it.

The decisions we make now, as human beings, and as
human beings who are members of groups with power to
act, may bind the future as no men's decisions have ever
bound it before. We are laying the foundations of a way of

life that may become so world-wide that it will have no rivals, and men's imaginations will be both sheltered and imprisoned within the limits of the way we build. For in order to think creatively, men need the stimulus of contrast. We know by sad experience how difficult it is for those who have been reared within one civilization ever to get outside its categories, to imagine, for instance, what a language could be like that had thirteen genders. Oh, yes, one says, masculine, feminine, and neuter—and what in the world are the other ten? For those who have grown up to believe that blue and green are different colours it is hard even to think how any one would look at the two colours if they were not differentiated, or how it would be to think of colours only in terms of intensity and not of hue. Most American and European women simply cannot imagine what it would be like to be a happy wife in a polygamous family and share a husband's favours with two other women. We can no longer think of the absence of medical care as anything but a yawning gap to be filled at once. Inevitably, the culture within which we live shapes and limits our imaginations, and by permitting us to do and think and feel in certain ways makes it increasingly unlikely or impossible that we should do or think or feel in ways that are contradictory or tangential to it.

So, as we stand at the moment in history when we still have choice, when we are just beginning to explore the properties of human relationships as the natural sciences have explored the properties of matter, it is of the very greatest importance which questions we ask, because by the questions we ask we set the answers that we will arrive at, and define the paths along which future generations will be able to advance.

The relationships between men and women and parents and children are the crucial areas of human relationships. As these relationships are patterned, so are they conveyed

to the infant at his mother's breast, who before he can toddle
has absorbed a particular style of sex relations and learned
to rule out other styles.

We can recognize how our experience limits our questions by exploring the possible results of asking different
questions. Suppose we ask: "Aren't women just as capable
of performing activity x as men are?" Or the reverse: "Aren't
men as capable of activity y as women?" Investigations of
this sort usually lead to quantitative comparisons, in which
it may be found that men are a little faster than women, or
women a little faster than men, or that there is no difference.
Or the answer may be a little more complicated, so that
women are found to be slower but more accurate, or men
quicker but lacking in small-muscle precision for the particular task. Once we have given such an answer, then, in
terms of our present culture, employers, or benevolent government agencies, or one sex pressure group will set to work
to exploit these differences or to minimize them, in order
to get better work for the same pay, or to invent a machine
that will equalize the difference. But in either case the discovered differences suggest no new uses of human resources.
They merely increase or decrease the probability that men
and women will work in the same factory; they will primarily be the background not for using differences constructively, but for inventing some methods for equalizing
the differences so that they do not matter, or for pigeon-
holing individuals in one job rather than another.

This is comparable to what we are doing with individuals
with different degrees of acuteness of sight and hearing.
Eye-glasses and hearing devices are eliminating the overt
differences in performance between individuals. Where
keenness of vision was once a vivid ingredient in the personality of a hunter, or a blessed myopia part of the equipment of a poet, we now know the effects upon the personality of having to wear eye-glasses or a hearing device. By

our inventive attempts to equalize the performance of individuals with different capabilities, we enormously increase the number of individuals whose functioning is externally comparable in society, but we disallow those subjective differences which might have also made a contribution to human civilization. The more we ask questions about sex differences only so that we can get rid of them, or exploit them quantitatively, the more likely we are to find ways of eliminating them, both as bases of inequality and waste in the world, and also as bases of diversification of and contribution to the world.

There are of course very many areas in which it is an obvious gain to ask just this kind of question and get a simple quantitative answer with which we can deal inventively. It is nonsense to debar women from activities where their physical strength is only slightly inferior to men's when some simple gadget would make them as efficient as men. It is particularly nonsensical when it is accompanied by elaborate social rationalizations about a task's being unwomanly, or—in the opposite case—unmanly. To the extent that all the members of a sex are automatically debarred from using their talents in some field in which a little objective research would show that they are perfectly fitted to contribute, it is obviously useful to society to break such myths down. If we recognize that we need every human gift and cannot afford to neglect any gift because of artificial barriers of sex or race or class or national origin, then one of the things we must know is where the assumed differences between the sexes are mere elaborations of unimportant differences that can be dealt with easily in this invention-conscious world.

There is perhaps an even more fundamental way in which the questions we ask about the sexes can affect the ground-plan of the world that, willy-nilly, with searching of heart or in utter carelessness, we are now engaged in building. We can ask our questions about sex differences in such a way that we focus on the limitations that sex imposes, and so very directly upon the limitations that our mammalian nature imposes upon us. When we focus on sex differences in terms of limitation, every word we say includes certain deeper assumptions. "How much protection from physical endeavour should a pregnant woman have?" "How much freedom from monotony should a healthy young man have?" "How much physical sex experience is necessary to mental health?" "How many opportunities should a small child—who after all should be likened to a bear-cub, biting and tossing among other cubs—be given to bite, kick, and tear things to pieces?" "And should small males have more such opportunities than small females?" "How much allowance should be made for the periodicities of a woman's life?" All such questions digging deep into our new willingness to come to grips with our biological past, and to build a world that will make due allowance for the limitations imposed by our mammalian nature, embody a sense of limitation. They stress those concessions we must make because *if* we do not make them, then many prices—in health, in happiness of individuals and of societies, in the symmetry and beauty of cultural traditions, in the peace of the world—will have to be paid. We find ourselves constructing a picture in which what have come to be called *basic human needs* are seen as boundaries beyond which we dare not pass, man-holes that must be skirted, or trap-doors that may be opening beneath our feet. Building a world in which human beings can live, or bringing up an individual family, becomes a task rather like building a house with one's eye on the zoning laws and the provisions of the health department, and cooking a dinner with charts of "loss of essential vitamins while cooking" as one's only cook-book. However much one may add to the list of basic human needs, seeing life in terms of needs—at least in our present climate of opinion—means essentially accepting a human nature as a statute of limitation. We may be promised that if we will only explore, list, and carefully satisfy these needs—for vitamins and minerals and so many grams of protein, for rest and liquids and oxygen, for the release of tensions (this is undoubtedly the most correct way to describe making love when the need category is uppermost), for continuous contact with one sensorily identifiable human being throughout the first two years of life, and so on, and so on—then we will be able to build a good society, rear healthy individuals, develop and perpetuate cultural traditions that have no snags or distortions, no murky ambiguities or falsely clear alternatives, and produce a peaceful world.

But such solutions leave us feeling empty and discontented. One has only to watch the faces of an audience while this point is expounded, and expounded as it so often is by those whose optimism and affection for the human race are unbounded and undauntable, to feel that even as the picture of the healthy child, the good society, the balanced, sane culture, and the peaceful world are unrolled before the watching eyes, a pall descends upon the spirits of the listeners. For back of the promise of sturdy little legs protected from the age-old threat of vitamin-A deficiency, of men and women whose clear eyes and jaunty gait assure us that they suffer from none of the pains and penalties of celibacy, the reading posture which shows that an eye-examination is given every year as a routine measure to every schoolchild—back of these looms a sense of limitation. If we take human needs as our only clues to the world we wish to build, we find in our mouths a flat taste. It is not a stale taste, because proper diet, rest, and sex hygiene have taken care of that, but simply a flat taste, and an insistent desire for the disallowed and so contrasting position—a desire for lips that "save themselves hungry and bite blessed bread." [1]*

For out of this demand that we examine our human na-

* Reference notes to all chapters are on pages 387-402.

ture, assess its needs, those of males and those of females, those of little males and little females, old males and old females, those of different physique or different rate of maturation, comes little positive drive. All the prescriptions are negative in the end: How *not* to get rickets, or be delinquent, or become a kleptomaniac, or get old maid's insanity. How *not* to be an aspiring dictator, or start a war, or be a nymphomaniac, or the torturing tyrant of a concentration camp. How *not* to be the wrong things, how *not* to dream—perhaps not the wrong dreams, but anyway how not to dream dreams that instead of functioning nicely to drain off antisocial wishes spill over into the day, and form the background of poetry—of the wrong kind. All these utopian plans neglect the other side of the picture, however much they may seek to bring it in: that as human beings we are not only interested in not doing wrong and evil and destructive things, but have also always cared terribly about our possibilities for doing good and right, constructive and beautiful, things.

But the answer does not lie for us, I think, at this period in history, in flinging ourselves to the opposite extreme. We can find no solace and no guide in ascetic or ecstatic commandments that flout the recognized biological needs of our mammalian nature. We have too recently come to understand the intricate connections by which a broken heart becomes a blocked nerve-track or a hyper-extended artery, by which an unpaid grocery-bill becomes something that an X ray can reveal in the stomach, and a forgotten girlhood memory, a severe attack of dysmenorrhoea. We know that when a little boy starts preferring to eat paper rather than food, it is not wise to wait until he has eaten all the theatre-tickets at Grandpa's birthday-party before taking him to consult a child specialist. However much we may want to proclaim that man does not live by bread alone, the results of the Federal nutrition program that ordered bread reinforced and helped banish pellagra from the American Southeast are part, and a very good part, of the stock of beliefs by which we live. Modern Americans, and probably a good proportion of modern western Europeans and modern Chinese and Japanese, are no longer able to flout our ever increasing knowledge of the cunning of our nervous system, or the sensitivity of our skin-tissues, or the responsiveness of our gastro-intestinal tract. Pictures of a world in which the clergy could say whole-heartedly, "We are not interested in civilization, we are interested in colonizing Heaven," may arouse a piercing nostalgia in all who love the Cathedral of Chartres, but by so doing they simply unman one more needed worker in the workshop of civilization. Those who give themselves to-day so whole-heartedly to the lovely and gracious task of colonizing Heaven that they have no time for public-health regulations or building-codes, by so doing cut themselves off from almost the whole band of colonists whom they would wish to lead gently into the eternal daylight of God's presence. Man's fitness for Heaven, which is perhaps one of the best ways we have thought of to describe man's potentialities that he does *not* share with any other known mammal, is no simple formula that will make modern men and women turn away from the dutiful attention to newly discovered ways of increasing man's fitness on earth.

But we need not accept any such dichotomy between earth and Heaven, between bodily needs and spiritual capacities, between limitations and potentialities. The potter who works with clay recognizes the limitations of his material; he must temper it with a given amount of sand, glaze it thus, keep it at such and such a temperature, fire it at such a heat. But by recognizing the limitations of his material he does not limit the beauty of the shape that his artist's hand, grown wise in a tradition, informed by his own special vision of the world, can impose upon that clay. Only if the potter ceases to remember the clay, and thinks to construct his pot by magic formulas that will work while he sleeps, or he who ceases to see a vision in his mind's eye and thinks that forceps and rules of proportions can replace that vision, is trapped and a failure. Because we are mammals, and male and female mammals at that, we have limitations, and we must know them, provide for them, keep them safely in our habits, if not continuingly and boringly in our minds. There are certain things that men cannot do because they are men, and women cannot do because they are women: begetting, conceiving, carrying, bearing, and suckling the next genera- tion are divided differently. As the bodies of the two sexes develop, to be ready for their different rôles in reproduction, they have basic needs, some of which are shared, some of which are different even in little children. All through our lives, the fact that we are creatures who are made not only to be individuals, but to continue the human race, is a persist- ent, unavoidable condition that we must meet. Failure to do so may express itself in innumerable ways: in a peptic ulcer or a temper tantrum, in a quarrel or a bad poem. (A good poem requires far more elaborate explanations to account for its existence.) But if we ask the question only in this way, ask only what are the limitations set by sex, the unavoidable conditions, the inevitable prices paid, then we invoke and reinforce the conflict, the traditional false dichotomy be- tween high and low, animal and spiritual, body and spirit.

So when we ask the very urgent questions we must ask about the differences and the similiarities, the vulnerabilities and the handicaps, of each of the sexes, we must also ask: What are the potentialities of sex differences? If men, just because they are men, find it harder to forget the immedi- ate urgencies of sex than do women, what are the rewards of this more urgent remembering? If little boys have to meet and assimilate the early shock of knowing that they can never create a baby with the sureness and incontro- vertibility that is a woman's birthright, how does this make them more creatively ambitious, as well as more dependent upon achievement? If little girls have a rhythm of growth which means that their own sex appears to them as initially less sure than their brothers, and so gives them a little false flick towards compensatory achievement that almost always dies down before the certainty of maternity, this probably does mean a limitation on their sense of ambition. But what positive potentialities are there also? If at each step we ask. consciously and articulately: What are the limitations, and what are the potentialities, the lower limits and the possible upper limits, of the fact that there are two sexes, and of the differences between them? then not only may we find answers that are in themselves rewarding about the place of the sexes in our present changing world; we shall do more. We shall make a contribution to the belief that on every question involving human beings we must concern ourselves not only with limitations, and not only with aspirations and potentialities, but with both. We will increase our faith in our full humanity—rooted in our biological ancestry that we dare not flout—capable of rising to heights of which each living generation can only glimpse the next step in the ascent.

II

HOW AN ANTHROPOLOGIST WRITES

IN THE JARGON OF MODERN AMERICAN COMMITTEE LIFE AND of general responsible social relationships, a phrase has crept in in the last few years, "from where I sit." It is often said half-jokingly, and yet it implies a total change in point of view. As one adds with a grin, or a half-smile, or perhaps a little rueful twist to the mouth, "from where I sit," this is an admission that no person ever sees more than part of the truth, that the contribution of one sex, or one culture, or one scientific discipline that may itself cross both sex and cultural lines, is always partial, and must always wait upon the contribution of others for a fuller truth. This book is being written from the standpoint of a woman of middle age, of an American, and of an anthropologist. It is part of the whole argument of the book that women will see the world in different ways than men—and by so doing help the human race see itself more completely. Necessarily, an American writes of America differently, with a different degree of involvement, than would a foreigner. The special contribution of an anthropologist, however, needs more comment.

An anthropologist's materials of study are the behaviours of living peoples living together in ways that they have learned from their forebears, who shared common patterns of behaviour. The anthropologist's laboratories are primarily primitive societies, small isolated groups of people who because of their geographical or historical isolation have remained outside the main stream of history, and preserved special practices of their own that contrast vividly with behaviour in large societies. The anthropologist does not study primitive peoples primarily to find out more about the origins of our present ways of behaving. The Eskimo and the Samoan, the Ashanti and the Cheyenne Indian, have histories as long as our own, only different. While a study of these primitive peoples may throw light on some of the relationships between a simple technology, an uncertain food supply, a small population, and other aspects of social life, in our thinking about social origins we can only use these relationships as suggestive; we can never be sure in which ways our own ancestral forms of society were similar. But we can study primitive peoples to provide us with the material with which to think about human behaviour, to give us clues as to when and how certain behaviours are learned. We go to these primitive societies to find material on the limits beyond which society cannot deny man's biological inheritance, and also to find variations in human behaviour that we might not otherwise be able even to imagine as possibilities.

Anthropologists have certain occupational peculiarities that arise from the kind of work we do. Because we have worked with primitive peoples who have no written language, we have developed ways of studying living behaviour rather than the traces of such behaviour that are found in a society like ours on papers, such as questionnaires, income-tax blanks, wills, certificates, and so on.

We have worked for the most part alone, or in pairs of opposite sex—and we have done this for a variety of reasons —because of lack of funds, because of the fewness of the workers and the urgency of the task, because most primitive communities are so small that the presence of two observers of opposite sex is all they can stand. Because we have worked alone, we have had to know a little about every aspect of the society, and a pattern of work that began with a simple desire to bring back some information on everything a people did—their art, their folk-lore, their kinship system, the way they made pots and prepared food, married, and buried their dead—has developed in time into a systematic point of view. The anthropologist has come to work always with a whole society as a back-drop. He does not specialize in the behaviour of infants, or the practices of advertisers, or the details of housing, as do students who work primarily within our own complex society. So anthropologists learn, by doing field-work, to think of many things together that most students of human behaviour are not accustomed to thinking of together. This way of thinking, which refers a whole series of apparently disparate acts—the way a child is fed, a house-post carved, a prayer recited, a poem composed, or a deer stalked—to one whole, which is the way of life of a people, this is a habit of mind that we carry over into work we do in our own cultures too.

This habit of reference to the whole society connects up, for instance, among the Iatmul of New Guinea the inconclusiveness of a mock weaning of a baby followed later by a real weaning, of shouts at dogs that the dogs never obey and of quarrels between groups that are never ended. By looking at the whole pattern it is possible to recognize in Bali that the construction of a Balinese house —a system of prefabricated independent parts put together, temporarily, in the house-building—expresses the same attitude that the Balinese always express towards the human body as a system of independent parts, assembled into one body but with the assemblage never quite certain. We look for regularities among many aspects of human behaviour within a single society, and we expect to find them because all these various acts are performed by human beings who in addition to their shared humanity share a common tradition, a common way of looking at the world.

In the next place, anthropology is a *comparative* science. We get our clues from comparing what people have done in one culture with what they have done in another. Explicitly, as a matter of training we send our students out to remote and exotic peoples, where they will be exposed to ways of behaviour quite different from our own, so different in fact that no effort of the mind will work that simply redefines the new ways in terms of the known old ways. Living among a people all of whose ways are alien, anthropologists make many adjustments. We learn to speak, or at least to hear and think, in quite different languages, in which there may be many genders or none, in which words may be put together in ways that defy all our attempts to fit them into our familiar grammatical categories, and which may be spoken with a phonetic system that is systematically related to the sounds our speech organs could make but not to the ones we have learned to make. Even our muscular habits take on some imprint of these other ways of life. In Samoa I learned to bend nearly double as I passed a seated person of high rank, and to-day when I must pass in front of some one whom I regard with deep respect, I feel a curious little itching in the small of my back. We learn to ask of crying children different questions from the familiar "What's the matter?" We learn to make other speculations about the meaning of clenched teeth, or slack hands, as we come to interpret human behaviour first in this one strange new context, and later more flexibly wherever we deal with it. Thus the student who as an anthropologist has once fully participated in learning about another culture is an altered instrument.

This particular thing which has happened to the trained anthropologist must not be confused with what happens to people who have the experience of moving from one culture to another, or marrying a member of another culture, or working with members of another culture closely, or even of speaking several languages. It is not the simple knowledge that the four-legged animal that is called *dog* in English is equally well designated by *chien, hund, nubat, maile,* and the rest. True, all people who have had the good fortune to learn several languages in childhood have a precious degree of sophistication and cross-cultural understanding. But the anthropologist learns that he has to think with and about the difference between a hand-shake among one people and the hand-shake among another, as well as to have the ability to adjust at once to the right hand-shake when confronted by some one of a given nationality. To the knowledge of other ways, and the ability to put these other ways on or off, the anthropologist adds a continuous consciousness of the differences—of the difference in tone of voice as well as of the words themselves, differences in sequences of behaviour, in the way a quarrel simply melts away in one country while in other countries a related set of initial interchanges would have led to a fist-fight or to a blank wall of silence.

If the reader is to enjoy anthropological discussion of our own society, especially the material in Part Four of this book, there is one issue that must be squarely faced. Is such an awareness of human behaviour cold and inhuman? We find a deep-seated suspicion in the hearts of laymen as to whether knowledge and kindness can go together, as to whether greater awareness does not always mean greater manipulativeness, greater coldness, or a greater seeking for power. We find this fear expressed in the stories so frequently told about the children of psychologists and psychiatrists, when every foible and every failure are seized upon and connected with apocryphal stories of experiments the scientist parents have performed on the children. The stories told about anthropologists in those primitive corners of the world where an anthropologist is almost as expected a part of the landscape as the trader, the prospector, the government official, and the missionary, are therefore particularly significant. For the current folk-lore about anthropologists in the Southwest Pacific almost always takes the form of accusing them of having taken off their clothes, and assumed native dress in one form or another. They are not accused of playing havoc with native society, of ruthless manipulation of native gardens so as to see some garden-magic, or of poisoning a few people of the right age or sex so that they can describe a series of funerals. But they are accused of having taken off the trappings of civilization, the toupee, the bush-shirt, the puttees, and put on a grass skirt or a loin-cloth, or of wearing nothing at all. I myself had to become accustomed to having a government official whom I had entertained as an anthropologist hostess clad in spotless white linen, primly seated behind a carefully laid tea-table, three months later describe in all good faith how I had looked in a grass skirt or a bath-towel. But after the first sense of outrage this particular set of myths about anthropologists can become quite comforting. For although they are all incredible slanders in detail, and no anthropologist ever goes to the extremes of comfort or native dress of which he or she is routinely accused, these stories make several points that are true in spirit. They say in the language of folk-lore that an anthropologist lays aside the trappings of his own culture and attempts to put on—to understand—the native culture; they say that he breaks down all the barriers of race and class and hygienic fears with which most Euro-Americans surround themselves in native villages, and that he receives food from the natives' hands simply. And finally these little folk-tales say quite clearly that the anthropologists' way of studying people is not to experiment, but to learn by observation and participation. The anthropologist not only records the consumption of sago in the native diet, but eats at least enough to know how heavily it lies upon the stomach; not only records verbally and by photographs the tight clasp of the baby's hands around the neck, but also carries the baby and experiences the constriction of the windpipe; hurries or lags on the way to a ceremony; kneels half-blinded by incense while the spirits of the ancestors speak, or the gods refuse to appear. The anthropologist enters the setting and he observes, but he does not change. So these folk-tales sum up very neatly the basic working principles of the field anthropologist, who regards the people among whom he works as human beings of no lesser and no greater stature than his own, who takes the trouble to learn their ways in meticulous detail, and who attempts to leave their way of life as untouched as possible, treating the whole living texture of that way of life as a valuable contribution to the science of man.

With the awareness, then, that has come from being exposed so thoroughly to another way of life, the anthropologist goes on to think with these contrasting details from many cultures. If one is fortunate, as I have been, one has an opportunity to study many comparable primitive societies, so that each new experience reinforces the distinctness of the previous experience and one's memory becomes almost as well stocked as one's note-books with contrasts and comparisons. But whether or not one studies many different societies, one learns to use material about many societies, to think with records of Eskimo life even if one has never been to the Arctic, and to read with new understanding the repetitions in a New Guinea tale of the phrase "Have you no bones?"—the phrase with which the women challenge the man to be a man.

When it comes to the question of what is maleness and what is femaleness, how male children differ from female children, men from women, anthropologists have their own special way of going at the problem. We do not devise tests of indistinct colour-forms in which men may see one kind of image, women another. We do not count the number of times that little girls build flat and cozy dwellings while little boys build towers. We do not line up groups of men and women and give them tests in tapping-speed or button-pressing. Nor do we take rats or guinea-pigs and inject sex hormones into them and watch the changes in their behaviour. We do not make detailed studies of the patients who come into our city clinic with such deep structural abnormalities that it is impossible to tell to which sex they belong. Nor do we follow out the life-histories of men who have decided to live as women, or women who have decided to live as men, to find what anatomical or endocrinological or psychological clues set them on these paths. All of these approaches to the question of how and where men and women differ are valid and important. Conclusions drawn from any one of these approaches must be checked against another.

But the anthropological approach is to go out into primitive societies without any too specific theories and ask instead open-ended exploratory questions.[1] How do male babies and female babies learn their social rôles in different societies? What types of behaviour have some societies classified as male, what as female? What behaviours have they failed to treat as sex-typed? How like have some societies felt males and females to be—and how unlike? We do not ask, initially, whether there are particular sex differences in personality that are systematically, and regardless of culture, associated with masculinity and femininity, such as passivity, initiative, curiosity, a capacity for abstractness, an interest in music. We do ask how different peoples expect infants to behave, how they use the difference in sex to define difference in rôle, and how they succeed in evoking the expected responses.

Such an inquiry does several things. First, it clears away our whole weight of cultural preconceptions about men and women, whether they are the traditional insistence on innate differences or the more contemporary attempt to deny many differences that have been accepted historically. This frees the mind from using the sort of arguments that have been invoked for and against the feminist movement, from hazy reconstructions of idyllic periods of history when women ruled and all was peace, and from querulous arguments about why women have not been great composers of music. The thousand and one statements that are made every day—"Isn't that just like a man?" "Men are just big children." "Women have such childlike minds." "Women are more sensitive than men." "Men are more sensitive than women." "Women are more variable than men." "Men are more variable than women"—have to be swept from the mind like tattered autumn leaves from the garden-paths before it is possible to think clearly at all.

But because the anthropological method is to go to live among a people, learn their language and all their ways, it becomes a very complicated matter to communicate the results of this *method* to others. The task of presenting a picture of one contrasting way of life is a fairly simple one. One can write a book describing in as much detail as possible the life of the Samoan or the Manus or the Eskimo or the Baganda, one can take the reader into native houses, to sit beside the mourners at a funeral, or follow the dancers' steps at a wedding, to listen in at conversations so unbelievable, so unexpected, that the reader experiences, though in very pallid form, something of what the anthropologist experienced initially. Sometimes it is hard going for the reader to plough through details of the fantastic kinship arrangements that classify granddaughter and grandmother together, prescribe special ways of behaviour for those cousins who are related through brothers and through sisters, but not through two brothers or two sisters, or the way in which father's ghost keeps his son's wife's tongue in order. Experience has proved that if the anthropologist is interested in that kind of communication, in bringing to the reader a sense of the living texture of another way of life, it can be done. Readers have consented, in fact, to having three cultures within one book, to making the enormous steps necessary to go from an Indian pueblo to a Papuan village, or from a mild parental people to a group of cannibals. Afterwards the names of the strange tribes, the incidents of life and death and sorcery and ceremony, may all merge together in a haze, but a residue remains. The reader has undergone the experience of realizing—if only for an hour—the extremely different ways in which our human nature can be patterned.

But so far, in seeking to make anthropological accounts useful to the sophisticated reader, who may be psychiatrist or biologist or geologist, judge or pediatrician or banker or mother of five children, we have tried to do only two things: either to convey that some one aspect of human behaviour could be organized differently—such as adolescence, or a proneness to heavy drinking, or a sensitivity to art—or to convey the extent to which cultures differ from one another. For the first task, to break down our culture-bound expectation that some aspect of learned behaviour is inevitably always as it is in our society, the description of one other culture is enough. For the second task, three or four cultures are sufficient.

In this book I want to do something rather different. I do not want merely to document vividly that different

peoples can cast males and females now for one rôle, now
for another, nor merely to show that the casting fits together very neatly, as between childhood training and
adult behaviour. I want somehow to give to the reader the
positive findings from a comparative study of culture about
similarities, about the essentials in maleness and femaleness with which every society must reckon, and regularities
as well as differences. I want to give results and yet keep
the sense of how these findings have been arrived at.

This is a much more difficult task, how difficult can best
be illustrated by an anecdote. I once wrote in an ethnological paper a paragraph that was to be published in a series
edited by a well-known geologist. In this paragraph I described the Samoan beliefs about the way in which pregnancy can be recognized, and these beliefs happen to
coincide accurately with present-day obstetrical conventions. The editor returned it to me with the statement, "same
all over the world." If I had been writing of a people who
believed that morning-sickness occurred only for first children, or that pregnancy took six months, the editor would
have let it stand because it differed from our own beliefs
and observation. So even a few sentences about a people
who believe that intercourse has nothing to do with conception, or that an infant in miniature form wanders about
in the snow and climbs into his mother's womb by mounting her shoe-laces, arrest the imagination, provide the
necessary shock. "Oh," says the reader, "then men haven't
always understood the biology of conception as well as
we do" (he will have to be very sophisticated indeed to
add that last phrase, for our usual assumption is that *now*
Science knows)—"hm, how interesting, and I can see that
would make a difference in how the family is organized, in
how willing fathers are to look after children," and so on.
And when I say very few human societies have been as
able to minimize the mother's rôle in child-bearing, although

the Rossel Islanders believe that the father lays an egg in the female,[2] who is regarded as a purely passive receptacle, and the Montenegrins are reported to deny to the mother any relationship to the child,[3] this is still arresting, because it is apparent to the reader how much more difficult it is to deny the mother's parental rôle than the father's. But when I say, "In all human societies it is recognized that women bear children," without first leading the reader through the series of starts and jumps appropriate to images of inch-size infants crawling chillily in the snow looking for their mother's boot-straps, or twins who wish to be reincarnated hopping about like little birds inspecting a group of women to see which mothers they will choose, there is an irresistible tendency to say, "So what, they do, don't they?" and dismiss the matter.

Yet between the statement made by the layman, "Naturally no human society would tolerate incest," which springs to his lips out of the traditional teaching of his own society, and the anthropologist's statement, "All known human societies have incest regulations," there lies a whole mass of experience that the second speaker has undergone, and that the first has not. When the first speaker says the word "incest" he means relationships between biologically related parents and children, or brothers and sisters. He will not, in our own society, include first cousins in his statement, although he may believe that cousin marriage causes insanity, or agree with some religious group that forbids first-cousin marriage without special dispensation. The anthropologist who speaks of incest will also be speaking of this same primary biological group, but he will have arrived at his statement after considering enormous and bizarre extensions of incest groups, perhaps including all the several hundred members of one's own clan, or a first-cousin grandmother under the heading of first cousin or under the heading of grandmother, as the case may be. After following over the face of the earth the diverse ways in which different people have extended and elaborated the incest taboos, his statement is a special kind of abstraction. Between the layman's "*Naturally* no human society" and the anthropologist's "No *known* human society" lie thousands of detailed and painstaking studies, made by hurricane-lamp and firelight, by explorer and missionary and modern scientists, in many parts of the world. But how are these observations to be introduced into the communication between writer and readers?

The method we usually use in bridging the gap between the observations of the scientist and the needs of those who are laymen to that particular science is the simple use of authority. I put on the jacket of my book, or safely on the title-page, all the appointments or fellowships I have ever had, or at least the most eminent. The reader inspects the list. If the reader is a carefully trained or a pedantic person, he may go further and look me up in some directory. Then, it being clear that I am myself, that I did once subject myself to the appropriate rituals for obtaining advanced degrees, that I have held fellowships and made expeditions and written monographs that have been published in learned series, the reader proceeds to read what I say with the respect due to some one who is what is called, revealingly enough, an "authority" on the subject in question. Later, when the reader wants to use the material, he may have to make a search to see if the other authorities agree with me, or how many authorities are on each side, and what explanations can be given for the differences among them, whether those differences are relevant or need to be explained in terms of political ideologies or historical adhesions. If the reader merely wants to use the findings of the authority in his ordinary human relations, he will find himself sooner or later in an argument in which he hurls his authority at some one else's head and gets some one else's authority hurled back at him. The results will be as simple to predict as the answer to the child's question: "Mummy, what happens when some one who just believes in God and some one who just believes in Science have a conversation about Nature?" And the deadlock that occurs in each such argument is only a symptom of the deadlocks that are occurring to-day in the minds of men who have accepted vitamins and atoms and endocrines and complexes—on authority—and find them poor material for thinking about a very difficult modern world.

I should like, somehow, to do more than this. I should like to be able to interpose between my statement and the reader's consideration of that statement a pause, a realization not of what authoritative right I have to make the statement I make, but instead of how it was arrived at, of what the anthropological process is.

To get some sense of the experience an anthropologist brings to the consideration of a human problem, let us take the simple statement "Love will find a way," a well-worn and well-loved adage of our own tradition. To a young American, this phrase will conjure up images of difficult transportation, a determined young man thumbing his way across the United States, or driving thirty-six hours stopping only for hot dogs, to get there in time to see his girl—before she sails, or decides to marry some one else. Or it may mean the way in which a girl plans, and saves, and even sews, to devise the dress that she then wears to the dance where she knows her estranged lover will see her and may choose her again. Through one's head will pass a variety of plots and incidents: motor cars, jobs, shortages of cash, failures of plane connections, occasionally even recalcitrant parents if the lovers are young enough or the parents rich enough for their views to matter. Mixed up with images from one's own experience will be snatches of scenes from movies, from novels, from radio serials, occasional images of Tom Mix riding across the plains, or Ingrid Bergman in some over-intense rôle, perhaps a line or so from *Romeo and Juliet,* or a couplet from an old valentine. If one is more sophisticated, some doubts about love itself—whether it is a sentimental word for "the hormones"—may crop up, to mix with the images of true-lovers' knots, pierced hearts, and "Johnny loves Alice" scratched on the wall of an empty city house. Love is an admitted emotion, felt by people who can be visualized as like ourselves, wearing clothes, driving cars, competing with rivals, fighting back depression when rejected, climbing to dizzy heights when accepted by the loved one. Even when the story of *Romeo and Juliet* is read carefully, Romeo and Juliet are seen as very like modern young Americans, with the feud between the Montagues and the Capulets as just part of the plot. After all, no one knows how Romeo and Juliet did feel. Shakespeare knew very little more than we as he, an English dramatist, wrote about them for a seventeenth-century English audience. A knowledge of the past may inform our tongues with lovely words, but they are recognized as including sentiments that are foreign to modern life, where fidelity even after death is regarded as a suspect emotion, hard on one's friends and family, and probably deserving the attentions of a psychiatrist more than those of a poet.

Between such a young reader who has never left America, and has seen the behaviour of other periods and other lands only through the special glasses provided by Hollywood and contemporary historical novelists—which make it seem just like his own—and the anthropologist who sits intimately in the thatched house of a New Guinea head-hunter, there are of course many shades of experience. In the United States we have millions of people who through the foreignness of their parents have felt in their very muscles that life could be and is different in other societies. We have uncounted thousands who have lived intimately in European or Latin American or Asiatic countries and learned, through close personal relationships with nurse or lover or friend, how differently the phrase "Love will find a way" would sound to them. Many of these experiences, with Serbian or Scottish parents, with German nurses or an Italian lover or French friends, have a quality of immediacy and intimacy that is not easily achieved between a twentieth-century Caucasian scientist and the people of a New Guinea tribe. These denizens of different emotional climates may well ask: Since what is wanted is vivid emotional relationships with peoples who see life very differently, have not those who have lived and loved abroad a better preparation for seeing behaviour in cross-cultural perspective than scientists who walk about with note-books, too busy writing down what they see to have time to see much? On the face of it this objection seems to have a great deal on its side. One conjures up the vision of a small American child, feet planted firmly and teeth clenched, straining in vain against the grip of a German aunt, or a young American painter leaning across a table in rapt intentness as he watches the play of expression on the face of his French wife. Then one compares these pictures with that of an anthropologist sitting at a table in a head-hunter's village writing down his observations among a people to whom the very act of writing is little short of magic, and surely it seems less likely that the anthropologist will ever learn what goes on in the head-hunter's head than that the small child and the lover will learn something significant and important about values very different from their own.

Still, the anthropologist does have an experience that is denied the young man who has lain awake all night making ardent love in another language, or the young woman who has followed her stranger husband to live with his family in a foreign land. For what the anthropologist does he does for reasons peculiar to his discipline. If you are six and Mama insists on a series of German Fraüleins as governesses, you may actually have made a pretty profound study of the ways of Fraüleins so as to get rid of the current one, if only for the excitement of having a different version of the same thing thrust on you at bedtime. If you are a factory-owner and the work of the plant is continually being disrupted by quarrels between two nationality groups, you may learn a lot about "how to get on with Italians," and if you are a political leader you may know just how to set the slate to calm or to profit from the existing national hatreds and alliances. But always, whether it is a matter of a child studying a procession of nurses, or a child in school in a foreign land, or a lover scanning his mistress's face, or a bride watching the strange behaviour of her foreign mother-in-law, always the observations are subordinate to the practical purposes of the child, or the lover, or the young wife. And this subordination gives them a different character from the observations of the anthropologist, rather as what one says to a new lover differs from what one says to a new psychiatrist. To both one may tell some harrowing childhood incident—how one waked alone in an empty house, or stood and watched the neighbour doctor amputate a hand from an injured man's arm, or watched one's father fall from the top of the windmill. But when one talks to the lover or the friend, one is building a relationship, putting in bricks of understanding and confidence for a structure that one hopes will last a lifetime. The story is shaped and pruned to fit the structure into which it is to fit, to be an appropriate reply to the last tale the other told, to lead on to further confidence. But when one talks to a psychiatrist, a conscious searching process, to which the relationship to the psychiatrist as a person is subordinated, is substituted for the intimate give-and-take of a whole relationship. If the psychiatrist is skilled and the patient sufficiently hounded by the terrors and anxieties that have brought him there, then this impersonal emphasis on understanding, and on using the understanding not interpersonally but personally, is maintained until some day the door of the consulting-room will close forever. The patient will be different. The physician's learning from the patient will be of quite a different order from the patient's learning from the physician, and one that they will not, in the normal course of things, discuss together.

When the anthropologist enters the village of a primitive people, either alone or as one of a married couple to set up a household among the other households, the situation is also a controlled and conscious one. He does not want to understand the culture *so that* he can get a house built, a garden dug, carriers for his gear, labourers on a new air-field, or converts for his religion. He does not even, as a doctor would, want to cure them of their diseases or change their ideas of public health, persuade them to bury their dead in a neat little cemetery instead of under the house, "where they will be less lonely." He does not want to improve them, convert them, govern them, trade with them, recruit them, or heal them. He wants only to understand them, and by understanding them to add to our knowledge of the limitations and the potentialities of human beings.* Just as the psychiatrist must limit himself to one aim, to heal, so the anthropologist must discipline himself to one aim, to observe and understand individuals as revealing their culture. To the layman, many of the discussions of psychiatric technique seem far-fetched. Why should there be a long discussion as to whether a psychoanalyst should or should not

* What I say here applies to the *study* of a culture. There is a developing science of applied anthropology, in which the anthropologist becomes a practitioner seeking to alter for the better the relationship between a native people and government, or between two ethnic groups in a community, or between co-operating units of two different nationalities. Here a different ethics applies.

shake hands, should ever go to his patient's house, should have a consulting-room with two doors? But it is just because the psychiatric relationship between doctor and patient is a partial and stylized one that all of these seemingly small details count.

So when the anthropologist goes to live in a native village, each detail of the way life is set up is considered carefully, and subordinated to the major task. Where is the house to be built? Not where it will have the best view or the most air or the least noise or the fewest pigs, not carefully isolated from the vicinity of Manngwon, a quarrelsome old widower who is always having temper tantrums, not far from the house of Kwowi Kogi Kumban, whose little boy Maggiendo has never got over crying because he was first adopted and then sent back in the middle of the night. None of the considerations of beauty, quiet, and health that one would normally consider in choosing a house-site can be taken into account. Instead, one makes a quick map of the village, noting especially where temples, men's houses, lounging-places, paths, are located. One considers the available sites, empty places where there have been houses before, and what the nature of these houses was. If, for instance, as was true of our house in Alitoa, it is the site of a former men's ceremonial house, the ground will be "hot," and visitors may be shy of coming there, for fear that some bit of their personalities will be tucked away in the earth that they believe is supersaturated with charms. Or, as was the case in Manus, one may acquire with a house-site the personality of some recently dead man, whose ghost may still be over-fond of haunting his former residence, and whose living female relatives may still be so afraid of him that they won't dare even to visit in the newly built house. But if one decides against a site because too much magic has been known to be whispered into the soil, or because a particularly aggressive ghost is going to be ubiquitous, that is not because one prefers neutral ground and quieter ghosts oneself, but because after careful consideration it appears that another site would introduce fewer complications into the work.

So our house-site in the village of Tambumum, on the Sepik River, was selected in 1938 for the following virtues: It was central enough to the village, but still over towards the end of the village that touched on the next village, and would increase contact with the next village. It was near enough to the big men's house so that one could hear the flutes play and—if one were the husband—go and see what was up. It was in a cluster of houses in all of which there were many little children, so—if one were the wife—one could listen for each child's cry, and if one marked a significant difference, hurry to the scene, as when I got out of my mosquito-net at 2 A.M. one morning when I heard a strange note in two-year-old Nemangke's voice, to find her facing a parental quarrel so deep that her mother had told her not to go near her father. Then too, our house lay neatly between the men's road, which ran along the river-bank, and the women's road, which lay inland. As I worked, I saw every one who passed from one end of the village to the other, not stopping to write down their names, not even stopping to note that I had noted their names, but registering them well enough so that when some group passed whose business I could not guess, or some combination of persons passed who would not normally be together, I could immediately jump up and find out what was happening. We built our houses without walls, so that we could always see what was going on, using only a great canvas ground-sheet, which had to be laboriously rearranged in the middle of the night when bad storms came. There was a convenient platform right outside the door, where people gathered and chattered volubly in the afternoon; again this was not what one would choose for that angry tropical hour when the sun is almost horizontal and invades every corner of such an exposed house; but it meant that the house was just that much better as an observation-post. Finally, one of the considerations in choosing that particular site was that Bangwin, our next-door neighbour, had a pregnant wife, and births are very hard to see in primitive society, where babies are likely to be born at 2 A.M. or when the mother is out fishing. True, in the end Bangwin's baby too was born when Tchamwole was out fishing, but I was near enough to hear Bangwin scold her because she had been pregnant too long, and Tchamwole answer: "Why do you rail at me? This baby will be born when it likes. It is a human being, and it chooses its own time of birth. It is not like a pig or a dog to be born when others say it should." We were able to film the quarrel when Bangwin chopped his other wife's woven sleeping-basket to bits—an act about equivalent to smashing up a grand piano or the new car in America—and the scene when Tchamwole, who was looking after her baby in another house, and raging with jealousy because the other wife was enjoying all the pleasures of matrimony, stalked back and placed a keep-off sign on the coconut-palm-trees that belonged to her, the first wife. So the choice of the house-site next to the house of a pregnant woman paid off, anthropologically.

As in the choice of a house and in its construction, the other details of living are consciously fitted together to increase one's powers and chances of observation. Servants are chosen not because they can cook, or because they are honest, although one is grateful when these coincidences occur, but because they will fit into the field-work, provide representatives from the two largest households, or from both sides of a divided community, or because they are the right age and sex to bring, or at least not to frighten, the kind of informant one hopes to attract. Thus in Manus, where I wanted to study young children, my entire house-staff was under fourteen, because with older boys problems of taboo relationships would have arisen, and small girls would have been kept away from the house. Twelve to fourteen is not an ideal age for a complete staff of servants, and sometimes the dinner went into the lagoon above which our house perilously perched, while vigorous fisticuffs raged in the kitchen. But among the many thousands of children's drawings that I collected there were girls' drawings as well as boys.

All this need to plan, to discipline one's choices to a single purpose, does not mean that one's relationships with a primitive people are coldly businesslike. But as one holds in one's arms the limp form of a drowned child, still working against hope to revive it, one is still obligated to observe the behaviour of that child's mother, who is off beating herself on the head with a wooden pillow, rather than to let one's mind stray in anguish to other little lifeless bodies one has held. One's own feeling, which might lead to a poem or a prayer for some one far away, or the decision to write a letter, or a desire to leave the scene of death and find that which never exists in the field, a moment alone—any of these must be subordinated to the obligation to watch, to listen, to record, to understand. Even a failure at such self-discipline—as when I burst into tears of helpless resentment when after sitting up all night with a very sick Balinese child, I went home for a moment, and came back in the chilly dawn of the mountain morning and was bitten by the family dog— must if possible immediately be used by the anthropologist as a stimulus point to discover what people will do when anger is shown in such and such a way.

Anthropologists differ very much in the ways in which they enter into the lives of their peoples, whether they bind up their sores, or help them mend their broken bits of modern machinery, or go out hunting with them, or provide cans of meat for feasts. But whatever the type of relationships that arises as one lives for many months open to the fears and to the joys of a whole village, the relationship must be disciplined to a single end—that of understanding the culture.

Thus the insights an anthropologist brings to the consideration of a subject like the relationship between the sexes are different from those of the sensitive man who has experienced more than one contemporary cultural setting, and are different from those of the historian, who must build his historical picture from the fragmentary documentary evidence that capricious accident has allowed to survive. It is a special order of material, and has a special usefulness, just as the clinician may often have far less range and richness of observation than the novelist, but because his observations are disciplined, he nevertheless makes a different type of contribution to our understanding of human behaviour.

The next important question is: *What* does an anthropologist observe as he works among a primitive people?

Perhaps the most important point here is that the anthropologist has to decide how he will analyze his results at the same time that he is making his observations. For example, if one wants to study the way in which the Irish, or the Queenslander, or the Kentucky mountaineer speaks English —each very different, very worthy of study—the linguist takes to his task his whole knowledge of the grammar and the phonetic system of English and other Indo-European languages. He asks, fundamentally, not what this language is, but how this language has varied within the framework of English. But when we go to a New Guinea tribe, we have to ask: What *is* this language? and from the discrete sentences that are drawn from a native perched uneasily so as to be eye to eye with the ethnologist, we have to derive the grammar. So in the behaviour of boys and girls, of men and women. To study the rôle of women in a South German village, one would bring all one's knowledge of the historical rôles of women in Europe, their place under Roman and old Teutonic law, the views of Catholicism and Protestantism on woman's place in the scheme of things, and, using this framework, find out just how this historical picture varies in this particular village. But when one approaches an un-known New Guinea tribe, there is no such formal way of thinking to guide one. As we anchor our pinnace, or halt our carriers—if we are going afoot—in some strange and unexplored village, we do not know which sex will be adorned and which unadorned, whether the shaved head peeping over a bush is that of a man or a woman, whether the distant figure inching its way to the top of a forty-foot coconut-palm is a man, because women should not do such dangerous and difficult things as climb palm-trees, or a woman, because climbing palm-trees is a job for children and women. We have to build our understanding directly from the behaviour of the people themselves, learn simul-taneously how a mother-in-law behaves and that there is a word for mother-in-law. To the anthropologist trained to surrender to his material, to wait and watch and listen until form emerges from the myriad small acts and words of the little group of people among whom he is living such a con-centrated existence, the material itself shapes his categories. So one escapes from the bondage of asking only the ques-tions that are based on our own and other known civiliza-tions.[4]

Then out of our storehouse of our own and other anthro-pologists' observations, whether these are held in solution in our memories as images, as phrases, as sounds, or neatly catalogued on cards that must be flicked carefully through searching fingers, we draw the material that will help us form hypotheses, check the usefulness of those hypotheses, and suggest new lines of work. This is the process which lies between the layman's sentence, "*Naturally* no human so-ciety," and the anthropologist's "No *known* human society," of which I should like somehow to preserve a sense in the reader's mind throughout the following pages.

Back of the word "man" stand in my mind a phalanx of images, men with white skins and brown skins and yellow skins and black skins; men with crew-cuts and shaved heads and great psyche knots; men in evening-dress in contemporary society and men wearing nothing but gleaming pearl-shell crescent ornaments on their chests; men with muscles that bulge and ripple and men with arms as slender as a girl's; men whose fingers are too clumsy to hold a tool smaller than an adze and men who sit threading tiny beads on a string; men whose manhood is offended by the smell of a baby and men who cradle an infant gently in a steady arm; men whose hands are always ready to fling upward and backward as if to throw a spear and men whose hands press easily palm to palm in a gesture of apology and entreaty; men of six feet six and men of five feet one. And beside them stand women, again with many-coloured skins; some with bald pates and some with long flowing hair; women with breasts that hang very low or can sometimes even be trained to a form which can be thrown over their shoulders and women with small high breasts like the figures on the Medici tombs in Florence; women who swish their grass skirts as they walk and women who handle these same grass skirts as if they were sheets of iron protecting their virtue; women whose arms look empty without a child in them and women who hold their children at arm's length as if they were clawing little wild cats; women who are readier to fight than their husbands and women who scatter like leaves before the sound of a brawl; women whose hands are never still and women who sit after a heavy day's work with hands flaccid in their laps. And in front and beside and behind them, in their arms, on their backs, clinging with hands tight around their necks, sitting on their shoulders, slung in slings and net bags and baskets, hanging on the tipi wall tightly laced in cradle-boards—there are the children. Children who may be dressed as tiny replicas of the adults, tripping over a long skirt as they learn to walk, and children who may go stark-naked until ten or eleven; children who relax into passivity as their carriers pound rice or play rough running-games and children who brace themselves tightly as the punted canoe jams and mother and child fall into the water; children for whom there is no word, who are first referred to as "mice" or "beetles" and then as "small men," children who have been wanted, children whose very words are treated as prophecy; children who are subhuman until they have teeth and children who are monsters if their teeth come in irregularly; children who have no toys and who cling sullenly to the legs of adults and children who are as gay and frolicsome as laughter itself.

This book is about males and females, as children and as adults. The reader's mind will be filled with images quite different from mine. The problem will be whether as I write from this background those who read can keep such words as "men," "women," and "children" open-ended words that carry an echo, although not the precise detail, of these varieties of human behaviour out of the knowledge of which I am attempting to communicate.

PART TWO

THE WAYS OF THE BODY

III

FIRST LEARNINGS

In this book I shall draw chiefly on the seven Pacific peoples among whom I have lived and worked. The Pacific Islands are an area where groups of men separated from each other by sea and mountain range, and lacking those political forms which bind men together into kingdoms, have developed strikingly different ways of life. Seven societies are a great many to keep simultaneously in mind. The details jostle confusedly, whether it be the kinship plan by which small Manus betrothed boys lie face down under a mat because their mothers-in-law are passing by, or Arapesh adolescent boys lead their child-betrotheds gently by the hand on all-night crayfish hunts, or young Mundugumor lovers come back with suitable explanations for the great scratches they have just received from the girl of the moment's choice; whether it be a Balinese elopement in the chilly dawn as the girl looks about to see whether there are witnesses before whom she must feign abduction with kicks and screams, or can go quietly with her chosen lover, or a

young Tchambuli husband who in sudden irascible lack of
understanding of his rôle thrusts a spear through the floor
crack into his wife's cheek, a Iatmul head-hunter calling in
his age-grade to rape his recalcitrant wife into submission,
or a Samoan girl whispering to her lover just where she will
meet him under the palm-trees.

I will attempt here to introduce each people briefly, as
was once done for the long caste of characters in an old
and complicated novel. These seven peoples, dwellers on
islands, in mountains, by lake and lagoon and river-bank,
are the actors—not as individuals, but as groups of individuals who share a common way of life. Their habituated and
age-old gestures are all parts of the weaving picture of
human life, new-woven itself from their behaviour, which
I must somehow attempt to bring before the reader. Perhaps
readers who do not grudge an occasional flip back to the
dramatis personnae on the theatre-program will also be
willing to turn back a page to reidentify a whole tribe.

THE SEVEN SOUTH SEA PEOPLES *

The Samoans

THE SAMOANS ARE A TALL, LIGHT-BROWN-SKINNED POLYNESIAN
people living on a small group of islands, part of which belong to the United States. Their way of life is formal and
stately. Chiefs and orators, village princes and village prin-
cesses, patterned groups of young and old, combine together
to plant and reap, fish and build, feast and dance, in a world
where no one is hurried, where food is plentiful, nature is
generous, and life is harmonious and unintense. They have
been Christian for over a hundred years, and have fitted
the tenets of Christianity into their own traditions, wearing

* See Appendix I.

beautifully starched cottons on Sunday, but still barefoot, and proud of their own way of life.

The Manus of the Admiralty Islands

THE MANUS PEOPLE ARE A SMALL, ENERGETIC TRIBE OF FISH-ermen and traders who build their houses on piles in the salt lagoons, near to their fishing-grounds. Tall, brown-skinned, lean and active, with nothing but their wits, their skill, and an ethics which says that the ghosts of the dead will penalize the unindustrious, they have built a high standard of living, which they maintain by continuous hard work. Puritan to the core, committed to effort and work, disallow-ing love and the pleasures of the senses, they take quickly to the ways of the Western world, to machinery, to money.

The Mountain Arapesh

THE MOUNTAIN ARAPESH ARE A MILD, UNDERNOURISHED people who live in the steep, unproductive Torricelli Moun-tains of New Guinea, poor themselves, and always struggling to save enough to buy music and dance-steps and new fash-ions from the trading peoples of the sea-coast, and to buy off the sorcerers among the fiercer people of the interior plains. Responsive and co-operative, they have developed a society in which, while there is never enough to eat, each man spends most of his time helping his neighbour, and com-mitted to his neighbour's purposes. The greatest interest of both men and women is in growing things—children, pigs, coconut-trees—and their greatest fear that each generation will reach maturity shorter in stature than their forebears, until finally there will be no people under the palm-trees.

The Cannibal Mundugumor of the Yuat River

THESE ROBUST, RESTIVE PEOPLE LIVE ON THE BANKS OF A swiftly flowing river. but with no river lore. They trade with and prey upon the miserable, underfed bush-peoples who live on poorer land, devote their time to quarrelling and head-hunting, and have developed a form of social organization in which every man's hand is against every other man. The women are as assertive and vigorous as the men; they detest bearing and rearing children, and provide most of the food, leaving the men free to plot and fight.

The Lake-dwelling Tchambuli

THE TCHAMBULI PEOPLE, WHO NUMBER ONLY SIX HUNDRED IN all, have built their houses along the edge of one of the love-liest of New Guinea lakes, which gleams like polished ebony, with a back-drop of the distant hills behind which the Arapesh live. In the lake are purple lotus and great pink and white water lilies, white osprey and blue heron. Here the Tchambuli women, brisk, unadorned, managing and in-dustrious, fish and go to market; the men, decorative and adorned, carve and paint and practise dance-steps, their head-hunting tradition replaced by the simpler practise of buying victims to validate their manhood.

The Iatmul Head-hunters of the Great Sepik River

ON THE BIG, SLOW-MOVING RIVER, INTO WHICH THE YUAT RIVER drains, for which the mountains where the Arapesh live is one watershed, to which the Tchambuli lake is connected by canals, are the swagger villages of the Iatmul people, head-hunters, carvers, orators, tall and fiercely, brittlely masculine, where women serve as spectators to the endless theatricality of the men's behaviour. Rich in sago swamps that provide them with a steady food-supply, well fed on fish that the steady industry of the women provides, they have built magnificent ceremonial houses, and beautifully carved war-canoes, and accumulate in their big villages the art-styles, the dance-steps, the myths, of all the lesser peoples about them, outstanding among their neighbours, and vulnerable in the intensity of their pride.

The Balinese

THE BALINESE, WHO CAN BE NUMBERED IN HUNDREDS OF thousands, not in a few thousands like the Samoans or a few hundreds like the New Guinea peoples, are not a primitive people, but a people whose culture is linked through Asia with our own historical past. Light, graceful, wavy-haired, with bodies every segment of which moves separately in the dance, they have a highly complex and ordered way of life that in its guilds and Hindu rituals, its written records and temple organizations, its markets and its arts, is reminiscent of the Middle Ages in Europe. Crowded on a tiny island with a beautiful, highly diversified, changing landscape, they have turned all life into an art. The air is filled with music day and night, and the people, whose relations to each other are light, without enduring warmth, are tireless in rehearsal for a play where these disallowed feelings will be given graceful stylized expression.

THIS IS THE CAST. THEY HAVE BEEN CHOSEN SIMPLY BECAUSE I myself have studied them and can compare one with another, counterpoint a Balinese witch-dance to the play of a New Guinea child, a Manus woman's muttered complaint over her husband's advances to a Iatmul woman's screamed accusation that her husband takes no interest in her. Nor were they chosen only to illuminate the problems that are to be discussed in this book, but for a variety of purposes, professional, practical, theoretical, and personal, through a quarter-century of research. They do not represent by any means all the ways in which the relationship between the sexes can be handled. Missing are societies where men threaten and bully their sons into helpless conformity, miss-

ing are societies in which women represent an evil supernatural force, missing are any societies in which there is
great religious intensity, or extreme economic exploitation,
tyranny, or class division. Missing also are any societies in
which men base their masculinity on forms of productive
achievement denied to women. But among these seven there
will be found enough to make one pause, to wonder, to question, enough to quicken our imaginations about what our
lives might be if they were not as they are.

In the discussion, these seven peoples will come and go,
now just a sentence invoking a bit of posture or the way a
man challenges a woman to love-making, or an old woman's
hand moves in a dance, now a longer description of a ceremony, or a scene between mother and child. These will not
be, however, the random bits of the older form of anthropology, where the arm-chair anthropologist quoted exotic
details from here and there without any knowledge of how
the given bizarre bit or human sacrifice or love-magic fitted
into the whole. Each detail is quoted from a whole, but I
will try to do the work of conveying that wholeness without weighing the reader down with the obligation to carry
a galaxy of strange social arrangements in mind. Out of the
differences, the contrasts, the strange and unexpected ways,
in which these seven peoples have ordered their lives, patterned the relationships between the sexes, between parents
and children, between men and women and their own creative skills, should come some greater appreciation of the
value for human civilization of the presence of two sexes,
of the importance of this counterpoint that we sometimes
ignore grievously, often distort, and have never used to the
full.

In discussing men and women, I shall be concerned with
the primary differences between them, the difference in their
reproductive rôles. Out of bodies fashioned for complementary rôles in perpetuating the race, what differences in

functioning, in capacities, in sensitivities, in vulnerabilities, arise? How is what men can do related to the fact that their reproductive rôle is over in a single act, what women can do related to the fact that their reproductive rôle takes nine months of gestation, and until recently many months of breast feeding? What is the contribution of each sex, seen as itself, not as a mere imperfect version of the other?

Living in the modern world, clothed and muffled, forced to convey our sense of our bodies in terms of remote symbols like walking-sticks and umbrellas and hand-bags, it is easy to lose sight of the immediacy of the human body plan. But when one lives among primitive peoples, where women wear only a pair of little grass aprons, and may discard even these to insult each other or to bathe in a group, and men wear only a very lightly fastened G-string of beaten bark, or—once they have killed their man—a flying-fox skin that is a fine homicidal decoration, but very unconcealing, and small babies wear nothing at all, the basic communications between infant, child, and adult that are conducted between bodies become very real. In our own society, we have now invented a therapeutic method that can laboriously deduce from the recollections of the neurotic, or the untrammelled phantasies of the psychotic, how the human body, its entrances and its exits, originally shaped the growing individual's view of the world. So the child analyst sits in his consulting-room and watches the child play with a fountain, make mud pies, pack nests of bowls together in sweet safety, or guide a miniature train into a tunnel with sure proud aim. He watches the disturbed child whose parents brought him there because his habit of eating everything became a nuisance when he ate the theatre-tickets stuff pieces of paper into his mouth and tear them to bits with his teeth. He watches the child take little lumps of Plasticine and put breasts on the boy-doll, and then angrily rip them off again, or equip the female doll with male genitals and castrate her

with a pair of toy scissors. In long slow sessions, interrupted
by the resistances of parents who long ago learned how to
hide any immediate relationship to their bodies from themselves, the child's imagery is reconstructed, and much of the
reconstruction seems to the mind of the average adult reared
in our society still a pretty fantastic affair. This is even more
so when the adult patient, lying relaxed on the analytic
couch, provides long and elaborate pictures of childhood
events that his parents know he could *not* have experienced,
living as he did safely tied down in his crib, in a room all by
himself. Those who have been healthily transformed into
functioning adults in our modern society cannot easily accept the symbols that come from the consulting-room or the
hospital ward. After all, although most people's children
may chew the fringe on the blanket and the tassels on their
hats, they do stop at theatre-tickets. And most adults, even
those who have been very carefully brought up, will be able
to laugh quite explosively at some simple vaudeville act that
involves carrots or asparagus. But to most of us most of the
time, theatre-tickets, comics, and baggage-tags are just—
theatre-tickets, comics, and baggage-tags; carrots, off the
stage, are a vegetable that good children are enjoined to eat
and adults need not. The all-pervading body imagery of the
little child is muted, overlaid, transformed into acceptable
social behaviour, and only a thin trickle of memory is left
as a hidden spring for giggling in adolescents and belly-
laughs in adults.

And this is as it should be. Civilization depends on such
an orderly transformation of the primary experiences of
childhood into the disciplined symbolism of adult life, in
which walking-sticks are decorations of class or individuality, umbrellas keep the rain off, hand-bags contain everything one needs for the day, and the distinctions between
food and not food are clear enough to make sword-swallow-
ing an amusing vaudeville turn. Those who have not suc-

ceeded in making these transformations go mad, and fill our insane asylums. Those who keep an easy access to their own early memories but who have also talent and skill become our artists and our actors; those who can combine these early basically human experiences with vision and love of mankind become prophets; those who combine this ready access to early images with hate become dangerous demagogues— Hitlers and Mussolinis. But for all, those who lead and those who listen, those who act and the applauding audience, the painter and those who replenish their less vivid imaginations with the scenes on his canvas, some veil between childhood and the present is necessary. If the veil is withdrawn, the artistic imagination sickens and dies, the prophet looks in the mirror with a disillusioned and cynical sneer, the scientist goes fishing. As for the audience, the schoolroom, the crowd in the street, they would be as irrevocably deprived. Long ago in a New England village one of the villagers received a revelation from God that every one was to do exactly as he wished. Sadly, with exemplary rambunctiousness, the villagers took off their clothes and ran around on all fours like animals, making animal sounds. No one had a better idea.

The whole significant and benign function of the transformation of primary body experience into culturally approved elaborations was beautifully demonstrated by a recent case of a child from a children's psychotic ward.[1] The little girl had lived with her mother in a brothel. When she entered the hospital she drew, over and over, pictures of a house and a tree and a church, but which she spoke of as herself, a phallus, and her mother's vulva, "and don't you say nothing against it." Slowly, as she regained her health and balance, the nightmare experiences of the brothel disappeared, and the house became just a house, the tree a tree with apples on it, and the church, a church—and the child could leave the hospital.

If this is so, if both the specially gifted and the healthy must strenuously preserve those veils of reinterpretation which lie between themselves and a deeply physical baby-hood, filled with impulses of ungovernable rage and appalling specificity, then what must be the procedure of the scientist who in order to clarify our understanding of the problems that confront us to-day must somehow—not tear these veils, for then they can only be falteringly and imperfectly reconstructed but—render them transparent. First, the scientist's intention must be clear as an exploration of early childhood in the name of a fuller humanity, a humanity more able to use the symbols of our great tradition. Second, the reader must realize that he can feel secure in the long years of living with a body that has been civilized, with teeth that chew food but do not bite other human beings, with body cavities that digest food in both sexes, gestate babies in women, and are not witches' caves in which enemies might be shut up or carved to bits, with genitals that are meant for love-making, and not for the obscure strange wars of tiny angry children trapped in a nursery world of giants. Because the clinic and the nursery-school provide us with evidence that the process of civilization is difficult and only proceeds slowly, and that children of four and five may still, if looked at carefully, show very marked signs of not being civilized, this does not mean that most of us have not been and cannot stay civilized. Bed becomes an irresistible temptation when one has a high fever, quaking limbs, and a racking head, but the average fatigued man or woman can shop all morning in a department-store filled with period furniture, or wander for an afternoon through the period rooms of Fontainebleau or Hampton Court or the American Wing of the Metropolitan Museum without flopping incontinently on some period bed-spread. If we are really to understand the basic differences between the sexes, and how these differences are built up in infancy and early childhood—as the growing child uses every inch of skin, every tensing muscle, every sensitive mucous membrane, to learn, to explore, to take in the world about him—this infancy, which lies well behind us and which lies ahead of all unborn generations, must be explored, without revulsion, without fascination, without partially averted eyes, for what it is: the process by which we acquire human stature.

But because we begin with early childhood, this does not mean that human cultures are created by children. Children's experiences in a world in which the adults already have a way of life become in turn the stuff out of which they, as adults, are able either to conform to and use, or to rebel against and change, their ways of life. In following the steps by which the infant learns his civilization, we are tracing a process of transmission, not one of creation; but the path is none the less revealing.

Of the child's first experiences within the womb, and the way in which different cultures pattern these experiences, we still know very little. The Arapesh say the baby sleeps until ready for birth and then dives out. The Iatmul believe an unborn child can hurry or delay, as it wishes. "Why do you rail at me?" said Tchamwole to her husband. "This baby will be born when it likes. It is a human being, and it chooses its own time of birth. It is not like a pig or a dog to be born when others say it should." "The birth is hard," said the Tchambuli, "because the mother has not gathered enough firewood." It is probable that in different societies, by the attribution of more or less autonomy of movement to the baby, by enjoining upon the mother active or placid behaviour, the process of learning may begin within the womb, and that this may be interpreted differently for the two sexes. It is possible that there may be deep biochemical affinities between mother and female child, and contrasts between mother and male child, of which we now know nothing. So, at birth itself, whether the mother kneels squat-

ting holding on to two poles or to a piece of rattan hung
from the ceiling—whether she is segregated among females
or held around the waist by her husband, sits in the middle
of a group of gaming visitors or is strapped on a modern
delivery table—the child receives a sharp initial contact with
the world as it is pulled, hauled, dropped, pitched, from its
perfectly modulated even environment into the outer world,
a world where temperature, pressure, and nourishment are
all different, and where it must breathe to live. Here there
may be cultural intervention, such as to save the boy-baby
and strangle the girl, but we know nothing as to whether
birth itself means something different to the boy-baby and
to the girl. There seems to be a differential sensitivity in the
skin of males and females; and a sensitive skin is one of the
clues that may make a male classify himself as a female, a
hard skin may tend to get a girl dubbed masculine, in her
own eyes and those of others. Skin-shock is one of the major
shocks of birth, and where there is a final difference, there
may be an initial one. In our own society, our images of the
carefully guarded rituals of the delivery-room, in which the
mind conjures up an even temperature maintained by a
thermostat, the most medically perfect oils and unguents,
and the softest of appropriate materials in which to wrap
the baby, overlay any realization of what a shock birth is.
The shock is easy enough to realize when the baby is born
on an unsheltered hillside, where the mother and attending
women crouch shivering over a tiny fire until finally the
baby falls with a soft little thud on a cold, dew-coated leaf
—to be left there, perhaps five minutes, while the mother
herself cuts and ties the cord, packs up the placenta, and
wipes out the baby's eyes and nose. Only then can the
squirming, exposed little creature be gathered up and laid
against the mother's breast. Whether or not this initial experience differs for the two sexes in any basic way, their
later realization of their sex can reinvolve the experience

they know has occurred. A longing for a world where pressure is even on the body and breathing is effortless, an experience that mystics of all times have sought, can be very differently woven into the phantasies of two parents expecting a child. To the expectant mother it means an increased sense of her sheltering relation to the child within her womb, to the expectant father such memories may come as a threat or as a temptation. For him, identification with the unborn child is at least partially unacceptable, for it turns his wife into his mother. For both expectant father and mother, such phantasies may arouse memories of the time before a younger child was born to his or her own mother, and then father and mother will defend themselves differently against these memories. What actual traces remain of the specificities of the birth-shock in the nervous system we do not know, but a careful examination of the ways in which new-born babies are handled—cradled gently against the breast, held up by the heels and slapped, wrapped so close that no light comes to them until they are many weeks old, stood out on the mother's iron-stiff arm to fend, like tiny frogs, for themselves—shows that these early ways of treating them are strictly congruent with later handling and later phantasies. However little the baby learns from its own birth, the mother who bears it, the midwife who assists, the father who stands by or walks the floor outside or goes off to consult a magician, all bear the marks of the birth experience and can again communicate it to the growing child. It will make a difference ultimately in our theories of human learning whether males and females are found actually to remember, differentially, their first shocking experience of temperature and breathing, or whether they learned about it from the imagery and poetry of the adult world. But in either case, whether the boy learns something different from his mother's voice because he has remembered, at some very deep level, a lesser shock upon his skin, or because he realizes that he can experience birth only once, while the girl pre-lives at that moment the day her own baby will be thrust out into the world—in either case, the birth experience becomes part of the symbolic equipment of women, who are formed to bear children, and of men, who will never bear them.

From the moment of birth—probably always from before birth also—contrasting types of behaviour can be distinguished in a mother's attitude towards her child. The infant may be treated as a whole little creature—little animal, little soul, little human being, as the case may be, but whole, and to a degree capable of setting its own will and needs over against those of its mother. Such behaviour may be called *symmetrical*;[2] the mother behaves as if the child were essentially similar to herself, and as if she were responding to behaviour of the same type as her own. Or she may treat the child as one who is different from herself, who receives while she gives, with the emphasis upon difference between the mother's behaviour and that of the child as she cherishes and shelters and above all feeds a weak, dependent creature. This patterning of the relationship may be called *complementary*, as each of the pair is seen as playing a different rôle, and the two rôles are conceived as complementing each other. A third theme occurs when the behaviour of the mother and the child is seen as involving an interchange when the child takes in what the mother gives it, and later, in elimination, makes a return. The emphasis is not on the symmetrical or the complementary character of the rôles, which include a feeling about the two personalities—as of the same kind or, in terms of the particular relationship, with different appropriate behaviours—but rather on an exchange of commodities between mother and child. Such behaviour can be called *reciprocal*.[3] In reciprocal phrasings of relationship, love, trust, tears, may become commodities, just as much as physical objects, but the interchange of physical objects remains the prototype. All these themes are present in every cultural phrasing of the mother-child relationship. To the extent that the child's whole individuality is emphasized, there is symmetry; to the extent that its weakness and helplessness are emphasized, there is complementary behaviour; and to the extent that the mother gives not only her breast, but milk, there is the beginning of reciprosity. But cultures differ greatly as to which they emphasize most.

So we may contrast mothers in different societies with these different emphases. The Arapesh treat a baby as a soft, vulnerable, precious little object, to be protected, fed, cherished. Not only the mother, but the father also, must play this over-all protective rôle. After birth the father abstains from work and sleeps beside the mother, and he must abstain from intercourse while the child is young, even with his other wife. When the mother walks about she carries the child slung beneath her breast in a bark-cloth sling, or in a soft net bag in which the child still curls as he curled in the womb. Whenever it is willing to eat, even if it does not show any signs of hunger, it is fed, gently, interestedly. The receptiveness of the mouth is emphasized in both boys and girls. Through the long, protected infancy, during which children are carried, slung in bags from their mother's foreheads or high on their father's shoulders, up and down the steep mountain trails, and are never asked to perform tasks that are difficult or exacting, their whole interest remains focussed on the mouth. Not even the almost ever present breast provides enough stimulation for a mouth that has been so heavily stressed, and small children sit playing endless gentle games with their lips, bubbling them, teasing them, puckering them lightly between their fingers. Meanwhile the grasping action of the mouth has never been developed. A readily offered breast does not have to be vigorously seized upon or bitten. The method of carrying places no emphasis on teaching the hands to grasp—which when it occurs can reinforce the grasping possibilities of the mouth. The Arapesh child, male and female, continues to take in, receptively, passively, what is offered it and to fly into tempers if food is ever refused—as it sometimes may be from necessity, for the people are very short of food.

Both boys and girls have learned about life from using their mouths. When they use their eyes, their eyes reflect the same passive expectancy. Eyes light up and mouths shout with excitement when some lovely colour is presented to them, but hands do not reach aggressively, eyes do not probe and seek with active curiosity. The Arapesh are a people among whom communication between infants and others has been very heavily specialized to one part of the body, the mouth, and to one aspect of that part, passive receptivity. Both sexes among the Arapesh, like other human beings, have the task of eventually learning to use their whole bodies in acts of sexual maturity that will procreate children. For the Arapesh female this is easy enough.[4] To transfer an attitude of pleasant expectancy from mouth to vulva, of soft, optimistic retentiveness, requires very little shift in attitude. Among the Arapesh, one may see a neglected wife eagerly bringing her neglectful husband food, touchingly grateful if he eats it; but I never heard a woman complain about a man's sexual competence. No accusations about low potency fill the evening air when a quarrel is on foot. When the usual pattern of marriage is followed, in which the husband as a boy of twelve or fourteen begins to feed his betrothed wife, himself playing a rôle that his mother has played to him—and his father also—and the marriage is not interrupted, the woman is in a psychological position that is the perfect development of her childhood experience—passive, dependent, cherished. In turn she treats her children in the same way.

But what happens to the Arapesh male? What kind of

preparation is it for living in the rough mountain country of New Guinea, surrounded by tribes who are fierce head-hunters and blackmailing sorcerers, to have learned that the major relationship to other people is either one of passive receptivity or one of provision of food and drink? He does not, within his own society, become a homosexual, although there is great ease and warmth and much giggling puppyishness among boys. But the reverse attitude—the desire to dominate, to intrude, which would provide a basis for active homosexuality—is too slightly cultivated, nor is there enough development of assertive resentment of passivity to fit into a type of homosexuality where active and passive rôles are interchanged. The men in adulthood develop into heterosexual males, extremely distrustful of strange over-sexed women from other tribes who will take part of their semen and keep it for sorcery. Even with their own young wives, whom they have fed and cherished, there is not complete trust, but a ceremony at which the genital secretions of each are entrusted ceremonially to the other. Even copulation within the well-defined domestic circle may in the end be dangerous. They engage very little in warfare, they permit themselves to be blackmailed and bullied and intimidated and bribed by their more aggressive neighbours; they admire so deeply the artistic products of others that they have developed practically no art of their own. When they hunt, they set traps and wait until the animal falls in, or else they "walk about in the bush looking for game," and quarrels between hunting-partners come over who first caught sight of the animals. Arapesh male ceremonies, from which women are excluded, stress symbolically the nature of maternity. The men cut their arms, draw blood from them, and mix the blood with coconut-milk and feed it to the novices—who thus ceremonially become their children (for the child at birth has only its mother's blood). The various sharp initiatory devices, sub-incision, beating with nettles, and so on, are all phrased as making the novices grow. Young males who have eaten carelessly of forbidden food—a phrase also used for sexual promiscuity—cut their penises and let blood from them to restore their health.

Thus the Arapesh form of child-rearing stresses complementariness in a form that is most easily transformed by women into an adult feminine sex rôle. Only that woman suffers who in spite of all this learning is still positively sexed and interested in climax for herself. But it is a society that makes it much more difficult to be a male, especially in all those assertive, creative, productive aspects of life on which the superstructure of a civilization depends. Where the upbringing fits most women, it fits only a few men.

But receptivity is only one of the two modes of behaviour that are appropriate to the mouth of the young child and which may be transferred to other parts of the body. The mouth is not only soft and receptive, the infant lips are fitted for more than pressing gently against the nipple; the mouth is also a grasping, demanding organ, and the smallest infant's toothless gums are already able to chew savagely on a breast that does not yield it satisfaction. As the mother first holds her baby in her arms, she may treat it as a receptive little creature, or as an active demanding little creature already armed with a will and teeth. This active relationship is still a complementary one; the baby takes, the mother responds, either resignedly or with active interplay, or she may even angrily withdraw her breast if the child is making too great demands. We find among the Iatmul headhunters both the receptive and the demanding behaviour well developed. From birth the baby is handled as if it were a separate little entity capable of a will of its own, and immediately after birth before the mother has milk the wet nurse thrusts her nipple into its mouth with cherishing care, but also with a touch of the gesture with which mothers later stop their babies' temper tantrums by thrusting their nipples into their mouths like corks into soda-water bottles.

As soon as the Iatmul child is a few weeks old, the mother no longer carries it everywhere with her, or sits with it on her lap, but instead places it at some distance on a high bench, where it must cry lustily before it is fed. Assured that it is hungry, the mother crosses to it and feeds it generously and easily, but a baby that has had to cry hard for its food eats more definitely, and the vigour with which the mother thrusts her nipple into its mouth increases. Before the baby has any teeth, it is given pieces of hard bird-meat to gnaw on, and when its teeth begin to come in, it cuts them on round shell ornaments that hang around the mother's neck. In this interchange between mother and child, the sense of the mouth is built up as an assertive, demanding organ, taking what it can from a world that is, however, not unduly unwilling to give it. The child learns an attitude towards the world: that if you fight hard enough, something which will treat you as strong as itself will yield—and that anger and self-assertion will be rewarded.[5] Children of each sex form images that will later inform their feeling about copulation, the girl-child forming a more active picture of her own rôle, the boy-child a more active picture of the female's rôle. Later, in the initiation ceremonies, giant model vulvas will be pushed down on the heads of the initiate males.[6]

On a tributary of the Sepik River live the Mundugumor, among whom the active attitudes found among Iatmul women towards their nursing children are carried much farther. The Mundugumor women actively dislike child-bearing, and they dislike children. Children are carried in harsh opaque baskets that scratch their skins, later, high on their mother's shoulders, well away from the breast. Mothers nurse their children standing up, pushing them away as soon as they are the least bit satisfied. The occasional adopted new-born child is kept sharply hungry, so as to suck vigorously on a woman's breast until milk comes in. Here we find a character developing that stresses angry, eager avidity. In later life love-making is conducted like the first round of a prize-fight, and biting and scratching are important parts of foreplay. When the Mundugumor captured an enemy they ate him, and laughed as they told of it afterwards. When a Mundugumor became so angry that his anger turned even against himself, he got into a canoe and drifted down the river to be eaten by the next tribe.

In all three of these tribes, the mouth plays an important rôle as a way in which adults communicate to the growing child their own organized attitudes about the world. It seems probable that as he is fed every child learns something about the willingness of the world to give or withhold food, to give lavishly or deal out parsimoniously. But for genuine communication of a type that lays the groundwork for the child's understanding of his culture and his sex rôle, the mouth must be of interest to the adult as well as to the child. When a woman has originally formed her own picture of her feminine receptivity from the way in which she was fed as a child, this process will be present as she thrusts her erectile nipple into her new-born baby's mouth, and it is from this interchange that the basic learning seems to occur. Children will of course differ in the sensitivity of their lips, in their hunger rhythms, in the strength of the sucking impulse. These individual differences, which may in fact be systematically related to constitutional type, will be very important in laying the groundwork of individual character, but each of these individualities will develop as a version of the general attitude prevalent in that society, or that class or region, where the child is reared.

In some cultures, the adults are less interested in the mouth and may instead be more concerned with training the child to an early control of his bowels. Feeding may be done in a less involved way, while the major learning of the child is focussed on the other end of the gastro-intestinal tract, whose modes of behaviour are not passive receptivity and active taking, as in the mouth, but retention and ejection. Here the emphasis shifts from the complementary relationship to an emphasis upon the relationship between the child and that which he first takes in and then gives out. Person-thing relationships are learned here, reciprocal rather than simple complementary relationships are stressed. The later transfer to the genitals of attitudes focussed on elimination makes for prudery, haste, lack of pleasure and foreplay in intercourse. This character-type in which the most emphasized communication between parent and child has been an emphasis on control of elimination is one that occurs fairly frequently in our own society. We find it writ large among the Manus tribe of the Admiralty Islands, a group of efficient puritans where women never swing their grass skirts—grass skirts after all are items in the endless exchange of goods that goes on—girls are never allowed to flirt, and all love, even the affection between brother and sister, is measured in goods. Here among these small Stone Age villages there was prostitution, and the owner of the war-captured prostitute made money. Here a woman never loosens her grass skirt even in the extremes of child-birth. Between husbands and wives sex is a hasty, covert, shameful matter; and otherwise it is adultery, heavily punished by vigilant, puritanical, ghostly guardians. Women's rôles and men's rôles are very slightly differentiated; both participate importantly in the religious system, both conduct economic affairs. If a man is stupid, his relatives seek for him a bright wife to compensate for his deficiencies. The sex act becomes a sort of shared excretion, and the attitudes that both sexes have learned during childhood come into play, not equally, for the female's sexual rôle is completely derogated, while the man is to a degree continuing an enjoined activity. But the general devaluation of sex and sex attraction is such that this difference in the images formed by males and females is less significant. A certain amount of sodomy among the young men is a natural concomitant of such a learning system.

Alternatively again, a people may show much less interest in either end of the gastro-intestinal tract. They may feed their infants in matter-of-fact fashion without emphasis, take their eliminations with the greatest casualness, and communicate with them instead by the way in which they carry them, confine their arms and legs, exert pressure on their skins, and pattern the interplay between child and carrier. The Balinese represent a people who conduct some communication with the mouth, but the emphatic part of this communication stresses pre-chewed (that is, by analogy, predigested) food, a mixture of bananas and rice piled in a little mountain on the helpless baby's mouth, and relentlessly pushed in wherever the baby opens its mouth to protest. This assault on the mouth is, not unexpectedly, followed by a great tendency to cover, or plug up, the mouth in later life. Eating is accompanied with great shame, while drinking, the prototype of which is drinking from an upturned breast, above which the infant is carried, is a matter of casual pleasure. A fundamental dichotomy runs through Balinese life between the light and the serious, heavy food and defecation on the one hand, light food and urination on the other, sleeping with one's wife and sleeping with a chance-met stranger. The infant first encounters the dichotomy in the feeding situation. But unlike the other four peoples whom I have just discussed, the Balinese place very early emphasis on the genitalia. A little boy's penis is being continually teased, pulled, flipped, flicked, by his mother, his child-nurse, and those around him. With the slight titillation go the repeated words, "Handsome, handsome, handsome," an adjective applied only to males. The little girl's vulva is patted gently, with the accompanying feminine adjective "Pretty, pretty, pretty." There is very little difference in the way in which a woman handles a male child and the way in which she handles her child's penis. The same flick, the same teasing, occur over and over again, while bystanders also handle the baby in arms just as they handle a small child's penis.

But most of the Balinese child's learning is focussed on his whole body, on his mother's carrying him as a part of her body; he is passive and relaxed, swinging in a sling as she pounds rice or works with rapid rhythmic movements. He develops a part-whole relationship to the world, in which each part of his body is a whole, and yet each is part of the whole. Valuation in sexuality is primarily a valuation of the penis itself. Male homosexuality is not a question of complementary assertiveness, but a search for as much maleness as possible, and where female homosexuality occurred—as it did in the palaces of the old rajahs—mock phalluses were part of the game. When small children put their fingers in their mouths exploringly, the emphasis seems to be on the sensation on the surface of the finger rather than upon the sensations from the lips or the mouth cavity. Love-affairs are matters of the eyes, foreplay is almost completely concentrated in a glance-exchanging courtship; the phrase for this eye-play is "as two fighting cocks looking at each other," and the sense of tension falls quickly from this first clash of feeling.

Even this very sketchy exploration of the way in which members of different cultures communicate some of their own elaborate historical cultural attitudes to their children should indicate how infinitely complicated the process of forming a picture of the adult sex rôle is for human beings who must be for so many years subjected to such elaborate adult pressures. The child's body with its orifices is open to endless pressures, stimulations, prohibitions, emphases. It may be handled only by women, or by men and women, or by little girls, or by little boys. It may be treated as part of the mother, as a whole separate person, as part of a person, as a beetle or as a god. But whatever the elaborations during learning, the adult sex act itself remains a complementary act; the male enters, the female is entered, however much these anatomical fundamentals may be overlaid and distorted. Each young child forms, from the way in which adults of each sex handle it, a picture of its own body and a picture of the body of the opposite sex, which will be in the end a part of its sex capacity and of its sex rôle. Probably emphasis on the mouth as a zone of intercommunication between adults and children gives the most vivid imagery for the sex act, but at the same time it carries extraordinary perils, because too vivid appreciation of the rewards of receptivity are incompatible with an adult male rôle, and may even lead to inversion; too much emphasis upon the assertive demanding aspects of the mouth may build a female picture that is over-active, over-demanding, and threatening. In marital quarrels among the Iatmul, the men complain bitterly that their wives demand too much of their copulatory powers.

So we have seen how emphasis on either the mouth or the genitals is basically complementary in character, and tends to build up attitudes towards activity-passivity, initiation-response, entrance and reception. We have also seen how emphasis on elimination may build most readily an emphasis on reciprocity, on taking in, retaining, and giving out, measured giving, measured receiving. To organize such behaviour into symmetrical behaviour, it is necessary to ignore or distort these partial relationships, all of which are essentially asymmetrical. Where the distortion is active, we find such situations as in a quarrel between Iatmul women when one says, "I'll copulate with you," and the other answers, with equal fury, "With what?" The Balinese man preserves symmetrical relationships by specific refusals of complementary situations. He covers his mouth, closes his ears, denies his responsiveness and receptivity, refuses to be worked on by oratory. He bends, and if his superior in status attempts any but the most highly stylized complementary behaviour, he suddenly exaggerates his own behaviour into complementary terms and offers his superior the danger of falling. The superior, to restore his own balance, must give up the complementary bit of arrogance.

But as important a set of learnings, and a set that will later be worked into the child's views of its own sex rôle, are offered to the child by the differences in size in the world around him. The differences in size between parents and children seem on the surface to be fixed, and therefore immutable; actually, however, cultures do very different things with them. The adult may stress the child's likeness to the parent, dress the child like an adult, minimize the difference in size and maximize the difference in sex. In parts of old Japan, the four-year-old male, because he was a male, could terrorize his mother and the other females of the household. His maleness overrode a difference in size that would have made it possible for any one of the females to have given him a sound thrashing. Every time that sameness of sex is stressed at the expense of contrast in size, the significance and the complementary character of the two sexes are emphasized. But when children are lumped together as all inferior in status or strength to adults of both sexes, then sex differences are minimized. Some cultures play hard on one theme, others play both. So among the Iatmul, where there is a strong preference for symmetrical behaviour, wherever symmetrical behaviour is not possible there are elaborate devices to keep the possibilities of complementary behaviour between males from getting out of hand. The young child learns simultaneously the possibilities of passivity and receptivity in the way in which his mother nurses him so assertively, and the advantages of self-assertion because he is not fed at all until he has asserted himself. Mothers not only treat their new-born as if they were separate wilful beings, but it is a common sight to hear a mother pitting her will against a two-year-old who runs away shrieking in terror from her raised stick—a stick, however, which will never fall. The child is allowed to escape, strained to the utmost; the mother returns to her interrupted work muttering over his great strength and intractability. Grown men scatter small boys with showers of stones, angry fathers pace the village breathing imprecations upon their eight-year-olds, who may just have burned down a valuable sago-patch. In a thousand ways the adult world says to the child: "You are very strong. Stronger than you look, stronger than you feel. So strong that you are our possible successful rivals." And when the mother picks up food to eat, the child shrieks with rage and makes her give it a piece first.

But despite this strong premium on strength, little boys are classified with little girls and women, vis-à-vis the men, who are strongest of all, or wish to believe they are. Little boys sit with their mothers in the houses of mourning, sit with backs that curve as gracefully as any girl's above her play cooking utensils, and carry babies around affection-ately. They hear any one of a dozen words for sodomy hurled about the village, irrespective of the sex of the user, but if two small boys attempt to act out what they have heard, older boys arm them with sticks and force them to fight each other. In adult life elaborate rituals in which men dress as women, caricaturing their lesserness, and women dress as men, caricaturing their glorious bombast, are a frequent fea-ture of ceremonial life.

And still in every society men are by and large bigger than women, and by and large stronger than women, and adults are bigger and stronger than children. A little boy may be made to feel that his maleness is deeply and finally in doubt because he is so much smaller than a grown man, or he may feel that his maleness is an inalienable and absolute possession because it gives him some position of dominance or preference over a much larger woman. A girl may spend her childhood wrestling on an equal basis with boys, many of whom are smaller or weaker than she, when children of both sexes are set against the adult world, and so learn to feel that she is as strong, or stronger, than a male. A girl may be treated with such exaggerated chivalry while she is still a mite that she sets a value on her female charms that could never be learned if it were not accorded her by males of so much greater size and importance.

So the three themes, complementariness, reciprocity, and symmetry, weave in and out of the long learning process, interpenetrating and informing each other, until one side of the complementariness may be so emphasized as to become a form of symmetrical behaviour, and with difference in age to provide the only asymmetry—as among the Arapesh, where husbands are ideally much older than their wives—because their receptivity and responsiveness are so much stressed. Or the assertive, invasive side of the suckling relationship may become dominant for both mother and child, with both sexes becoming assertive and demanding. Through the body, the ways of the body are learned.

IV

EVEN-HANDED, MONEY-MINDED,

AND WOMB-ENVYING PATTERNS

In the last chapter we followed the way in which the child's intercommunication with the rest of human society, particularly its nursing mother, formed its earliest expectations and understandings of the complementary character of sex relations. We look next at the way in which these seven South Sea peoples have patterned, in ritual and in ceremony, the relative rôles of men and women, how they have valued, or devalued, the basic anatomical sex differences.

There are two ways in which we can get enlightenment from these records of men's houses with towering carved pillars, of women fishing while men make speeches, or men driving oxen while women make offerings, of men who wear curls while women are brisk and bald and businesslike, or women who walk so that their stiff grass skirts almost melt around them and men who grow old from bearing children. Not only do they give us clues to possibilities in our own society, or in any society well known to us, but also they make it

possible for us to see more clearly some of the basic relationships between men and women that are obscured by the
complexity and diversity of our modern ways of life.
Walls separate us from each other at most of the important
moments of our lives, schools separate one age from another,
clothes separate us from our own bodies as well as from the
bodies of others. The few occasions on which we take down
the walls—the one funeral to which it is impossible not to
go; the one wedding where the meaning of marriage is still
somehow forced upon the wine-befuddled consciousness of
the wedding-guests and they weep, resenting their weeping
and not knowing why they weep; the one birth for which
clothes and fuss adequate for a hundred Samoan babies
muffle the unpreparedness with which the father and mother
enter parenthood—all these serve to make our picture of ourselves and of the opposite sex more rather than less fantastic,
less rather than more immediate.

Perhaps in the mid-twentieth century in the United States
of America it is harder to think about the simple bodily outlines of our humanity than it was in earlier periods, because
we are living in one of those temporary swings of the pendu-
lum when reflecting the snatched promiscuity of war we are
going in heavily for undecorousness in our advertisements
and in our speech. But the pin-up girl, however long her
legs, does not make the man who pins her to his wall feel
more at home with his body, or with hers. We are trained by
our society to keep our bodies out of our minds. We have to
make considerably more of an effort to do so if we are confronted everywhere with pictures of partially dressed seductive women. The puritan, in his off moments, may sin more
frequently, but not more easily, and closeness to the bodily
self is still felt, inevitably, as a threat to those whose standards of control and responsibility and decency have been
built on its denial. The solution for the peculiar difficulties
of a puritan society does not lie in a series of pin-up girls

whose breasts, tailored for love, are explicitly *not* meant for the loving nourishment of their children. It lies rather in developing greater ease with our clothes on; taking them off only increases our anxiety.

When we study exotic peoples whose whole way of life has been built up differently, and who live, moreover, in a climate in which nakedness is adaption and not simply lack of ability to make leather garments or put soles on shoes, we have an opportunity to follow the body through its growth, watch adults and children communicate through the way in which the child's body is treated, and yet—keep our own clothes on. Without direct reference to our own selves, far enough removed from the uplift bras and the way Grandfather looks when Granddaughter wears one of them, the ways of the body may be followed in delicate, far-away outline, and perhaps some new understanding of what human beings are and have the power to be may be learned as no stripping to a tingling and sensitive skin could ever teach us at home. The search of the eighteenth century for the noble savage, for the inhabitants of Eden still untouched by the serpent's wiles, can be seen as an escape, or a piece of voyeurism, or a search for understanding. And even the most hardened and disassociated business man who is a model of behaviour at home has one long debauch when he goes to the big city, and when he went to Bali because of the exposed breasts in the advertisements, stayed in Bali to ask, "Why are the people so contented?"

If we return then to the small boy and the small girl living in a world where the bodies of males and females of all ages are slightly clothed and simply accepted, we find that the small girl learns that she is a female and that if she simply waits, she will some day be a mother. The small boy learns that he is a male and that if he is successful in manly deeds some day he will be a man, and will be able to show how manly he is. When he looks at girls and women, and compares their bodies with his, he has the choice of saying simply, even-handedly, "I am a male, and she can never be a male," or "I am a male, but may be transformed into a female," or "Aren't the women really males too?" It seems possible that the presence of so many unmarried and child-less women in Western society may be one of the factors that mute the male's sense that women bear children and he does not, and increase his feeling that women are imperfect men, castrated, incomplete, partial males, who can never be as important as he because they lack his full equipment. Similarly, in modern society the little girl, watching the women around her, is no longer given the sure sense that "because I am a girl some day I will have a baby." The dif-ference between the sexes that is forced home on children in our world of walled-in, self-contained flats has to do with differences in occupation, in dress, in privilege. All women do not have babies, but most men don't have to wash dishes. It is men who are flyers and gangsters and ship-captains and policemen, men who win the ski-jumps and become Presi-dents. Significantly, the United States has been as unable to find a suitable rôle for the President's children as for the President's wife; both are temporary and derivative.

But in societies where every woman marries, and even the sterile woman is likely to adopt and even suckle a child, where pregnancy is an obtrusive and interesting event, little boys do learn that they cannot have babies, however much they may play that they can and express those wishes later collectively in ceremonies that imitate gestation and child-bearing. True, the social scene, the arrangements of men and women into families, the words of kinship, tell them that they will be fathers, but being a father is much harder to grasp than being a mother. The little girl places her hand firmly against her mother's swelling belly; there is a baby, and some day within her own body, shaped like her mother's, there will also be a baby. She goes away to sit playing in the sand, drawing sand up to cover her vulva, closing herself in, she who is to become a vessel for a new life. She places a doll, or a puppy, or a toy cucumber, or her baby-sister gently in some enclosed place, and she can directly project herself into the future. Her present sexual capacity is negative where her brother's is positive. He can flaunt his masculinity, she can only wait for her maternity.

His equipment for love is manifest to the very small boy—but what is it to be a father? This is something that goes on outside one's own body, in the body of another. Furthermore, it takes a very long time. One of the reasons why it is so hard to convince people of the importance of nutrition, as compared with the importance of mere nourishment, is because the effects of a vitamin-C deficiency take so long to manifest themselves that many adults find it impossible to believe in them. For small children, whose time-span is much shorter, whose grasp of the future is much more precarious, the whole question of impregnation, followed so many months later by birth, is far more difficult to grasp than are gestation and birth. Detailed symbolic analysis of small children's play suggests that little boys who take their cues from adult life play at copulation, and play at pregnancy, but they play less at impregnation, at a sequence that they initiate and another must finish. Man, the lover and the achiever in order to prove his manliness, and woman, the maker of babies, sometimes seen as a lesser, sometimes as a greater, achiever, are what catch the small boy's imagination. "Why don't you copulate with your wife instead of beating her?" shouts the six-year-old little Manus boy. His notions of the sex act are many and various, as many and various as the practices and emotions to which the adults in his society allow expression, but his conception of paternity is vague, unvalidated by his own body.

Whether or not the adults show an active or a prohibitory interest in infant genitalia, children themselves become differentially aware of them. Both sexes experience moments of heated orgiastic pleasure, and boys seem to associate these more easily with their genitals than do girls. Both sexes learn gradually—or sometimes perhaps suddenly—that the differing names and phrases and behaviours that have been meted out to them as a boy or a girl, a "small male" or a "small female," a "male thing" or a "female thing," are specially relevant to their genitals. This learning will have very different meanings, however, to the extent that the small child is able to experience directly the continuity between its small child's body and the adult's.

In the wave of earnest attempts to sweep away some of the taboos that were no longer appropriate to a society which had changed radically since they were developed, recently in the United States there was an epidemic of parents' attempts to protect their children from some of the misconceptions that psychoanalysis had discovered in neurotic patients by letting their children see them nude. When the next crop of neurotics, this time small children, reached the consulting-room, a new alarm was set up, because the clinicians reported that this was not necessarily the panacea it had been expected to be, that children were still frightened and confused and unaccepting of their sex.

These well-meaning reformers had missed a serious link in the chain of learning. What the small child receives in a primitive society, and what he is coming closer and closer to receiving on our bathing-beaches to-day, is the assurance that there is a continuous series of steps between his small body and that of an adult. The little boy needs to see the changes in body form and hair, the gradually developing genitals, the spreading hair on chest and armpits, the first soft facial down that no razor will recognize, to bind his sense of himself, still so small and undeveloped, to the man that he will become. And the little girl, to be equally assured, needs to be one of a series of girls, up through the nubile girl with budding breasts to the mature young woman, and finally to the just pregnant, the fully pregnant, and the post-parturient and suckling mother. This is what happens in those primitive societies in which the body is hardly covered at all and most of the major bodily changes are present to the child's eye. The adult may be modest, in the deepest sense of modesty, never intruding on the unprepared eye of another any exposed body part that would shock or embarrass him—as when the male Balinese, after bathing naked, walks away from the bath shielding his genitals lightly with one hand. But to the eye of the child, when that eye has been left free to see and is neither frightened nor bribed into blindness, the full pageant of human development from early childhood to full maturity is visible. The worried and frightened comparisons between the small boy and his father—the only exhibit of maleness that is vouchsafed him in the one heavily enlightened home—are not the characteristic features of such an experience.

Such experiences can of course be made frightening, even in a society in which there are no clothes. Primitive peoples can introduce very deep fears into the growing little boy. The imagination of man has developed so many subtle ways of embroidering upon the mysterious conditions of his existence that in South America, in Africa, and in the South Seas there are tribes in which the old men's antagonism to the springing sexuality of the young induces fears that are later reduced in pantomime, cruel initiatory rites in which the young men are circumcised, their teeth knocked out, and, in various ways they are reduced and modified and humbled, and then permitted to be men. The contrast between small and large, especially when joined with a recognition that some day action will be required, is one that is always there either for a whole culture or for a single child's disordered or over-sensitive imagination to play upon.

But let us consider those societies in which the small child does experience all the normal growth and expression of the adult body, and in which the initiatory rites are not accompanied by any such overwhelming castrative feelings. The little naked boy walks about the village, his steps uncertain, his balance precarious. When he slips, his hand goes to his penis, to keep his balance. Or after he has tripped, his hand goes to his penis as if assuring himself that it is still there, and also to clutch for support. There are no blind spots in the language that prevent any one's calling his penis by any name at all, or which devalue it and make it seem to vanish away, as can happen in languages in which prudery has robbed the human tongue of any words for the organs of procreation or the acts of procreation—usually through an unfortunate over-association with acts of excretion. People speak to him of his penis as they do of his arms or legs, his eyes or nose. It is something that he has, indubitably, definitely. He is male. He is small, but some day by the steps he sees represented by the growing boys about him he will be an adult. He will be a man and he will not be a woman.

The reader who is well versed in the literature on middle-class neurotics of contemporary Occidental society may wonder why I do not discuss first the experience of the little girl, the wounding experience that she is less equipped than her brother for the battle of life. But this Western experience, which undoubtedly does occur often enough to be a very frequent characteristic of the woman who finds her way to the analyst's couch, occurs against a background of a prudishly clothed society, and in a society that has so over-rewarded male positions that an envy for the rôle which is played by the father can coalesce with an experience of the little brother's or a boy companion's more conspicuous anatomical equipment. As we shall see later in a discussion of the elaborations of the sex rôle that society has developed, envy of the rôle of the opposite sex is almost unavoidable in some individuals, in any society, but sharp envy of opposite sex anatomy is quite another matter that may or may not develop.

To the small naked children, running lightly in the sun beneath the palm-trees, the little girl's sex membership is as clear as her brother's, but there is less that she can do with it. When she trips and falls, she clutches at her head, or tries to fold her arms across her chest. Her femininity is concealed deep within her, nothing that she can touch and see, depend upon or flaunt. In those societies where children's sex membership is recognized by adults, in which the men treat the little girls with flirtatious attention and the women tease and challenge the small boys, the little girls respond by movements of the entire body, which undulates and postures in delicious indulgence of feminine response. The small boy struts, sometimes with emphasis on his penis, more often carrying hatchet, knife, stick, pole, in upward positions as he marches, parries, performs. His behaviour, however symbolic, is to the extent that it is male a concentrated phallic exaggeration, while his sister's is more diffuse and involves the whole body. The little boy is sure about his specific maleness, but seems not to be so sure of his adequacy to operate it. He supplements with various symbolic objects. Very often he also shouts, adding the vigour of his voice to the vigour of his posturing.

The little girl in such a society also sees pregnancy treated with the greatest openness and simplicity. Child-birth itself may be shrouded from all but adult eyes: children may stay away from child-birth, as in Bali, because they have been frightened by tales of witches abroad to snatch the newborn; they may be firmly kept away by the adults as in Arapesh; they may be shooed away with a shower of small stones and return to peek through the cracks in the blinds, as in Samoa. But nowhere in any of these seven societies is pregnancy concealed, and indeed it requires heavy clothing and shuttered houses and an economic system that can withdraw women from almost all productive work, to make it possible to conceal pregnancy from the eyes of the world as was done for certain classes in Europe in the last century. "I Wajan is pregnant, some day you will be pregnant. My! what a fat little tummy you have! Are you perhaps pregnant now?" In Bali, little girls between two and three walk much of the time with purposely thrust-out little bellies, and the older women tap them playfully as they pass. "Pregnant," they tease. So the little girl learns that although the signs of her membership in her own sex are slight, her breasts mere tiny buttons no bigger than her brother's, her genitals a simple inconspicuous fold, some day she will be pregnant, some day she will have a baby. And having a baby is, on the whole, one of the most exciting and conspicuous achievements that can be presented to the eyes of small children in these simple worlds, in some of which the largest buildings are only fifteen feet high, the largest boat some twenty feet long. Furthermore, the little girl learns that she will have a baby not because she is strong or energetic or initiating, not because she works and struggles and tries, and in the end succeeds, but simply because she *is* a girl and not a boy, and girls turn into women, and in the end—if they protect their femininity—have babies. Her society may enjoin certain precautions on older girls—they may have to observe food taboos, or rub themselves with stinging nettles to ensure that their breasts will grow; but throughout the emphasis is on protecting a natural unfolding, at the most a slight enhancement of breast-size, not on effort and struggle. Her sex membership may not be so conspicuous now as her brother's, but she has only to wait, to be, and—some day—she will have a baby.

Meanwhile, what does his present and future male rôle mean to a little boy brought up in a society where women's

procreative rôle is so conspicuous? Here we can draw sharp
distinctions among these seven societies. Not between those
societies in which men's achievements are the most conspicuous, as compared with those in which they are the
least conspicuous, for the great men's houses of the Sepik
River are the most grossly conspicuous achievements of
any of our seven societies. The distinctions do not divide
those societies in which the physiques of men and women
have been most clearly differentiated. In Bali, where, if
there is any envy at all, it is anatomical maleness that is
valued, the two sexes look extraordinarily alike. The men
are almost without large muscular development and have
well-developed breasts, the women are slight, with small
high breasts. What we find within these seven societies is
that those societies which have emphasized suckling, the
most complementary relationship of all the bodily learning
experience, there is the greatest symbolic preoccupation
with the differentials between men and women, the greatest
envy, over-compensation, ritual mimicry of the opposite sex,
and so on. With the emphasis on the suckling relationship
goes naturally enough a greater emphasis on the relationship between mother and child, or at least between lactating
woman and nursling. The baby cannot be left too long in
the charge of a father or a grandparent or a child-nurse; the
tie to the breast is strong and central. When in addition
male separateness from women has been developed into a
strong institution, with a men's house and male initiation
ceremonies, then the whole system becomes an endlessly
reinforcing one, in which each generation of little boys grows
up among women, identified with women, envying women,
and then, to assert their endangered certainty of their manhood, isolate themselves from women. Their sons again
grow up similarly focussed on women, similarly in need
of over-compensatory ceremonial to rescue themselves.

For however clear the small boy may be that he is a

male and that some day he will be a man, there still remains
the problem of identification with an adult. He may know
he will be a man, but this is no surer guarantee that he
wishes to be a man than in our equally lop-sided Western
society a girl's knowledge that she is a girl is any guarantee
that she will *want* to be a woman. In fact there is a strong
possibility that the unsatisfactoriness of one's own sex rôle
—as an adult—is all the more vivid if one's sense of sex
membership is clear and unequivocal at the age when only
the most salient and conspicuous aspects of the opposite
sex rôle can be seen: that women make babies, and that
men ride horses, and kill enemies. Only later will the girl
learn that the fear that one may not kill a lion makes the
game hardly worth the candle, or the boy conclude that
child-bearing is a slow, patient, nine-month-long price to
pay for a few moments of dramatic achievement.

These seven South Sea societies give us practically every
variation on this particular theme. In Samoa and in Bali,
where the emphasis is on handling the child as a whole,
with the suckling relationship specific and undiffuse, and
there is practically no preoccupation at all with elimination,
the young child grows up in a two-sex world, a world in
which neither men nor women are treated in ways that
are not significant and even-handed. In Samoa the baby
learns to respect the head of the household not because he
is a man, but because he is the *matai*. Both boys and girls
are equally shooed away, and both creep back to watch a
feast or a pair of lovers in the moonlight. In ceremonials,
the men have their feasts and the women theirs, but the
greatest feasts of all are when the *taupou*, the ceremonial
princess, and the high chief, or the *manaia*, the heir apparent,
dance together, each wearing head-dresses of human hair.
Neither boys nor girls are hurried or pressed. The boy who
would flee from too much pressure on his young manhood
hardly exists in Samoa; the girl who is ambitious and man-

aging has plenty of outlets in the bustling, equally organized life of the women's groups. Sureness of one's own sex, a separation between care, discipline, and suckling, no emphasis on elimination to shroud sex relations in shame, and a picture of the adult world in which men and women both have satisfactory rôles, all combine to make it possible for Samoans to develop into easy, balanced human beings, with a balance so sure that even years away from Samoa does not disturb its essential symmetry.

Bali, in many ways, contrasts sharply with Samoa. Samoan life is characterized by ease, by lack of elaboration, by long moonlight evenings in which people dance the same simple dances and effortlessly applaud a joke heard many times before. The Christian religion has been taken simply as a pleasant and satisfying social form in which choirs sing and married women wear hats and pastors pray and preach in the most beautiful language. Balinese life is instead a highly elaborated razor-edge, in which people whose emotions during childhood have been first tautened and then slackened turn from personal relationships to endlessly complicated and interwoven artistic and religious forms, in which women spend days making intricate offerings, men practise for months to perfect some orchestral piece, small children may be trained to dance in trance on live coals, and every one lives a life so dependent on knowing his exact location in time and space and caste that even moving twenty miles away is traumatic. Yet here also men and women are not segregated, except as men sometimes have their ceremonies and women have their counterparts of them. As in Samoa the wife of the talking chief is also a talking chief, so in Bali the wife of the Brahman high priest may be a high priestess, and the chief elder of the village temple rite may be replaced by his wife. Division of labour is definite, but when it is reversed no one minds. The slight over-emphasis on maleness, which accompanies the slightly greater rôle played by the mother as compared with the father in the upbringing of the child, is a symbolic anatomical one, an overvaluation and over-interest in the responsiveness of male organs rather than an interest in the greater achievement of men.

Among the Manus also there is a fair degree of even-handedness in the economic and religious life of a village. Trade is emphasized more than war—which was primarily engaged in to acquire property, or occasionally to avenge a death—and in trade and in religion a woman can play a conspicuous rôle. What is most significant in Manus culture is a devaluation of sex, and of the husband-and-wife tie. The prudery, the equation of the sex act with excretion, the close tie between women and property, the pivoting of all economic arrangements on marriage so that adultery is always a threat against the economic system, all serve to make the woman's lot less attractive than man's. As the representatives of the disallowed activities of the body, as the sex in fact that does more with its body, women are the more hedged-in. If women gossip, the male ghosts get very angry; if women sin with anyone, the ghosts make trouble. But Manus men may sin freely beyond the borders of the tribe, beyond their own tribesmen's economically important women. All of this reacts on the children. When children are asked to draw males and females, the males are drawn with penises, the girls with grass skirts. When a woman has a child, she is isolated from her husband for a whole month, until he can redeem her with a large payment to her brother, and meanwhile he is free to play about the village with the dispossessed child. The tie between father and son formed in these early years is warm and durable, but the small girl first becomes attached to her father, and then, at five or six, must return to the women, because the avoidances and taboos connected with marriages and prospective marriages would embarrass the men and boys among whom her father and brother move freely. Her identification with the female group is never as happy or as complete as her brother's identification with the male group. As a grown woman she walks with no swing of the hips, the heavy ornaments that weigh her down as bride or at her later wedding anniversaries are money rather than adornment; she may grow so tired of carrying them that she slips home not even noticed if the strings of shell money have already been counted. It is the exchange of property, not the bride, that is the centre of the wedding-feast.

This Manus example is very instructive because it represents a case where women do not enjoy being women, not because public rewards given males are denied to them—influence, power, wealth, are all open to women—but because the sensuous creative significance of the female rôle of wife and mother is so undervalued. The sense of touch itself is regulated and regimented; the one woman with whose breasts a man may play is his female cross-cousin, with whom he has no tender relations—tenderness is for his sister—and with whom he may not copulate. In our current Western theorizing, it has been too often ignored that envy of the male rôle can come as much from an undervaluation of the rôle of the wife and mother as from an overvaluation of public aspects of achievement that have been reserved for men. When all achievement is outside the home, women of enterprise and initiative hate to be told that they must confine themselves there, but when the home itself is undervalued, then also women will cease to enjoy being women, and men will neither envy nor value the female rôle.

On the New Guinea mainland most peoples practise some variety of male initiation within similar formal patterns. I have worked in four of these initiatory cultures—Arapesh, Mundugumor, Tchambuli, and Iatmul—and it is instructive to compare what has happened as four different groups of people have worked within a common framework. An initiatory culture, with a men's house in which the men gather for ceremonial and from which women and uninitiated boys are excluded, is a social institution of very great strength, so interwoven with every other aspect of the culture that usually when the initiatory system breaks—as it does before mission influences, for instance—the whole cultural system collapses also. Groups of people may through time, by accident of personality, or epidemic, or the effects of contact with their neighbours, deviate in many directions from the original culture with which their particular initiatory system was congruent. As a result, the record of the way in which different New Guinea societies living close together, eating the same foods, speaking languages that show many signs of relationship, modify and change this strongly integrated institution of the men's house and initiation—this record gives us valuable clues to the relationship between a social institution and the development of attitudes towards sex membership and sex rôles.

We may take the Iatmul culture of the Middle Sepik River, with its huge houses, its impressive villages, its splendid art, its great canoes, as a type of culture in which the initiatory system is stabilized by the very complexity and eclecticism of the culture itself. Each paternal clan has its own strip of land in the village, with the tall dwelling-houses set back among the trees, the gables surmounted with great carved faces and high well-built ladders leading to the upper stories. Closer to the great sluggish river, which at high water floods the village so that people go about in canoes, stands the men's house, taboo to women, and at the water's edge canoes, used by men and women, are lined up on the mud banks. In addition to the small men's houses, each village boasts one large men's house or more, built with the effort of several clans, strong enough to stand for many decades if not burned down in an enemy raid, with

its attic filled with the great slit gongs, flutes, masks, and all
the impressive ritual paraphernalia of the men's cult. Inside
the ceremonial house, all the important events of the men's
elaborated ritual, war-making, and debating go on, and
here occur the preludes to the crocodile-hunt and the war-
party. Usually the lower storey is left open so that women
and children, kept at a respectful distance, can see something of the everyday activities. But for initiations and
other ceremonies, a great enclosure of leaves is built. Into
this, sometimes through a gate itself shaped like a crocodile,
the novices are finally taken, after bullyings, scarifications,
and humiliations, to take their places with the adult men
in the men's house, which is appropriately enough called
a womb. The initiatory myths recount how the sacred noise-
making objects were originally discovered by women, who
gave the secret to men, and even entreated the men to
kill them so that they, the men, might keep the secret for
all time.

Meanwhile, in the great, spacious dwelling-houses the
daily life of the village goes on. The women come and go
about their fishing and their basket-making, moving in
troops up and down the village, and with them go the small
girls and the small boys. When the men go home to their
own houses, they have no special rôle. They quarrel with
their wives and their wives quarrel back with fine symmetrical fury. Vis-à-vis a group of men, the women, except
on special occasions, are admiring spectators, but individually they are upstanding viragos. The father inside his own
house will often hold his infant or dandle his two-year-old
on his knee, but with the same gestures and the same general tone of voice as the mother. Like the mother, he shouts
at the children, pretends that they are stronger than he
is, pushes them to the limits of their strength, rewards them
for assertiveness, and helps to build up the capacity to enjoy
passivity, a part of Iatmul character that as men they must

not indulge. The period is one in which they share in the full life of the women, even to attendance at the great mourning ceremonies from which the men are excluded, while they see the life of men either as a pallid version of their mothers' lives—when their fathers are at home in the dwelling-houses—or from a distance as a magnificent, fantastic spectacle. Later, after the boys have been initiated, their conscious memories of this childhood period will dim. They will say: "My mother must have taken me to mourn over the dead, for I see women take other small boys. But I do not remember." Yet when we gave eleven- and twelve-year-old boys toys to play with, it was mourning games that they liked to play best, turning in phantasy back towards the childhood that they shared with their mothers, not forward towards the splendour and dash of male public life. Little boys take almost as much care of infants as do girls, and even young adolescent boys spend a good deal of time playing with babies. In manner, they are surprisingly feminine, willowy, giving very little premonition of the bombast and high, headstrong behaviour that will characterize them as adults.

Their identification has been, inevitably, first with women, with women who treat boy and girl babies alike, symmetrically, as angry little bundles of will power, and complementarily, as objects whose mouths can be stopped by an intruding nipple. Later, in their early teens, and long before they wish to go, they are whisked away to be initiated, and then afterwards spend several miserable months, or sometimes years, during which the women chase them away—as a cluster of modest nymphs might rout an intruder into the women's bathing-pool—while they themselves are loath enough to join the men.* Meanwhile, in the men's

---

* This description is as of 1938 in the village of Tambunum. The practice of going away to work as indentured labour on plantations has considerably reduced the age of initiation, as returned work-boys are likely to be too old and too assertive for the initiatory rites.

group there is loud, over-definite masculine behaviour, continuous use of verbs that draw their imagery from phallic attack on men and women alike. But there is also a very strong taboo on any display of passivity, and there is no development of male homosexuality within the society. The slightest show of weakness or of receptivity is regarded as a temptation, and men walk about, often comically carrying their small round wooden stools fixed firmly against their buttocks. A male child from any outside village or tribe becomes a ready victim, and Iatmul work-boys are said to become active homosexuals when they meet men from other tribes away at work. But within the group, the system holds, and demonstrates vividly how it is possible to distort the upbringing of every male so that his capacity and temptation to introduce sex into his relationship with other males is very strong and yet kept closely in control.

Sex relations with women are active and vigorous. A woman's seduction techniques are either to question the man's virility—this can be done by sending some little love-token and one of the mocking questions already noted, "Have you no bones?" or "Are you a man or woman?" through a go-between, or by presenting herself in an attackable posture. The balance between defence against attack and readiness to attack runs through the whole upbringing. Children are so alert that, to reach its object, a slap must be delivered absolutely without warning. At the slightest tensing of an adult's body, a whole group of children will scatter like leaves. To stir the men into any sort of activity, showers of abuse and challenge are necessary, either from another moiety or another clan, while the individual wife whose larder is empty will rave at the top of her voice against her husband, whose laziness, improvidence, and general lack of energy are bringing her, his children, himself, to shame before his brothers-in-law.

When we follow this same initiatory structure that divides

women and children from men into three other smaller, less swagger New Guinea cultures, we find valuable clues as to the way in which so strong an institution can be modified. The Tchambuli villages of the lovely ebony-black lake that lies to the southwest of the Sepik River have superficially the same structure as the Iatmul: clusters of clan houses with men's houses down by the lake, initiation, and elaborate ceremonial put on by the initiated males for the wonder and admiration of the women. But Tchambuli female character is made of much sterner and more matter-of-fact stuff than that of Iatmul women. Where the Iatmul woman treats her child as strong, as capable of wilfulness and assertiveness and useful anger as she herself is, the Tchambuli woman stresses her own strength. She feeds her baby lightly, gaily, either from her breast or with a variety of lollipops, lily-roots, sweet seeds, and fruits. Where the Iatmul mother chases her erring two-year-old with a ten-foot paddle with which she threatens to kill him when she catches him—and never does kill—the Tchambuli mother simply tucks small offenders under her confident arm. In Iatmul, it is the women and the children who wear strings of ornaments; in Tchambuli it is the men and the children; the women go with shaven heads, unadorned, determinedly busy about their affairs. In Iatmul a man is a master in his own house, albeit he has to fight for it against a wife practically as strong as he; his wives quarrel among themselves, and make his rule easier. In Tchambuli, a man marries the daughter of one of his mother's clan brothers, so that a young girl enters as a bride the house of her father's sister. As aunt and mother-in-law, his mother treats the young wife well. The women of the house form a great solid mass, always together, working briskly while the little boys tumble unconsidered among them, and the young men sit gingerly on the edge of the women's group and then flee to the men's house. Instead of the great collective initiations of the Iatmul, Tchambuli small boys are initiated and scarified one at a time in a family ceremonial, in which the emphasis is upon the ceremonial and exchange of valuables, not upon them. Iatmul boys are made into men, their pre-manhood feminine-like state is ruthlessly overstressed, masked figures are poked ignominiously into their mouths and giant vulvas are clapped down on their heads; but Tchambuli boys are simply scarified and kept in a kind of purdah for several months.

Adult males in Tchambuli are skittish, wary of each other, interested in art, in the theatre, in a thousand petty bits of insult and gossip. Hurt feelings are rampant, not the violent angry response of the Iatmul male challenged in his most vulnerable point, but the pettishness of those who feel themselves weak and isolated. The men wear lovely ornaments, they do the shopping, they carve and paint and dance. Before the coming of British control headhunting had been reduced to the ritual killing of bought captives, and they put up no effective resistance against the depredations of the neighbouring Iatmuls, but fled inland instead, only to return when the Pax Britannica made it possible. Men whose hair was long enough wore curls, and the others made false curls out of rattan rings.

This is the only society in which I have worked where little girls of ten and eleven were more alertly intelligent and more enterprising than little boys. Even the confusions of Iatmul upbringing do not prevent the little boys from being bolder and more exploring of mind than the girls, but in Tchambuli the minds of small males, teased, pampered, neglected, and isolated, had a fitful fleeting quality, an inability to come to grips with anything.

The initiatory cult of New Guinea is a structure which assumes that men can become men only by men's ritualizing birth and taking over—as a collective group—the functions that women perform naturally. The Tchambuli have nevertheless modified this cult to fit the special emphases of a people who have lost interest in the warlike ideal. They have only partially adjusted their society to fit their chief interest—the arts. The Tchambuli male is made into an artist vis-à-vis a strong practical woman who spoils and manages him. The long-nosed black and white masks he carves are some of the loveliest masks from the whole area, but they remind one inevitably of werewolves.

Meanwhile two rivers and some fifty miles away, the Mundugumor of the Yuat River have done something quite different with the initiatory system. Upon the kinship patterns of the area, which always seems to hesitate between emphasizing ties through the mother and ties through the father, they have built a system that has divided man from man more thoroughly than any other known kinship system. Lineages are called ropes, and consist of a man, his daughters, his daughters' sons, his daughters' sons' daughters, and so on. All valuables, including the sacred objects that belong to the men's cult, pass down these lines. Even when a girl elopes, she tries to steal the heavily ornamented sacred flute that is her father's. If a woman has two sons, who will then belong to the same rope, a taboo divides them which says they must never eat from the same dish, nor speak to each other except in anger. Boys and girls alike grow up in a world that is hostile and divided against itself. Boys are taught their place in society, their kinship terms, and elaborate sets of kinship prohibitions by their mothers, girls by their fathers. Both sexes are independent, hostile, vigorous, and both boys and girls come out with very similar personalities. There is no men's house in which all the men gather, for no two men sit down comfortably together. The unit of society is the compound, where a man's wives maintain an uneasy co-operation and his daughters a certain degree of solidarity, while each mother turns her son into an enemy both of his father and of his half-brothers. Initiation is no longer a collective act in which males are welded together, but a display given by an important man, in which those who have not been initiated, whatever their age, can be cut and bullied by the already initiated. Girls are permitted to be initiated merely by observing taboos.

In such a society women are handicapped by their womanly qualities. Pregnancy and nursing are hated and avoided if possible, and men detest their wives for being pregnant. Men see women as a kind of human beings over whom they will have to fight and through whom they can be injured. If one has no sister to give in exchange one will have to pay a valuable flute for a wife, and so we come to the curious position that flutes, those excessively male symbols of the male cult, which elsewhere can never be seen by women without endangering the entire male society, are equated with women, are nearly but not quite as valuable as women, and are something that women are permitted to see with less fuss than boys. The boys' whole concept of their identity is that of fighting males tied precariously through women to other fighting males. Women are masculinized to a point where every feminine feature is a drawback except their highly specific genital sexuality, men to a point where any aspect of their personalities that might hold an echo of the feminine or the maternal is a vulnerability and a liability. The division of society into two groups, grown men on the one hand, women and children on the other, has been practically shattered, but at a price which, as in Tchambuli, threatens the very survival of the group. For the Mundugumor's habits of hostility were such that they had begun to eat people of their own language group. There was virtually no tribal solidarity, and it was probably a mere accident of history that they capitulated to the mission before they were destroyed by marauding neighbours.

The Mountain Arapesh are the fourth of our groups of

people whose social life is built upon a division between men and women, in which males have to be made into men by initiation into the adult male group. The Arapesh possessed the same paraphernalia of the men's cult as the other tribes I have described: the bull-roarer, the sacred flutes, the masks, the enclosure in which the novice is scarified, the special relationship of the initiator to the novice. But where the Tchambuli system crumbled under a reversal in the ethos of men and women, and the Mundugumor system was invaded and disintegrated by an emphasis on a common hostile ethos that lacked counterpoint or any complementary character beyond the bare facts of sexual anatomy, the Arapesh system is rendered innocuous by an emphasis on the maternal, parental aspects of both men and women. Arapesh men and women are both snugly at home in their small mountain huts, caring together for their children. They have no use for a men's house except for ceremonials, and large houses are hard to build. Labour is always scarce and might better be put into feeding children. All the rites have been rephrased as protective, and the men keep the fierce impersonations of the supernatural guardian of the men's cult from showing his fierceness towards the women, and if possible, towards the initiates.

In such a society, small boys and girls grow up together, with parents of both sexes always before their eyes as models. Boys know that they are boys by their bodies, their names, and the skills they learn. Girls know they are girls by their bodies, their names, and the little carrying-bags that their mothers place on their heads. Both sexes sit happily around the fires on chill mornings and bubble their lips. Little girls see their mothers carry loads in net bags, and little boys see their fathers carry them on carrying-poles. Later, little boys know, they will participate in men's affairs, and perhaps even have to make speeches or engage in fights. These are duties laid upon men, and they see how tired the men are who come out from the rare occasions when the flutes play in the village and the men have to sit up all night with them. Women have to flee over the edge of the village when the flutes are installed or when the mythical monster of the men's cult walks around the village leaving his giant leaf-anklets or marks on the ground where his testicles have bounced. Men have to stay away from the edge of the village where women bear their children, and wonder, with anguished curiosity that will never be satisfied, what it is like to bear children. Both boys and girls have to guard their growth so that they will both be good parents. They will both be depleted by parenthood, a man no less than a woman. "You should have seen what a fine-looking man he was before he had all those children."

No complexities of identification disturb this rhythm, but it does mean a probable greater modification of innate behaviour for most of the men than for the women. Even here, although the men's house has virtually been replaced by a home in which parents of two sexes rear children of two sexes, even here, the alteration of the basic institution of the initiatory cult is not effected without some penalty in adjustment to sex rôle.

It will be profitable to examine now, after following these four variations on the initiatory theme, the underlying structure of this initiatory cult, because it provides such cogent counterpoint to our Western ideas of the relationship between the sexes. In our Occidental view of life, woman, fashioned from man's rib, can at the most strive unsuccessfully to imitate man's superior powers and higher vocations. The basic theme of the initiatory cult, however, is that women, by virtue of their ability to make children, hold the secrets of life. Men's rôle is uncertain, undefined, and perhaps unnecessary. By a great effort man has hit upon a method of compensating himself for his basic inferiority. Equipped with various mysterious noise-making instruments, whose potency rests upon their actual form's being unknown to those who hear the sounds—that is, the women and children must never know that they are really bamboo flutes, or hollow logs, or bits of elliptoid wood whirled on strings—they can get the male children away from the women, brand them as incomplete, and themselves turn boys into men. Women, it is true, make human beings, but only men can make men. Sometimes more overtly, sometimes less, these imitations of birth go on, as the initiates are swallowed by the crocodile that represents the men's group and come out new-born at the other end; as they are housed in wombs, or fed on blood, fattened, hand-fed, and tended by male "mothers." Behind the cult lies the myth that in some way all of this was stolen from the women; sometimes women were killed to get it. Men owe their manhood to a theft and a theatrical mime, which would fall to the ground in a moment as mere dust and ashes if its true constituents were known. A shaky structure, protected by endless taboos and precautions, enforced by the women's shame in Iatmul, by fluttery fear for their child-bearing qualities in Arapesh, by good-humoured indulgence of male vanity in Tchambuli, and by blows and buffets and the curious reversed identification of flute and woman in Mundugumor, it survives only as long as every one keeps the rules. Iatmul men who see their whole social order threatened by the coming of the European threaten in tearful rage to complete the ruin by showing the flutes to the women, and the missionary who shows the flutes to the women has broken the culture successfully.

To the Occidental, bred in a society that has exalted the achievements of men and depreciated the rôle of women, this all seems far-fetched, perhaps the more far-fetched when he realizes that the men who depend for their sense of manhood on a phantasy structure of bamboo flutes, played within leaf hedges imitating man-made wombs, are not peaceful shepherds, but bold and fierce head-hunters, men often six feet tall, well set-up, and capable of magnificent anger. But if whole societies can build their ceremonial upon an envy of women's rôle and a desire to imitate it, then it should be easier to explore the possibility that envy of the other sex, or doubt of the authenticity of one's own sex, is a possibility in the life-history of both sexes, a possibility that may be immensely fostered by cultural arrangements, but which is always present.

V

FATHERS, MOTHERS, AND

BUDDING IMPULSES

IN EACH SOCIETY, THE GROWING CHILD ENCOUNTERS NOT ONLY the changes in his own feelings—his feeling about himself and about other human beings—but also the feelings which those other human beings, and especially his parents, have about him. As children reach four or five years of age, their own preoccupation with their sex and the preoccupation with it of the adults around them increases. It may include harsh disapproval of touching the genitals and a beginning insistence on wearing clothes, especially for girls. Adult behaviour towards children alters. The fact that in all these societies it is girls who are permanently clothed first is again an expression that they are waiting women, while the boys have manhood still to achieve. Older boys and men find little girls of four and five definitely female and attractive, and that attractiveness must be masked and guarded just as the male eye must be protected from the attractiveness of their older sisters and mothers. It seems that the more completely women's femininity—as a positive point, not a mere negation of maleness—is recognized, the more they are taught to protect it. A small girl, chic and entrancing, is sufficiently a temptation to a grown man so that societies usually have devices to protect her, circumscribe her, teach her not to exhibit her sex, which she herself lacks the wisdom to moderate. A small boy, on the other hand, however much his mother may treat him as a male, is less a temptation to her femininity than an extension of her maternity, while in the boy himself strong protections against his attraction to his mother have already been built. Mother-and-son incest is the rarest form of incest in the world, and it takes fairly elaborate cultural arrangements to make genuinely attractive any affairs between older women and men young enough to be their sons. Undoubtedly the groundwork for the greater attractiveness of the younger female to the older male and of the older male to the younger female is laid down firmly in early childhood.

With the boy, there is another emphasis. One has only to watch the tormented little boy carefully skirting a group of men in Bali who might otherwise give a pull at his penis as he passes, or the furious little Iatmul boy being ceremonially mauled by his father's sister, to realize that sexually toned contacts with adults are frightening to him, and must draw, if they draw on anything, on his passivity, on evoking memories of what he learned as an infant receptively and passively accepting the breast. Every contact arouses in him the triple fears: of losing his penis, or of never being an adequate man, or of becoming again a passive, dependent child at the breast. When the fear of passivity is also present in the minds of the adults—that is, when homosexuality is recognized in a society, with either approval or disapproval— the fear is exacerbated. The parents begin to pick at the child, to worry about his behaviour, to set him trials, or to lament his softness. Why did the eight-year-old little Balinese boy Gelis sit around all day with the women and girls, his head cradled against any convenient knee, instead of taking the oxen out to the fields? His peasant parents in the Balinese village of Bajoeng Gedé had very probably never seen a transvestite homosexual in the flesh—a *bantjih*, as they are called in Bali—still, they worried. With an initiative and a responsibility that Balinese parents, schooled to treat life like an already exposed film that will develop in due time, seldom display, they decided that perhaps Gelis' passivity had some connection with the seller's stall set up in front of their house, where he could always stuff his mouth with sweets; so they persuaded the seller to move. Too great softness, too great passivity, in the male and he will not become a man. The American Plains Indians, valuing courage in battle above all other qualities, watched their little boys with desperate intensity, and drove a fair number of them to give up the struggle and assume women's dress.

There seems in fact every reason to suppose that with the exception of the occasional anatomically confused hermaphrodites, homosexuality is a combination of adult expectations and fears and a possibility latent in many children that will never be fully expressed if it is not given social recognition or if the complementary position is not allowed for —as among the Iatmul. The worry that boys will not grow up to be men is much more wide-spread than that girls will not grow up to be women, and in none of these South Sea societies does the latter fear appear at all. As long as the female is seen as the mother, and not as a potential rival in some achievement field or as a possibly unwilling wife, a touch of boyishness in a small girl may be one of the ways in which she is protected from adult male interference until she is older. The American Indians did worry, in some instances, for fear their women would manifest male behaviour, but they paid a price for it; an Omaha Indian girl left alone was a soft, compliant victim. As counterpoint to having insisted on such yieldingness in the girl, the adults had to chaperon her, while the men took such aggressive advantage of the promiscuously yielding woman that a woman of uncertain virtue was subject to rape by groups of men.

So as little boys and little girls reach the age at which they are experimenting with their own budding sexuality, they also reach a crisis in their relations with adults that in psychoanalytical theory has been technically called the Oedipus situation, named for the Greek myth of Oedipus, who killed his father and married his mother. Stated most generally, this is the period of development in which children who are capable of intense feeling and capacity for pleasure, but without the degree of maturation necessary for adult procreative relations, must come to terms both with their parents and with their own immaturity. The boy must give up part of his passionate attachment to his mother and his rivalry with his father, the girl her attachment to her father and her rivalry with her mother. Each must accept the own-sex parent as in some way a model for his or her own future behaviour. At the same time they must accept a postponement of full sex satisfaction, and this includes a recognition that their parents belong to each other, and not to the children. When the surviving forms of this conflict are explored in dreams and by free association, the images that are exposed are difficult for the adult to cope with. The term "Oedipus conflict" has assumed an aura of unacceptability because it has taken its name from failure—from the unfortunate Oedipus who failed to solve the conflict—and not from the successful, though often compromised, solutions that each civilization has worked out.*

---

* It is interesting to turn to an American poet's statement, written before Freud, and unselfconsciously sure that this was a problem which men mastered: "To a Usurper," by Eugene Field.[1]

> Aha! a traitor in the camp,
>   A rebel strangely bold—
> A lisping, laughing, toddling scamp,
>   Not more than four years old!

[Continued on page 109.]

In all known societies, we find among boys some manifestations of what psychoanalysts call latency, a period in which overt interest in sex is discontinued, and the boys live in a world of their own, indifferent or openly hostile to girls, concerned with gaining strength and mastery one over another. They have outgrown the eagerly accepted sensations of childhood, and they are not yet ready for the more sophisticated pleasures of adulthood. Whether there is any internal psychological mechanism that would make a child "go into latency" we do not know, but certainly the age of five or six does present the child with a dilemma as to what

---

> To think that I, who've ruled alone
> So proudly in the past,
> Should be ejected from my throne
> By own son at last!
>
> He trots his treason to and fro,
> As only babies can,
> And says he'll be his mamma's beau
> When he's a "gweat, big man"!
>
> You stingy boy! you've always had
> A share in mamma's heart;
> Would you begrudge your poor old dad
> The tiniest little part?
>
> That mamma, I regret to see
> Inclines to take your part—
> As if a dual monarchy
> Should rule her gentle heart!
>
> But when the years of youth have sped,
> The bearded man, I trow,
> Will quite forget he ever said
> He'd be his mamma's beau.
>
> Renounce your treason, little son,
> Leave mamma's heart to me;
> For there will be another one
> To claim your loyalty.
>
> And when that other comes to you,
> God grant her love may shine
> Through all your life as fair and true
> As mamma's does through mine!

he is going to do for the next seven or eight years about his relationships with adults, with the other sex, and with his own body. This dilemma is sharpened when the child lives in a small biological family, his only female companion a mother who has fed and tended him lovingly and has developed in him a great dependency, and his male companion a father who, however friendly, is yet a rival for that mother's love. There comes a moment—when the little boy is sent away to boarding-school in an upper-class English family, or when the next baby is born, or when he loses his milk-teeth—when the relationship to his mother can no longer be defined in terms of his being a baby and she the succouring female. The more adults emphasize maleness and femaleness, the more sharply the little boys will feel the pressure of the situation, the rivalry of the father, the potential sex-contrast with the mother. The more, also, the mother, intent upon her sex relationship as a female to adult males, will be willing to let him go. It is a different matter when it is the femininity of the woman and the masculinity of the man that are emphasized. Then the mother may cling to the growing boy, and his masculinity have to develop as counterpoint to her maternity rather than as rivalry to his father. Where the masculinity of the men is harsh and their parental feelings slightly developed, their capacity to see even a most diminutive male as a rival is enhanced, and the father will treat the son-rival in ways calculated to diminish his own fears of that rivalry, often by forcing his son to act more like a man and less like a baby, which is another way of saying, "Go away from your mother." Thus even before birth a child is a potential threat and rival to both Mundugumor parents, intent as they are on their masculinity and femininity, and disliking parenthood. Among the Mundugumor the prenatal taboos that in other near-by societies protect the baby protect the parent; if the husband copulates with his pregnant wife, he will get boils, or beget another baby and be faced with the double catastrophe of twins. But among the Arapesh, where parental rôles over-shadow sexuality, intercourse and pregnancy go together for a long time while the baby is built up bit by bit, and only when the baby is thought to be completely formed does the husband cease to sleep with his wife, as a protection for the wanted child. So as far back as before the baby is born the form of the Oedipus situation is foreshadowed and there is already an indication of how the potential rivalry between father and son, or mother and daughter, will be handled.

The child at the age of five or six is also at a stage of con-solidating all that he or she has learned so far and reshaping it into an approach to a wider world. Still close to the mother, at whose breast there is another baby—if not her own, then a neighbour's—shepherding younger brothers and sisters whose control over their elimination is still uncertain, faced with a realization of his or her sex, the child's be-haviour now will shape its later life deeply. The necessity for this lies in the long interval which intervenes between human beings' capacity to feel sex emotions and their readi-ness for parenthood. But it lies also deeply in the nature of the human family, in the circumstance that parents were once children, and that their adultness is built upon their childhood experience. Thus, in any society, the way in which five-year-old children deal with their springing, premature, socially functionless sexuality is embedded in the parental character. As the father watches his five-year-old son postur-ing with a spear, sending an arrow straight and true to its mark, bidding for the mother's breast or being pushed sharply away as too old for such indulgence, he lives over again his own feelings when he at the same age was treated in the same way.

In homogeneous, slowly changing societies, this revival of memories works well enough, for the adults whom the little

boy encounters will all have had experiences that are regularly related to each other. In Mundugumor, the father will
have been treated harshly by his own father and mother,
and received some passing indulgence from other males,
half-grown boys, mother's brothers, and from neighbouring
women. He is prepared to treat his own son as harshly as he
was treated, and so perpetuate the pattern. No irregular indulgence will confuse the small boy struggling with a world
that he learned was hostile as he was given his mother's
grudging breast. Mundugumor children of five may already
be sent as hostages to live for several months among temporary allies in another tribe. The little boy, whose life will
be forfeited if the war-plans change, has to be able to hate
the people among whom he lives well enough to learn their
language, and spy out their roads, so that later, when he
grows up and they are enemies and not allies, he will be a
valuable scout in war. No softness, no protectiveness, have
interfered with his capacity to stand such a test. When his
younger brother was born, his mother may have admitted
him again to the breast, for the first time ungrudgingly, for
the pleasure of watching the struggle between the two little
males. Against his father, his mother is his partisan. She tries
to save his sister for her son to exchange for a wife, and to
keep the father from exchanging the sister for another wife
for himself. Conversely, the father watches jealously over
the daughter, and if he can, while his son is too young to
oppose him exchanges the daughter for a young wife. The
issues are clearly drawn, the Oedipus situation is solved in a
way that sets every man's hand against every man. The
Mundugumor grows up to live in a harsh world, but his
laughter is vigorous; he grins when he describes biting into
an enemy's flesh. His legend of how death came into the
world is that mankind lost the secret of stopping the flow of
blood and so wounds became mortal. He has a hostility towards all males, a rapaciousness towards females, that would

land him in deep difficulty in a modern society, or would find expression in covert and probably criminal ways so well fitted together that they defied re-education, conversion, or psychoanalysis. But in Mundugumor the pattern holds, and each father, reliving the hot anger of his own childhood, rears a son who can meet the rigours of life angry and laughing.

So in primitive societies we study the rôle of the father not from the memories of the individuals who are sufficiently disturbed to end up in the office of a psychiatrist or of a social worker, but by watching living people interacting, by watching fathers pet or push, approve or taunt, their young children, by watching children respond, by analyzing the taboos that define their inter-relationships. We find that the rôle the father plays towards the child, the rôle of the mother, the rôle of the wife, are sufficiently stylized so that each individual father, be he young and strong, old and weak, or old and strong, each individual mother, whether her breasts flow generously with milk or can only give a few meagre drops so that she must depend upon other women to supplement them, stands against the stylized picture. Thus it is possible to describe in some detail the form the Oedipus solution will take. One often hears in our society, "If his father had been a different sort of man, then his problems would have been quite different." But it would be even truer to comment also: "If he had been born into a society with a different form of fatherhood . . ." Where the style of fatherhood calls for great strength and self-contained dignity, a weak father threatens the development of the son so that that son has a lesser chance than his neighbours. But where the style of fatherhood calls for a friendly, easy-going, ally father, then a strong, self-contained, powerful father becomes the threat. Even in our highly diversified society, in which each small family is so isolated from others that no one knows how peculiar or how usual are the feelings and the behaviours that are shut behind each Yale lock, there is still a style to which individual actions are referred, albeit faultily.

Cultures differ very much in the extent to which children are permitted to play out and experiment with their sexuality, and in how the onus of reserve is placed. In Samoa, the expected personality is one to which sex will be a delightful experience, expertly engaged in, and which still will not be sufficiently engrossing to threaten the social order. The Samoans condone light love-affairs, but repudiate acts of passionate choice, and have no real place for any one who would permanently continue, in spite of social experiences to the contrary, to prefer one woman or one man to a more socially acceptable mate. The demand that one should be both receptive to the advances of many lovers and yet capable of showing the tokens of virginity at marriage is sufficiently incompatible, and was solved first by placing the onus of virginity not on the whole young female population, but on the *taupou,* the ceremonial princess of the village. She was then better guarded than other girls and thus freed from temptation. As an additional protection, the blood of virginity could always be counterfeited. The *taupou* who failed to warn her chaperones that she was not a *taupou,* and so on her wedding-night shamed her village, risked being beaten to death—not for her frailty, but for her failure to make an adequate provision of chicken-blood. Marriages were arranged between families, with some attention to the wishes of the young, and the young in turn conducted with suitable partners the long liaisons that led to pregnancy and were regarded as appropriate preparations for marriage, and reserved quick affairs "under the palm-trees" for the unsuitable mates. Premarital affairs and extra-marital affairs were conducted with enough lightness not to threaten the reliable sex relationships between married couples, sex relationships so reliable that they have now underwritten one of the highest population increases recorded in the modern world.

When we examine how this capacity for reliable sex responses that nevertheless do not threaten or disrupt a social order which is firmly built into quite stable marriages, we find that the relationship between child and parent is early diffused over many adults. The Samoan mother nurses her child generously, or if she lacks milk a chosen wet nurse nurses him; nursing is a slight but very specific physical relationship. However, he is given food, consoled, carried about, by all the women of the large households, and later carried about the village by child-nurses who cluster together with their charges on their hips. He is fed when he is hungry, carried when he is tired, allowed to sleep when he wills. If he does wrong—cries and disturbs the dignity of some consultation going on among the elders, defecates in the house, or has a temper tantrum—it is not he who is punished, but the child-nurse whose duty it is to keep him out of such difficulties and to lug him out of earshot when he cries. Children are too young to know how to behave, but they may be trusted to develop sense—*mafaufau*—in time. In the meantime adult society is protected against them, and they do not need to fear that they themselves, by their unsteady sphincter control, their loud wails or importunate demands, will endanger the normal order of existence. As they grow older, their elders may waste considerable time telling them to do what they are already doing. I used to grow impatient as the ten-year-olds told the four-year-olds, or the twenty-year-olds the ten-year-olds, "*Soia! Soia! Soia!,*" "Keep quiet! Keep quiet! Keep quiet!" when the children in question were already sitting like frozen mice, legs demurely crossed, eyes fixed in a respectful stare. In fact a great many positive injunctions are given that are unnecessary, so that the child in a sense rattles a little within a framework that he fits with room to spare. He hardly ever has the

experience of being asked to do something that is too difficult, which demands too much self-control or too long a
period of sitting cross-legged and cross-armed with never a
flick at a fly under his chin. Rather he is almost held back
from doing what he can do well, as if this margin were used
not only as a margin of safety, but as a kind of leverage on
the perfection of his performance. All adults partake somewhat of the dignity of the head of the house, in whose
presence one eats only very formally, and does not scratch,
or tickle, or giggle, or loll. But eating between meals, greed-
ily, loosely, as also scratching, tickling, giggling, and lolling,
are all permitted outside the circle of formal life, outside
the house, or even in the house if there is no formal life going
on there. The developed formality between parents and
children never breaks down completely; parents do not discuss sex with their children, although parents and children
together will be audience at a dance of quite uninhibited
frankness. The formality is thus a spatial one, and one for
which for a long time the child is given no responsibility.
The parent does not repel, the child is not required to inhibit, the child-nurse simply drags away the child who shows
signs of yelling out of earshot of the adult whose dignity
would be impaired by the yelling. The child learns: "You
have a body and a set of impulses that may do inappropriate
things, but this is just a matter of your being young. No one
is angry at you for it, but they will be very angry at your
small guardians if they let you, who are innocent, do harm."
The "not-yet" quality of childish emotion is reinforced at
every turn by a system which regards this essential unreadi-
ness of the child as both natural and desirable. The pilgrimage towards maturity is paced so slow that the urge to
slip back is unusually undeveloped. Once a Samoan child
has learned to sit still, and is therefore allowed to stay peacefully where he wants to be, he expresses very little desire to

turn into a kicking, screaming menace to the dignity of the occasion.

When children are five or six, they shift from being protected against the damage their own exorbitant demands and unregulated impulses might inflict on the dignity of life. The little girls in turn become child-nurses, who must themselves carry other babies out of earshot. The little boys begin to tag after the bigger boys, learning to fish, swim, handle a canoe, climb trees, and all the other lesser male skills. The girls' attention is focussed on the rôle of facilitating domestic life and caring for babies, who are regarded as pretty tough and so more of a burden than a responsibility. The boys' attention is shifted to being at the bottom of a ladder of skill and virtuosity, eager to be accepted by the older boys. Permission to accompany older boys seems to provide a potent incentive to good behaviour, and the seeming miracle of transformation from demanding, uncontrolled, temper-tantrumish youngsters to sober little child-nurses and sober little water-carriers and bait-collectors goes on.

The break between the boys' group and the girls' group is fairly strong at this stage, and is reinforced by the strongest taboo of Samoan society, the brother-and-sister taboo. This includes not only one's own sister, but cousins, and of course all the girls of one's own household. Brothers and sisters must never talk together casually or lightly, must never walk together or touch each other, or participate in the same informal pleasure-seeking group. As a fourth or even a third of the girls in one's own village may be called "sister," this effectively divides the older children's groups bent on mischief and fun into one-sex groups. It also breaks the tie between child-nurse and young charge if the young charge is a boy. The term *tei*, younger sibling, is a term affectionately used by women. The brother-and-sister relationship is the focus of the male child's break from a lusty emotion-indulging early childhood in which he had his slightly older sister at his beck and call to a later childhood as a very small, very unimportant, very unskilled male in the older boys' group. The imposition of the taboo is left in the young boy's own hands: "when he feels shy, when he feels ashamed," then he will gradually avoid his older sister or cousin or young aunt who has so uncritically ministered to his childish needs. Nothing is enforced hurriedly; he simply learns, by watching others, by the remarks of others, by the looks and glances of those around him, that he is reaching the age where on his own initiative he sets a barrier between himself and his impulsive and irresponsible childhood, and declares the taboo to be in force. Throughout the whole period of childhood and early adolescence, boys and girls move in separate groups, maintaining their separateness by a certain degree of ceremonial hostility, sometimes verbal, sometimes in pitched battles with light missiles. Later, as each becomes ready, the girls are chosen for first love-affairs by older boys who have been initiated into full sex experience by older girls. In each sex partnership, one of the partners is expected to be sure and practised. The only serious maladjustment I observed in Samoa came when two inexperienced adolescents had a first sex-affair with each other and became traumatized by their own clumsiness.

The Samoan adult sex adjustment may be said to be one of the smoothest in the world. Passion and responsibility are so blended that children are loved and cared for and reared in large stable families that do not rely on some slender tenuous tie between two parents for their only security. The adult personality is stable enough to resist extraordinary pressures from the outside world and keep its serenity and sureness. The price they pay for their smooth, even, generously gratifying system is the failure to use special gifts, special intelligence, special intensity. There is no place in Samoa for the man or the woman capable of a great passion, of complicated aesthetic feeling, of deep religious de-votion. The price paid for the disallowance of all of these intensities, which accompanies the premium on slowly de-veloped sureness, may be seen to be reflected in a certain amount of malicious gossip, slander, and low-grade but very astute political intrigue. The misfits are the gifted, those whose superior intensity could have dealt with the full force of an Oedipus situation that both parents played out as major drama. But the drama is not there. A Samoan father is far too occupied with the even-paced relationships to his whole social group, his emotion is too well diffused over his entire family group, to feel the insistent desire of his small wriggling son for his mother as anything that either threatens him or interests him. He is not afraid of his own sexuality, he is not afraid of his own ability to satisfy his wife, he does not see his wife as unstable and demanding, so no impulses, originally self-protective, arise in him to chal-lenge or to protect his little son. Similarly, mothers do not turn from an unsatisfactory life with their husbands, to which they have brought demands that can never be ful-filled, to a hopeless craving that their sons may satisfy those demands instead. Perhaps more sharply than in any known society, Samoa culture demonstrates how much the tragic or the easy solution of the Oedipus situation depends upon the inter-relationship between parents and children, and is not created out of whole cloth by the young child's biological impulses.

If Samoa and Mundugumor are thought of side by side, we see two societies that prepare their children to be adults, one by underplaying any intensity between parents and children, the other by overplaying the hostilities and sexual specificities between parents and children. Both prepare their children to be adults who can function in the on-going society. But the two societies are not equally viable. The Samoans have made one of the most effective adjustments to the impact of Western civilization of any known people. From the European's technology they took cloth and knives, lanterns and kerosene, soap and starch and sewing-machines, paper and pen and ink, but they have kept their bare feet, their cool short sarongs, their houses built of native materials fastened together with coconut-fibre cord. When the hurricanes come, the metal roofing sheets on the white men's house fly off and sometimes kill people, the house itself is wrecked, but the Samoan house collapses gracefully before the storm, later to be rebuilt of the same posts. They accepted Protestant Christianity, but gently remoulded some of its sterner tenets. Why repent so bitterly, says the Samoan preacher, "when God is just waiting to forgive you all the time"? Neither literacy, nor missions, nor modern technology have finally disturbed the evenness and flexibility with which this group of people, their culture based on diffuse but warm human relationships, has adapted to change. The Mundugumor have always been in danger of not reproducing themselves, of splitting into so many small groups that the culture would vanish, of neglecting so many of their ceremonies that the ceremonies themselves would be forgotten. A solution of the Oedipus conflict that sets every man's hand against every other man may be a perfectly tolerable solution for the individual. The Mundugumor spends his time in hostilities towards all the world, but he is cheerful and laughs often. It is when we consider a society from the point of view of the capacity to face emergencies and change, and to form larger social units, that the difference between the two ways becomes so striking.

The Mundugumor have faced new events brittlely. They fought rather than adapted. A man who at five has defied his father and left home, at six has been a hostage among the enemy, and at fifteen has a wife whom he must defend against grown men, does not bow easily even to natural events. They say that when the river upon which they now live changed its course, and finally divided the Mundugu-mor-speaking peoples in two, the Mundugumor continued to hate and fear the water and to handle canoes clumsily.* They have not adapted their methods of child-rearing to life on the banks of a rapidly flowing river, and village life has been riddled with a tiresome attempt to keep small children away from the water instead of teaching them not to fall in. From time to time, some one yielded to impulse and pushed some one else's child or feeble-minded dependent into the water to drown. No one claimed that children were watched over to protect the children, but it was inconvenient to have to fetch water from elsewhere, and after a drowning the water of the river was taboo for drinking. They say that when the water separated them from members of their own group, they saw them less often; they say that some one suggested that perhaps it might be possible to eat even members of one's own language-group without dire results. The Mundugumor may be regarded as a people whose adjustment was within the range of bearable adjustment for individuals, but which was nevertheless expressed in institutions that required very favourable environmental circumstances for survival. As long as the Mundugumor could prey upon their much less aggressive neigh-

* The reconstruction of past events when one is dealing with a preliterate people is exceedingly unsatisfactory. The change of course of the river, which the Mundugumor claim happened and which fits a large part of their behaviour in regard to canoes, is plausible in terms of the known behaviour of New Guinea rivers. It is also possible that the extraordinary clumsiness in handling canoes, the inability to swim, the fear of children's drowning, the split between the tribesmen living on one side of the river and the other, may all have occurred as an increasingly clumsy adjustment to an unchanged environment; or they may merely be the result of an unrecorded and forgotten migration. The Mundugumor may have moved closer and closer to the river and finally crossed it themselves, and then later accused it of having divided their territory and complicated their lives. In either case the gist of the argument remains the same—whether the change was due to the river or to their own migration, they handled the resulting new situation clumsily.

bours, who also did most of their necessary craft-work for them, and as long as food was abundant and mainly collected by women, who could express their active aggressive impulses by fishing and eating better than men, or serving dishes tastier than their co-wives to a common husband, the society survived. When the Europeans came, they first tried to subdue the Mundugumor by punitive expeditions. But the Mundugumor laughed at burned villages or village members shot down by a punitive police-party. That was the way men were meant to die. It was only when big men —men with many wives—were gaoled instead that they submitted to government controls, for inactivity, coupled with violent jealousy over who had their wives, was something that the dominating big men could not stand.

The Arapesh solution of the Oedipus situation is as specialized as the Mundugumor, and also fits a society dependent upon a specially favourable environment to survive. Where the Mundugumor stress the fierce cross-sex tie between parents and children, and the resulting jealousy and competition between all males and between most females, the Arapesh mute all interest in cross-sex ties between adults and children. It is good that children should be of both sexes, and fathers and mothers treat children of both sexes in virtually identical ways. A child endowed with more intensity of feeling may attempt to precipitate a sharper relationship with the parent of the opposite sex, but only if that parent has also some intensity will it come to anything. Both boys and girls are drawn into the networks of a number of small related families, each family intent on raising food, feeding pigs and children, and responding to the plans of others. Children of five and six may have furious temper tantrums if refused food, tantrums that adults appease rather than attempting to curb them or to retaliate. These same gusts of rage which sweep the child whose exorbitant demands have not been met recur in later life, and lay the adult society open to danger. The angry adult whose request for help at a feast or the loan of food has been refused will steal the personal leavings of his offending relative and send them to a sorcerer. The child learns that temper tantrums are unbearable and disruptive. As an adult, he joins in punishing the man who provokes another, not the one who, provoked, engages in violence. With the continuous interpersonal emphasis on food, on the alternating request to feed and be fed, the difference in the rôles of father and mother—both mild, both loving, both irrationally bad-tempered occasionally—is very slight. It is the adolescence of their children that the Arapesh view with some alarm, and not their behaviour at five or six, when they are thought of as too young, too weak, to be really troublesome.

Characteristically, there is no formalization of latency. The small boys are not driven away from a home in which the mother is over-accepting or over-demanding of their masculinity, or in which the father insists on treating them as rivals or potential victims. Instead, the children trail about in ones and twos, with older boys and men or with women, as the case may be. Only as they approach adolescence do they cluster together a little more, as the girls learn the rites of the menstrual hut and whisper together, flutteringly, of how their breasts are growing, while the boys begin the serious business of tabooing certain foods to protect the growth of their genitals. It is at adolescence that the taboos by which parents have curbed their own sexuality to protect their children are reversed. The adolescents must protect their parents and, especially after their long-arranged marriages are consummated, must be careful not to give parents or parents-in-law food cooked on the fire beside which they have had sex relations. In this society where the nexus between males is not their competition for women, but their common enterprise of feeding people of all ages

and both sexes, attention is shifted from the specificity of
the Oedipus struggle to the internal battle that each individual must fight with his own impulses if he or she is to
be in turn fertile and able to grow human beings. The
parents remain allies in the child's battle, laying no heavy
prohibitions, not fighting back, not stimulating the child by
providing him with a strong and dangerous opponent. Any
struggle in one's own life can be transmuted into activity
on behalf of children, as when the tribe-brothers Wabe and
Ombomb, both rather intractable, deviant personalities,
capped their quarrels with their own wives with plans for
helping their nephews get wives, and in Wabe's case with
a plan to adopt a child.* So among the Arapesh the six-year-
olds are treated gently, their sex underplayed, their need
for food and shelter emphasized, until they can become the
custodians of their own growth, the boy of his child-wife
whom he feeds, the girl of her own body and so of her
future children.

The system is vulnerable. It does not allow sufficiently
for accident or for death. The Arapesh are gentle and hard-
working, they climb up and down the mountains in the
cold morning mists to help one another and feed one another, they restrain their own impulses, and focus their
attention on others. In such a system there is no allowance
for "bad happenings." When every one wants to feed children, there should obviously always be food. But sometimes there is no food. The land is poor, the system of horti-
culture very inadequate. When a man is willing to grow
his wife and wait patiently many years for her to mature
so that his and her capacities for parenthood will be safe,
and she in turn is willing to acknowledge by obedience this
debt of waiting and feeding, it is patently unfair that one

* Detailed descriptions of these deviant personalities are given in *Sex and
Temperament,* Part One, and in *The Mountain Arapesh,* Part IV, *passim.*
See Appendix IIc.

of them should die and upset the whole structure. Death itself, except for the very old or the child with a congenital defect, is not intelligible. The combination of no adequate explanation for death and the impulsive rages that are precipitated in childhood by the refusal of food—by those who claim they want to give it—makes the Arapesh vulnerable to sorcery, and to the internal strife that comes with the suspicion of sorcery. It is not enough that parents should be loving and gentle, preoccupied with their most parental functions, in a world like New Guinea, where food is scarce and hunger and cold are the daily accompaniments of life. It is not enough that parents should try to convince their children that the anger in their voices when they refuse the children the food they do not have is anger not at the children, but because there is no food—for their voices will contain also their own childish anger against their parents when *they* were refused food. The outside world, the sorcerers of the next tribe, heavy-set men with scowling faces, trade easily upon the childish pique or the undisciplined behaviour of the stupid or the maladjusted among the Arapesh, and discord follows. If their lands were fertile and their forests filled with game, they would be able to feed their children. No child would lie face down and tear-stained in the dust of the village square screaming for a coconut because the only coconuts in the village must be kept for the rare meagre feast at which all of his own relatives as hosts will still have to go hungry. But also, if their lands were fertile and their forests well stocked, it is most improbable that these lands would belong at all to people like the Mountain Arapesh. All through New Guinea, the fertile plains, the fish-filled rivers, the high lands where coconuts grow, and the sago-swamps that are bountifully self-replenishing, belong to the more aggressive people. The very parental behaviour that makes the shortage of food in the mountains such a breach in their carefully built

wall of social defences also unfits them to compete openly
with their more warlike neighbours, whose choice it is
whether they shall blackmail them or attack them more
openly. Blackmail, which exacts hospitality for the plains-
men on the long treks from plains to coast, pays their
neighbours better, and the Mountain Arapesh survive in
a world so much less satisfactory than their dreams with a
persistent nightmare that in each generation the children,
the children whom they have worked so hard to feed, are
getting smaller and smaller.

Another solution of the Oedipus situation is the three-
child system, by which each child of each sex is first the
favoured, then the ousted, and finally remains in the family
group to see the usurper's place in turn usurped.[2] This
system of child-rearing focusses the attention of the child,
who must finally move out of the Oedipus situation and
take a waiting place in the world of childhood, upon a
complex drama in which both parents and younger siblings
play a rôle. In both Iatmul and Bali, the "yard-child," the
third from the bottom, is the focus of the drama between
the parental world and the child itself. Where the Mundugumor and the Arapesh begin to define the relationship
between parent and child before birth, and extensive tension arises at the weaning period when the next baby is
born, in Bali and Iatmul the weaned child remains near
the mother, enclosed in a quartet of mother and three children in which the next oldest child plays the rôle of nurse
to the youngest.

There are many other solutions than those found among
these seven peoples. Boys may be sent away to their maternal
grandparents for all the years between early childhood and
initiation, and then, after years of indulgence, away from
fathers whose rôle is sternness, be harshly recalled to the
realities of adult life by initiation ceremonies, as among the
Ba Thonga. Or the sexual readiness of small children may

be exploited casually by adults, as among the Kaingang of Brazil. But no known society has been able to ignore completely this most conspicuous aspect of our humanity, this premature double blooming of sexual feeling, in the child so unready for procreation.[3] Each adult carries within him, ready for reawakening or even on the tip of his tongue, his own memories of childhood, and these in co-operation with the impulses of the child provide the dynamics for the drama through which each new generation must live. The nature of the drama is distinctive for each culture. In a changing society, the parts of the system get out of step; a childhood suited for an expressive adolescence may be followed by a restricted one, or a restricted childhood be followed by a demand for an expressive adolescence. Then the patterns become confused, more children fail to experience the sequence of events which, in that culture, are the appropriate prelude to adulthood. The task by which human societies, changing and meeting other societies that change, have to readjust through the living adjustments of the human beings who compose them is endless and recurrent. The capacity to make such adjustments, like the capacity to crystallize in culture a set of viable nutritional habits, is part of our human inheritance, part of the mechanism of evolution that his unique mentality has given to man. Used without insight, it is a blunt, uncertain, fumbling capacity, producing sometimes civilizations of great beauty and strength, sometimes civilizations that twist and distort and disallow even those aspects of our humanity which are permitted expression at all. But we have yet to prove that we can develop an insight that, disciplined by faith in a free humanity, can economize on the wastefulness of the ages of innocence and still build not a reactive cynicism, but a new innocence that will not have foundations in human sacrifice.

VI

SEX AND TEMPERAMENT

UPON THE SOLUTION OF THE OEDIPUS SITUATION WILL DEPEND a great deal of the way in which a boy or a girl accepts primary sex membership. But it is not enough for a child to decide simply and fully that it belongs to its own sex, is anatomically a male or a female, with a given reproductive rôle in the world. For growing children are faced with another problem: "*How male*, how female, am I?" He hears men branded as feminine, women condemned as masculine, others extolled as real men, and as true women. He hears occupations labelled as more or less manly, for a man, or more or less likely to derogate her womanhood, for a woman. He hears types of responsiveness, fastidiousness, sensitivity, guts, stoicism, and endurance voted as belonging to one sex rather than the other. In his world he sees not a single model but many as he measures himself against them; so that he will judge himself, and feel proud and secure, worried and inferior and uncertain, or despairing and ready to give up the task altogether.

In any human group it is possible to arrange men and women on a scale in such a way that between a most masculine group and a most feminine group there will be others who seem to fall in the middle, to display fewer of the pronounced physical features that are more characteristic of one sex than of the other. This is so whether one deals entirely in secondary sex characters, such as arrangement of pubic hair, beard, layers of fat, and so on, or whether one deals with such primary sex characters as breasts, pelvic measurements, hip-torso proportions and so on. These differences are even more conspicuous when one considers such matters as skin sensitivity, depth of voice, modulation of movement. Also, one finds in most groups of any size that there are very few individuals who insist on playing the rôle of the opposite sex in occupation or dress or interpersonal sex activities. Whether full transvestitism will occur seems to be a question of cultural recognition of this possibility. Among many American Indian tribes the *berdache*, the man who dressed and lived as a woman, was a recognized social institution, counterpointed to the excessive emphasis upon bravery and hardiness for men. In other parts of the world, such as the South Pacific, although a large number of ritual reversals of sex on ceremonial occasions may occur, there are many tribes where there is no expectation that any single individual will make the complete shift. Peoples may provide sex-reversal rôles for both sexes—as among the Siberian aborigines, where sex reversal is associated with shamanism; they may permit it to men but deny it to women; or they may not provide any pattern at all. But between the conspicuous transvestitism of the Mohave Indians [1]—where the transvestite men mimic pregnancy and child-birth, going aside from the camp to be ceremonially delivered of stones—and the Samoans—who recognize no transvestitism, but among whom I found one boy who preferred to sit among the women and weave mats—the contrast is clearly one of social patterning. A society can provide elaborate rôles that will attract many individuals who would never spontaneously seek them. Fear that boys will be feminine in behaviour may drive many boys into taking refuge in explicit femininity. Identification of a little less hairiness on the chin, or a slightly straighter bust-line, as fitting one for membership in the opposite sex may create social deviance. If we are to interpret these experiences, which all children have, we look for some theory of what these differences mean.

We strip away all this superstructure when we have invoked the presence or absence, the recognition and toleration, of transvestite social institutions, or the explicit suppression of homosexual practice, but we still find differences that need explanation. After we have gathered together the insights from detailed case-histories in Western society that show how accidents of upbringing, faulty identifications with the wrong parent, or excessive fear of the parent of the opposite sex may drive both boys and girls into sexual inversion, still we are left with a basic problem. Set end to end, standing in a line, the men of any group will show a range in explicit masculinity of appearance as well as in masculinity of behaviour. The females of any group will show a comparable variety, even more, in fact, if we have X-ray pictures to add to their deceptive pelvic profiles, which do not reveal their feminine reproductive capacities accurately.[2] Is this apparent range to be set down to differences in endocrine balance, set against our recognition that each sex depends for full functioning upon both male and female hormones and the interaction between these hormones and the other endocrines? Has every individual a bisexual potential that may be physiologically evoked by hormone deficit or surplus, which may be psychologically evoked by abnormalities in the process of individual maturation, which may be sociologically invoked by rearing

boys with women only, or segregating boys away from
women entirely, or by prescribing and encouraging various
forms of social inversion? When human beings—or rats—
are conditioned by social circumstances to respond sexually
to members of their own sex as adults and in preference
to members of the opposite sex, is this conditioning playing
on a real bisexual base in the personality, which varies
greatly in its structure as between one member of a group
and another?

At first blush, it seems exceedingly likely that we have to
advance some such hypothesis. If one looks at a group of
little boys, it would seem fairly obvious that it would be
easier to condition those who now appear "girlish" to an
inverted rôle, and that from a group of little girls, the "boyish" girl would be the easiest to train into identificatoin with
the opposite sex. And does not "easiest" here mean the greatest degree of physical bisexuality? Yet the existing data
make us pause. The most careful research has failed to tie
up endocrine balance with actual homosexual behaviour.
Those rare creatures who have both male and female primary sex organs present of course major anomalies and confusions, but so far they have thrown little light on the general problem. The extraordinary lack of correlation between
physique that can be regarded as hypermasculine and hyper-
feminine and successful reproductivity is marked in every
group. The man who shows the most male characteristics
may have no children, while some pallid, feminine-looking
mouse of a man fathers a large brood. The woman with
ample bosom and wide hips may be sterile, or if she bears
children she may be incapable of suckling them. Yet we
are still continually confronted with what looks like a correlation between the tendency towards sexual inversion of
the men and women who deviate most towards the expected
physique of the opposite sex. In the primitive tribe that
does not recognize inversion, the boy who decides to make

mats will look more like the female type for that tribe, the woman who goes out hunting will tend to look more like the male. Does this apparent physical correspondence mean nothing, is it sheerly an accident within a normal range of variation? If the tribe sets hairiness up as a desirable male characteristic, will the less hairy become confused about their sex rôle, while if the tribemen think that hairiness is simply a brutish characteristic, the very hairy may be almost sexually ostracized and the most hairless will not thereby be regarded as less male? This would be the extreme environmental answer, while the invocation of some very subtle, as yet unplumbed structural and functional variation in the biological basis of sex membership would be the extreme genetic answer.

I suggest another hypothesis that seems to me to fit better the behaviour of the seven South Seas peoples whom I have studied. A Balinese male is almost hairless—so hairless that he can pluck his whiskers out one by one with pincers. His breasts are considerably more developed than are a Westerner's. Almost any Balinese male placed in a series of western-European males would look "feminine." A Balinese female, on the other hand, has narrow hips and small high breasts, and almost any Balinese female placed among a group of western-European women would look "boyish." Many of them might be suspected of being unable to suckle children, perhaps accused of having infantile uteruses. But should these facts be interpreted to mean that the Balinese is more bisexual, less sexually differentiated, than the western European, that the men are less masculine, the women less feminine, or simply that the Balinese type of masculinity and femininity is different? The extreme advocates of a varying bisexual balance would claim that in some races the men are less differentiated, are more feminine and so on, than in others, and might also apply the same argument to the women. But on the whole, it would be agreed that at least some of the respects in which a Balinese male would seem feminine are matters that do not really affect his masculinity at all: his height, girth, hairiness, and the like. So it might be fairly readily admitted that as between racial strains that vary as greatly as Balinese and northern Europeans, Andamanese pygmies and Nubian giants, not only would certain of the criteria for masculinity and femininity be inoperative, but also that actual cross-correspondence might occur, as all Andamanese males would fall within the height range for females in some much taller group.

But all human groups of which we have any knowledge show evidence of considerable variation in their biological inheritance. Even among the most inbred and isolated groups, very marked differences in physique and apparent temperament will be found, and despite the high degree of uniformity that characterizes the child-rearing practices of many primitive tribes, each adult will appear as more or less masculine, or more or less feminine, according to the standards of that particular tribe. There will be, further-more, orders of variation that seem, at least on inspection —for we have no detailed records—to apply from one group to another. Although almost every Balinese would fall within the general configuration that might be classified technically as asthenic, yet the asthenic Balinese continues to contrast with the Balinese who is heavier in bony struc-ture, or shorter and plumper. Within the limits set by the general type, these same differences occur, in both men and women. Not until we have far more delicate methods of measurement, which allow not only for individual consti-tution but for ancestral strains, will we have any way of knowing whether there is any genuine correspondence, on a behavioural level, among the slender, narrow-bodied of the Arapesh, Tchambuli, Swede, Eskimo, and Hottentot, or whether their behaviour, although possibly in some way constitutionally based, is still in no way referable to something they may be said to have in common. Until such measures are developed, and such studies made, one can only speculate on the basis of careful observation, with no better instrument for comparison than the human eye. But use of this instrument on seven different peoples has suggested to me the hypothesis that within each human group we will find, probably in different proportions and possibly not always in all, representatives of the same constitutional types that we are beginning to distinguish in our own population. And I further suggest that the presence of these contrasting constitutional types is an important condition in children's estimate of the completeness of their sex membership.

If we recognized the presence of comparable ranges of constitutional types in each human society, any single continuum that we now construct from the most masculine to the least masculine can be seen to be misleading, especially to the eye of the growing child. We should instead define a series of continuums, distinguishing between the most masculine and the least sexually differentiated male within each of these several types. The slender little man without beard or muscle who begets a whole brood of children would not then seem such an anomaly, but could be regarded as the masculine version of a human type in which both sexes are slender, small, and relatively hairless. The tall girl whose breasts are scarcely discernible, but who is able to suckle her baby perfectly satisfactorily as her milk seems to spread in an almost even line across her chest, will be seen not as an imperfectly developed female—a diagnosis that is contradicted by the successful way in which she bears and suckles children, and her beautiful carriage in pregnancy—but as the female of a particular constitutional type in which women's breasts are much smaller and less accentuated. The big he-man with hair on his chest, whose masculinity is so often claimed to be pallid and unconvincing, will be seen to be merely a less masculine version of a type in which enormous muscularity and hairiness are the mode. The woman whose low fertility contrasts so strangely with her billowing breasts and hips may be seen as only one of a type of woman with very highly emphasized breasts and hips—her low fertility only conspicuous because most of the women with whom she is compared have smaller bosoms and less full hips. The apparent contradiction between pelvic X-rays and external pelvic measurements might also be resolved if it were considered from this point of view.

And as with physical type, so with other aspects of personality. The fiery, initiating woman would be classified only with fiery, initiating men of her own type, and might be found to look like not a lion, but merely like a lioness in her proper setting. When the meek little Caspar Milquetoast was placed side by side not with a prize-fighter, but with the meekest female version of himself, he might be seen to be much more masculine than she. The plump man with soft breast-tissue, double chin, protruding buttocks, whom one has only to put in a bonnet to make him like a woman, when put beside the equally plump woman will be seen not to have such ambiguous outlines after all; his masculinity is still indubitable when contrasted with the female of his own kind instead of with the male of another kind. And the slender male and female dancers, hipless and breastless, will seem not a feminine male and a boyish female, but male and female of a special type. Just as one would not be able to identify the sex of a male rabbit by comparing its behaviour with that of a lion, a stag, or a peacock as well as by comparing rabbit buck with doe, lion with lioness, stag with doe, and peacock with peahen —so it may well be that if we could disabuse our minds of the habits of lumping all males together and all females together and worrying about the beards of the one and the breasts of the other, and look instead for males and females of different types, we would present to children a much more intelligible problem.

A great number of very puzzling theoretical questions would fall into place also. Take for instance the question of degree of sex activity, and the greater activity reported by men who mature early. Are such men more masculine, or simply another type? Take the women who even among a people like the Arapesh, who have no concept of orgasm for the female, are actively demanding in sex, and specific in their sexual appetites. Or take the women who among peoples like the Mundugumor, who cast women as sexually specific and unmaternal, are still diffusively responsible and maternal. These deviations would no longer be regarded as signs of greater or less femininity, but of different types of women, types so biologically rooted that all the apparatus of cultural conditioning is insufficient to mould them completely to the type which that particular culture has come to regard as really feminine or masculine.

The growing child in any society is confronted then by individuals—adults and adolescents and children—who are classified by his society into two groups, males and females, in terms of their most conspicuous primary sex characters, but who actually show great range and variety both in physique and in behaviour. Because primary sex differences are of such enormous importance, shaping so determinatively the child's experience of the world through its own body and the responses of others to its sex membership, most children take maleness or femaleness as their first identification of themselves. But once this identification is made, the growing child then begins to compare itself not only in physique, but even more importantly in impulse and interest, with those about it. Are all of its interests those of its own sex? "I am a boy," but "I love colour, and colour is something that interests only women." "I am a girl," but "I am fleet of foot and love to run and leap. Running and leaping, and shooting arrows, are for boys, not girls." "I am a boy," but "I love to run soft materials through my fingers; an interest in touch is feminine, and will unsex me." "I am a girl," but "My fingers are clumsy, better at handling an axe-handle than at stringing beads; axe-handles are for men." So the child, experiencing itself, is forced to reject such parts of its particular biological inheritance as conflict sharply with the sex stereotype of its culture.

Moreover, a sex stereotype that decrees the interests and occupations of each sex is usually not completely without a basis. The idea of the male in a given society may conform very closely to the temperament of some one type of male. The idea of the female *may* conform to the female who belongs to the same type, or instead to the female of some other type. For the children who do not belong to these preferred types, only the primary sex characters will be definitive in helping them to classify themselves. Their impulses, their preferences, and later much of their physique will be aberrant. They will be doomed throughout life to sit among the other members of their sex feeling less a man, or less a woman, simply because the cultural ideal is based on a different set of clues, a set of clues no less valid, but different. And the small rabbit man sits sadly, comparing himself with a lionlike male beside whom he is surely not male, and perhaps for that reason alone yearning forever after the lioness woman. Meanwhile the lioness woman, convicted in her inmost soul of lack of femininity when she compares herself with the rabbity little women about her, may in reverse despair decide that she might as well go the whole way and take a rabbity husband. Or the little rabbity man who would have been so gently fierce and definitely masculine if he had been bred in a culture that recognized him as fully male, and quite able to take a mate and fight for her and keep her, may give up altogether and dub himself a female and become a true invert, attaching himself to some male who possesses the magnificent qualities that have been denied him.

Sometimes one has the opportunity to observe two men of comparable physique and behaviour, both artists or musicians, one of whom has placed himself as fully male, and with brightly shining hair and gleaming eye can make a roomful of women feel more feminine because he has entered the room. The other has identified himself as a lover of men, and his eye contains no gleam and his step no sureness, but instead an apologetic adaptation when he enters a group of women. And yet, in physical measurement, in tastes, in quality of mind, the two men may be almost interchangeable. One, however, has been presented, for example, with a frontier setting, the other with a cosmopolitan European one; one with a world where a man never handles anything except a gun, a hunting-knife, or a riding-whip, the other with a world where men play the most delicate musical instruments. When one studies a pair such as this, it seems much more fruitful to look not at some possible endocrine difference, but rather at the discrepancy, so much more manifest to one than to the other, between his own life preferences and those which his society thinks appropriate for males.

If there are such genuine differences among constitutional types that maleness for one may be so very different from maleness for another, and even appear to have attributes of femaleness—as found in some other type—this has profound implications not only for interpretation of variation within each sex, and for the forms of inversion and sex failure that occur in any society, but also for the pattern of inter-relationships between the sexes. Some simple societies, and some castes within complex societies, seem to have chosen their sex ideals for both sexes from the same constitutional type. The aristocracy, or the cattle-men, or the shopkeeper class may cherish as the ideal the delicate, small-boned, sensitive type for both males and females, or the tall, fiery, infinitely proud, specifically nervously sexed man and woman, or the plump, placid man and woman. But we do not know whether the male and female ideals of a given culture complement each other in this way. When the ideals for the two sexes do seem to be consistently inter-related, it is probable that a more finely meshed, more biologically direct relationship can be established as the ideal marriage, and the marriage forms will have a greater consistency. When those men and women who do not con-form to the ideal type try to use the marriage forms—the delicate interwoven ballet, or the fierce proud reserve, or the comfortable post-prandial hot milk, which have become the appropriate and developed forms for that ideal type—they are at least faced with a consistent though alien pattern which it may be easier to learn.

Let us imagine for instance an aristocracy in which for both men and women the ideal is tall, fiery-tempered, proud specifically and very sensitively sexed. Into such an aristo-cratic household is born a boy who is plump, easy-going, fond of eating, diffusely sexed. All through his childhood he will be trained in the behaviour appropriate to a type very different from himself, and this will include accepting as his feminine ideal a girl who is fiery-tempered, reserved, spe-cifically sexed. If he marries such a girl, he will have learned a good part of his proper rôle, which she in turn will have learned to expect of him. If he marries a girl who deviates as much as he from the expected standards, each will never-theless have learned a consistent rôle, he to treat her as if she were sensitive and proud, she to treat him as if he were sensitive and proud. Their life may have more artificiality in it than that of those who actually approximate the types for which the cultural rôles are designed, but the very clarity of the pattern of male and female rôles may make them rôles that can be played. In every such tightly patterned picture there will be some who will rebel, will commit suicide—if suicide is a culturally recognized way out—will become promiscuous or frigid or withdrawn or insane, or, if they are gifted, will become innovators of some variation in the pattern. But most of them will learn the pattern, alien though it be.

So in each of the societies I have studied it has been possible to distinguish those who deviated most sharply from the expected physique and behaviour, and who made different sorts of adjustment, dependent upon the relationship between own constitutional type and cultural ideal. The boy who will grow up into a tall, proud, restive man whose very pride makes him sensitive and liable to confusion suffers a very different fate in Bali, Samoa, Arapesh, and Manus. In Manus, he takes refuge in the vestiges of rank the Manus retain, takes more interest in ceremonial than in trading, mixes the polemics of acceptable trading invectives with much deeper anger. In Samoa such a man is regarded as too violent to be trusted with the headship of a family for many, many years; the village waits until his capacity for anger and intense feeling has been worn down by years of erosive soft resistance to his unseemly over-emphases. In Bali, such a man may take more initiative than his fellows only to be thrown back into sulkiness and confusion, unable to carry it through. Among the Maori of New Zealand, it is probable that he would have been the cultural ideal, his capacity for pride matched by the demand for pride, his violence by the demand for violence, and his capacity for fierce gentleness also given perfect expression, since the ideal woman was as proud and fiercely gentle as himself.

But in complex modern societies, there are no such clear expectations, no such perfectly paired expectancies, even for one class or occupational group or rural region. The stereotyped rôles for men and for women do not necessarily correspond, and whatever type of man is the ideal, there is little likelihood that the corresponding female type will also be the ideal. Accidents of migration, of cross-class marriage, of frontier conditions, may take the clues for the female ideal from quite another type from which the male ideal is taken. The stereotype may itself be blurred and confused by several different expectations, and then split again, so that the ideal lover is not the ideal brother or husband. The pattern of inter-relationships between the sexes, of reserve or intimacy, advance or retreat, initiative and response, may be a blend of several biologically congruent types of behaviour instead of clearly related to one. We need much more material on the extent to which this sort of constitutional types may actually be identified and studied before we can answer the next questions about the differential strength and stability and flexibility of cultures in which ideals are a blend, or a composite, or a single lyric theme, ideals that are so inclusive that every male and female finds a rather blurrily defined place within them, or so sharp and narrow that many males and females have to develop counterpointed patterns outside them.

A recognition of these possibilities would change a great deal of our present-day practices of rearing children. We would cease to describe the behaviour of the boy who showed an interest in occupations regarded as female, or a greater sensitivity than his fellows, as "on the female" side, and could ask instead what kind of male he was going to be. We would take instead the primary fact of sex membership as a cross-constitutional classification, just as on a wider scale the fact of sex can be used to classify together male rabbits and male lions and male deer, but would never be permitted to obscure for us their essential rabbit, lion, and deer characteristics. Then the little girl who shows a greater need to take things apart than most of the other little girls need not be classified as a female of a certain kind. In such a world, no child would be forced to deny its sex membership because it was shorter or taller, or thinner or plumper, less hairy or more hairy, than another, nor would any child have to pay with a loss of its sense of its sex membership for the special gifts that made it, though a boy, have a delicate sense of touch, or, though a girl, ride a horse with fierce sureness.

If we are to provide the impetus for surmounting the trials and obstacles of this most difficult period in history, man must be sustained by a vision of a future so rewarding that no sacrifice is too great to continue on the journey towards it. In that picture of the future, the degree to which men and women can feel at home with their own bodies, and at home in their relationships with their own sex and with the opposite sex, is extremely important.[3]

VII

BASIC REGULARITIES IN

HUMAN SEX DEVELOPMENT

But different as are the ways in which different cultures pattern the development of human beings, there are basic regularities that no known culture has yet been able to evade. After excursions into the contrasting educational methods of seven different societies, we can sum up the regularities that must be reckoned with by every society. Every attempt to understand what is happening in our own society, or in other societies, every attempt to understand ourselves, or to build a different life for our children, must take these into account.

Thus we see that the child's sense of its own sex membership, and the way the importance of that sex membership is estimated, must be referred to a series of conditions. There is the structure of its own body, in which the girl finds that the reinterpretation of impregnation and conception and birth fits easily into her early experience with the intake of food, while the boy with the same initial experience can at most use it to interpret the female rôle, but will find himself heavily confused if he attempts to use it to interpret his own. The girl-child who has received her mother's breast happily need make no new or structurally different adjustment to accept an adult sex relationship. Inception is a form of behaviour that fits the essential biological rhythm of her being. Because one part of the body can so easily replace another in the imagination, if its form or its mode of behaviour is congruent, the girl may develop uncongenial clues if in addition to her human desire to run and leap, explore and handle, she becomes overly interested in her vestigial phallus, the clitoris. Evidence from many societies, however, does not support the common assumption of students whose researches are limited to our own society that this "phallic" stage in girls is a regular hurdle with which they have to contend, or that it even presents such a systematic difficulty in full sex adjustment as does the extension of receptivity—initially associated with eating—in the boy. When such disturbances do occur, neither a boy's inappropriate emphasis on inception nor a girl's over-emphasis on intrusion can be referred directly to the human body. Both must be seen as interpretations of the bodily experience of two small creatures who live in a two-sex world, in which the two sexes are of all ages, and in which copulation, pregnancy, birth, and lactation—behaviours that demand sex specialization—are as significant as eating and drinking, digestion and elimination, which are unspecialized.

The clues that the child's own body gives, in its tensions and its modes, its capacities to take in, to keep, to give out, and to interact, either partially and complementarily or symmetrically as a whole, with other human beings or reciprocally, can never be seen alone, as a mere developmental sequence. Always, beside the child who is experiencing the sensation of biting something to bits with newly erupted teeth sits the adult who has developed highly patterned feelings about biting, tearing, cutting up, dissection, analysis. The child bites, innocently, exploringly, into an apple. The adult hand tightens sympathetically to the remembered tingling of the flesh of the apple on the teeth; apprehensively in a first realization that soon this baby will be able to bite or attack others, and must be curbed; furtively in enjoyment of a hidden angry day-dream that has been whisked out of consciousness for many years. That slight tautness of the mother's arm, the little gesture of moistening her lips, the sound of her teeth as they grind together, the constraint of her encircling hand—all these enter in to tell the child what the nature of biting is. Sometimes the adult phantasies are so far removed from the observed realities that the child's own body intrudes into the child's consciousness some organ or some mode that the surrounding adults are attempting to deny totally. Then we may find it important to re-emphasize the fact that whatever the adults say, or feel, or repress, the child does have a body; that mouths first suck and later bite, and are capable of spitting, of squirrelling food in the cheek all night; that the child is not only not a tabula rasa, but a vigorous, maturing organism with modes of behaviour appropriate to its age and strength. But it is not a maturing organism in a glass box, or in a consulting-room. The artificialities of the well-lit cubicle in which the child can be photographed from six angles are useful ways of getting an abstract picture of the behaviour pattern that the child has developed as it grows up among other human beings. The other human beings may be subtracted for the nonce, and the child viewed as a developing organism pushing its own way towards adulthood. But in the whole of human experience this never happens. No boy is asked to interpret his maleness except in relationship to other human beings of both sexes; no small girl ever sits attentive only to the rhythm of her own heart. If the mother who holds a child in her arms is so conscious that some day it will bite that she meets the sucking vigour of the new-born *as if it were biting*, very possibly the child may learn about biting before it has any teeth. But it will not have learned about biting from its gums, nor from its latent desire to eat its mother up, but rather from the way in which the mother, who has teeth, feels about anything that the mouth of another human being does to her or to an object, or even from her response to the simple tensing of its body under restraint.

When the dependence of the child upon other human beings for interpretation of the modes of its own body is ignored, it often seems as if the clinician in our own society were engaging in the most fantastic constructs. The clinician reports some not unusual case of a little boy who believes that children are born from the anus, and supports the account with vivid play material, verbal statements, perhaps nightmares in which the little boy thinks he is having a baby. The reader or listener who tries to make sense of this material thinks that what the clinician has said—and often the clinician himself thinks that is what he has said—is that out of his own bodily experiences of eating, digestion, and elimination the little boy has evolved a fine phantasy of anal birth. Actually probably nothing so simple has happened. Out of his whole experiences with males and females of all ages, combined with what clues he could get from his own body, the little boy has then, and only then, elaborated his own phantasies. The more society obscures these relationships, muffles the human body in clothes, surrounds elimination with prudery, shrouds copulation in shame and mystery, camouflages pregnancy, banishes men and children from child-birth, and hides breast feeding, the more individual and bizarre will be the child's attempts to understand, to piece together a very imperfect knowledge of the life-cycle of the two sexes and an understanding of the particular state of maturity of his or her own body.

But even in societies where few of these obscuring conditions occur, where the child sees human bodies of all ages and in all stages, including death, the particular ways in which the adult acceptance or rejection, or mixed acceptance and rejection, of their own sex membership has developed will be communicated to the child, and so reinstate in each generation the expected pattern of character or some systematic distortion of it. Each such system carries within it not only a central pattern, or several patterns for different castes or classes, but also the limits of possible deviation. A Manus boy may grow up to rape strange women, to be a voyeur, to be a satyr, and still be sane, but he will not grow up to be gentle and considerate as a lover. Such a possibility is not contained within the limits of what he learns from the adults around him. An Arapesh may become a passive homosexual in contact with a member of an outside tribe, he may be impotent, he may develop the hygienic rituals enjoined upon him into an autoerotic ritual, but rape and active homosexuality are outside his pattern—unless he is completely insane.

So we must conceive of children as continuously reinterpreting experience as their own bodies develop among the developing and developed and involuting bodies of members of both sexes. And when we do so, when we think always of a two-sex world, always of human beings of different ages and sizes, we find that there are certain biological regularities that cannot fail to play a part in these interpretations.

The first of these regularities is that both boys and girls are nursed by the mother, which means that one sex receives a picture of muted complementary behaviour within its own sex, and the other—the male—initially encounters a complementary relationship with the opposite sex. However much or little the three-month-old infant may be capable of realizing alone the difference between the sexes, the mother is fully capable, and her smile, her arm, the whole position of her body, are conscious—albeit in different ways in different societies, and for different temperaments—of that contrast. The little female is a small replica of herself. "As she feels now, so I once felt" is an introspective comment by the mother that is easily enough communicated to the child. It lays the basis in a girl for an identification with her own sex that is simple and uncomplicated, something that exists, requires no elaboration, can be accepted simply. But for the boy, the mother's comment must inevitably be, "This is different for him." Inception is not the same for the male as for the female. Transmuted into adult terms, this is a reversal of the male and female rôles, in which "I insert, and he receives. Before he is a man he will have to accomplish a change from this passive inception." So the female child's earliest experience is one of closeness to her own nature. Mother and female child together fit one pattern, the mother's assumption that their pulses beat to the same rhythm provides an immediacy to the child's development. The little girl learns "I am." The little boy, however, learns that he must begin to differentiate himself from this person closest to him; that unless he does so, he will never be at all; that he must find out—says his mother's smile, the slight coquettishness or perhaps aggressive tightening in her arms, or the extra passivity with which she yields her breast—who he is, that he is male, that he is *not* female. So at the very start of life, effort, an attempt at greater self-differentiation, is suggested to the boy, while a relaxed acceptance of herself is suggested to the girl.

The discussion that has gone before has suggested some of the ways in which different societies have twisted and distorted and over-emphasized, overvalued or devalued, membership in one sex or the other. In this chapter, however, I am emphasizing the biological regularities that underlie these enormous diversities. Whether women like being women or deeply resent it, they will teach their girl-children that they belong to the same sex, whether that sex is regarded as fortunate or unfortunate, and their boys that they belong to a different one. This fundamental regularity is of course tied up with lactation, and with the carry-over into social patterns that because women breast-feed children, they are also the ones to care for them. If breast feeding were completely superseded as a form of feeding infants—always a possibility in our mechanically oriented society—and fathers and brothers were to take over an equal responsibility for the child, this biological regularity would disappear. Instead of girls learning that they simply were, and boys that they must become, emphasis would shift to such matters as relative size and strength; the preoccupations of the developing child would alter, and so might the whole psychology of the sexes. At present, the by-products of lactation still hold universally, for in all societies the care of infants is believed to be more women's work than men's, and we have therefore no way of telling whether or not the male drive towards assertion of maleness by differentiation from females through achievement has any other base beyond this earliest one. Cultures like the Arapesh show how easily, where parents do not discriminate strongly between the sexes of their children and men take over a nurturing rôle, this drive in the male may be muted. But this muting on the whole seems expensive enough so that it makes one question whether there are not a number of other, perhaps more phylogenetically determined, roots for assertiveness in the human male. However that may be, the mother-child situation at present provides a perfect learning context in which girls learn to be and boys learn the need to act.

At the next step in development, the stage at which the relationship to the breast becomes an active one, the child seeking, the mother according or withholding the breast, the learning situation is to a degree reversed. The mother may interpret as male behaviour the active seeking of her male baby and reinforce him in this seeking, demanding attitude, or she may still be sufficiently preoccupied with the reversal to feel that his seeking is rapaciousness, emptying her rather than replenishing her femininity. The girl-baby may similarly be treated as if her eagerness is unseemly in a female, or as if it is merely a phase of natural female receptivity. This period, then, when the infant shifts from passive receptivity to active, eager pursuit of the breast, is one in which there is a possible confusion, in terms of the basic relationships between developing mouth and offered breast. It is not surprising that here many elaborations of mother-child relationships, many complications of attitudes towards others, seem to develop, and that a detailed exploration of the nursing situation from the second half-year of life to weaning is always rewarding.

Then comes weaning, always somewhat loaded with emotion, whether it come while the child is still majorly preoccupied with intake, too young to walk, or after the child can walk and talk and fend for itself. When the break comes, the girl leaves her mother-child relationship, although she will some day repeat it. The boy leaves it forever, reliving it only inasmuch as intercourse may express symbolically re-entry into the womb. Among the possible male-female relationships, that between mother and suckling son may be the one that women find most rewarding, and if they do, this feeling will be communicated to their small sons. "Yet another month" of this most precious relationship will be implicit in the mother's voice as she repels the advice of bystanders, "He's big enough to be weaned." The boy in turn will learn that this is the relationship which women value most, and as a man expect his wife to prefer nursing his son to sleeping with himself, and so repeat the cycle. But to the girl, the diagrammatic statement is: "You must begin to change places. You must stop being a baby, suckled by a woman, and start on the road to being a woman who yourself nurse babies." Among the Arapesh, little girls share their mothers' extreme valuation of nursing, and are as unwilling as little boys to be weaned. In Manus, mothers have already communicated their lack of enthusiasm for the maternal rôle to their small daughters, and the girl-child on the point of weaning treats the mother's breast in a slightly jeering cavalier fashion. But whatever the nuance, for the boy it means the end of a type of relationship, while for the girl it means the end of one side of a complementary pattern and the beginning of preparedness for the other.

The period when small children are learning to regulate their elimination again provides a natural basis for interpreting sex membership. There are certain ways in which the modes of behaviour of the anus are related to behaviours learned with the mouth. Although ejection from the mouth is due either to sickness, to emergency behaviour, or to unpleasant emotion, still ejection is a mode the mouth can practise. The reversal of direction in the oesophagus that results in vomiting has the same convulsive quality as sudden violent defecation, and the unacceptability of vomiting may be transferred in feeling to attitudes towards defecation. If the child has already learned in the period of nursing definite attitudes towards taking in, towards defending his mouth from attack by persons or things, or habits of holding food in the mouth and refusing to swallow, these in turn may be reinterpreted into his eliminative behaviour. Cultures in which there is a strong preoccupation with the shamefulness of elimination tend to obscure the recognition that the gastro-intestinal system is a single system, open at both ends, in which food is meant to move one way, but in which it may move either way. So the child's interest in taking in, keeping, and giving out, almost always aroused to some degree by the shift from milk to food and by the exigences of sanitation—all known human societies have some rules of sanitation—is another point where the conception of maleness and femaleness, of what it is like to be a member of one's own sex and of the opposite sex, is again given new emphasis. The recognition that objects are not only taken in, but after being taken in may be altered, and emerge in a different form, is a recognition that may profoundly affect one's estimate of conception, gestation, and birth. If the emphasis on the product is that it is in fact a production for which the child is permitted to feel some identification and interest, the tie-in with birth can be close. But if a general prudery insists on disallowing the products of digestion, then the emphasis on the way in which food is destroyed or turned into something unacceptable may be so great that only the destructive nature of intake is left, and males and females alike reinvest all intaking organs, vulvas as well as mouths, with dangerous, destructive properties. Or the whole matter may be solved on a cultural level by a denial that the change in form is of any significance or that the body takes anything from the food. So among the Trobrianders, conspicuous for their denial of the father's biological rôle in procreation, any utility is also denied to food, which is said merely to enter the body and come out again in a less pleasant form. The extreme other elaboration of identification of eating and copulation may come with the phantasies found in adolescent girls in our society who refuse to eat because of a deep unconscious fear that eating will lead to pregnancy.[1]

The dual character of the eliminative tract also provides a background for re-emphasizing or de-emphasizing sex differences. If all elimination is treated in the same way, which occurs when there is such extreme shame about either exposure or elimination that urination must be as private and as heavily surrounded with taboos as defecation, sex differences as they refer to copulation are muted, although sex differences as they refer to child-bearing may be exaggerated. Here the likelihood of children and faeces being equated is enhanced. Where a more casual attitude towards urination exists, the difference in structure between males and females is likely to be much more conspicuous. Although under such circumstances women usually stand to urinate and so the expected expression of female envy that is found in the West—the little girl who insists on standing up to urinate—is missing, still small boys are likely to be highly exhibitionistic about urination, and to flaunt their achievements in the eyes of little girls, if the culture permits it, or at least before each other. Here is undoubtedly one of the points where simple male pride in the possession of a male organ can be developed or permanently damaged, and in which some bitterness or despair, or sense that it is no use trying, may be engendered in the female.

In any discussion of the way attitudes towards elimination pattern attitudes towards sex, much more than in the discussion of nursing behaviour, it is necessary to qualify the discussion in terms of different culturally allowed possibilities. The whole operation of eating, digesting, and eliminating is very complex, and may be interpreted in many different ways. The difference in structure between boy and girl can be very heavily muted by cultural convention, and there is no one clear and simple way in which this stage of childhood can be said to contribute to a sense of maleness and femaleness, although some important contribution may always be expected.

However, it is important to emphasize that the gastrointestinal system as a whole is the system by which the body is related to objects rather than to persons, in which food is taken in and absorbed, and waste products are given out. On the other hand, the child's first feeding relationships are primarily relationships to a person, although the child's discrimination between itself and its mother's breast may be as dim as many students of infancy believe it to be. Where the mother gives the child food as well as nursing it, the re-

lationship of child to object and child to person will have
one character; where she nurses it without supplementary
feeding it will have a different one. Teething procedures
may then intensify these distinctions. In Iatmul, as has been
noted, the child cuts its teeth on large round white shells
that hang around the mother's neck. When the baby's teething pains might lead it to bite, to protect her breast from
bites the mother does not have to depersonalize her relationship completely; she can merely shift the aching little gums
to her necklace. But in Bali, the baby's teether is a silver
box hung around his own neck, in which traditionally a piece
of the umbilical cord was once kept. When he wishes to bite,
he learns, in so far as he experiences this as a personal act
at all, that it is personal towards extensions of himself, and
not towards others. After his mother has overstimulated him
by teasing, the same baby will often prefer to suck his own
toe, even though he could turn to his mother's breast.

Whatever the transition, the distinction between mother's
body and the own body, as satisfying or dissatisfying in interpersonal terms, and in person-object terms, is an important one. Where the nursing situation is not emphasized
and the whole process of eating and elimination is the centre
of adult-child communication, the child may form a picture
of the world in which things are more important than
people, in which relations with others are seen primarily as
interchange or reciprocity, in which the production of children is equated with the production of any other object, so
that birth itself becomes a sort of externalization. In the
imagery of our industrial society, the human body becomes
a factory that manufactures human beings rather than the
factory's becoming an imperfect model of a human body
itself. The products of the body become identified as non-
personal, and the orientation of the individual to the outside
world is made more predominant as the relationship to the
own body shrinks. This is the Manus character structure,

as well as being a character that develops in modern society rather frequently, but its occurrence at such a primitive level as among the Stone Age, ghost-guarded, pile-dwelling Manus people of the Admiralties suggests that while it is congruent with the machine and the factory, the dynamics lie deep in the relationship of individuals to their own bodies. This externalization shows up vividly in the Manus' handling of miscarriages and abortions, all of which are named, and treated as if they had been full individuals. Years afterwards the mother will not distinguish in retrospect between a miscarriage at three months, a stillborn infant, and a child who died several days after birth. All have been seized upon by the outside world, property was exchanged in their names, and they are equated in her expressed memories about them

So to the interpretation of its own sex through its own sex organs the child brings these earlier experiences through which inter-relationships with others have reinforced the cues of its own body. If the adults have differentiated, and differentiated happily, between the two sexes, the boy will be able to take pride in his realization that he is a male, and will find the structure of his body impressive, worthy of exhibitionism and boasting. The girl will be considerably less sure that the immediate structure of her body is something to be proud of. She definitely has less conspicuous genitalia than her brother. However well she may be identified with her mother as a female, still she has no breasts, her little belly is very small indeed, even though she walk with it protruded and have the rather doubtful experience of being poked and prodded with the playful exclamation, "Are you pregnant?" Whereas the boy perhaps is given maximum certainty that he *is* a male as long as he keeps his mind on the simple phallic position and does not let it dwell too much on problems of paternity, which are beyond his imagination, the girl has to take on faith the fact that she *will be* a mother. Motherhood is more easily grasped than fatherhood, the rewards of simple anatomical masculinity are more positive than the rewards of anatomical femininity. The more biologically accurate the earlier stages have been, the more the mother has made her male child feel his maleness and the female child her femaleness, the more this period is likely to be one of assurance for boys and uncertainty for girls.

But it likewise makes the whole Oedipus solution a different matter for boys and girls. At the height of his sense of his own maleness the boy has to face the fact that he is, in actuality, not ready to take any woman unto himself, either a grown woman or a small girl. He has to face the need to grow, to learn, to master a great variety of skills and strengths, before he can compete with grown males. This may be frightening if his father feels his incipient masculinity as a threat, or communicates to him his own fears about the whole danger of ever being masculine at all. It may be infuriating to the boy if grown men have been presented to him as creatures of so little importance that competition with them should be easy. It may be terribly discouraging if the grown man in his society is seen as a creature of incomparable strength and bravery, fierce and warlike like a Plains Indian. Growing-up may be phrased in terms of physical growth, or taking a head, or having collected enough property to purchase a wife. But almost always the attainment of the full rights of a male to the favours of women becomes conditional on his learning to act in specified ways, some of which will seem difficult. Some societies do not concern themselves to forbid his playing sexual games, exhibitionist games with other boys, mock-marriage games with other little girls. But whether he is allowed to play sex-games or not, he is taught, sometimes explicitly, sometimes implicitly, that there is a long, long road between the lusty, exhibitionistic self-confidence of the five-year-old and the man who can win and keep a woman in a world filled with other men.

Here again the phrasing that growing-up receives reverses the position of boys and girls. The boy learns that he must make an effort to enter the world of men, that his first act of differentiating himself from his mother, of realizing his own body as his and different from hers, must be continued into long years of effort—which may not succeed. He still carries his knowledge of child-birth as something that women can do, that his sister will be able to do, as a latent goad to some other type of achievement. He embarks on a long course of growth and practice, the outcome of which, if he sees it as not only being able to possess a woman but to become a father, is very uncertain.

But the little girl meets no such challenge. The taboos and the etiquette enjoined upon her are ways of protecting her already budding femininity from adult males. She learns to cross her legs, or tuck her heels under her, or sit with her legs parallel and close in. She is dressed to enclose her further against attack, against premature defloration. Implicit in the abundant rules that are laid upon her, the prohibitions against the freedom, the exhibitionism, the roaming and marauding, permitted to her brother, is the message "It might happen too soon. Wait." And this comes at the very time when her brother is permitted far more exposure in public, when he may go about naked, unkempt, uncared-for, the very negligence of the adult world proclaiming aloud that nothing is going to happen *from him* yet that can possibly matter to any one. So in Iatmul, in Arapesh, in Mundugumor, in Tchambuli, the little boy puts on a G-string when he feels like it, but the girl has a grass skirt carefully tucked around her diminutive waist. And as adolescence approaches the prescient signs that surround the girl increase: chaperonage will increase in those societies which value virginity, approaches from older men will increase in

boldness in those societies which do not. Upon the initial
uncertainty of her final maternal rôle is built a rising curve
of sureness, which is finally crowned—in primitive and
simple societies, in which every woman marries—with child-
bearing, with an experience that is so real and so valid that
only very few and very sick women who are bred in societies
that have devalued maternity are able wholly to disavow it.
So the life of the female starts and ends with sureness, first
with the simple identification with her mother, last with the
sureness that that identification is true, and that she has
made another human being. The period of doubt, of envy
of her brother, is brief, and comes early, followed by the long
years of sureness.

For the male, however, the gradient is reversed. His earliest experience of self is one in which he is forced, in the relationship to his mother, to realize himself as different, as a
creature unlike the mother, as a creature unlike the human
beings who make babies in a direct, intelligible way by
using their own bodies to make them. Instead he must turn
out from himself, enter and explore and produce in the outside world, find his expression through the bodies of others.
His brief period of simple sureness that he is fully armed
for the fray—seen as simple copulation or as simple feats of
strength and power—is brought to naught by the awareness that he himself is not ready to act. This imposed uncertainty, this period of striving and effort, never really end.
He may grow up, take a head, or collect for himself a bride-
price; he may marry, and his wife may have a child, but the
child his wife bears is probably never the absolute assurance to him that it is to her. Possibly cultures like the
Arapesh, which associate the creation of a child with ardu-
ous and continuous work on the part of both parents as the
child is built up of steady accretions of semen from the
father and blood from the mother, come the closest to giving the male who has fathered a child a sense that he has

accomplished something in his own right. But the Arapesh version of paternity is after all a myth, a myth congruent with the great value set on parenthood by the Arapesh. At the simplest level of human society, men have had no way of estimating the relationship between copulation and paternity; as the habit of making correlated and exact observations has increased, his own rôle has been specified as a single copulatory act that was successful. While modern genetic theory has again dignified the paternal rôle to a genetic contribution equal to the maternal, it has not increased our ability to prove that a given man is, in fact, the father of a given child. Genetic theory has simply increased our capacity to prove that a given man could *not* be the father of a given child. It may protect a man against a lawsuit and help him verify his suspicions of his wife's infidelity, but it does not increase his certainty of his paternity. Paternity remains, with all our modern biological knowledge, as inferential as it ever was, and considerably less ascertainable than it has seemed to be in some periods of history. So while in the end the female in societies in which every woman marries is practically certain of resolving all the doubts about her own sex membership that were implanted in her in the natural course of her long infancy and childhood, the male needs to reassert, to reattempt, to redefine his maleness.

In every known human society, the male's need for achievement can be recognized. Men may cook, or weave or dress dolls or hunt humming-birds, but if such activities are appropriate occupations of men, then the whole society, men and women alike, votes them as important. When the same occupations are performed by women, they are regarded as less important. In a great number of human societies men's sureness of their sex rôle is tied up with their right, or ability, to practise some activity that women are not allowed to practise. Their maleness, in fact, has to be underwritten by preventing women from entering some field or performing some feat. Here may be found the relationship between maleness and pride; that is, a need for prestige that will outstrip the prestige which is accorded to any woman. There seems no evidence that it is necessary for men to surpass women in any specific way, but rather that men do need to find reassurance in achievement, and because of this connection, cultures frequently phrase achievement as something that women do not or cannot do, rather than directly as something which men do well.

The recurrent problem of civilization is to define the male rôle satisfactorily enough—whether it be to build gardens or raise cattle, kill game or kill enemies, build bridges or handle bank-shares—so that the male may in the course of his life reach a solid sense of irreversible achievement, of which his childhood knowledge of the satisfactions of childbearing have given him a glimpse. In the case of women, it is only necessary that they be permitted by the given social arrangements to fulfil their biological rôle, to attain this sense of irreversible achievement. If women are to be restless and questing, even in the face of child-bearing, they must be made so through education. If men are ever to be at peace, ever certain that their lives have been lived as they were meant to be, they must have, in addition to paternity, culturally elaborated forms of expression that are lasting and sure. Each culture—in its own way—has developed forms that will make men satisfied in their constructive activities without distorting their sure sense of their masculinity. Fewer cultures have yet found ways in which to give women a divine discontent that will demand other satisfactions than those of child-bearing.

PART THREE

THE PROBLEMS OF SOCIETY

VIII

RHYTHM OF WORK AND PLAY

WE MAY NOW TURN FROM CONSIDERING THE WAYS IN WHICH
the child learns about his or her sex rôle and look at the
whole question from a different point of view. If any human
society—large or small, simple or complex, based on the most
rudimentary hunting and fishing or on the whole intricate
interchange of manufactured products—is to survive, it must
have a pattern of social life that comes to terms with the
differences between the sexes. If we look over the whole
known human world we may ask: What are the problems
that must be solved if a society is to survive? One of these
problems is how to set up a rhythm of activity and rest,
which in most societies becomes transformed also into the
way in which work—activity that is purposeful and directed
towards ends that lie outside the activity—and play—activity
which is self-rewarding—are alternated.

The relationship between the physiological rhythms of
human beings and the way in which mankind has patterned
day and night, months and years, seen life as a continuum

endlessly subdivided or as a series of cycles of life and death, brings into sharp relief the different contributions of the two sexes. We may look at the physiological rhythms themselves and note the contrasts between the life of a woman, with its sharply defined transitions of menarche, defloration, pregnancy, birth, lactation, and menopause, and the life of a man, shading imperceptibly from childhood into youth, from youth into manhood, with the first seminal dream or the first intromission leaving no mark upon the organism except such meaning as the individual gives to it himself. Or we may look at the elaborate cultural expressions in which time has been patterned into intricate periodicities, of mathematics and music, fields in which women have played almost no creative part. We may look at the monthly cycle through which women pass, one of heightened and lowered tension and receptivity, as the body prepares itself tirelessly for the impregnation that may come, but does not, and compare it with the fitful states of zest and moodiness in men, which unless pegged to their wives' periodicity, seem to have no rhythm out of which a calendar could be built. Finally, we have the claims of students of endocrinology and fatigue who suggest that women have a capacity for continuous monotonous work that men do not share, while men have a capacity for the mobilization of sudden spurts of energy, followed by a need for rest and reassemblage of resources.

So striking are these contrasts that one can see at a glance that if a culture were built to the rhythmic specifications and capacities of one sex, it would become a pattern that fitted most unevenly and grossly the other sex, and that all cultures in which men and women share the work of the world must somehow be a compromise between the rhythmic periodicities of men and the rhythmic periodicities of women. But the ways in which different cultures have achieved these compromises are various and differently rewarding.

Consider first the question of monotonous, repetitive work compared with working in spurts of effort and rest. The capacity for spurts can be definitely tied in with our endocrinological knowledge of the male; conceivably it might be physiologically induced in the female, but at the cost of masculinization in secondary sex characters. The rest of the assumptions—that because men are more capable of working in spurts, monotony is more expensive for them, and that women are biologically more naturally capable of enduring monotony without psychic expense—seem without any present foundation in the research material.

The Balinese manifest less fatigue than any people of whom we have a record. Day and night the roads are filled with men and women running lightly under loads so heavy that it takes several people to lift them to the bearers' heads or shoulders. Day and night the air is filled with music, men practising tirelessly, after many hours of work when they stood ankle-deep in the mud of the flooded rice-field. Activity goes on, hour after hour, swift and yet unhurried, and marked usually by a steady light pace rather than by any heavy spurts of energy. The arms of the men are almost as free of heavy muscle as those of the women, yet the potentiality for the development of heavy muscle is there; when Balinese work as dock-coolies under the insistent driving supervision of the European, their muscles develop and harden. But in their own villages they prefer to carry rather than to lift, and to summon many hands to every task, so that when a house is moved from one place to another or a giant forty-foot cremation tower is carried to the cemetery, a hundred men are assembled for the task, and none strains beneath it. For a house-building, for a temple feast, for a ceremony, there are always more workers than are needed, and there is almost always time to spare.

Without pressure, on tasks that are divided and subdivided to give some task to every one, men and women work, pause to smoke, chew betel, take a stroll, play with the baby, play a few notes on one of the musical instruments that are ready to the hand—and fall back into the pattern of work again. There is no word for "tired," but only a word that can be better rendered as "too tired," used on the rare occasions when there is pressure, as when the men plough in the great exhibitionistic ploughing events, each man racing his bedizened oxen across the high, dry rice-fields in the mountains, and then going home to sleep for many hours, exhausted by the very spurt of effort that Westerners think of as congenial to men. Here in Bali this capacity for spurt, for the sudden mobilized effort that can lift a heavy weight, or dash at top speed, has been neglected, and men and women carry and make offerings, walk long distances under loads they cannot lift but under which they can maintain a light swift walk, work many hours in the field, and refreshed by a few minutes of what is called "to walk about forgetting," go on to many more hours of practice for a dance, or cutting out leaves or meat for offerings. If we knew no other people than the Balinese, we would never guess that men were so made that they could develop heavy muscles, and work in alternating heavy energetic spurts and periods of recovery.

But just as the work-rhythm of Bali does not draw on the capacity of men to put forth special effort, so also the calendar makes no compromises with female periodicity. Menstruation and pregnancy are both ceremonially disqualifying—a menstruating woman may not enter the temple, even the small garden-temple courtyard in her own home; pregnant women, and women who have recently given birth, may not enter the houses where special gods are kept, or approach too closely to a priest, whose ceremonial purity must be preserved. But the calendar, an intricate pattern in which weeks of one day, two days, three days—up to ten days—turn upon each other, and each recurrent intersection marks a certain appropriateness for ceremony, brooks no readjustment to suit these feminine rhythms. The feast arrives, and the menstruating women cannot attend. The child is born, and the parents who would have been an integral part of some great calendrically fixed feast simply are not allowed to participate. The dance is set, and the day before the event, one of the little girl trance-dancers menstruates for the first time and drops out forever from that particular dance. Unconcedingly the calendrically determined life proceeds, and women, and men through women, are debarred from participation. Perhaps it is not surprising that women customarily define menstruation as being unable to enter the temple, and speak of pregnancy in the same breath with a wound or a mutilation that debars them from ceremonial life.

But almost as if the failure to come to terms with the possible climaxes of both sexes—with the cyclical and orgiastic climaxes of maternity, with the orgiastic climax of copulation, and with the capacity to put forth mighty physical effort by the male—had to be met in some other way, we do find in Balinese religious ceremonial violent paroxysmal seizures. These are extremely violent, but without specific sex manifestations. Men and women, armed with krises, turn the krises against themselves, and after spurts of furious simulated self-attack, fall twitching and in spasm to the ground. After the trance is over, the women's hair is twined again on their heads—as is done during childbirth to calm them—cool holy water is poured on the faces of both men and women. They return to ordinary life, which is unhurried and non-climactic in character, a life through which both men and women move quietly occupied through days that are infinitely subdivided by an artificial system which ignores the known but unremarked lunar year, itself perhaps too much of a natural rhythm to be as satisfactory as the two-hundred-and-ten-day cycle on which their main calendar is based.

But we need only turn to another culture to find a dif-- ferent rhythm. In the steep mountain wildernesses of the Torricelli Mountains of New Guinea, where food is scarce and gardens are far removed from each other, the underfed Arapesh men and women spend much of their time going up and down the steep slopes, the women's jaws shut tight against the loads that hang from their foreheads. When a feast is given, it means too much work for too few people, long hours in the sago-swamps from which men and women come back with bloodshot eyes, weary, and disinclined to any activity. All work is heavy work, all roads are too steep and too long, and all loads too heavy for the carrying. Women do all the routine carrying, their heads are said to be stronger; men carry pigs and large logs, and their shoulders chafe beneath the carrying-poles. In the village, on the occasional off-day both men and women sit with hands empty and unoccupied, the women with their babies at their breasts, and the phrasing is, "To-day we are weary, we will sleep in the village." As women share in the heavy, exacting spurts of work, so also men share in the small routines of everyday life, care of children, making the fire, fetching small things from the bush. But on the whole, the rhythm of the work is closer to the supposedly male type of spurts of energy; characteristically, the handwork that has occupied women's industrious hands in so many socie- ties is absent. Women's hands lie as inert as men's after the day's long climb.

There is no calendar to lay on the passing days a scheme born of man's imaginative patterning of time, or of his careful observation of moon and stars. The movement of the Pleiades is marked, but for no set purpose; and yams, elsewhere harvested by a calendar, so that there are times of plenty and times of hunger, are among the Mountain Arapesh planted at any time of year. The rhythm of work that we think of as feminine, the work that is never done, responsive to the recurrent needs for food and care of others, especially of children, is here combined with the rhythm of work that we call masculine, in which irregular outputs of energy alternate with irregular periods of rest.

To the female periodicities, both men and women adjust. During menstruation the woman rests in a small, badly built shelter over the edge of the hillside, and the man must fend for himself, care for the children, and abstain from entering his yam-garden, from which she is debarred. So during pregnancy he shares her taboos, and after child-birth he lies beside his newly delivered wife, resting from the labour, from the hard work of child-bearing, which ages a man as much as it does a woman. Looking only at the Arapesh—and the Balinese—it would still be hard to form any picture of a biological difference in rhythm for the two sexes. Looking at the Arapesh alone, one would judge women wholly capable of heavy spurts of work, and men somehow subject to the physiological penalties of menstruation and child-bearing.

To the Balinese, there is also no strong distinction between work and play. The distinction between one kind of work and another is primarily a matter of its sacredness, so that although cutting up meat in the temple is work for the gods, cutting it up at home is just work. But the pile-dwelling Manus fisher-folk of the Admiralty Islands make distinctions between work and idleness very close to those of our Puritan ancestors. Both sexes work hard, the men fishing, house-building, and trading on long voyages; the women cooking, smoking fish, attending the local market, making bead-work and grass skirts. Idleness is a sin permissible only when earned by special hard work—as when the men loll around the village after a long night of fishing waist-deep in the cold lagoon; or when a woman sits with her new-born child, temporarily immobilized while her husband accumulates enough sago to ransom her back from her brother. But here, just one degree from the equator, both men and women work hard, busy and troubled by many things, urged on by the requirements of captious and exacting ghosts—every illness is interpreted as ghostly punishment for some economic failure to pay a debt or build a house or initiate some new undertaking. Menstruation is regarded as so shameful that it must be hidden; a woman is neither penalized nor given respite. Taboos on the new father permit him a period of partial idleness while the food needed to complete the exchanges for the new child is accumulated. On the whole, the Manus picture is fairly even-handed between the sexes. Husbands and wives are associated, although separated, in a brief period of idleness after birth. Women carry somewhat more of the routine activities of life, but men are so industrious that the contrast does not stand out. Where work is a matter of duty, duty reinforced by heavy religious sanctions, women's possibly greater capacity for small monotonous tasks and men's possibly natural capacity for irregular work spurts can both be overlaid with a type of activity that takes its pattern from a learned duty to be industrious.

Among the Iatmul head-hunters of the Middle Sepik River we find a division of work-rhythms that approximates very closely present theories of sex differences. Here the women work fairly steadily but cheerfully, in groups, without any sense of being inordinately driven. They are responsible for the daily catch of fish, for the fish that is taken to the market, for gathering firewood and carrying water, for cooking, and for plaiting the great cyclindrical mosquito-baskets that are miniature rooms to protect human beings against the ravenous mosquitoes. For most of their waking hours they are occupied, and they display very little fatigue, or irritation against the continuous exactions of housekeeping and fishing. Men's work, however, is almost entirely episodic—house-building, canoe-building, communal hunts for crocodile in the dry season or for small rodents by burning down the grass-land, or devising the elaborate theatrical settings for ceremonial. Hardly any of these activities need be done at any given time, and all are done in response to long preliminary harangues, threats, challenges, dares and counter-dares, under pressure of which the group of men who will finally perform some activity get excited and angry enough to go to work with a will. There are a great many abortive attempts at large-scale work that the angry, exhibitionistic will to work is not sufficient to carry through. When tasks are performed, they are performed with a great display of energy and effort, the whole body is involved, and Iatmul males complain vigorously of being tired after such efforts.

When the small boys and girls play together, they mimic adult life. The boys hunt for small birds, the girls cook them, together they mime mortuary ceremonies or shamanistic events. Then the narrator will often add: "We returned to the village. The little girls said, 'Let's play again to-morrow,' but the little boys said, 'No, we are too tired; let us rest to-morrow.'" The ability of the Iatmul woman to work steadily at unexciting tasks, without boredom or serious disturbances in rhythm, and the disinclination of Iatmul men for any such tasks were prettily illustrated by an episode when we first came to the village of Tambunum. We asked Tomi, one of the native men who was working for us as an informant, to get some clay from the river-bank and stop up the crevices between the mosquito wire and the unevenly laid cement floor of our mosquito-room. Tomi fetched the clay, and half-heartedly started to fill up the cracks. Then he sent for his five wives. He divided the clay into two parts, and gave one part to his wives to continue the tedious, useful work of filling up the cracks. With the other part, he modelled a very handsome crocodile to adorn the door-step.

Thus if the theorist about men and women's natural work-rhythms had based his theories on Iatmul, he would easily have come up with a picture of man as the lineal descendant of a nomadic hunter, capable of strong output of effort, but demanding long periods of recuperation, and a picture of women as better fitted by nature for the routine tasks of everyday life, unresisting and unrebelling against a world in which their work was never done and their hands were hardly ever at rest.

The Iatmul take menstruation lightly; a menstruating woman is not supposed to cook for her husband unless she is out of temper with him and wishes to do him some mild harm. But due to the way in which Iatmul households are organized, with two families living in opposite ends of one house, and usually several spare women—extra wives, widows, and unmarried daughters—about, this works no hardship for any one. At child-birth the mother may return to her own family, where she will be relieved from work, but no heavy taboos are laid on the husband. Social pressure is mainly exerted against the iniquity of getting more than one wife pregnant at the same time, and men may be publicly rebuked by the elders of their clan: "Who do you think you are, to have three wives pregnant at once? Who now will do the work in your house? Who will bring the firewood? You, I suppose!" Men must be aroused into working sago even to feed their own families. The village air is shrill with the vituperations of wives goading their husbands by insult and invectives to work sago for their households.

Among the Samoans, work-rhythms are again more evenly divided. Although the men do have occasional spurts of fishing for turtle or shark that take all their energies, both men and women do heavy, exacting gardening and tiring fishing. Both men and women cook, both men and women do handwork, and even the hands of a chief of the highest rank are seldom idle. As he sits among his councillors, his hand is busy rolling sennit (coconut-fibre cord) on his thigh, or braiding it into the thousands of yards needed to fasten houses and canoes together. Women spend many hours plaiting the mats as fine as linen that are to be the dowries of the daughters of chiefly families, or the coarse mats that provide bedding for the whole village. Work is scaled primarily to age and status rather than to sex. Both men and women are strong and muscular, both climb, both carry, both alternate vigorous work with periods of quiet industriousness and long relaxing hours of singing and dancing. The busy, contented, industrious life is counterpointed with periods when a whole village goes on a visit to celebrate a marriage, or simply for an interchange of festivities. Then perhaps for two or three months no work will be done at all and the entire time is given over to feasting, which will have to be repaid in kind later, and will mean much hard work. But men and women, old and young, share in the work and in the festivities. There is no sense of great pressure or hurry, although sometimes there is much trumped-up excitement over matters of etiquette and ceremonial, and children of five rush about exclaiming, "Oh, great complications in our household!"

Thus even a survey of five societies shows how arbitrarily the work-rhythms of men and women can be arranged. If research finally demonstrates any genuine differences in the capacity to tolerate monotony, or to benefit by working in irregular spurts of energy, we will still have to consider whether the most felicitous results are obtained by constructing a society in which women's work, while more monotonous and demanding, is also keyed to the cycles of menstruation and pregnancy, and men's work, less monotonous and demanding, is the work that can be depended upon in any emergency, since men are subject to no such periodic rises and falls in capacity as women. Possibly we may find instead that if all work is keyed low enough so that women do not suffer too inappropriate demands during their periodic fluctuations in capacity, but men are not prevented from constructing crises if they find them congenial, the gain in adaptation of rhythm between the sexes may be greater than any loss that comes from not pitching the work-rhythm of each sex as perfectly as possible to their distinctive periodicities.

So far we have been considering the distribution of effort in time, and the possible differences between the two sexes in innate capacity and in learned behaviour, But there is another contrast between the sexes that is as striking as their different diurnal and monthly rhythms and the presence and absence of pregnancy, and that is the contrast in the plot of their lives.

Women's biological-career line has a natural climax structure that can be overlaid, muted, muffled, and publicly denied, but which remains as an essential element in both sexes' views of themselves. For it cannot be stressed too heavily that children of each sex form their pictures of their sex rôles from experience with *both* sexes; whatever the peculiar nature of the other sex, it is then phrased as "something I am not," "something I can never be," "something I wish I were," "something I might become." This special female climax-structure carries with it the possibility of a greater emphasis on states of *being* than does that of the male. A girl *is* a virgin. After the breaking of the hymen, physically in case she has one, symbolically in case her hymen is structurally negligible, by extension she is *not* a virgin. The young Balinese girl to whom one says, "Your name is I Tewa?" and who draws herself up and answers, "I am Men Bawa" ("Mother of Bawa"), is speaking absolutely. She is the mother of Bawa; Bawa may die to-morrow, but she remains the mother of Bawa; only if he had died unnamed would her neighbours have called her *"Men Belasin,"* "Mother bereft." Stage after stage in women's life-histories thus stand, irrevocable, indisputable, accomplished. This gives a natural basis for the little girl's emphasis on *being* rather than on *doing*. The little boy learns that he must act like a boy, do things, prove that he is a boy, and prove it over and over again, while the little girl learns that she *is* a girl, and all she has to do is to refrain from acting like a boy.

Against the set of physical certainties that make up the biological picture of a woman's life, the virgin and the childless stand out in sharp relief, a contrast that can be given to men's lives only by definite cultural elaboration.

The little girl is a virgin; after defloration she is no longer a virgin; something definite, identifiable, has occurred that is very different from the boy's gradual experimentation with copulation. Only in societies that postpone sexual experimentation until very late, so that a boy may never have touched a girl's body until as an adult he attempts to copulate with her, is it possible to regard first intercourse for boys as equivalent in dramatic incisiveness to defloration for girls. Puberty for the girl is dramatic and unmistakable, while for the boy the long series of events come slowly: uncertain and then deepening voice, growth of body hair, and finally ejaculations. There is no exact moment at which the boy can say, "Now I am a man," unless society steps in and gives a definition. One of the functions served by the variety of male initiation ceremonies that occur over the world—when the adult males incise, sub-incise, circumcise, scarify, or otherwise mutilate and knock about the young adolescent males—is that the rituals serve to punctuate a growth-sequence that is inherently unpunctuated. Whether or not there would be any desire for such punctuation, such definiteness, without the sharp irreversibility of the female menarche, we do not know. At any rate, the girl's first menstruation marks a dividing-line between childhood and womanhood. Whatever any given culture may have done in patterning this event, no recorded culture has ever patterned it out of existence.*

Menarche is an important ceremony among the puritanical Manus, who from then on conceal all menstruations between menarche and marriage. There is no word for "virgin" in the language, and bleeding from the rupture of the hymen is simply equated with menstruation, which is itself believed to be reactivated by marriage. So extreme is the prudery of the people—women in the last stages of illness will not loosen their grass skirts—that any visual inspection of the genitals is unthinkable, and the chances of rediscovery of the hymen are slight. The phrase for menstruation is *kekanbwot* ("leg"—third person possessive —"broken") so that menarche contains the idea of injury that among some peoples is reserved for their attitudes towards defloration. At her first menstruation the Manus girl is given a great ceremony; the other girls of the village come to sleep in her house, there are large exchanges of food and ceremonial and splashing-parties in the lagoon; men are excluded and the women have a few jolly parties together—then absolute secrecy descends upon the girl's later menstruation. But the corresponding ceremony for boys, in which their ears are pierced and comparable

* We can, of course, from our experience of the extreme ingenuity with which man has rephrased his own physiology, imagine ways in which this could be done. A baby-girl could be ritually bled each month from birth, so that actual menarche would fit evenly and smoothly into the already established behaviour. An even more artificial social practice is the manufacture of virginity in brothels, reported for certain parts of Europe. In any consideration of the relationship between the innate and the culturally patterned, such bizarre possibilities must be taken into account, but they should not be overstressed.

charms are said over them, is a pallid affair. Something has happened *in* the girl, which has changed her from one physical state to another; something has been done *to* the boy, which puts him in a different social status.

Among the Arapesh, first menstruation occurs several years after a young betrothed girl has gone to live with her husband's kin, where he and his kin will hunt and garden to provide food to make her grow. Her first menstruation is occasion for ceremony; her brothers come and build her menstrual hut, placing it safely beyond the edge of the village to keep the village safe from the dangerous supernatural strength attached to menstruating women. The girl is cautioned to sit with her legs in front of her, her knees raised. Her old grass skirt and her old armlets are taken from her and either given away or destroyed. Older women of her family attend her and instruct her in rolling stinging nettle-leaves and inserting them into her vulva to make her breasts grow. This practice explains why there will be no experience of defloration unless a young husband "steals" his wife before her first puberty ceremony. The girl fasts for five or six days, and then emerges to be painted and decorated.

The women put her old net bag on her head, freshly decorated with *wheinyal* leaves. They place a bright-red, heart-shaped leaf in her mouth. This leaf is also worn by novices in the *tamberan* ceremony. Her husband has been told to bring a rib of a coconut-leaflet, and some *mebu*, the scented flowers of sulphur, on a pair of *aliwhiwas* leaves. He waits for her in the middle of the *agehu;* she comes up slowly, her eyes downcast, her steps lagging from her long fast, supported beneath the arm-pits by the women. Her husband stands in front of her. He puts his big toe on her big toe. He takes the coconut-rib and as she looks up into his face he flicks the old net bag from her head—the old net bag that his father placed on her head as a child when he arranged the betrothal. Now the girl drops the leaf out of her mouth and puts out her tongue, furry and heavy with her fast. Her husband wipes it off with the *mebu* earth. Then the girl sits down on a piece of sago-bark; she sits down carefully, lowering herself with one hand, and sits with her legs straight out in front of her. The husband gives her a spoon wrapped in a leaf, and the bowl of soup that he has made. For the first spoonful he must hold her hand to steady her, and so for the second. By the third she will be strong enough to hold it for herself. After she has eaten the soup, he takes one of the *wabalal* yams and breaks it in half. She eats half and half he places in the rafters of the house; this is the earnest that she will not treat him like a stranger and deliver· him over to the sorcerers. Lest she do so, tradition provides him with part of her personality also. The piece of yam is kept until the girl becomes pregnant.[1]

The Sepik peoples—Iatmul, Tchambuli, and Mundugumor—make little of menstruation ceremonies, more preoccupied as they are with elaborating male initiatory rituals than with worrying about ensuring women's fertility.

In Samoa, there is no social stress on menarche, but an elaborate ceremonial recognition of defloration. A permissive attitude towards sex is combined with an inordinate pride in the prerogatives of rank, and the daughter of a family of rank should be a virgin at marriage; the official counsellor of the bridegroom should be able to show to the assembled guests his fingers bound in blood-stained white; a large white bark-cloth banner stained with blood should be hung outside the house. But if the girl is not a virgin, then she must have the courage to tell the old women of her family, and they will provide a proper amount of chicken-blood. Here a people who have shown themselves especially skilful in combining the demands of the body with the formalities of a gracefully ordered way of life have achieved a way of regarding defloration as socially, if not physiologically, repeatable if not reversible.

In Bali, the stress is again on menstruation, with little girls who menstruate early seeking to conceal it for fear they will then be married off to husbands of their parents' choice, while girls who menstruate late—especially among the upper castes, where elaborate and beautiful ceremonies are held—become over-anxious, and are deeply pleased when menarche arrives.

In Bali, the circumstance of childlessness is assimilated to a sense of choosing different paths. A Brahman girl may become a virgin priestess—and then she must not marry—or marry, and later become a priestess. In the mountain villages, men and women who are childless can reach the next to the highest point in the social hierarchy, but if they have any children, then one must be a boy, or their status is socially crippling. One may reach almost the highest status by childlessness, and the woman who remains unmarried is spoken of as "seeking heaven," but for full status in this world a man must have a child, and that a male. The Manus attempt to proclaim that having children requires only will rather than bodily participation. Women adopt children and claim them as their own, negating every detail of the child's biological origin—as they smother in economic details the memory of their miscarriages, as if these had been full-term children.

But however much cultures may refashion the fact of child-bearing, pregnancy remains conspicuous and unconcealable—except within the confines of great cities or complex societies—and the difference between the woman who has borne a child and one who has not remains absolute. Some societies may classify any conception—even a miscarriage of two or three weeks—as putting a woman over on the child-bearing side; others may insist on the birth of a live child; and others may classify a woman whose children

have all died, almost at any age, as virtually on the childless side. But a distinction remains, absolute, irreversible.

Again at the menopause a sharp, irreversible change
takes place. Where reproductivity has been regarded as
somewhat impure and ceremonially disqualifying—as in
Bali—the post-menopausal woman and the virgin girl work
together at ceremonies from which women of child-bearing
age are debarred. Where modesty of speech and action is
enjoined on women, such behaviour may be no longer
asked from the older woman, who may use obscene language as freely as or more freely than any man. But again
something happens to the woman, finally, in a way that
nothing happens to a man.

So women's lives are arranged in sharp, discontinuous
steps, with the emphasis almost inevitably on being—a virgin, a girl who has ceased to be a virgin, a childless woman,
a woman who has borne a child, a woman (past the menopause) who can no longer bear a child. Their lives cannot be
infinitely subdivided into steps of lost virginity, partial
menarche, or a series of increasingly successful attempts to
carry a baby to full term, without enormous efforts, enormous cultural constructions denying the physiology of reproduction.

To achieve comparably dramatic sequences in a man's
life, either something may be done to his body—circumcision,
incision, sub-incision, teeth-excision, scarification, tattooing—
in which members of his culture, armed with cultural tools,
no longer following any clear rhythm of their biological inheritance, alter, deform, or beautify his body. Or the society
must itself introduce artificial social distinctions, require that
an unmarried male remain forever associated with the young
boys—as in a Balinese mountain village—or refuse him a fishing and hunting license,[2] as in the early days when French
Canadians were constructing a society that would have a
guaranteed competitive birth-rate. Some cultures go so far

as to introduce synthetic male menstruation, blood-letting for males in which they also can rid themselves of their "bad blood" and so be as healthy as females. We have seen how New Guinea societies have built whole ritual systems on the imitation by males of child-bearing and child-rearing, but throughout these are artificial systems, creations of the imagination of one sex to which the life of the other sex has appeared dramatic and challenging. As the expectation of life lengthens, the menopause, unrecorded among the primates—probably because of their short life-span—becomes increasingly more conspicuous, and we find again an attempt to emphasize the male analogue; for while only one male in a hundred may experience any physical analogue of a "change of life," still a climacteric, with accompanying tensions and crisis behaviour, is available to any bank president.

When human beings view their biological inheritance and consider to what extent they are bound by it, women appear at once as the more intractable material. Conception and birth are as stubborn conditions of life as death itself. Coming to terms with the rhythms of women's lives means coming to terms with life itself, accepting the imperatives of the body rather than the imperatives of an artificial, man-made, perhaps transcendentally beautiful civilization. Emphasis on the male work-rhythm is an emphasis on infinite possibilities; emphasis on the female rhythms is an emphasis on a defined pattern, on limitation. The immigrant who comes to America from a small European country in which the possibilities of building anew are all defined by the, to him, irrevocable past—as each new road must follow, in effect, a prehistoric path—finds the unpatterned plains of Kansas an exciting challenge upon which anything can be built. Human beings may also find the less patterned biology of the male an open challenge. It is not surprising that the age which saw continents opened up, the earth mined, and the skies turned into ordered traffic ways should have regarded the rhythms of the female as primarily a nuisance and a handicap, to be muted, transcended, ignored. It is not surprising that such an age should have concentrated on painless child-birth for "junior Mom," pills that keep you "looking at your best even on those days," television baby-tenders, artificial feeding, and "looking like a girl though a grandmother." When human beings have been fascinated with the contemplation of the beating of their own hearts, the more intricate biological pattern of the female has become a model for the artist, the mystic, and the saint. When mankind turns instead to what can be done, altered, built, invented, in the outer world, all natural properties of men, animals, or metals become handicaps to be altered rather than clues to be followed. Much of the ill-tempered railing against women that has characterized the popular writing of the last two years is a half-hearted attempt to find a way back to a more balanced relationship between our biological selves and the world we have built. So women are scolded both for being mothers and for not being mothers, for wanting to eat their cake and have it too, and for not wanting to eat their cake and have it too, as one might say, "What has become of the irreversibles that have given part of the meaning to human life?"

IX

HUMAN FATHERHOOD IS A

SOCIAL INVENTION

MEN AND WOMEN OF ALL CIVILIZATIONS HAVE BEEN IN SOME way preoccupied with the problem of what constitutes the specific values of humanity—in what ways, how irrevocably, how reliably, human beings are separated from the rest of the animal world. This preoccupation may take the form of an insistent emphasis upon man's kinship with the animals that he hunts and upon which he depends for food—as among those primitive peoples who as they circle their camp-fires wear the masks of the hunted beasts. It may contain such a strong repudiation of the animal tie as is found in the Balinese ceremony when an incestuous pair are forced to crawl on hands and knees wearing the wooden yokes of domestic swine upon their necks, and after eating from a pig-trough with their mouths, take leave of the gods of life and go to live in the land of punishment, serving only the gods of death. In the wide-spread custom that is technically called totemism, divisions of societies, clans, or other organized groups in society signalize their differences one from another by special claims of kinship to particular animals, which they may treat as mascots, be allowed a monopoly in eating, or taboo forever. Among almost all peoples, the animal world is drawn on liberally for terms of abuse and often also for terms of love; the parent abuses the child for behaving like a pig or a dog, carelessly calls it a kitten or a dove, reproaches it for behaving like a wild beast or admires the ferocity or swiftness that it shares with some creature of the wood. Long before Darwin phrased the kinship between man and beast in evolutionary terms that were as repugnant to many of his generation as the Balinese find it to see a child crawl like an animal, men dealt with their recognition of man's similiarities to and differences from other animals.

The question has been elaborated in the great religions, translated into poetry, as when St. Francis preached to the birds, into a whole way of life, as when the Jain refuses to drink from water that may perhaps contain some gnat; dramatized in the trials of animals in the Middle Ages; given horrid twists and turns in the special sensitivities of those who although brutal towards men have sometimes been unduly careful of horses. Children dream and wake shrieking from their dreams of strange and terrifying animals that may destroy them—counterpart of the parental recognition of impulses in the child that are called animal. Beneath the poetry and the symbolism, the evocative beauty of the great sacrificial symbols in which the Lamb of God suffers for men or man's kinship with all living things is reaffirmed, behind the profanity and abuse that can degrade men no further than by accusing them of being animals or of following the sexual practices of animals, there lies the recurrent question "In what does man's uniqueness consist, and what must he do to keep it?" Long before there were philosophers to think systematically about the question, men with matted hair and bodies daubed with mud realized that this humanity of theirs was somehow something that could be lost, something fragile, to be guarded with offering and sacrifice and taboo, to be cherished by each succeeding generation. "What must we do to be human?" is a question as old as humanity itself.

In this continuing question lies man's recognition that his physical humanity, his erect stature, his almost hairless body, his flexibly opposable thumb, and the potential capacities of his brain still do not constitute the full secret of his humanness. Not even in the long period of gestation, during which a single human child is brought slowly to a birth that finds him still sufficiently unformed so that he may receive the full imprint of a complex civilization, lies any guarantee of continued humanness. We speak in our current folk-language of the beast in man, of the thin veneer of civilization, and either statement simply means that we do not trust mankind to be continuously human.

For our humanity rests upon a series of learned behaviours, woven together into patterns that are infinitely fragile and never directly inherited. The ant we discover imbedded in a block of Baltic amber, which the geologist dates 20,000,000 years ago, may be trusted to reproduce its typical ant behaviour wherever it can survive. It is trustworthy for two reasons: first, because its complex behaviour, by which its society will be divided into minute castes that carry out predetermined tasks, is built into the very structure of its body, and second, because even if it should learn something new, it cannot teach it to the other ants. The repetitious pattern in which countless generations of a single species repeat a pattern more complicated than the dreams of a technocratic Utopian is protected by these two circumstances: behaviour imbedded in physical structure and an inability to communicate new learnings. But man does not even carry the simplest forms of his behaviour in such a way that a human child without other human beings to teach it can be relied upon to produce spontaneously a single cultural item. Long before his small fist is strong enough really to deliver a blow, the angry gestures of the human child bear the stamp not of his long mammalian past, but of the club-using or spear-throwing habits of his parents. The woman left alone to bear her child calls not upon some reliable instinctive pattern that will guide her through the complexities of cutting the umbilical cord and cleansing the new infant from the traces of birth, but fumbles helplessly among bits of folk-lore and old wives' tales that she has overheard. She may act from the memory of what she has seen animals do, but in her own living nature she finds no reliable cues.

We may cherish our noses or our lips, our relatively hair-less bodies, our graceful arms and cunning hands, but when we shrink from some human deformity that makes a human being look more like an animal, when we shudder away from members of other races and identify them by the par-ticular ways in which they may be felt to be more animal than we—for example, the thin lips and hairiness of the Caucasian, the bridgeless noses of some Mongolians, the pigmentation of the Negroid type—under the manifest fear of miscegenation lies the knowledge that all forms of cul-tural behaviour can be lost, that they are dearly purchased and dearly kept. Whenever men's fear is expressed in social terms—in great group rituals in which the sun is sought to shine again, in the Balinese New Year when all men are quiet for a day that life may flow on, among the Iroquois when once a year men lived out their dreams, confessed their sins, and plunged naked into icy rivers at the behest of a dream—the expression of the fear becomes also a way of assuaging it. These rituals are ways of restating that only together *can* men be human, that their humanity depends not on individual instinct, but on the traditional wisdom of their society. When men lose this sense that they can depend upon this wisdom, either because they are thrown among those whose behaviour is to them no guarantee of the continuity of civilization or because they can no longer use the symbols of their own society, they go mad, retreating slowly, often fighting a heart-breaking rear action as they relinquish bit by bit their cultural inheritance, learned with such difficulty, never learned so that the next generation is safe.

This is a fear that may indeed be counted to men for wisdom and not chalked up under some attribution of peculiar irrationality. It is so deep that it may include the most minute and the most irrelevant actions. The smallest details of manners—which food is eaten, when it is eaten, with whom and on what-shaped plates—may become the conditions on which man feels his humanity is held. In caste societies, such as India or the Southeastern United States, where one's culturally defined humanity is inextricably bound up with membership in a caste group, to associate with the other caste in forbidden ways means the loss of one's humanity itself. The sense of membership in one's own sex is deeply imbued with such attitudes. So the Cossack woman in Sholokhov's novel, prying into the ways of the strange Turkish woman brought among the Cossacks, reports: "I saw them myself. She wears trousers. . . . When I saw them my blood ran cold." In cultures where table-manners are the insignia of humanity, people may be unable to eat their food at the table with some one who eats differently—especially if the table-manners are also class- or caste-marked so that the presence of one who eats differently automatically classifies one with that other. The strong men of western Europe feel unmanned when they meet people from eastern Europe, where men squat to urinate, and in modern Australia women feel strangely embarrassed when American women tell their husbands to fetch the cocktails. Each little courtesy to or restraint or deference from others is cherished for what it is, something laboriously learned and easy to lose.

Against such a background we can look at the arrangements that surround the relationships between the sexes which have been essential to the preservation of human society. Beneath the thousand fleeting and irrelevant symbols —the lifted hat of the gentleman, the downcast eyes of the lady, the geranium on the window-sill of the German burgher, or the scrubbed white steps of the mill workers of the English Midlands—is there a core of common practice to which all societies everywhere have had to cling in order to keep the dearly bought, learned aspects of their humanity?

When we survey all known human societies, we find everywhere some form of the family, some set of permanent arrangements by which males assist females in caring for children while they are young. The distinctively human aspect of the enterprise lies not in the protection the male affords the females and the young—this we share with the primates. Nor does it lie in the lordly possessiveness of the male over females for whose favours he contends with other males—this too we share with the primates. Its distinctiveness lies instead in the nurturing behaviour of the male, who among human beings everywhere helps provide food for women and children. The sentimental figures of speech so common in the modern Western world in which the bees and the ants and the flowers are invoked to illustrate the more suspect aspects of human beings have obscured our recognition of how much of an invention this behaviour of human males is. True, father-birds do feed their young, but men are a long way from birds on the evolutionary tree. Male fighting-fish do make bubble-nests and only capture the female long enough to squeeze her eggs out of her, and then, after driving her away, devote themselves, rather unsuccessfully, to retrieving the eggs that fall out of the bubble-nest, and—when they don't eat up the eggs or the young—some young survive. But these analogies from the world of birds and fish are far from man. Among our structurally closest analogues—the primates—the male does not feed the female.[1] Heavy with young, making her way laboriously along, she fends for herself. He may fight to protect her or to possess her, but he does not nurture her.

Somewhere at the dawn of human history, some social invention was made under which males started nurturing females and their young. We have no reason to believe that the nurturing males had any knowledge of physical paternity, although it is quite possible that being fed was a reward meted out to the female who was not too fickle with her sexual favours. In every known human society, everywhere in the world, the young male learns that when he grows up, one of the things which he must do in order to be a full member of society is to provide food for some female and her young. Even in very simple societies, a few men may shy away from the responsibility, become tramps or ne'er-do-wells or misanthropists who live in the woods by themselves. In complex societies, a large number of men may escape the burden of feeding females and young by entering monasteries—and feeding each other—or by entering some profession that their society will classify as giving them a right to be fed, like the Army and the Navy, or the Buddhist orders of Burma. But in spite of such exceptions, every known human society rests firmly on the learned nurturing behaviour of men.

This nurturing behaviour, this fending for females and children instead of leaving them to fend for themselves, as the primates do, may take many different forms. In almost all societies women also keep some food-gathering or food-cultivating tasks, but among people who live almost entirely on meat and fish the woman's activities may shrink to skinning and cooking and preserving the catch. Where hunting supplies only a small part of the diet and men's food-getting

rôle is principally hunting, women may take over nine-tenths
of the task of gathering staple food. In some societies, where
men go away to work in large cities for money, all of the food
itself may be raised by the women who are left behind on the
farm, while the man buys tools and machine-made gadgets
with the money he earns. The division of labour may be
made in a thousand ways—so that the men of a given society
are very idle, or the women left disproportionately free of
effort, as in the childless American urban home. But the core
remains. Man, the heir of tradition, provides for women and
children. We have no indication that man the animal, man
unpatterned by social learning, would do anything of the
sort.

Which women and which children are provided for is entirely a matter of social arrangements, although the central
pattern seems to be that of a man's providing for the woman
who is his sexual partner and whatever children she may
happen to have. Whether the children are believed to be
his, or merely the children of a man of the same clan, or
simply the legitimate children of his wife by some earlier
marriage, may be quite irrelevant. They may also have been
added to his household by adoption, by election, by orphan-
ing. They may be the child-wives of his sons. The home
shared by a man or men and female partners, into which
men bring the food and women prepare it, is the basic common picture the world over. But this picture can be modified, and the modifications provide proof that the pattern
itself is not something deeply biological.[2] Among the
Trobriand Islanders, each man fills the yam-house of his
sister, not that of his wife. On the Island of Mentawie, each
man works in his father's household until his own surreptitiously conceived children are old enough to work for him.
Meanwhile, the children are adopted by their mother's
father, and their mother's brothers feed them. The net social
result is the same; each male spends a large part of his time

nurturing females and their children, in this case his sisters' instead of his own. Under extreme forms of matriliny, a man may work for his wife's maternal household, and in case of divorce have to return to his own maternal house, there to subsist on foods grown by his sisters' resident husbands, as in the pueblos of Zuni. But even here, where it might be argued that the social responsibility of males for females had almost broken down, the males do continue to labour to feed women and children. A more extreme form of a society in which men continue to work to feed children, but the relationship to the children's mother has grown faint indeed, can be found in modern industrialized societies where large numbers of children live in broken homes, supported by taxes levied on the males and working females of higher income brackets, so that the hard-working well-employed members of society become the providing fathers of thousands of children who are public charges. Here again we see how tenuous the urge of the male to provide for his own children is, for it can so easily be destroyed by different social arrangements.

The mother's nurturing tie to her child is apparently so deeply rooted in the actual biological conditions of conception and gestation, birth and suckling, that only fairly complicated social arrangements can break it down entirely. Where human beings have learned to value rank more than anything else in life and where attaining rank is valued more than anything else, women may strangle their children with their own hands.[3] Where society has so overdone the rituals of legitimacy that men are kept good providers only at the cost of social ostracism of the unmarried mother, the mother of an illegitimate child may abandon it or even kill it. Where bearing children is penalized by social disapproval and a husbandly sense of being wronged, as among the Mundugumor, women may make every effort not to bear children. If a woman's sense of appropriateness of her sex rôle is badly distorted, her delivery masked in anaesthesia that prevents her realizing that she has borne a child, her suckling of the child replaced by a formula pediatrically prescribed—then also we may find very serious disturbances in maternal attitudes, disturbances that may spread over an entire class or region, and which may become of social as well as personal importance. But the evidence suggests that we should phrase the matter differently for men and women —that men have to learn to want to provide for others, and this behaviour, being learned, is fragile and can disappear rather easily under social conditions that no longer teach it effectively. Women may be said to be mothers unless they are taught to deny their child-bearing qualities. Society must distort their sense of themselves, pervert their inherent growth-patterns, perpetrate a series of learning-outrages upon them, before they will cease to want to provide, at least for a few years, for the child they have already nourished for nine months within the safe circle of their own bodies.

So at the base of those traditional forms through which we have preserved our learned humanity is the family, some form of the family within which men permanently nurture and care for women and children. Within the family, each new generation of young males learn the appropriate nurturing behaviour and superimpose upon their biologically given maleness this learned parental rôle. When the family breaks down—as it does under slavery, under certain forms of indentured labour and serfdom, in periods of extreme social unrest during wars, revolutions, famines, and epidemics, or in periods of abrupt transition from one type of economy to another—this delicate line of transmission is broken. Men may flounder badly in these periods, during which the primary unit may again become mother and child, the biologically given, and the special conditions under which man has held his social traditions in trust are violated and distorted. So far, in all known history human societies have always re-established the forms they temporarily lost. The Negro slave in the United States was bred like a stud bull, and his children were sold away from him, and the marks of lost paternal responsibility are still to be found among working-class Negro Americans, where the primary nurturing unit is the mother and the mother's mother, a unit to which men may sometimes attach themselves even without making any economic contribution. But as soon as education and economic security are reached this disorganized way of life is abandoned, and the American Negro father in the middle class is perhaps almost overly responsible. Often the settlement on the edge of a new country is first made by men, then for a few years the only women may be prostitutes, but later women are imported and the family is re-established. So far no break in the family pattern has been prolonged enough to eradicate men's memories of how valuable it was.

This continuance of the family to date, its re-establishment after catastrophic or ideological destruction, is not however any guarantee that this will always be the case, that our generation can relax and take it for granted that this will always be so. Human beings have learned, laboriously, to be human. They have kept their social inventions through a thousand small vicissitudes; partly because, isolated in small groups, separated by rivers and mountains, oceans, strange languages, and hostile border watches, some group could always cherish the dearly bought wisdom that other small groups flouted, just as some escaped epidemics that wiped others out quickly or nutritional errors from which others slowly weakened and died. It is not without significance that the most successful large-scale abrogations of the family have occurred not among simple savages, living close to the subsistence edge, but among great nations and strong empires, the resources of which were ample, the populations huge, and the power almost unlimited. In ancient Peru, the state moved people about at will, took many girls away from their villages, the unfavoured to become weavers in great weaving nunneries, the more favoured to be the concubines of the nobility. In Russia before 1861 the serfs were married off by order of the landowners, treated like cattle rather than like human beings. In Nazi Germany, illegitimacy was rewarded with specially sunny nursing-homes for mother and child, the state taking over completely the male nurturing tie. We have no reason to believe that such procedures, if persisted in long enough by nations that could insulate their members from knowledge of any other previous or contemporary way of life, might not prevail. Soviet Russia after a brief experiment in loosening marriage-ties and reducing parental responsibilities has returned to an insistence on the family, but this has occurred in a world-context and in competition with the rest of the world. The abortive attempts in history to build societies in which *Homo sapiens* would function not as the human being we have known, but as a creature who could be more profitably compared to an ant or a bee, though with learned instead of inherited rigidities, stand as new types of warnings—sharper than the analogies that primitive men sensed between their behaviour and that of the furry creatures of the wood—that we hold our present form of humanity on trust, that it is possible to lose it.

If we recognize, then, that the family, a patterned arrangement of the two sexes in which men play a rôle in the nurturing of women and children, has been a primary condition of this humanity, we can explore what are the universal problems that human beings who live in families must solve, beyond the primary one of providing males with habits and patterns of nurture. First, some order of permanency must be established, some assurance that the same individuals will work together and plan together at least through a harvest, usually with the expectation that the association will last a lifetime. No matter how free divorce, how frequently marriages break up, in most societies there is the assumption of permanent mating, the idea that the marriage should last as long as both live. Wives may be returned because they are infertile, or another wife may be demanded from the wife's clan; brothers may give their wives to younger brothers with whom they get on better; women may leave husbands or husbands leave wives for the slightest cause—and yet this assumption remains. No known society has ever invented a form of marriage strong enough to stick that did not contain the "till-death-us-do-part" assumption. On the other hand, very few primitive societies have carried this assumption to the point of refusing to recognize a variety of marital failures. The legal insistence on marriage for life under all circumstances fits best into just those societies which have become so organized that the group can impersonally coerce the individual whatever the actual relationships between the sexes may happen to be. To date, one of the conditions of establishing and maintaining the family as a form has been the offer of a normal lifelong pattern—in a few cases as a relationship to a sister rather than a wife, but the lifelong pattern remains.

To ensure a stability and continuity of relationship that would constitute a family, each society must solve the question of competition among males for females so that they will not kill each other off, or so monopolize the females that a large number of males have no wives, or drive away too many of the young males, or maltreat the females and the young too grossly during competitive mating.[4] When we imagine two men armed with clubs facing each other over the shrinking form of an unarmed female, we think of this problem of competition as belonging to our primordial past and not as characteristic of modern society. But patterns that regulate competition in the choice of sex partners are learned patterns, and so can break down at any time, and must be continually readjusted if they are not to break down because they are no longer adaptive. It is said that one of the factors which led to the growth of the Nazi Party was the Weimar Republic's self-defeating practice of giving what jobs there were to older men, leaving the young men unable to compete for women's favours. In World War II, the differential pay of the American GI and the British Tommy was primarily important in Britain because it gave the first group an advantage over the second in courtship and solicitation. Whenever there is violent change in the pattern of life, in the division of labour, in the proportion between the sexes —as in Pacific Island army garrisons during the last war— the recurrent competitive problem returns. It may not lead to individual battles with stones or knives between two men fighting for a single mate; it may lead instead to disturbances in group morale, to aggravation of labour troubles, to the formation of revolutionary parties. It may upset the relationships between allies or the chances for success of a democratic revolution.

In modern societies where polygamy is no longer sanctioned and women are no longer cloistered, there is now a new problem to meet, the competition of females for males. Here we have an example of a problem that is almost entirely socially created, a product of civilization itself imposed upon an older biological one. At the simplest human level, the male with his persistent attraction to females, his greater physical strength, unencumbered by offspring, was in the natural battling position. The females, though not necessarily either passive or uninterested in the battle, were nevertheless to a great degree pawns in the game. But as civilization has replaced fist and teeth, first with stone axe and knife and gun, then by subtler weapons of prestige and power, the problem of competition of two members of one sex for one member of the other has become progressively removed from its biological base. So in those societies in which there are more women than men—our normal Western sex ratio—and in which monogamy is the rule, we find the struggle of men over women shifting to include a struggle of women over men also. Perhaps there is no more vivid demonstration of what can be socially accomplished than this particular shift, which can put the sex most biologically disadvantaged for battle into an active competitive rôle.

There is great variety in human solutions of the problem of which men are to have which women, under what circumstances and for how long, and the less usual but modern problem of which women are to have which men. Some societies permit periods of licence in which those who feel that they are able to cope with more members of the other sex than are normally permitted to them have a chance to act out their day-dreams without disrupting the social order. Some societies practise wife-lending, exchange of wives between friends, so that co-operation between males is reinforced by this sexual tie. Some societies permit all the men who belong to the same clan to have access to each other's wives, and one may find the quaint admonition that during pregnancy a woman may have sex relations only with her own husband. Among the Usiai people of the Great Admiralty, boys and girls have been permitted a year of supervised gaiety together, at the end of which each might choose a mate for a single night, after which the young girls were married off to older men and the young men ultimately married widows with property and experience. In some societies the stronger males, strong as fighters or hunters or agriculturalists or as the repositories of traditional lore, have been allowed to have more wives than other men. And in all societies it is necessary to deal not only with real situations, such as the relative shortage of men or of women, but with the day-dreams that are bred of the particular social arrangements. A Mundugumor male will treat his single wife as if she were one of several wives, because the ideal male in Mundugumor is a man with several wives, although he himself, puny and ill-equipped, may have only one lame wife with ringworm, while his elder brother has eight or nine. But an Arapesh man with two wives, one of them inherited from a dead brother or a runaway from the more aggressive plains people, will continue to treat each wife as if she were his only wife, the wife whom he had fed and cherished through a long betrothal. The Manus people, themselves puritanical monogamists but surrounded by cheerful polygamists, believe that there is a terrible shortage of women in the world, and they not only betroth their sons as early as possible but report a most unseemly scramble in the spirit world for the soul of each newly dead female. The Kiwai Papuans practise complicated magical rites to ensure their boys success in marriage, and the Eskimo practise both female infanticide—on the theory that there are too many girls —and polygamy, which involves taking other men's wives away from them, because there are not enough women to go around.

All of these competitive situations, however, affect adults, whether the focus be upon the struggle between stronger older men and weaker younger men or between more attractive younger women and more entrenched older ones, or upon a struggle between contemporaries. But there is another problem that every human society must solve—the protection of the sexually immature, which is at its core the problem of incest. We have seen the various ways in which the developing sexuality of the child is handled, how the Samoan child enters his years of sex inactivity through invoking the brother-and-sister taboo, how a child's identification with a parent of its own sex carries with it specific types of strain and prohibition on the relationship to the parent of opposite sex. The protection of the children from the par-

ents, once established as desirable, involves the need of protecting the parents from the children also. The protection of
a ten-year-old girl from her father's advances is a necessary
condition of social order, but the protection of the father
from temptation is a necessary condition of his continued
social adjustment. The protections that are built up in the
child against desire for the parent become the essential counterpart to the attitudes in the parent that protect the child.
Usually the primary incest-taboos are extended in various
ways, so that the immature child is protected from all adults,
although the protection may be minimal, as among the
Kaingang, where all children receive a greal deal of sexual
stimulation from adults, or maximal, as in the traditional
French upbringing of the *jeune fille*. These prohibitions become elaborated into informal taboos against "cradle-rob-
bing" and legal definition of an "age of consent," which
mothers a generation ago explained to their daughters as the
age at which "a girl can consent to her own ruin."

The basic incest rules cover the three primary relationships within the family: father-daughter, mother-son, and
brother-sister. The social necessity for rules that prevent
competition within the family is vividly illustrated by conditions in Mundugumor. The taboo on marriage between
different generations broke down, overstrained by a too-
complicated marriage system, and this left men free to exchange their daughters for extra additional young wives for
themselves. But this put father and son into competition for
the daughter-sister, both of whom wanted her to exchange
for a wife. Mundugumor society became a jungle, with
every man's hand against every man's, surviving merely
through the memory of earlier social forms that some men
still attempted to observe, and so unable to adjust because
of those very memories. As the primary task of any society
is to keep men working together in some sort of co-operation, any situation is fatal that sets every man against every

other. If the male is to remain a nurturing parent within the family, he must nurture, not compete with, his dependent sons, nephews, and so on. If he is to co-operate with other men in the society, he must form patterns of relationship to men in which direct sexual competition is barred.

Societies that have come to emphasize helpfulness between males rather than competitiveness can rephrase the incest-taboos so that they stress not the need to keep related men from fighting, but the need to establish new ties by marriages. "If you married your sister," say the Arapesh, "you would have no brother-in-law. With whom would you work? With whom would you hunt? Who would help you?" And anger is focussed on the antisocial man who will not marry off his sister or his daughter, for it is a man's duty to create ties through the young females of his household. But getting oneself a brother-in-law to hunt with, as among the Arapesh, or a daughter-in-law to dominate, as among the Japanese, or even permitting royal incest between brother and sister, as among the ancient Hawaiians and Egyptians, are all elaborations of incest rules. So too are the extensions that cover half the tribe, or in an extreme case, as among Australian aborigines, so extending the rules that only by the most far-fetched fictions can certain young people marry at all. At the core incest rules are a way in which a family unit can be preserved and the relationship within it be personalized and particularized. The extension of incest rules to a variety of protections for all the young—the children of a whole society—against any exploitative or inhuman treatment is but one instance of the way in which the conserving, protective inventions of our human history serve as a model for wider social behaviour.

X

POTENCY AND RECEPTIVITY

BUT ALTHOUGH THE HUMAN FAMILY DEPENDS UPON SOCIAL IN-
ventions that will make each generation of males want to
nurture women and children, these inventions are based
upon the specific physical sex relationships between men
and women, which are themselves biologically determined.
Without a mating-season, without explicit receptivity in
the female that periodically waxed and waned, human
beings could make continuing sex relations the basis of permanent association.

Among the primates full sex activity is still subject to the
periodic readiness of the female. The primate male's interest
in the female is of little avail except at the periods in which
she is receptive. There is some evidence to suggest that this
cycle of readiness is still operative in the human female,
but it no longer has the same effects on mating and child-
bearing.[1] When anthropologists began studying primitive
societies carefully, we discovered societies in which there
was great premarital sexual freedom but practically no il-

legitimacy. Yet after marriage, the girls who had lived a life of complete freedom conceived and bore children, and furthermore conceived and bore many children. Samoa and the Trobriands are two of the best-studied examples of such gay premarital freedom, and both are fertile peoples. As a first explanation it was suggested that there might be, for some stocks, or in some climates, or for some sections of a population, a lag between menarche and ovulation, so that girls might appear mature one or two years before they were actually able to conceive.[2] But while this may be a partial explanation, it does not seem to be a complete one. Perhaps more important is the shift in the control over the timing of intercourse from the female to the male that comes with marriage, and which is symbolic also of what seems to have happened in human history. In these primitive societies, before marriage, it is the girl who decides whether she will or will not meet her lover under the palm-trees, or receive him with necessary precautions in her house, or in her bed in the young people's house. He may woo and plead, he may send gifts and pretty speeches by an intermediary, but the final choice remains in the hands of the girl. If she does not choose, she does not come, she does not lift the corner of her mat, she does not wait under the palm-trees. A mood, a whim, a slight disinclination, and the boy is disappointed. But in marriage all this is changed. A man and his wife share bed and board. The bed may be a mat on the floor, a hammock in the jungle, a mosquito-basket on the Sepik River, one-tenth of the family sleeping-bag—but the man has, subject to various rules of etiquette and taboo, access to his wife by right. It is his unperiodic, insistent desire that sets the stage, not her more fitful moods, which are so differently spaced in different females that they cannot be referred even to any sex-wide regularities.

Many writers on the sexes and the human family lay great emphasis upon the fact that the human male is capable

of rape. This is an abrupt and startling way of putting something that is actually much subtler. In the human species
the male is capable of copulating with a relatively unaroused
and uninterested female. We have no evidence that suggests that rape within the meaning of the act—that is, rape
of a totally unwilling female—has ever become recognized
social practice. It may develop as a form of deviance under
a variety of special social conditions, when men are segregated from women under conditions that breed extreme hostility, in caste situations that do not have adequate, deep
social sanctions to make them tolerated, or when rapist or
victim is definitely insane. But for a woman to be actually
raped—that is, copulated with against her entire conscious
and unconscious choice—by a sane unarmed man, special
circumstances are necessary, such as unusual differences in
size, differences in culture so that the girl is paralyzed or the
man misled by the unfamiliarity of the situation, or some
other unexpected or unusual element in the setting. By and
large, within the same homogeneous social setting an ordinarily strong man cannot rape an ordinarily strong healthy
woman. There are many primitive societies in which rape
is a day-dream of one sex or the other, or of both, but there
are adequate social measures to prevent its happening in
reality. Even in our own society, in the days when for a lady
to be alone on the street late at night would be likely to
invite attack—that is, to suggest willingness rather than unwillingness—there was a well-developed lore of hat-pins. The
Dobuan male dreamed of rape, and the Dobuan female had
well-developed techniques to prevent his success. Iatmul
males constantly talk of rape, day-dream of situations in
which a woman's exposed helplessness will give a setting
for rape, but in actuality they have to call in their entire
age-grade to discipline—by rape—women whose husbands
have utterly failed to bring them to order. Rape does occur
in modern societies, where there are many levels and sec-

tions with different social mores, in which some members of both sexes are utterly unable to interpret the behaviour of members of the other sex who come from a different setting, or where our techniques for diagnosing or institutionalizing the criminally insane are inadequate. But it is a very different act from any behaviour that can be postulated for the small groups of creatures who at the dawn of our history were just inventing social patterns.

Yet there is a very great shift from the simple, periodically determined mating of the primates, in which males must compete with each other and also obtain favour in the eyes of a female at the precise moment when she is physiologically receptive, and the human family, within which the male is able to press his desires in the face of the female's disinterest, boredom, fatigue, aversion, or actual repugnance and rejection. When this shift is made from female readiness to male readiness, a responsibility for readiness is laid upon the male that he did not face at earlier animal levels. In the primate horde, females periodically show receptivity, and the males who respond mount them if they are accepted. To the male who does not become aroused nothing happens at all. He doesn't get into fights with the other males that day, he sits peacefully grooming himself. Or he may even get a better share of the food because his more sexually active contemporaries are busy elsewhere. He doesn't need a wife. Aside from his sexual activities, he is extraordinarily self-sufficient; he finds and consumes his own food, he can pick out his own scurf. He does not, like the Eskimo, need a wife to chew his boots, or like the Papuan one to feed his pigs, or like men in other societies one to give him a place in the social swim, or mend his socks, or dress the skins of the game that he brings home. Nor does he, of course, need a wife to care for his children. He doesn't have children—in that sense. The females have the children and the females look after them. So while the over-active male struggles with his contemporaries for access to receptive females, the temporarily or permanently less active male can sit. Nobody reproaches him, the females do not tease him. He will very likely live longer than his more active group-mates. He is not worried by impotence.

But from the moment that actual long matings between human beings develop in which male and female live together, and her receptivity is such that she is accessible to his desire at any time, a host of new problems face human beings. The male's achievement as a lover becomes tangled with his need for a wife, with his tie to the children whom he has learned to nurture, with his standing in the community. While the primate needs a female for immediate physical reasons and for no other, a human male at the simplest social level of which we have even a hint needs a wife. And a wife is always, in all societies and under all known circumstances, regarded as something more than the object or the means of satisfaction of physical desire. So a variety of derived learned behaviours enters in to complicate and pattern a human male's attitudes towards women. Stripped of every social convention, or surrounded by a set of social conventions that defines her only as an immediately available sexual object without any other social attributes, the actively receptive human female can still arouse in most human males the same sort of response that we find among the primates. The male who is active sexually will respond actively, the sluggish male more sluggishly, or perhaps not at all. Even among white rats there are active males and inactive males. But the instant that human relationships are patterned with implications of courtship, marriage, prestige, affinal exchanges, a good street address, and the rest, the male's intrinsic spontaneous sex choice is compromised by his other desires. He wants to keep his wife—this may mean sleeping with her more or sleeping with her less. "Do you wives think," demands the exacerbated Iatmul husband, "that I am made of ironwood that I am able to copulate with you as much as you want?" "Copulation is revolting," say Manus women. "The only bearable husband is one whose advances one can hardly feel." Each culture stylizes the preferences of men and women in wives, husbands, and lovers, and permits more or fewer individual differences to develop. Men and women reared in the same culture will share the same sexual ideals. A male knows what sort of man is regarded as a good lover, he knows under what circumstances his wife is likely to throw a pot at him, or slap the baby, beat the dog, kick the house ladder down so that he can't climb into her hut, or suggest that he sleep on the sofa in his dressing-room. Instead of a simple uncomplicated urgency kept in check by the periodicity of the female, as among the primates, the human male finds his urgency endlessly implicated with other considerations. But male sexual functioning seems to work most easily when it is most automatic, when the response is to a simple set of signals that have been defined as sexually exciting, whether those signals be bodily exposure, a special perfume, a woman's reputation for compliancy, or simply a woman alone—on a bush path or in an empty apartment. Once male sex functioning is complicated by sets of ideas about sentimental love, or by prestige, moral qualms, theories of the relationship between sex activity and athletic prowess or religious vocation, or between virility and creativity, that sex functioning may become that much less automatic and reliable. It is not an accident that in the élite groups—the aristocracy, the intellectuals, the artists—of all cultures there have developed a variety of subsidiary and supplementary practices designed to stimulate male desire, whether these be perversions, a new concubine every night, homosexuality, or dramatizations of obscure daydreams. They occur with startling regularity, while in those portions of a population where there is less choice, less taste, and fewer confusing ideas, copulation is a simpler matter.

Viewed against his mammalian background, man may be seen to have, vis-à-vis the female, far greater powers of initiative than do the primates. But, perhaps as one of the choice dilemmas that stud the history of living things, the very circumstance that consolidates his initiative, the institution of human marriage, introduces many new complications. Put very succinctly, the more he thinks, the less may he copulate, unless copulation and thought are skilfully integrated at each level.[3] In those cultures in which all goods are regarded as limited, the investment of "energy" in sex activity is very likely to be conceived as loss, and as antithetical to success in some other field. On the other hand, where sheer active maleness, as in a hunter, a fighter, a lover, is emphasized, potency may be high. In general, however, it may be said that the more interpersonal sex relations become, the more the actual personality of each partner, their mood, state of fatigue, feeling about the world and the other person, are taken into account, the more possibility there is that some reduction in actual sex activity may occur. Some of the American Plains Indians developed the tie between husband and wife more explicitly and more personally than any other primitive groups of which we have records. Courtship sometimes lasted for years, and the bride was wooed for weeks after marriage before the marriage was finally consummated. Old warriors spoke with nostalgia of those early nights of marriage when they lay awake all night just quietly talking to their young wives. And it is among American Indians that the fantastic institution of the chastity-blanket developed, the pierced blanket that had to be obtained from an elder of the tribe whenever any married couple wished to have intercourse. Here, too, couples could take enormous pride in the gaps between their children.

Much of the thoughtfulness of the other's mood that is implicit in marriages with a strong interpersonal emphasis can of course be crystallized in cultural forms that take the onus of thought, and so of restrictive self-control, or expected calendrical activity, off the individuals concerned. All of these Pacific cultures, except Bali, taboo intercourse during pregnancy. The male does not have to consider his wife's moods; intercourse is simply taboo with a variety of heavy sanctions. When the men of a Iatmul village are preparing for a head-hunting raid, they sleep together in the men's house away from temptation. Menstruating women in Arapesh are isolated in huts away from the village, and if they walk about take little-known trails. Among many aristocracies, husband and wife have separate sleeping-quarters, so that the dignity of the lady need not be considered from minute to minute and is protected from importunity inappropriate to her rank. The presence of competing activities, child-bearing and suckling, hunting, fishing, fighting, praying, making artistic products the outcome of which is uncertain, have often been stylized as times of abstinence, and thus the burden of choosing between sex activity and other activities has been taken off the individual.

So it is fairly easy for a culture to regulate the active behaviour of human males, to stylize it, isolate it, confine it to certain times and certain places; all of this tends to reduce the amount of actual activity. But it is far less easy to deal with the loss of spontaneity when sex activity is enjoined in spite of the individual desire of the moment. Some positive patterning must of course occur. The males in each society must learn to modulate their potency, shorten or lengthen the time or frequency of intercourse, to the expected behaviour for which both males and females are reared and upon which successful sex relationships in that particular society depend. But if the culture is patterned so that men are *required* to make love to a particular woman at a particular time and place, then rebellion may set in. The folk-custom of a marriage-night where the consummation of the marriage is subjected to public scrutiny and approval will break down when demands on the bridegroom's conforming spontaneity are *too* great. In fact it is on the male's capacity to resist or to refuse patterns that regiment his spontaneity too heavily that the welfare of the individual and the welfare of the race meet. The male can maintain, in all honesty, that a culture which does not protect his spontaneous sexuality will in the end perish, because there will be no children conceived to carry it on. He can demand, and demand most vehemently and with full social responsibility, that social forms which hamper and over-define his impulses must be altered. The need for cultural forms in which spontaneous sexual impulse can be happily expressed serves as a testing-point in every human society. This is perhaps one reason why men are so often regarded as the progressive element in human history.

The human female, as distinguished from the primate female, has gained in her control over her sexuality, and has learned to substitute many other forms of behaviour for simple impulse. The female primate is the creature of her oestrus cycle; when the periodic upsurge of sexual receptivity occurs, she is receptive; otherwise she is not. She may occasionally, like a young male, offer herself in return for food or protection, but this appears to be the grossest prostitution. But the human female who has learned through a long childhood education to value a great variety of rewards, and fear a great variety of punishments, finds that her receptivity—although perhaps retaining a slight degree of periodicity—is actually subject to a great deal of modulation. Where receptivity requires so much less of her—merely a softening and relaxing of her whole body, and none of the specific readiness and sustained desire that is required of the male—she can learn to fit a simple compliancy together with a thousand other considerations of winning and keeping a lover or a husband, balancing the mood of the moment against the mood of to-morrow, and fitting her receptivity into the whole pattern of a relationship. There seems little doubt that the male who has learned various mechanical ways to stimulate his sexual specificity in order to copulate with a woman whom he does not this moment desire is doing far more violence to his nature than the female who needs only to receive a male to whom she gives many other assents, but possibly not active desire.

The institution of marriage in all societies is a pattern within which the strains put by civilization on males and females alike must be resolved, a pattern within which men must learn, in return for a variety of elaborate rewards, new forms in which sexual spontaneity is still possible, and women must learn to discipline their receptivity to a thousand other considerations. In monogamous societies, the strain on the man is seen as the monotony of sleeping always with one woman, but in polygamous societies, the man complains of the demands of too many wives. In monogamous societies, the wife complains because her husband makes too great demands, but in a polygamous society one finds each wife trying to tempt her husband back to her hut. So in rapidly changing societies the articulate and the concerned will be likely to start writing novels and evolving philosophies about the way this balance is working at the moment, and in so doing rediscover that the basic strain introduced by civilization, compound of man's possible continuous access to a mate and women's capacity for controlled receptivity, remains.

In certain societies and at certain periods of history, strong emphasis is placed upon the strain put upon men. In a culture where individuals are as crystallinely impersonal as in Bali, so that even the members of the audience of a play that all enjoy have no rapport either with each other or with the dancers, the question of impotence becomes very important. The wedding-joke is the pantomime of the kris that bends even before the lightly woven leaf mat, and men worry lest there will be such slight nexus between the social conventions in terms of which they take a wife and the uncertain rhythms of their own bodies that they will never have children at all. Appropriately enough, there are heavy sanctions to make men marry, to penalize socially those who do not have children. Potency is seen in Bali as a problem of wavering male response, with the male always turning back disarmed by the fearful female, able to respond initially to her beauty, unable to sustain the relationship, because all too often she turns out to be not the beautiful sister, but the ugly sister, who is dressed in the theatre like the mother and the mother-in-law.

Among the Arapesh, the problem is seen not as maintenance of potency but as resistance of seduction by strong positively sexed women. "She will hold your cheeks, you will hold her breasts, your skin will tremble, you will sleep together, she will steal part of your body fluid, later she will give it to the sorcerer and you will die." Beyond the safe borders of the home, beyond those stopping-places on a journey where one finds an aunt, a cousin, or a brother's betrothed, lies the world of strange women who may easily seduce one into death. No Arapesh came to the door of the field clinic asking for medicine to restore his potency; instead he came for emetics to undo the harm that sorcery —following seduction—had done him. But his reliable potency is not necessarily a satisfaction to all Arapesh women, because the occasional Arapesh woman who, despite the cultural framework, is actively, specifically sexed is only too likely to fit into the suspect pattern of a woman who wishes to seduce in order to kill.

The Manus, trapped in the so frequent phrasing of copulation as a form of excretion (or "outlet," as Dr. Kinsey prefers to call it), find little pleasure in marital sex relations for men or women. The ideal home setting, from the standpoint of both husband and wife, is a household with two children, a child to sleep with the husband on one side of the fire and a child to sleep with the wife on the other. When men and women have aged together, and their children are half-grown, they may relax and talk together, and even eat together, freed from the distasteful burden of a relationship that is phrased in terms of repugnance and shame for both. The Manus birth-rate is very low. Potency again is not a recognized problem. There are no overt hints that men have much expected of them, and their wives' disinclination towards sex possibly acts as a sufficient stimulus to overcome the burden of shame, just as the captured prostitute, shared by a group of men, is their symbol of a satisfactory sex adventure.

Among all the peoples I have studied, the Samoans have the sunniest and the easiest attitudes towards sex, putting their whole emphasis on the specific interpersonality of the sexual act. Man as a successful lover is defined as a man who is able to make a woman sexually contented, and who is also himself contented in so doing. A male's pride can be terribly hurt if a girl receives a second lover the same night; he does not reckon up his defeats in terms of potency, however, but in terms of personal clumsiness. With characteristic Samoan emphasis on slowness, love-making is seen as something that must be approached gradually, the girl's body prepared to enjoy a lover, and the attention of the lover himself is shifted from anxious inspection of his own adequacy to his relationship with her. The sexual misfit in Samoa is the *moetotolu*, the sleep-crawler, the man who must steal, and that surreptitiously, what he cannot win for himself, the man who counts on a girl's waiting for her lover and slips in ahead under cover of darkness and takes advantage of her receptivity. But this Samoan ease in sex relations is made possible by the whole system of child-rearing that has been described earlier, by a widening of the circle of personal relationships within which the child is reared until the emotions of childhood are diluted, rather than broken, as in Bali. Competition is muted and controlled; few strong demands for individual success are made on either male or female. Love between the sexes is a light and pleasant dance, in which one may be either very graceful, or alas! awkward and so lacking partners. Later in life it is a good meal, eaten together often, with ease and good humour, uncomplicated by shame, or striving, or any capacity to care deeply or even to inquire into the other's soul. In Bali the air is never empty of music, in every village ritual and offering occupy the people's time; the sculptor works on the partly finished temple relief; cremation towers that take weeks to complete rise in perishable splendour above the palm-trees. In Samoa the dances, of which the people themselves never tire, are simple, depending on grace rather than plot, on the sheen of human skin rather than on costume. Within Samoan culture, each child learns to ask for simple things, and is given the means to satisfy his desires completely.

I have called this chapter "Potency and Receptivity," in order to stress the difference in the problems that face males and females who live in human culture. The civilized male always runs the risk that civilization may dictate to and so reduce his spontaneity. The female's capacity for receptivity can as a rule be enhanced by civilization, by her ability to plan, her desire for home, marriage, children, food, companionship, or the continuance of any relationship that is not expressly keyed to her manifestation of physical desire. The failure of female ardour can of course be crucial under some circumstances, where the conditions of a human society are temporarily reproduced, and there is no genuine mating but only temporary association between males and females, as in an occupied town in wartime, and in extra-marital love-affairs that are built about passion. In such circumstances, the active ardour of the woman counts just because the man's potency is uncomplicated by any of the thousand little considerations that intervene in normal human life. The soldier who finds a woman cold will turn to a woman who is less cold, if such a one is available. The passionate lover will turn from a cold mistress. But man as a prospective or contemporary husband, which is what most men are decreed to be most of the time by the nature of human civilization, always has other things on his mind. He is not looking for a female to match a per-fectly running mammalian urgency, such a match as the female primate in heat is able to offer to a male, but for a wife whose receptivity will match, after a fashion, his unperiodic potency, a potency that may be increased or reduced by irrelevant considerations of shame and hope and pride, of success and saving, of prestige and power, whether he wins his point in the men's house, at the boar-hunt, or at the committee-meeting.

There are many primitive societies in which women's receptivity is all that is required or expected, in which little girls learn from their mothers, and from the way their fathers pat their heads or hold them, unworriedly, close to their bodies, that women are expected to be receptive, not actively or assertively sexed. That whole societies can ignore climax as an aspect of female sexuality must be related to a very much lesser biological basis for such climax. It is true that it is possible for human society to build viable cultural systems that are extraordinarily detached from any biological base. Much of our learned behaviour, such as walking, only develops after the reflex behaviour that is its structural prototype has disappeared,[4] and Gesell, who believes in virtually inevitable sequences of human matura-tion, found credible the story of the wolf-child who ran on all fours with the wolves.[5] Our whole eating behaviour is so completely disassociated from any specific wisdom of the body that each artificial pattern of nutrition, in which adequate nourishment may depend on one or two special foods that are the only carriers of a given nutrient, has to be reinforced by social learning, by deeply entrenched habits in which certain foods served in certain ways are right for certain times of the day. We know from experiments that human children, faced with a variety of foods *all* of which are suitable nutritionally will make well-balanced but individual selections, compensating one day for an over-emphasis of the day before, an over-emphasis that is known to the nutritionist who has analyzed the particular food.[6] We know that rats given artificial nutrients—vitamins and minerals in clear glass tubes—can make a better choice than can the biochemist who plans for them a stock diet.[7] But we also know that rats kept without food or water will retain enough wisdom to go *towards* water rather than towards food if both are out of sight and smell, but if the two are placed *side by side*,[8] will choose a liked food that will increase their state of thirst and discomfort rather than the more neutral but more needed water.

We may assume, from the rather slender evidence available, that human beings have the capacity to choose among foods that contain various essential nutrients so as to make a biologically good pattern of nutrition, but that this capacity will not assert itself except under very special conditions that have never existed until the present century, when nutritional analyses and nutritional isolation of elements could occur. Meanwhile, human infants in society learn to eat the foods that, because of a long process of social experimentation and accident—almost all outside the range of rational control—have become the standard and dependable diet of their own society. The child learns to eat those foods, and not to eat others, by relying not on any latent biochemical sensibilities to a particular vitamin, although this latent sensibility may be the biological base for crucial discoveries, but by the parents' invoking disgust and pleasure, reward and punishment, the whole battery of sanctions and settings for learning. The child finally learns: "This is food for me. That may be food for others, but not for me," and, "That is food for animals but not for human beings." "That is inedible." The teeth, the shape of the pelvis, the resistance against certain diseases, the wound-healing capacities of a whole people, may depend upon the meticulousness with which they use learned, not specific inherent, capacities.

It is therefore quite credible, given what we know of human culture, that learned behaviours absolutely essential to reproduction should have replaced the biologically given ones. The human female shows a capacity for sexual stimulation, and it might be argued that the lesser frequency of masturbation among young females that is reported for our own society, and characteristic of all the South Seas societies I have studied, is merely a structural matter. The female child's genitals are less exposed, subject to less maternal manipulation and self-manipulation. If masturbation is not socially recognized and taught, either by parents to children or by older children to younger, it may escape the spontaneous learning of the female child. But this part of the argument aside, there are no data that tie the capacity to conceive with an orgasm in the female in the same direct way that capacity to impregnate is tied to ejaculation in the male. Sheer physical potency, however disassociated, however artificially stimulated, is essential for impregnation. If a society should invent methods of child-rearing that completely inhibit the erectile and ejaculatory capacities of all its males, it would simply not reproduce itself. There seems no simple reason for believing that orgasms in females are of comparable importance for conception, in at least the majority of females. There seems therefore to be a reasonable basis for assuming that the human female's capacity for orgasm is to be viewed much more as a potentiality that may or may not be developed by a given culture, or in the specific life-history of an individual, than as an inherent part of her full humanity. The necessity for the female's fitness to be impregnated is as indubitable as the necessity for the male's fitness to impregnate. The male capacity for intromission may much more suitably be compared with the female's fitness to carry through the whole reproductive sequence, to conceive, to carry, and to bear a child, than with any assumed female capacity for orgasm. There have been some interesting experiments on rats in which the investigator, taking simple copulation as his unit for comparing male and female performance, found capacity to copulate and learning ability positively related for male rats and without any relationship for female rats.[9] Some of the interpretations tended to emphasize that the male copulatory act was after all so much more complicated— and exacting—than the female's. However, when the experiments are pursued a little further and the learning ability of the female rat is compared with her performance not as a copulator, but as a mother, the same order of relationship is found as is found between superior copulation and superior learning ability in males. The female's biological contribution lies in her maternal functions as a whole—not only in the copulatory act, which requires only the capacity to remain still.

But we are still faced with a certain amount of conflicting evidence. There are societies in which women are quite actively sexed, recognize and seek orgasms with the same freedom as males, and in which the woman who is not so actively sexed is penalized. Mundugumor is the society I know best in which women are expected to derive the same kind of satisfaction from sex that men do. The fact that some women still do not find such satisfaction in sex would of course be easy to explain in terms of low tonus, or unfavourable learning situations, and so on. But then we have to deal with societies like the Arapesh, in which in spite of most women's reporting no orgasm, and the phenomenon's being socially unnamed and unrecognized, a few women do feel very active sex desire that can be satisfied only by orgasm. If all innate urge towards orgasm is denied for the whole female humanity, what has happened to these particular women? Are they, as some theories might assume, more masculine, in the sense of having a different pattern of endocrine functioning? Certainly when compared with many other women in the same society, the highly sexed woman will sometimes appear closer to the masculine type. Have they learned, through some accident of childhood experience, that orgasm is a potentiality of every human body, and then developed a specific appetite, as human beings of both sexes can develop appetites for special ways of preparing food, although such food pattern may not have any primary biological relevance? This is also possible, and some such theory lies back of the puritan phrasings of the difference between good women, who are "unawakened," and bad women, who are "awakened." But the theorist who believes that orgasms are a primary response for women can easily dispose of the "unawakened" woman as a distortion produced by a puritan civilization.

An alternative theory would suggest that the capacity to learn a total orgasmic response is present differentially in all women, and that the differentials are perhaps very slight, depending on such details as the relative sensitivity of a variety of erogenous zones. It is possible that in the much more diffuse patterning of a woman's sexual receptivity now one part of the body, now another, now the nipples, now the lips, and so on, may be sensitive enough to develop a trigger effect. Societies like Samoa that emphasize a highly varied and diffuse type of foreplay will include in the repertoire of the male acts that will effectively awaken almost all women, however differently constituted they may be. But in cultures in which many forms of fore-play are forbidden, or simply ruled out by social arrange-ments that insist on both partners being clothed, or on the absence of lights, or on the muffling of all body odours by scented deodorants, this potentiality, which all women can develop under sufficiently favourable circumstances, may be ignored for a large proportion or for almost all of them. It is important also to realize that such an unrealized poten-tiality is not necessarily felt as frustration.

It may be useful to consider here some of the other potentialities and variations of the female reproductive cycle that may be ignored or developed through cultural emphases. Morning-sickness in pregnancy may be com-pletely ignored, or it may be expected of every woman, so that the woman who displays no nausea is the exception, or it may be stylized as occurring for the first child only. But in those societies which either ignore it or stylize it as for the first child only, there are still a few women who have extreme nausea. Nausea may be a sign of rejection of the newly conceived child, but in a society like our own, where every social expectation is keyed to morning-sickness, and a woman's female friends immediately begin setting the stage for how terribly she is going to feel, any simple hypothesis that nausea indicates an unconscious rejection of the coming child is probably barred out. Nausea with postponed menses may, instead, be a sign of extreme hope that one is pregnant, the nausea being taken merely as a socially recognized symbol and imposed on the body by very strong wishful thinking. In societies that do not recog-nize nausea as in any way suitable for pregnant mothers, or which expect only mothers of first children to manifest it, nausea *may* be an expression of rejection. but it may also be a less psychologically specific disturbance that is within the range of normality, but still statistically unusual, which manifests itself in spite of any cultural expectation. (The very rare occurrence of hot flashes in men as a climacteric phenomenon also *may* be hysterical female identifications, but they may also have a basis in some rare imbalance in the organism.) So we may say of morning-sickness that where it is culturally stylized as appropriate for any period of pregnancy or order of pregnancy (such as first pregnancy only), a large majority of women will show this behaviour; where it is not, only a very few will. Convulsive vomiting is a capacity of every human organism, which can be elaborated, neglected, or to a large degree disallowed.

The same sort of observation can be made on the subject of dysmenorrhoea. The Samoans recognize some mild pain as a normal accompaniment of menstruation, and a large number of girls report its presence.[10] The Arapesh do not recognize menstrual pain at all, possibly because the extreme discomfort of sitting on a thin piece of bark on the damp, cold ground in a leaky leaf-hut on the side of a mountain, rubbing one's body with stinging nettles, obscures any awareness. Careful studies of dysmenorrhoea in America have failed to reveal any consistent factors among women who manifest pain except exposure during childhood to another female who reported menstrual pain. Although the possibility of end-organ change has not been ruled out, there seems reason to believe that here we may possibly be dealing with a phenomenon of attention, perhaps comparable to some of the phenomena of causalgia, in which reverberating circuits are set up so that a given individual suffers because she is aware of uterine contractions that occasion other women no pain.[11] Cultural expectation can be an important factor in bringing such an awareness about, just as practices like Yogi can accustom individuals to experiencing consciously bodily processes that are normally below the level of conscious attention.

There is still another related hypothesis that may be introduced to explain the basis upon which some societies develop in women an active, seeking type of specific sexuality culminating in orgasm, while others develop women whose sex responses are less climactic and more diffuse. It is possible that there may be a genuine difference associated with constitutional type, a difference that may have specific structural correlates—such as a larger or more exposed clitoris or a clitoris nearer the mouth of the vagina, more erectile nipples, and so on—or which may be a much subtler matter of tonus or the tempo and timing of the whole nervous system. Here as elsewhere a culture can take its clues from one type and impose on other constitutional types a learned behaviour that is less congenial to them than it is to those from whom the clue was taken. So Balinese nursing procedure, in which the baby is held high on the mother's hip and leans over at will to drink from the mother's small high breast, fits the prevailing constitutional type in Bali, and is awkward and difficult for the woman with more pendent breasts. But in those groups where breasts are stretched to a degree of pendency that makes it possible for some women to throw their breasts over their shoulders, the typical Balinese woman with high firm breasts would be at an even greater disadvantage. In small inbred populations, the proportions in the population of one constitutional type or another may be radically altered, and so constitutional cues may continually reinforce a cultural learning. In large heterogeneous populations like our own, such selectivity is hardly possible, and very extreme forms of learning, plus actual external interference with the form of the body, may occur, as in the current demand for plastic surgery on women's breasts, and the dietary disciplines to which women submit to approximate the contemporary American ideal of slimness. If a real constitutional difference in capacity for orgasm were found to be associated with constitution, this might provide a clue to the lines upon which in some cultures women's responses are happily diffuse, in others as happily specific, with the deviants in each trailing more or less miserably behind the prevailing style.

Comparative cultural material gives no grounds for assuming that an orgasm is an integral and unlearned part of women's sexual response, as it is of men's sexual response, and strongly suggests that a greater part of women's copulatory behaviour is learned. Theories that attribute either great specificity or great lack of specificity to women as "natural," and ignore the great importance of learning, are likely not only to fall down scientifically, but to promote various social attitudes that do violence to the nature of female sexuality, and place an unnecessary burden on the relations between the sexes.

XI

HUMAN REPRODUCTIVITY

LIVING AS WE DO TO-DAY IN AN URBANIZED SOCIETY IN WHICH children are expensive luxuries and societies so large that one often thinks of rising or falling birth-rates rather than of the significance of single children, the problem of reproduction has come to mean to many people the problem of population limitation. There seems to be a deep-seated belief that conception is an almost automatic process, and that unless drastic measures are taken every sexual act will result in a child. The story of the king and queen who had no children is replaced by jokes based on contraceptive failures. Even in the face of rising sterility rates and the occasional sterility clinic, the popular mind is still focussed on how not to have children rather than on how to have them. There is nothing mysterious in this one-sided emphasis. Any period in history when social change is taking place faster than can possibly be registered in the character structure of the people who must live within the changing order will show lop-sided emphases of this sort. In the

United States a mobile population, prevailingly rural two generations ago, is faced with a social demand for small families, but our attitude towards parenthood is studded with dedications to the mothers of innumerable children, sometimes featured as all living, sometimes with a liberal number of infant deaths, and modern woman is seen as escaping by a hair's-breadth from a fate worse than death --bearing in rapid succession some dozen children.

But explicable as the contemporary attitude towards reproduction is—that is, that reproduction will always occur unless it is prevented, a view shared by both the advocates and the opponents of planned parenthood—it is, of course, one-sided. Every human society is faced not with one population problem but with two: how to beget and rear enough children and how not to beget and rear too many. The definition of "enough" and "too many" varies enormously. In a young colonial country, or a rising military state, there cannot be too many healthy children. When fecundity threatens vigour, social pressures against childbearing may become apparent. Agrarian peoples with a limited amount of land are automatically faced with the necessity of keeping the population stable, or of letting their young people emigrate, or of developing some form of industry. Primitive peoples living on small infertile bits of land struggle incessantly with the question of balance: how to get the right number of boys and girls, how many children to save and rear, when the life of one child should be sacrificed to the life of a sibling—even in rare cases by giving the baby to the elder sibling as food. And at the primitive level, as in our complex modern societies, there is also the fear that the reproduction rate will fall so low that the society will die out. Faced with any sort of new situation—the coming of the white man in the Pacific, the disappearance of the buffalo on the American plains, the introduction of fire-arms, even simply the need to cope with a river when a group had formerly been a bush people—a group may find its social arrangements so altered that it is impossible to keep the population moving in a stable or desirable direction. Many small South Seas populations, without any new contraceptive practices, began to die out in the face of the white man's advance. When the groups were very small they sometimes died out altogether. Larger groups reeled for a generation before the impact of a new world, and then regained sufficient stability to make it worth while to go on.

Such reductions in the birth-rate may be an accurate measure of despair, but we still know very little about the mechanisms that are involved. Very often they cannot be referred to such simple social conditions as a later age of marriage or a lower marriage rate, or to overt practices like contraception, abortion, and infanticide. Behind all of these age-old devices there lies a subtler factor, a willingness or an unwillingness to breed that is deeply imbedded in the character structure of both men and women. How these relative willingnesses and unwillingnesses function, at what point in the reproductive process blocks are introduced, we still do not know, but the evidence leaves little doubt that they are there.

Beneath population trends that are registered in statistics, behind articulate anxieties as to the size of the village fighting-force or hunting-party, or the shrinking amount of land available for each child, there lie the developed attitudes of men and women towards child-bearing. We have seen that there seems good basis for believing that men's desire for children is learned, learned in perhaps all cases as a very small child, either by identification with or envy of the mother as a child-bearer or by identification with the father in his complete socially defined rôle as the begetter of and provider for children. As we have also seen, this particular piece of learning is one of the most basic to the

preservation of a human society. In any society that has
provided the conditions under which men desire to father
and care for children, the man who does not desire children
will find himself to some degree anomalous and deviant.
He may label his lack of learning as inversion and become
a homosexual; he may choose some status where he himself is still fed and cared for as if he were a child, and live
out his life in a monastery, in a cloistered college, or in
the army. If a psychiatrist examines him, he will usually
be found to be deeply deviant from the expected character
structure of men in his society, and so vulnerable not
because he is unnatural, but because he has not learned
something that most other males of his age and class and
level of intelligence and type of sensitivity have learned.
He is no more "unnatural" than the intellectual American
on a small salary who insists upon having a large number
of children. In such a patriarch, an equally searching psychiatric examination would probably reveal equally important failures to learn, although such a man would no
doubt worry less about himself and come less often to the
psychiatrist because he has the support of former ages
behind him. Both failure to learn and over-learning may
involve serious bodily penalties; somatic accompaniments
of aberrancies in the individual career-line are frequent
enough.[1] We have no way of knowing whether the cost in
discernible bodily symptoms of denying some basic biological function is greater than the price some individuals
pay in similar coin when they are not allowed to write a
certain kind of music, or to dress as they have learned
members of their class should dress. So that when it is
said that men have no natural urge to paternity and so
do not necessarily suffer from refusing paternity, we still
must recognize that refusing the responsibilities of parenthood in most societies is a very expensive matter for the
individual.

Bali is an excellent example of a society in which the very lavishness of detail by which marriage is rewarded underlines the expectation that human beings will not enjoy it. In the village of Bajoeng Gedé a man who does not marry is denied full social status. He remains forever at the foot of the ladder, the oldest of the youths; he is an old young man instead of a "flower youth." A childless man can never rise to the top of the hierarchy, to full sanctity, but must retire one degree from the top. Even worse, however, is the penalty for the man who attempts paternity and fathers only girls. For example, in Bajoeng Gedé if a man has four daughters and then there is an interval of four years with no more children, he is retired from active citizenry. His position is, however, redeemable at any time if he fathers a son. In marriage he is always worried about whether or not he will desire his wife sufficiently to beget children. Social arrangements are endlessly separating husband and wife; "one goes, one stays to guard the courtyard," "one in the village, one on the farm." Marriage is formal, socially enforced, a way of producing children whom one must have to be socially complete. And in Bali there are men who refuse to marry, and women who refuse to marry, and there are men and women who take their childlessness, or more often their position as the parents of one dead girl, so hard that they become moody and antisocial, take to gambling, and destroy the material structure of their lives. The whole setting is such that it produces both people who so respond to the negative phrasings that they refuse to marry and have children, and people who respond to them so intensely that their personalities are ruined without successful social paternity. I know no instances of any extreme response to the condition of being the bereaved parents of a single dead male child. This is in fact the most socially rewarded position in Bajoeng Gedé, for one has attained a degree of completion as an individual that only death can interrupt. Men with living children have to face retirement from all active life when their youngest child marries or when their first great-grandchild is born. But a man and woman with a dead male child are safe for the rest of that incarnation. This single circumstance dramatizes vividly the nature of the pressures towards paternity in Bali. It is also desirable to have a male descendant to carry on one's line of ancestral prayers, and families with daughters adopt their sons-in-law; childless families sometimes, but not always, adopt a son. The need for prayers from descendants is not as heavily enforced as the need for social completion as a person in this incarnation. The sequence of completion is interesting: first, the unmarried, who are by definition incomplete except in the case of a Brahman girl who has become a priestess in her own right, and who is then debarred from marrying (that is, she has attained the status normally acquired only by a limited number of Brahman women in marriage, and has no farther to go; marriage in a temporal sense would be a step down); then there are the married who have begotten girls only; the married who are childless; and finally the married who have begotten at least one male child.

The Marind-Anim have carried to violent extremes the fear that men and women will never find heterosexual activity sufficiently rewarding to indulge in it. Their young men are given a period of highly conventionalized homosexual experience, and then in the ritual that prepares a whole initiatory group to be men a heterosexual pair locked in an embrace are cast into a pit and killed as a necessary sacrifice. The fear that no one will ever prefer heterosexual love is a very extreme attitude; it dramatizes one end of the scale, while those peoples who place the heaviest possible restrictions on heterosexual activity (in the explicit fear that otherwise it will get out of bounds) lie at the other end. There are no known primitive peoples who do not show in some way a recognition that copulation is related to reproduction, even though they may phrase it as merely making a path for the spirit of the child to enter, or feeding it after it has entered, the mother's womb. So the institutionalized attitudes towards the intractability of heterosexual impulses, or need for their stimulation, provide one index of the attitude towards reproduction. These may often be counterpointed, and prayers for fertility may be accompanied by taboos on heterosexual activity so that the new lives may have a chance, or prayers and rites of fertility may be accompanied by rites to stimulate heterosexual desire. The relationship in the male between his innate sexual impulses and reproduction seems to be a learned response to which the presence of this great variety of conflicting cultural solutions testifies. Male sexuality seems originally focussed to no goal beyond immediate discharge; it is society that provides the male with a desire for children, for patterned interpersonal relationships that order, control, and elaborate his original impulses.[2]

In the female, however, we are confronted with something very different. The male sex act is immediately self-resolving and self-satisfying, but the female analogue is not the single copulatory experience, however self-resolving that may appear to be, but the whole cycle of pregnancy, birth, and lactation. Although women can actually devote only about half of their lives in societies where women die young, and a third in societies where they are long-lived, to childbearing, most societies persistently emphasize the childbearing aspect of femininity as the significant one. In many societies girls before puberty and women after the menopause are treated very much as men. A society that has not defined women as primarily designed to bear children has far less difficulty in letting down taboos or social barriers. It is very significant that the Mundugumor, even though they have an institutional framework based on the exclusion of women from initiation into the men's cult, both repudiate women's child-bearing functions and let women into the mysteries of the sacred flutes. To parallel this we may turn to the American Indian pueblo of Zuni, where men had been denied by the cultural phrasing any activities that were not of a constructive, conserving, child-rearing aspect, where also there was no objection to women being initiated into the men's societies. But whereas in Mundugumor only the very casual indolent girl was likely to refuse the small trials of initiation, in Zuni few of the women took advantage of their privileges. In pre-Soviet Russia there seems to have been extraordinarily little valuation placed on women's child-bearing character, and it is striking that the Russians find little difficulty in letting women share occupations normally defined as male, even to using rifles and machine guns in war. In Tchambuli, where women have taken over the bulk of the providers' rôle, the men chafe against the burden that the care of children puts upon their women, and the young men importuned us to bring goats to the tribe. "We could milk the goats and feed the babies," they said. "The women are busy and have other things to do." We shall see later how in the United States, where a large part of a woman's education is identical with a man's, and the dogma of equal economic opportunity is far advanced, the married state is still expected to carry with it a specialized child-bearing, home-making rôle almost completely differentiated from the shared experience of boys and girls about choices in life.

Put very simply, men have to learn as children to want to beget and cherish children, and to maintain a society in which children are provided for as well as simply protected against enemies. Women, on the other hand, have to learn to want children only under socially prescribed conditions. The small male looks at his body and at the bodies of other males of all ages and realizes his potentialities to explore, to take apart, to put together, to construct the new, to penetrate the mysteries of the world, to fight, to make love. The small female looks at her body, and at the body of other females of all ages, and realizes her potentialities to make, to hold, to suckle, to care for, a child. The simple logic of "breasts that do not give suck" can only be escaped by the most elaborate forms of cultural learning. Girls can be placed in learning contexts where every one of them will wish to be a boy and resent being a girl; girls can be placed in learning contexts in which being a woman and bearing a child is a synonym of having one's body invaded, distorted, and destroyed. Girls can certainly learn not to want children, but such learning seems always to be socially imposed. Every delicate detail of the female body may of course be reinterpreted by the culture. The vulva may be stressed as an immediate pleasure-giving part of the body, and no longer be recognized as the doorway of a new life. The breasts may be labelled as erotic zones, to be trained and cherished only because they are valuable supplements to love-making, not because they will some day feed children. The softness of a woman's body may be seen not as the surface against which an infant nestles its over-sensitive, womb-soft skin, but as something contemptible to be overcome by "hardening." The womb may come to seem not a point of glad expansion, but a menace to be shrunk even farther by eating magical roots that will make one barren—as in Tewara, a Dobuan settlement—or a spot to be isolated from the rest of the too-fertile body by the tube-tying operation. The beauty of infertile women may become so meaningful to a whole people that the witch is defined as the woman whose daughter is rejected in marriage, as in Bali, and who then in revenge trains beautiful, sexless little girls to spread death over the land.

The witch figure, which recurs with dreadful monotony over the entire world, among the civilized and the uncivilized, in the far reaches of jungle and at the cross-roads of

Europe, is a woman who has ridden away on a broomstick or a peeled wand leaving her empty skin by her husband's side to deceive him into believing that she is still there. It is not without significance that we have no such recurrent monotonous image of the male who does evil magically. Sorcerers, witch-doctors, and black magicians appear and disappear through history and in different cultures. The witch remains as a symbol so deep that she seems to resist dethronement by even the most vigorous cultural imagination.

In Bali, the witch is the principal figure of drama, pictured as wearing the trappings of female maternity and male maturity: pendent breasts, and abundant body hair. Children re-enact her with clutching hands, as a being ready to destroy them, but on the adult stage she is herself the figure of fear, both frightened and afraid. Alone, curiously moving, she stands within the magic circle that the friendly male dragon has drawn around her and the people of the village. She is within them, but they are safe as long as she can draw no other witches to join her. And in the *djoget*, the charming street-dance in which a little pre-adolescent girl dances to delight the men of the village, the dancer may, standing as she does for the desirable, the irresistible, in women, take a doll, and turning it into the witch, place her dainty, slender maiden foot firmly on its head, crushing it to death in the dust. Far away from Bali, up the Sepik River in New Guinea, where witches are only a verbal folk-lore theme, I once found a little five-year-old girl dancing over her baby brother, whom she had placed in a shallow hole she had hollowed out of the earth. With never a visual clue, never a traditional dance-step to guide her, she re-enacted the steps that in Bali have been raised to the level of a dramatic form. The figure of the witch who kills living things, who strokes the throats of children till they die, whose very glance causes cows to lose their calves and fresh milk to curdle as it stands, is a statement of human fear of what can be done to mankind by the woman who denies or is forced to deny child-bearing, child-cherishing. She is seen as able to withhold herself from men's desire, and so to veil the nexus with life itself. "She may ride away leaving her empty skin by her husband's side." Women, like men, are creatures who learn; their behaviour as adults is as dependent upon their childhood experiences. They can so learn not to want children that they become dangerous to all life on earth.

But there seems no reliable evidence to suggest that learning not to want children necessarily introduces such a deep conflict into a woman's nature that the conflict is insoluble and she must inevitably pay a price, in frustration and hatred of her fate, that will in turn reverberate in the lives around her. A psychiatrist working in the United States once summarized his clinical experience: "I have never seen a woman who was socially and physically able to have children, and who refused to have children, who did not suffer, psychologically, from that refusal." This statement may be interpreted, as it would be by some of the more extreme writers of the day, as meaning that woman's urge to have children is so basic that interference with it inevitably produces disorder, if not disease. They would have it mean that just as human beings cannot learn not to breathe, not to eat, not to sleep, but only to modulate and regulate these assembled activities, so also women cannot learn not to want to bear children. But if one examines the psychiatrist's statement again one finds a neglected adverb, "socially." It is equally easy to interpret his statement as meaning that those will suffer who having put themselves in a situation that they have learned to believe calls for child-bearing, *then* reject it. So it is also with the eldest son of a king who cannot bear the responsibility of the throne, or the mate who funks at his task of taking over the ship at sea when the captain dies, or the young student who accepts the music fellowship to study in Europe and then fritters it away without learning any music. All of these will also show serious psychological disorders. Human society has a great accumulated store of ways of teaching human beings what they should do, and a corresponding battery of punishments, externally and internally imposed, for those who fail to do what they have learned. Women in our society have learned that marriage and child-bearing go together, that except under exceptional circumstances—such as hereditary disease, the ill-health of one partner, extra financial burdens of a succouring sort, such as care of parents or brothers and sisters—avoidance of parenthood is avoidance of responsibility. Under such circumstances, women, and men, who purposely avoid the responsibility will show the marks of having chosen a socially disallowed course.

Even the evidence from the clinics that suggests, not too conclusively, that the menopause is more severe, and that carcinomas may take a different form, in women who have never borne children does not substantiate any simple theory of the female body's avenging itself for non-use of the maternal function. To the unmarried woman who has wanted children, and to the childless married woman who has wanted children, the menopause comes as a final closing of the gates of hope, and so may bring with it despair and disease. We still have to insert the phrase "who wanted children" into the statement to make it fit into a framework of comparative discussion. Those who learn to want will suffer if they do not attain their desires, unless they have also learned to derive high rewards from self-abnegation.

The institution of the monastery, in which in the service of God men deny their procreative and women their child-bearing potentialities, is an example of a socially approved tradition in which women may learn not to want children. Wherever it is possible for little girls to sit beneath a tree and chat together of their future, with one saying, positively and definitely, "And I shall be a nun, and wear a fluted coif and take care of hundreds of babies," or "nurse the sick" or "teach" or "pray all day," society has offered a phrasing within which women may deny their reproductivity without damage to themselves. Sometimes later loss of religious belief, or even a doubt of her own religious vocation, may shatter this learning, and the once dedicated nun may become a poor mad creature, listening to voices no longer of angels, but of her unborn children. Still, it is possible to set up vocations for women that do not include child-bearing and which little girls can learn to embrace as full human solutions for themselves. When these solutions are uncomplicated by any denial of femininity, any rejection of children or the maternal rôle, this process of learning is probably simpler than when a small girl, because it has some deep appeal to her, selects a way of life that is labelled as male. The dynamics of choosing to-day to be a doctor in Soviet Russia and in the United States are still necessarily different, for here the woman doctor is the somewhat disapproved exception, while in Russia she is in the approved majority. But we do not have the material to insist that those rôles in which women have been contented although childless must be rôles that may be interpreted as sublimating the desire for children. We still do not know how completely any given girl-child, or any group of girl-children, may learn *not* to want children.

Nor have we any evidence yet as to whether learning not to follow some bodily defined path is more destructive than learning to follow some socially defined path that has no bodily base. If a society teaches its men to be constructive and peaceful and mild at the expense of their active enjoyment of their sexuality—as in Zuni and Arapesh—then those males will pay a price for the new learning. But the Samoans, equally peaceful and constructive as a people, paid no such price. Male sexuality was never defined as aggressiveness that must be curbed, but simply as a pleasure that might be indulged in, at appropriate times, with appropriate partners. It seems safer to say that in every society, both males and females learn the meaning of their bodily differences, the significance of their reproductive equipment. During this learning a culture may define the behaviour asked of either sex in such a way as to impose either heavy burdens or light ones.

Perhaps the most conspicuous instance of such phrasing is the handling of child-bearing itself. Some societies define child-bearing as ultimately dangerous, and the Aztecs saw the heavens red with the blood of men who died in battle and that of women who died in child-birth. Others may handle child-bearing as so simple that it is only the mother herself who calculates hopefully that her baby will be born in camp, and so have a chance to live, and not on the cold march during the day, when it will surely die. The rigours of child-birth may be so exaggerated that the father shares them and has to lie beside his wife "resting" afterwards, or after pacing the floor of the hospital waiting-room take a trip to Bermuda. Old wives may fill children's ears with stories of pain and witchcraft so that they fall into frightened sleep if there is a birth in the house, or children may scamper through the village looking for an interesting birth to watch. Women may be expected to groan or shriek in a manner designed to make all young female spectators indisposed towards birth and definitely predisposed to shriek when their own "time" comes. Or women may learn that a woman in labour should behave with quiet decorum, paying attention to the business in hand, and certainly not dissipating her strength or disgracing her family with a lot of loud-mouthed yelling. So child-birth may be experienced according to the phrasing given it by the culture, as an experience that is dangerous and painful, interesting and engrossing, matter-of-fact and mildly hazardous, or accompanied by enormous supernatural hazards. Whether they are allowed to see births or not, men contribute their share to the way in which child-birth is viewed, and I have seen male informants writhe on the floor, in magnificent pantomime of a painful delivery, who have never themselves seen or heard a woman in labour. To the phrasing of any piece of human behaviour, however sex-limited it may seem to be, both sexes contribute their imaginations, and also members of either sex with special bents may give it the dominant note. Men who feel copulation as aggressive may have different phantasies about the dire effects on their wives of their dreadful uncontrolled aggressive desires from men who feel copulation as pleasant, who may share in a cultural phrasing which insists that the child "sleeps quietly until it is time to be born, then puts its hands above its head and comes out."

It has been suggested that one of the most significant changes in modern times has been the reduction of women's fear of death in childbed, because statistics show reduced death in childbed.[8] But I find this—in the light of primitive material—a culturally limited point of view. Whether childbed is seen as a situation in which one risks death, or one out of which one acquires a baby, or social status, or a right to Heaven, is not a matter of the actual statistics of maternal mortality, but of the view that a society takes of child-bearing. Any argument about women's instinctive maternal behaviour which insists that in this one respect a biological substratum is stronger than every other learning experience that a female child faces, from birth on, must reckon with this great variety in the handling of child-birth. It cannot be argued that child-birth is both an unbearable pain and a bearable pain, both a situation from which all women naturally shrink in dread and a situation towards which all women naturally move readily and happily, both a danger to be avoided and a consummation devoutly to be desired. At least one aspect must be regarded as learned, and it seems simpler in the light of present knowledge to assume that women's attitudes towards child-bearing and men's attitudes towards child-bearing have complex and contradictory elements in them, and that a society may pick up and elaborate any one, or sometimes even a contradictory, set of such attitudes. And as with all learned, culturally elaborated behaviour, the farther away from the biological base, the freer the imagination is. There seems some reason to believe that the male imagination, undisciplined and uninformed by immediate bodily clues or immediate bodily experience, may have contributed disproportionately to the cultural superstructure of belief and practice regarding child-bearing. It is perhaps not without significance that in those Polynesian societies where the male participates in his wife's delivery as a husband, not as a magician or a priest, there is an extremely simple, uncomplicated attitude towards birth; women do not scream, but instead work, and men need no self-imposed expiatory activities afterwards.

But back of acceptance and rejection of reproduction, of child-bearing itself and of the cherishing and fostering of children, there lies always a cultural tradition within which boys and girls learn to accept a two-sex world, and the rôle of each sex within it. Societies may be differently successful in teaching each sex its reproductive rôle, and when both sexes set their hearts against reproduction, then such societies die out—even without benefit of contraceptives.

So through many thousands of years people after people have struggled with the problems of fertility and infertility, making one faulty and haphazard adjustment after another to the relationship between the number of children they want, the number of children they can afford, and the number of children who will be born—unless in some way interfered with—under their existing social practices. It is possible that we may some day evolve a culture in which there will be such a good communication within each paired relationship that no other control will be needed than the female's own natural monthly rhythm of fertility. It seems clear enough that the female's sensitivity to the changes within her own body, while it may counsel her safely to stay away from a moonlight tryst in a society in which love is taken lightly, is not strong enough to resist the thousand pressures of a complex social organization such as ours, in which natural impulses are stretched and fitted into a world defined by alarm-clocks and factory-whistles and commuters' trains, months in which marriage is auspicious, the season for Bermuda, the strain of an annual directors' meeting, or a play about to be produced. But as we witness the desperate expedients to which simpler peoples have had to resort to fit their survival rate to their social structure—as we see new-born female babies among the Todas laid in the mud for the buffalo to trample them to death while the surviving excess of males then share a common wife with elaborate precautions to make the household amicable—we may realize that it is not civilization, in the sense of modern urbanization, alone that has alienated human beings from the rhythm of their own bodies. Between the period when our foraging ancestors could be trusted to spit out at once an evil-tasting berry and perhaps find a root that contained the salt they badly needed, and to-day, when we begin to know enough to arrange a proper self-selective diet for a human baby, human beings have fumbled, eagerly, imaginatively, clumsily, at the problem of fitting a man-made way of life upon an organism that has the skill to design such ways of life but no automatic capacity to fit them on. Between the first artificiality—the first bed made of dry grass, the first boulder rolled to provide a wall against the wind, or the first branch actually fashioned into a tool, or perhaps the first female who lay, herself quiescent rather than desirous, beside a chosen mate, or the first male who began regularly to share his fruity plunder with her—and the most modern gadget of the atomic age—the radio nurse, vitamin-D homogenized milk, or the part of an eye transplanted from the dead to the living—men have travelled the same road; and none of it has been natural. It is a piece of sentimental nonsense to talk about the Eskimo squatting in a fur suit carefully tailored by his wife's needle, shod in boots that she has chewed with wifely love, holding in his mittened hand a cunningly fashioned harpoon as he watches for a seal, as *natural;* and about modern man, in factory-made boots that his wife bought at a sale, dressed in a factory-made suit of factory-woven cloth made of wool from Australia as he tends a meat-canning machine, as *unnatural.* It is like the arguments that rage among the nutritionists against reinforcing bread with vitamins, because it is an "unnatural" way of treating natural bread—bread that is grown from domesticated wheat, by artificial tools, milled in a modern mill and baked in a man-made oven. Our problem is not to be natural, which would mean in effect to strip off every vestige of civilization, abandon speech, and return to an animal life; and it is not to be *more* or *less* artificial, and accept some simple figure of speech, some fake rural gesture, or a hunting-trip with an air-mattress, or badly ground whole-wheat bread, as redeeming us from our horrid artificial state. Our problem is to develop and elaborate this new method of evolution, this precious system of invention and learned social practice that man alone of all living things has begun. We need not "more natural" bread, made of a wheat at least approximately more like the food of wild animals, though a little the worse for a few hundred years of cultivation and fertilization. We need bread in which we can combine more "unnaturalness," more, not fewer, results of research and skill and learning.

Our humanity depends upon our relative infertility, upon

the long period of human gestation and dependency possible only where there are few children, who can be reared long and lovingly. It depends upon the presence of warm human responses in both sexes that are not tied tight to a reproductive cycle in the female. But to pattern and discipline this potentiality for mating, to balance the children whom we learn to want with the children we can afford to have so that no abrupt and incongruous measures are necessary, so that no section of the population need be reared to psychological childlessness, so that no lives need be begun only to be flung beneath the feet of blind gods—this requires more knowledge and a more finely wrought pattern of human relationships than mankind has yet conceived.

PART FOUR

THE TWO SEXES IN

CONTEMPORARY AMERICA

XII

OUR COMPLEX AMERICAN CULTURE

LOOKING OVER THE GREAT EXPANSE OF THE UNITED STATES, the complicated and diversified landscape, the hundred sets of folk-customs that reign in pockets in the Southern mountains, on bare New England promontories, in lonely shacks on the plains, it would seem almost impossible to write about the American people as a whole. Are there not unbridgeable gaps between the immigrant mother who sets her baby gently in a cradle that she brought from the Old World and the young American mother imbued with ideas of schedules and hygiene who sternly lets her baby in its thumb-sucking-proof blanket cry its heart out because it is not time for the next feeding, and the ultra-modern mother who has abandoned schedules and feeds her baby on self-demand? If it is true that in the experiences which help to prepare the child for its adult sex rôle every detail of the world that surrounds it is almost inestimably important, whether it be the feather or the flower in a small boy's hair, a beaded nose ornament, or a band of pigment on the little girl's forehead, the softness of a piece of fine weaving on the smooth skin of a buffalo embryo or the scratchy surface of a harshly plaited basket—then how indeed can one say anything at all about American babies, and about how American babies become men and women, able—or unable—to love and beget children? But if you enter the simplest, the most deviant American house, the unsealed sharecropper's cabin with the pine knots blazing on the hearth, the cold-water flat without furniture except rugs brought from the Near East—even in these settings, which differ so sharply from the two-story white house with the green shutters that the papers picture as "the American home," you are likely to find, if not a modern crib, at least a mail-order catalogue or a calendar with a picture of a modern crib. Where the material objects and the new ways that go with them have not penetrated, because the way of life of that family is too firmly rooted in some old tradition, or because the way in which that family earns its bread leaves no money to approximate an American standard of living, you find that the image of the new ways, of the modern ways, of the standard American ways, has come. It has come in the mail-order catalogue, over the radio, in the moving pictures, even if they are seen but twice a year. The women may still wear long calico skirts as their grandmothers did, but their daughters wear cheap but authentic versions of the styles that are found on Fifth Avenue and Hollywood Boulevard. Beside the traditional foods in the rural child's lunch-basket, there must be a piece of store bread or that child will be ashamed and not take its lunch to school. Subtly, insistently, continuously, the standard American culture is presented, to rich and to poor, to newcomer and even to aborigines whose ancestors roamed the Plains before the Spaniards brought the horse to the New World.

But it may well be asked: Is the mere presentation of the new ways enough? Surely the mother who lolls in a sagging frame doorway idly turning the pages of a catalogue that shows the best type of orange-squeezer to make the baby's orange-juice, but herself simply thrusts the sugar-tit deeper in her child's mouth when it cries—surely she is a different mother from the trim young housewife, clad in a charming apron, brightly measuring out the orange-juice for the baby. The nutritional effects are very different. One child will perhaps have a serious vitamin-C deficiency—especially if its mother gets a little fussier and forbids it to eat raw vegetables pulled up in the garden; the other probably will not. Even if the child of the cabin-dwelling mother grows up and goes to high school, and in the end becomes superficially indistinguishable from the child of the city dweller in the immaculate little flat, there will be a difference. These two children as mothers themselves may follow the prescription of the same pediatrician for their children, but one will do so secure in the sense that she is doing what her mother did. The other will lament over her neglected teeth, and hide shamefacedly from her own eyes the memory of what her mother did not do. In the shadows of the consulting-room, the two will have very different stories to tell of the childhood memories that formed their images of what the relations between father and mother were. One will remember voices behind the carefully shut door, interrupted perhaps by a telephone call that made it necessary to open the door and give the straining childish ears a glimpse of tense faces, a memory of a single half-understood sentence. The other will have memories of quarrels of parents who shared the same room, and perhaps the same faded quilt, whose blows and whose making-up were both visible to the child's eyes. The anguish of not being asked to the box-supper, or of failing to make the high-school sorority, will seem very far apart in every detail, even to that most important detail of whether the story is told at all. Nor will the backgrounds of two boys who grow up to be husbands be less strikingly

different, although—and this is significant—they may be reversed. For the girl from the slovenly unkempt cabin may
grow up to marry a boy from the town, the town-bred girl
to marry the cabin-bred boy. So in one home it will be the
father who will remember vaguely, perhaps with no outlines
at all but just a sweet-sour taste between his teeth, the sugar-
tit of his babyhood, the drag of wet pants that no one
bothered to change; in the other home it will be the mother.
And which parent remembers which way of life will make a
difference. The father may feel more estranged from his
small son, so clean and neat and starched in his play-suit—
a rather girlish-looking play-suit—than he will from his
daughter, because the lines of memory lead back to such
a different little boy, less surely to a different little girl. The
mother from the cabin will find her fingers grow suddenly
stiff with desire as she runs her electric iron over the fluted
ruffles of her little girl's dress and remembers the faded little
hand-me-down that her mother was too tired, or too spirit-
less, to shorten. But the mother from the urban flat, facing
a husband who can't see why money should be spent the
way she spends it, will tighten her lips with anger remembering the carefully fluted ruffles of her childhood, hardening her heart against his unwillingness to give his child what
that child has a right to.

Each home will present a different picture. In the America
of to-day only in the by-ways, in the mountains, in the villages from which the young men go away, among back-
woods communities of freed and abandoned slaves, or little
clusters of Spanish-speaking peoples who cling to the ways
of the sixteenth century—only here is there found the sort of
relationship between the parents and the child, between
grandparents and grandchild, that is found in primitive societies. Everywhere else in the United States the striking
characteristic is that each set of parents is different from
each other set, that no two have exactly the same memories,

that no two families could be placed side by side and it could be said: "Yes, these four parents ate the same food, played the same games, heard the same lullabies, were scared by the same bogeys, taught that the same words were taboo, given the same picture of what they would be as men and women, made ready to hand on unimpaired the tradition they received, whole, unravelled, unfaded, from their parents."

Every home is different from every other home, every marriage, even within the same class, in the same clique, contains contrasts between the partners as superficially striking as the difference between one New Guinea tribe and another. "In our family we never locked the bathroom door." "In our family you never entered another person's room without knocking." "Mother always asked to see our letters, even after we were grown." "The smallest scrap of paper on which one had written something was returned unread." "We were never allowed to mention our legs." "Father said that 'sweat' was a good deal honester word than 'perspiration,' but to be careful not to say it when we went to Aunt Alice's." "Mother said my hands would get rough if I climbed trees." "Mother said girls ought to stretch their legs and get some exercise while they were young." Side by side, next-door neighbours, children of first cousins, sometimes children of sisters or brothers, the ways of each household diverge, one family bringing up the children to prudery, privacy, and strongly marked sex rôles, another to an open give-and-take that makes the girls seem tomboys. Then again comes marriage between the children with the different upbringings, and again the clash, the lack of timing, the lack of movement in step, of the new set of parents. Every home is different from every other home; no two parents, even though they were fed their cereal from silver porringers of the same design, were fed it in quite the same way. The gestures of the feeding hands, whether of mother, grandmother, Irish cook, English nurse, Negro mammy, country-bred hired girl, are no longer the assured, the highly patterned gestures of the member of a homogeneous society. The recently come foreigner's hand is unsure as it handles unfamiliar things and tries to thrust a spoon into the mouth of a child who acts and speaks strangely; the old American's hand bears marks of such uncertainties in former generations, and may tremble or clench anew over some recent contact with some newly arrived and little-understood stranger.

But just because every home is different from every other home, because no husband and wife can move effortlessly in step to the same remembered cradle-songs, so also is every home alike. The anthropologist who has studied a New Guinea tribe can often predict down to the smallest detail what will go on in each family if there is a quarrel, what will be said when there is a reconciliation, who will make it, with what words and what gestures. No anthropologist can ever hope to do the same thing for the United States. What the quarrel will be, who will make up and how, will differ in every home; what the highest moment between parents and child will be will differ. But the form, the kind of quarrel, the kind of reconciliation, the kind of love, the kind of misunderstandings, will be alike in their very difference.[1] In one home the husband will indicate his importunate desire by bringing flowers, in another by kicking the cat playfully as he enters, in a third by making a fuss over the baby, in a fourth by getting very busy over the radio, while the wife may indicate her acceptance or rejection of his erotic expectation by putting on more lip-stick or by rubbing off the lip-stick she has on, by getting very busy tidying up the room or by sinking in a soft dream into the other overstuffed chair, playing idly with her baby's curly hair. There is no pattern, no simple word or gesture that has been repeated by all husbands in the presence of all the small children who are to be future husbands, and all the small girls who are to be wives, so that when they grow up they will be letter-perfect in a ballet of approach or retreat.

In America the langauge of each home is different, there is a code in each family that no one else knows. And that is the essential likeness, the essential regularity, among all these apparent differences. For in each American marriage there is a special code, developed from the individual pasts of the two partners, put together out of the accidents of honeymoon and parents-in-law, finally beaten into a language that each understands imperfectly. For here is another regularity. When a code, a language, is shared by every one in the village, spoken by the gracious and the grim, by the flexible-tongued and the stubborn, by the musical voice and the halting and stammering voice, the language becomes beautifully precise, each sound sharply and perfectly differentiated from each other sound. The new-born baby, first babbling happily through his whole possible range of lovely and unlovely noise, listens, and narrows his range. Where he once babbled a hundred nuances of sound, he limits himself to a bare half-dozen, and practices against the perfection, the sureness, of his elders. Later, he too, however stumbling his tongue or poor his ear, will speak the language of his people so that all can understand him. The perfected model made by the lips and tongues of many different sorts of people speaking the same words holds the speech of each new-comer clear and sharp enough for communication. And as with speech, so with gesture, so with the timing of initiative, of response, of command and obedience. The toddler falls in step with the multitude around him and cannot fail to learn his part.

But in a culture like modern America, the child does not see any such harmonious, repetitive behaviour. All men do not cross their legs with the same assured masculinity, or squat on wooden stools to protect themselves from a rear-guard attack. All women do not walk with little mincing

steps, or sit and lie with thighs drawn close together, even
in sleep. The behaviour of each American is itself a composite, an imperfectly realized version, of the behaviour
of others who in turn had, not a single model—expressed in
many voices and many ways, but still a single model—but a
hundred models, each different, each an individually developed style, lacking the authenticity, the precision, of a
group style. The hand held out in greeting, to still a tear, or to
help up a strange child that has stumbled, is not sure that
it will be taken, or if taken, taken in the sense in which it
is offered. Where patterns of courtship are clear, a girl knows
the outcome if she smiles, or laughs, casts down her eyes, or
merely walks softly by a group of harvesting youths cradling
a red ear of corn in her arms. But in America, the same smile
may evoke a casual answering grin, embarrassed averted
eyes, an unwelcome advance, or may even mean being followed home along a deserted street, not because each boy
who answers feels differently about the girl, but because
each understands differently the cue that she gives.

So although each home is different, there are many things
that it is possible to say about each American home, especially if we concentrate on the great stream of American
life, and allow for, but do not follow too closely, the little
shallows and inlets of colonies from a remote past, or a new-
come strangeness. The details will differ, differ enormously,
but the underlying response to these differences has itself
assumed shape and form. The speech, the gestures, of Americans include the tentativeness, the possibility of being misunderstood whenever relations go deep, the possibility of
building a quick code that for the moment will do roughly,
the need to feel out the other person, to find some slight,
over-explicit, imperfect, immediate communication.

There is another sense in which American homes, however strikingly different, are alike in ways that homes as different can seldom be said to be alike in Europe. For the

American family is oriented towards the future, towards what the children may become, not towards the perpetuation of the past or the stabilization of the present. In a caste society, each parent sits eyeing a son who will, for better or worse, repeat the parental way of life, marry a girl from the same caste, walk and dress and think, save money or spend it, make love and be buried, in the manner of his ancestors. Even if the son's way of life changes, it changes in step with the other members of his caste, and so he is still, in a sense, faithful to the ancestors. In a mobile, fluid class society like America, the parents who sit on the high steps of a brown-stone house in Hell's Kitchen or in the spacious houses of Hyde Park, Illinois, on a Nevada ranch or in a Pennsylvania mining town, when they look backward, invoke memories that have no shared details. But when they look forward they may see almost the same vision, sons identically clad in Brooks Brothers suits, hats set at the angle recommended to win the approval of the fairest girl, a bank-book in the vest pocket, success in the eye, the same make of car waiting at the door. If the grandparents were there—proud Hungarian landowners, English squires, Welsh miners, skilful Swiss craftsmen, Scots with a vision of perfectibility to hold up before their children—the grandparents would shake their heads, and each in his own way deny the shining vision. "In a thousand years no one from our valley ever went away but died in the attempt." "No member of our family has ever soiled his hands with manual labour." "The men of our family ride horses, not machines." From the past, difference, and paralysis, hope narrowed to a single thread of ancestral expectancy, would have been laid upon the children's shoulders. But the great-grandparents and the grandparents are far away, in another country, or another city, or another class, brushed aside in spirit if not in fact, and parents of many kinds, themselves too disparate to sit comfortably around a dinner-table, nevertheless dream the same dream. Where each little village, each separate caste or dialect group, in Europe or Asia has been standardized by the experience of the past, faultlessly transmitted to each new generation, the people of America, North and South, East and West, are being standardized by the future, by the houses all hope to live in, not by the houses where they were born, by the way they hope their wives will look, not by the folds of Mother's skirt in which they hid their faces.

There are of course many exceptions, on Beacon Hill in Boston and on the Main Line near Philadelphia, where birth transfixes the new generation in a world in which the lives of those about them are fluid and changing. There are exceptions in the mining towns where the people, transplanted straight from Europe, have not yet learned that a miner's son need not be a miner. There are exceptions among the sharecroppers of the Southeast, who heard with amazement—in the Share the Meat Campaign during World War I—that common folk could be expected to eat two pounds of lean meat a week, and among the slum dwellers who ride on their first train at sixty and find it "just like a street-car, but it goes when it says it will." But the restrictedness, the impoverishment, of the lives of these exceptions among the self-conscious old families, the isolated miners, the remote sharecroppers, is itself a comment on the fluidity of the rest of American life. The tragedy of an upper class that has nowhere to go but down because in American culture there is no real concept of simply maintaining position, or the bitter intransigency of a million miners trapped in an occupational enclave that negates almost every expressed value in American life—these simply serve to bring into relief the prevailing, compelling quality of the dream of the future. This dream will linger about the grimy little ankles of the cabin child, the knobby knees of the slum child, as well as around the sturdy, vitamin-shaped legs of the children of the carefully nurtured middle class. All of those children, however their legs are misshaped from lack of sunlight and vitamins, however malformed from wearing the wrong shoes, expect to wear the nylons that dazzle from magazine page and newspaper, from car ad and bill-board. It is not the certain sensuous feel of wool or silk or air, of scratchy black cotton or sealskin, that gives to the American girl a sense of the surface of her growing legs. She does not feel as the strongest, most compelling image, what she has worn, its cling, or scratch or caress, or the bumps in the sole where Mother darned; she walks clad in a pair of stockings made of a material that she may never have actually touched at all. Not unnaturally her legs become a visual image seen through her own eyes rather than a memory of skin and moving muscles fretted or soothed by the stockings worn in childhood.

Associated with the compellingness of the dream, of the ideal to which Americans aspire from a thousand different backgrounds and special, atypical experiences, is a carking dissatisfaction with the version of one's own family and one's own childhood. Groups of students sit together in bull-sessions raking over their pasts and the mistakes that each family made, one too strict, inhibiting spontaneity, the next too lenient, leaving no room for healthy rebellion, the third too anxiously attempting to evoke a spontaneity that then became a burden. By the very nature of the dream, none can attain it, and each particular household falls short of the ideal. Each house lacks some detail that is included in the ideal house which no one lives in. No mother can be all that an American mother should be, no romance have all the qualities that true love should show. And this, not because the ideal is so high, but because it is a dream of the future rather than an attempt to reproduce the past. In societies that attempt to reproduce faithfully, lovingly, the patterns of the past, a few of those who try to build their houses on the ancient model fall short for a variety of reasons—because of poverty, because of slothfulness, because of ill luck and illness and inability to organize their lives; a few have an imagination that goes beyond the old model and creates a new one. But in societies that live by an unrealized future pattern, the falling-short is of quite another order. The style of life held up to the growing child is a style that could be realized only by a method of child-rearing that was itself based on that style of life. You can in fact learn to live in a given kind of house, effortlessly, gracefully, only by having been reared with just that set of rooms, that arrangement of furniture, that slant of lighted lamp, of flickering candle. On the terrace of the Leopoldskron at Salzburg in the summer of 1947, great candelabra filled with lighted candles were set out for the Austrian musicians to play by. The American listeners could only half-attend for worrying and wondering about the candles—would they go out, would the musicians be able to see their notes as the candle flames wavered uncertainly in the light wind? To-day we can no longer have candles on Christmas-trees, not because candles on Christmas-trees have become more dangerous, but because people no longer have the necessary habits to use candles safely, habits that include a sharp awareness of blowing curtains, or a child's loose hair. Perfect relationships between oneself and one's surroundings, between oneself and other people, depend upon this long loving habituation, as first the infant's eyes, then those of the child, absorb the same patterns, as layer over layer of meaning is laid down in its mind, each layer being consistent with each other layer, however counter-pointed or apparently contrasting.

So it is not only not possible to describe in consistent detail all the steps taken by all the different sorts of Americans in the journey towards adulthood, but it is also not possible for any one of us to feel that the steps were perfectly taken. This discrepancy between the actuality and the ideal is experienced as a discrepancy between "myself and the others," a falling-behind the standards of the block, the clique, the school class, the other men in the office, the rest of the faculty; and also as a discrepancy between what one should be and feel and what one does feel. "I have a husband I am devoted to, a lovely child, plenty of money, brains and beauty, but," complains the young wife, "I am not one hundred per cent happy." "Somehow I don't seem to be getting what I should out of life." "I feel as if life were passing me by." "Am I as happy as I ought to be?" The old perfectly realizable Puritan imperative for the moment, "Work, save, deny the flesh," has shifted to a set of unrealizable imperatives for the future, "Be happy, be fulfilled, be the ideal."

It is very difficult to live all one's life in a way for which one has not been actually prepared, to move in relationships never fully experienced in childhood, raising a spoon to one's lips that has no power to evoke memory by the pressure of the handle on clasping fingers. It is so difficult, especially for new Americans whose parents or grandparents came as strangers to these shores, or for those Americans who have left one class position for another, that most of them meet the problem by denying its existence. The grandparents who did not fit, the parents with the broken accents, are forgotten, denied, obliterated. Shallow pictures closer to the American ideal are pinned, untidily, over the sharp accurate memories of real faces and real postures. The one-room shack, the cold-water flat, the thousand deviations from the American home, are glossed over as accidents, as having nothing to do with the picture of the self. So American soldiers in Europe in World War II looked with perfect honesty at British slums and said, "No American lives like that." The British who had seen pictures of the Dust Bowl, of the Back of the Yards area in Chicago, or the back-streets of Southern cities, quite naturally thought the Americans were lying. But they were not lying, they were simply speaking, as they had always learned to speak, about the ideal, which to them was the truth about Americans. People in America of course live in all sorts of fashions, because they are foreigners, or unlucky, or depraved, or without ambition; people live like that, but *Americans* live in white detached houses with green shutters. Rigidly, blindly, the dream takes precedence. The process of denial is continuous, not one great act of repudiation of a past that has not led to the expected goal, but a day-by-day readjustment from what life actually is to what one believes that life should be. The real living-room, with the worn furniture, the out-of-date crocheted arm-rests, the lamp with the hideous red-and-green tropical scene in bloated opaque glass, become shadowy precursors of this year's model living-room in the department-store down town. The shawl that Grandmother still ties around her head becomes a half-hat, and is transformed completely the year kerchiefs come in style. In and out the imagination weaves between what is experienced with all the senses and found to be wanting and what may be seen in the mind's eye as complete and perfect.

According to their separate constitutions and life experiences, Americans meet these discrepancies in many different ways. There are those who refuse to deny them and who express their burning realization of the discrepancies in American culture either in cynical rejection of all values, or in warm partisanship of minority groups and energetic efforts to improve the community, to make the actual come closer to the ideal. These latter are the liberals, the yeast within the body politic upon which American society relies to keep its dream worth following. Without them, we should be lost. Yet with them, we are uncomfortable. For they draw their strength from the discrepancies in the very heart of

American life. It is not only that we do have glaring social inequalities, fantastic contrasts between rich and poor, unbearable contradictions between ideal and practice, in our society. Other societies have had just such contrasts and faced social change quite differently. But because American character structure is itself built upon the need continually to reconcile the actual present and an unrealizable future—in personal life—the social discrepancies have a peculiar poignancy. When they are pointed out they trouble the hearts and consciences of almost every one: some only stir nervously in their sleep, most put their hands into their pockets to give to some good cause; a few—those with the least capacity to tolerate discrepancies—get angry, defensive, and organize a counterattack. Recent studies at the University of California have explored the contrast in character structure between those who show themselves to be actively partisan towards all underprivileged groups (labour, Jews, Negroes, and so on) and those who show themselves to be actively anti-minority.[2] In the pro-minority group are found those who would be classified as neurotics; that is, those who have faced and incorporated in their own characters the discrepancies present in the culture. In the anti group are found those whose need for consistency is very great, who cannot tolerate ambiguities, who have smoothed out their perception of reality into a tight and perfect structure, which presents a smooth extra-well-adjusted aspect, but which contains the possibility of a psychotic break.[*]

These groups represent three emphases in American life: The liberals have not softened their view of actuality to make themselves live closer to the dream, but instead

[*] The contrasts between these types of character structure, both associated with rapid social change, is probably not confined to the United States, but the special forms they take in the United States are associated with the nature of change in American culture, the combination of a future-oriented ideology and the circumstances of such extensive migration from other cultures, from rural to urban, and from class to class.

sharpen their perceptions and fight to make the dream actuality or give up the battle in despair. The members of the great central majority blur their perceptions, sacrifice the sharpness of their experience, in order to live as if they had been bred to live in the dream. And finally the reactionaries, since they can neither bear the discrepancy nor deal with it by half-measures, deny it altogether and even favour action that will deny it. In personal life, this last group take refuge in projections and phantasies and in blaming other people: in political life they advocate various forms of reaction that would substitute for our traditional political dreams the acceptance of social inequality, racial caste systems, violence and ugliness in social life. The publication of the Kinsey report has brought the contrast among these groups into sharp focus. The reformers redouble their efforts to bring sex education more in line with what the individual will have to face in actual sexual practice; they do not lower their sights, they simply double their efforts. The vast majority stir uneasily at having to face figures that suggest that the discrepancies, which they both practise and deny, are so wide-spread, and so difficult to ignore in cold black print. If a man knows that his own marital infidelity, about which he feels ashamed and guilty, is to be pigeon-holed in a table with percentages of males of his age and class, his whole defence system is threatened, that system in terms of which he has both sinned and repented of his sinning, and so in his repentance made it possible for the unrealized ideal to survive. The reactionary and the cynic make common cause in suggesting that what is, is right, and that laws and ideals should be re-tailored to recognize the deviations and discrepancies between ideal and practice, abandoning the effort towards the ideal.

Any attempt to describe the way in which American boys and American girls become men and women, learn the ways of life that will both express and define their sex rôles and themselves, must take all this into account. To discuss the regularities in the way in which Americans grow up when each grows up differently means devising a way of dealing with these differences. If I describe the non-sensuousness of a Mundugumor child, I can relate it directly to the lack of skin contact with the mother or other human beings, to the harshness of the carrying-basket, to the way in which the child is nursed and carried. But when one discusses the impaired sensuousness of American women, one refers it not to being held or not held as babies, wrapped in burlap or swan's down, stroked or not stroked—for some Americans have each of these experiences—but rather to the gap that all Americans face when the actual sensuous experience must be adjusted to the visual ideal that is held up before them. No sensuous actuality fits the dream, each must be to a degree denied, blurred, or critically rejected, so that one may continue to live. The break in sensuousness is at another level. It is no mere habituation to harsh surfaces, followed by avoidance of any soft cheek-to-cheek contact, no mere puritanical denial of the body, no mere smothering against a mother's too-insistent breast. All these occur, all these will turn up in the detailed case-history of the psychiatric case-worker or the psychoanalyst, but when we speak of the lack of skin sensuousness of Americans as a group, the non-sensuousness upon which the European comments, the non-sensuousness that makes looks and appearance loom so large in love and love-making, the description moves away from the particular experience of each American to the regularities that appear in the experiences of practically all Americans as they approximate a sex ideal for which each lacks the particular necessary antecedent behaviour.

Then there is a second way in which it is possible to discuss sex rôles in America and relate them back to childhood experiences. This time to childhood experiences that

most Americans who live them out never had. Human
beings are able to feel, in some degree, what must have
been the forerunners in experience of any present state.
We look at a ravaged face and reconstruct the grief and
shock that laid those lines down; we sense in a frightened
and truculent child the harsh treatment which made that
child so wary; we see behind the softness and relaxation in
a woman's body the love-making that left her thus. So
around the pictures of the ideal American man and woman
there form in the minds of all the actual men and women
pictures of what kind of experiences in childhood and youth
could have led to this finished result. Behind that school-
girl complexion, for example, could be phantasied many
sorts of conditions—a baby's face gently washed with a
supersoft wash-cloth, fresh air blowing through a window,
a steaming pan on the radiator that kept the room atmos-
phere from being too dry, creams "blended by our own
secret formula," lotions for the little skin protective against
sunburn and windburn, a regular digestion ensuring that
the body never keeps a bit of poisoning waste product
beyond the allotted hour; by a diet properly compounded
of protein breads, free of too many sweets and fats, con-
sisting of things that are good for you and good to eat too;
sheets of soft material laundered with soaps that contain
no harsh chemical; a sex life free from those indulgences
which are still believed somehow to affect the complexion.
Out of the procedures of the moment recommended for
the care of infant and child and maiden, out of the threats
and warnings and promises of the advertisements, out of
the dark admonitions of childhood, a picture is fashioned
of how one should treat one's daughter so that when she
grows up she will have a complexion as faultless as that of
the girl on the magazine cover. Current practice, the scientifically supported dicta of pediatrician, dietitian, physical
therapist, and health-educator, the styles set by current

fiction and movies and radio, the underlying assumptions and innuendoes of the advertisements—these coalesce to form an imaginary past for the pictured ideal, the imaginary future. And so in the way in which the mother washes the soft pink cheeks of her baby-girl a new relationship is established between the way she treats the child and what the child will become that is quite different from the repetitious, faithful child-rearing of old and settled societies. The methods that the two mothers use will be diverse, contradictory, and doubtfully related to the attainment of a beautiful complexion, but they will have in common the desire to give the child the complexion; the expressed purpose is a sort of common denominator of the different practices.

And finally, Americans are continually presented with a picture of how Americans are brought up, make love, marry, beget children, that is itself the ideal for which their training has so doubtfully and unreliably fitted them. While we cannot follow back each American man and woman through all the separate and contradictory steps that brought them to adulthood, we can follow with fair accuracy the picture of this assumed development—the recommended, applauded, underlined pattern assumed by film and educator, radio commentator and advertiser. This is the picture to which adults are both readjusting their memories of their own past and are attempting to approximate in relation to their children. It is possible to describe the routine of a baby's day, in that little white house with green shutters in which hardly anybody really lives, or the words of the proposal between the boy in the faultlessly fitting white flannels and the girl in the perfect date-dress, the way the new father expresses his feeling about his new baby-boy. In this idealized picture there will be gaps, for there are parts of life that are never mentioned in popular or even in fine art. "Why," asks the uninhibited American child of 1949, "does

no one ever go to the bathroom in a book?" These gaps
can only be very partially filled for any culture, even when
it is a homogeneous and relatively unchanging one. But the
significance of the gaps, of the ignorance that each woman
has about the sex life of each other woman, of the ignorance
of any birth except the delivery of one's own child, of the
appearance of any sex organs except those of lover or husband or wife, of the disturbing phantasies of the woman
next door—or do other people ever think of such things?—
these can be described and placed in their context to help
build up an understanding of the sexes in our changing
American culture.

So in attempting to apply anthropological insights to the
problems of the two sexes in America, we shift our observations to different levels, study the regularities among the
great number of apparent sharp contrasts and differences,
and describe the impact of the ideal upon American expectations.

XIII

EXPECTED CHILDHOOD EXPERIENCE

THERE IS NO MAGIC IN AMERICA TO DETERMINE THE SEX OF an unborn child. Parents may refuse to consider a boy's name or a girl's name, or, following out the logic of the idea that carrying an umbrella will prevent rain, consider only the name of the sex that they do not want. There are no social reasons why one sex should be preferred above the other; women are not more honoured as mothers of sons, men are not regarded as less virile for begetting only daughters. True, an attempt of a Girl Scout leader to organize a group of "Dads of Daughters *Only*" in a Far Western community met with only shamefaced half-acceptance; but it is doubtful whether any American would be pleased to belong to any group limited by the word "only," even "Owners of Rolls Royce Only." The expectation that a son will carry on his father's life-work is so slight that the emphasis of other societies on the need for an heir to the land or the family craft tradition is lacking.

The difference in American life is simply between having

a child and not having a child, and a caustic critic has labelled the one child of middle-class families as a "status child," a child that merely gives the parents the status of *having had* a child. For this status, the sex of the child is irrelevant. There is a greater tendency to name the son for the father than to name the daughter for the mother, thus perpetuating our patrilineal tradition, reinforced by the complications of having to refer to the mother as "big" or "old" Susan, neither adjective being attractive to women. The rather widespread preference that the first-born be a male is heavily offset by the frequent picture in advertisements of the American family with two children, the girl older than the boy. Little sisters remain a masculine daydream, counterpoised against the general feeling that sisters in America are always big sisters to their brothers, more likely to represent law and order, prunes and prisms, privilege and manipulation, than to be tender little creatures deserving of chivalry and guidance.

But there is a feeling that the sexes should be mixed. People who have only boys or only girls are pitied, and there is always a danger that the third or fourth child of a run of girls or boys will feel that it has disappointed its parents. Thus the very simple accidents of sex distribution inside any family give a structure within which a child can feel unwanted, and specifically unwanted because of its sex. Ineffective contraception and unsuccessful amateur attempts at abortion lurk in the background of many Americans' pictures of the beginning of their lives. To the bitterness of feeling "I was only an accident," "I was an unwanted child," "I would never have been here at all if some one hadn't been too lazy to go out to the drug-store," can always be added, "They only wanted another child if it was a girl," "They never would have bothered to have another child if they had been sure it would be a boy." The age-old intractability of the sex of a child has ruined dynasties and bedevilled the painstaking social arrangements of many peoples. In the United States it provides one facet of the possible acceptance or condemnation of one's own past—either "I was the sex they wanted," or "I wasn't." Undoubtedly, it is the rejecting parent who tells the child that another sex was hoped for, but because there is some rejection at some time in almost every parent, even without being explicitly told the child may construct from the general picture all about it in society a sense of having failed to meet its parent's expectations.* Not every child has the security to say, like the little girl who, after hearing her mother say she had always wanted twins, said to herself, rocking dreamily: "Oh, I wanted to be twins, but I couldn't be twins, so I just ordered me."

The sex of the child, marked by a name, is the way in which the fact of birth is fixed in the minds of friends and relatives who have not seen the child. Before birth, hopeful mothers may use the planned name for the baby, but only after birth does the child move, and at once, from "it" to a named, fully sexed individual. In Bali, a new baby is not named, and is referred to by a name like Mouse or Caterpillar, little interest being taken in its sex except in those cases where the birth of a boy makes the father sociologically safe (that is, if he has already had a daughter, a son is absolutely necessary). But the sociological service or disservice that the baby's sex does to the father is on the whole divorced from the child itself, which is essentially sexless until its naming ceremony at one hundred and ten days. But American practice leaves no room for attained sex; the child is absolutely and completely named and identified from birth. The recurrent sentimental colour-note, blue

---

* This may explain in part the rather surprising results in the *Fortune* poll in the autumn of 1946, in which 3.3% of men said that if born again they would like to be born as women.[1]

for a boy and pink for a girl, runs through announcements, gifts, and nursery decoration.

Meanwhile, the child's body is undergoing a long series of experiences that will influence each sex's view of its own body, of the body of the opposite sex, and of the relations between them. Birth in America is ideally in a hospital. More and more frequently actually in a hospital. This means that but for a few exceptional cases, the father is absent and the mother has been given over to the care of professionals, doctors and nurses. For months before the birth she has been preparing to leave her home and her husband, not for the home of her parents or her brother, as in many primitive societies, but for a strange, segregated spot, where she and many other women unknown to her will lie together, giving birth among strangers. When the baby is born, it is born against the force of gravity, on a delivery table designed not to let the child's own weight assist the birth, but rather to facilitate the ministrations of the obstetrician. Its first cry is often induced by a vigorous slap. The mother deep under an anaesthetic does not hear this cry, although recent research has suggested that the cry has a function in making her uterus contract. The infant is taken away to a row of cribs; its lips, ready for sucking, are left to press helplessly against each other; crying brings no surcease. The primary bodily capabilities with which the child enters the world are initially unrewarded. It can suck, but no breast is given it; it can cry for help, but no one holds it close and feeds it. Its body is wrapped completely in soft cloth, the first lesson in expecting cloth to intervene between one body and the next. The second lesson will come when it is taken to its mother, at the proper hour for its birthweight, neatly laid out on a moving table, and placed against her fully clothed body, with the carefully sterilized breast exposed just a few inches, and persuaded to suck. This persuasion is often a grim business; the nurse knows how to take the baby, who very often is so exhausted with hunger that it no longer wants to eat, and holding it by the scruff of the neck, put it on the mother's breast. Whether it eats or not, it is supposed to be taken away again after the appointed number of minutes. The mother is left—sometimes with nipples sore from its hungry little jaws, sometimes worried and engorged because the baby would not eat, having very doubtfully enjoyed the routinized, cloth-enveloped experience. During the nine or ten days that follow, the mother handles her baby clothed, and only at regular hours. The father does not handle it at all. Breast feeding is frequently abandoned altogether, and by the time the child goes home, the mother, if not the baby, has learned that contacts between mother and child have a certain form. The failure of milk, the failure of the baby to nurse, the obstetrical and pediatric pressure towards at least supplementary feeding, are all natural enough in a setting where the new child is treated as if its health and well-being depended on the machine-like precision with which it is fed, and on what it is fed. The mother learns impatience with her milk, which is too rich or too weak, too much or too little, pouring through nipples that are inverted or sore or otherwise unobliging. She can turn with some relief to the bottle and the formula, the reliable rubber nipple with a hole that can be enlarged with a pin, the graduated bottle into which just the right formula, at just the right temperature, can be measured. No recalcitrant individual unregulated human body here, to endanger her baby's gain in weight, the chief criterion of its healthful existence. At once, or in a few weeks, most American mothers reject their own bodies as a source of food for their children, and in accepting the mechanical perfection of a bottle, reaffirm to themselves, and in the way they handle their babies, that the baby too will be much better the more it learns to use the beautifully mechanical bottle—accurately, on time, in the right amounts—the more it accepts an external rhythm, and abandons its own peculiar rhythms that it brought into the world. For the primary learning experience that is the physical prototype of the sex relationship—a complementary relation between the body of the mother and the body of the child—is substituted a relationship between the child and an object, an object that imitates the breast, but which is not handled as either part of the mother or part of the baby. If the mother holds the baby as she gives it the bottle (a practice that has been recommended as a way of giving the child more of what is inaccurately called body contact), the bottle in most instances becomes an implement, an extension of her hand so that it holds food, rather than an extension of her breast. At what age the child distinguishes the exact difference between a glass bottle and a rubber nipple, loose in space, and a human breast we do not know, but the mother experiences the difference from the start, and her experience is available to the child, in her voice, in her hands, in the very tempo of her being. She is not giving the child herself; she is faithfully, efficiently providing the child with a bottle, external to both of them, substituting for a direct relationship a relationship mediated by an object.

During the first months of its life, the mother is continuingly concerned with the health and growth of the child, to feed it the right foods, to bathe it correctly, to keep its skin from being chafed, to keep it from being overexcited, to keep it from catching cold, to keep it away from all infections of any sort. Its bath is a ritual that may dominate the whole day, but it is a ritual of anxious concern rather than of pleasure. American babies probably get as perfect physical care as any infants in the world, the infant death-rate steadily decreases, babies are, on the average, plumper, and show fewer signs of vitamin deficiency. The well-fed, well-bathed, well-powdered, well-clothed baby lies in its crib and drinks its well-pasteurized milk out of its well-sterilized bottle. After crying, perhaps, because no one will spoil it by picking it up, it falls into a properly regulated sleep, one nap on one side, the next on the other, to keep the shape of its head. Meanwhile it is weighed and watched and assessed. It is fitting into the norms—whether these be the Gesell norms used by the reading mother or the neighbourhood gossip of the unliterate. Its mouth, which has never—or only a few times—fastened with eagerness on its mother's breast, must be watched for the first signs of teeth arriving earlier or later than the average. Then there is the matter of thumb-sucking. Will the child suck its thumb? The very modern pediatrician may recommend a pacifier—the same old pacifier that still lingers on the back-street, in the little overcrowded, littered neighbourhood drug-stores—but if he recommends it, it will be so that the child shall *not* suck its thumb. He may even press the pacifier on the contented occasionally breast-fed baby, because he is convinced that satisfying the sucking reflex in this way will prevent thumb-sucking. The taboo on thumb-sucking is phrased in terms of health and good looks, but principally health. It will spoil the child's breathing, ruin the shape of the teeth. The mouth is primarily for taking in the right food, and must be kept clean. No rubber toys from the floor, no grimy little thumb. And children fall asleep hugging a bit of an old toy dog or a broken doll, dependent for comfort and pleasure upon objects that are parts of no one's body, neither of their own nor their mothers'.

In these early months, the genitals are kept specially clean; there must be no irritation, for irritation would enhance the child's consciousness of them and might lead to masturbation.* Meanwhile the child is actively encour-

---

* The most significant comment on the attempts of some child specialists to break down the masturbation taboo is the present-day aberration in which parents and teachers have shifted from the taboo on masturbation to an

aged to grow, to learn to move, to use its hands and feet, to follow things with its eyes, to respond to sounds. Regardless of sex, particularly regardless of sex because there is such a slight particular nexus between the mother's body and the infant's, the child is encouraged to be active and vigorous. As the mother bathes her child, she puts out of her mind the conspicuous differences in sex. The overt behaviour of most adults makes no open distinction between the treatment of boys and that of girls. It is probably always there, for quite small children show marked differences in their treatment of members of their own sex and of the opposite sex; but all such distinctions remain below the surface as long as the child is an infant in its mother's hands. In the ritual of dutiful mother-love, there is no place allowed for differential tickling or teasing. This would be disapprovingly classed as "over-stimulation."

So boy and girl alike learn that their mouths, like their hands, are something with which you take—active body parts that come in contact with the outside world for a purpose. Mouths are not a way of being with some one, but rather a way of meeting an impersonal environment. Mother is there to put things—bottles, spoons, crackers, teethers—into your mouth. Deep in the child's inarticulate picture of the relationships between men and women lies the image of his original satisfaction through having things put into his mouth. Later, when the American soldier goes abroad, puzzled foreigners speculating on American morale will decide it is orange-juice or Coca-Cola or some other familiar item of American food or drink that is basically important. For the complementary relationship of the child at the breast is substituted a pattern that can be easily made an alternating one—"Give baby a cracker," "Baby, give

almost obsessive insistence on it. It seems doubtful which method is more guaranteed to extinguish the child's simple exploratory pleasure in its own body.

mother a cracker"—in which a satisfying object intervenes between the two, and deep structural differences between their masculine and feminine rôles is lost. Child-studies in the United States have noted that both boys and girls propose to their mothers at a certain age, with a suggestion that it is a mistake to over-interpret the small boy's proposal as sexual, for does not the small girl propose too? But what does the proposal lead into? "When I grow up I'll marry you, Mother, and buy you a beautiful house, and a great big automobile and a fur coat." The game of "I give you something and you give me something" is not necessarily cross-sexed when it is based on bottles and zwieback rather than upon the deeply specific experience of the breast.

In the second year comes the next piece of learning, for boy and girl alike—learning to control elimination. Here the differences in structure between boy and girl intrude more sharply on the mother's attention. "Boys are harder to train"—with an imputation of something recalcitrantly masculine. But also, "Well, it's easier to take a boy out all afternoon in the park. You can send a boy behind a tree," which is echoed later in the small girl's comment when she first saw a little boy urinating, "Wouldn't that be a convenient thing to take on a picnic!" The beginning of an egoistic valuation of the male organ begins here, as an organ of which the female body has no counterpart and which is capable of doing specific things, and sets the stage for the little girl's envy that will frequently appear a little later— envy that is like her envy of another child's bicycle or roller-skates, an active seeking envy for something you can do something with rather than the deep narcissistic wound described in classical neuroses cases of European background. Later it will be expressed most vividly in one form in women's insistence on driving their own motor cars, and in another form in the cult of the high breasts and legs, one aspect emphasizing the activity and power points, the other, body parts to be admired and valued. In adulthood the typical American woman will walk like some one fully equipped, neither trotting along behind her spouse with steps appropriate to such a different creature, nor using her way of walking to induce some male to complete her. The American woman may believe that she needs something called *sex* satisfaction—which one can need the way the healthy person "needs exercise"—and she may want a husband, but neither in walk nor in manner does she suggest that she is one part and a conflicting part of a possible union of two persons.

But the little boy and girl, being "trained" by anxious and dutiful mothers, learn other things besides the differences in their body structure. They learn that the act of defecation in the right place, at the right time, is good, while the products of elimination are so bad that if they are kept in the body beyond their proper time, they will cause all sorts of troubles. Learning to tell Mother in time becomes of heart-breaking importance to the small child, especially to the small boy, to whom bladder control is more complex than for the girl. Foresight rather than impulse, anxious planning to deal with unforeseen situations, long automobile rides, street-car rides, visits to the moving pictures, or a visit to Grandma's—all these have to be planned for and dealt with. Failure to remember, to tell Mother in time, is punished by a withdrawal of maternal love, a love that the child has already learned is conditional upon performance. "Mother loves her little boy when he remembers." So the child learns that it is very important to eliminate, and it is important to think about it enough so that there will be no accidents. American streets contrast with the street arrangements of France or Italy, more indulgent to immediate impulses in males, more insistent that female impulses should be house-bound. Public latrines in the United States are there for emergencies, for the people who failed to plan, who got caught out in a traffic jam—not for the ungrudged relief of impulse.

This association of elimination and virtuous healthful behaviour is congruent with the peculiar character of the American bathroom, in which the utensils for washing, bathing, and eliminating are all grouped together, and are often used communally. Other cultures have been much more obsessed by a repudiation of the products of elimination, by disgust and uncleanliness reactions, and have placed the bathing-place far away. But the American inclusion of elimination in the ritual of health has meant replacing the dank, unattractive latrine by maximumly efficient and pleasant plumbing, plumbing that whisks away the products, now properly eliminated, and leaves one triumphant, in good shape for the day's work.

The enormous importance the mother attaches to toilet-training makes this period one in which the child forms a sort of archetype of what the body can do. In the earlier stage, it learned to take in, now it has learned to give out, to keep nothing inappropriate or harmful. Modern architecture spares no effort to make the entire process sanitary, attractive-looking, and free from discomfort. The clean white-tiled restaurant and the clean white-tiled bathroom are both parts of the ritual, with the mother's voice standing by, saying: "If every rule of health is complied with, then you can enjoy life."

But while the mother so faithfully avoids showing any favouritism as between girl and boy, and through the helpful intermediacy of objects is able to treat them almost exactly alike—with an occasional sigh of weariness over the boy's greater intractability, his lower amenability to the pattern—the father does differentiate his behaviour; he plays up to his rough-housing little boy and pays mild courtship to his little girl, selecting gentler games. Older boys accentuate the father's recognition of the difference in sex, poking and prodding, teasing and daring, the small boy into truculence and retaliation, ignoring small girls as not their game. With enormous variations in class and region, there is still a tendency for little boys to learn about maleness by a vis-à-vis rough-house with their fathers and older brothers that is carried over later into the approved rough-housing, jocose insult, and endless hearty banter of male groups. From his mother he has learned that rewards—in the shape of food and praise—come when he grows, is healthy, achieves, learns independence, control of his body, skill in the management of things. If he does what she asks, she will reward him. Later, as a husband, his rewards will come when he earns a good living, fixes the screen-door on Saturday, and takes his wife out to the movies. Without his mother's approval he is miserable, worried, fearful of loss of love. But from his father he learns that relationships with men require putting forth all your strength, taking buffets good-humouredly, getting in and pitching, small as you are —and that this is fun. Both father and mother demand that he should act up to—and a little beyond—his full strength, and he is always a little anxious for fear the strength that is demanded isn't there. Both father and mother hope that he won't be a baby and that he won't be a sissy, that he will make good at school, in sports, and later on in his job. All three hopes have an underlying note of fear of failure in them.

Meanwhile the little girl learns about her sex in two ways. She too must not be a cry-baby or a sissy, she must never act the way a boy acts who is acting like a girl. And she learns from her father how to play the only game he knows how to play with women, the game in which he teasingly asks and she teasingly refuses. It is significant that for American girls the older man is characteristically the victim, the sugar-daddy, rather than the exploiter. Fathers are soft towards their daughters, likely to let them stay up late and to buy them extra candy. Mothers have to be continually watchful to see that daughters aren't spoiled. So the small girl learns that she must manage her father in spite of what another woman does. This is a lightly played conflict for the little girl, but blossoms into a much sharper conflict at adolescence when girls see their mothers as interfering with their relationships to boys.

Meanwhile the prohibition against being a sissy leaves the girl with a very confusing picture. She is not told not to behave like a boy, not to be a tomboy. This admonition of girls, which was so prevalent even two generations ago, while it angered the active and especially gifted girl, was at least clear and simple. To be a tomboy meant to run wild, climb trees, steal apples from orchards, fight, play boys' games, rather than stay closer to home, keep one's hair-ribbons on, play dolls and house, and sit quietly with legs crossed, bursting into tears on appropriate occasions. Conversely, for the boys it was fairly simple to be told not to play with dolls, or fuss about having one's clothes clean and neat, or run away from open encounters with other boys. As long as each sex was asked to avoid the well-defined pattern of the other sex, a few members of each sex suffered, sometimes acutely, and grew up to be misfits and inverts, misanthropists and hermits, but the majority were able to adjust to the pattern. Women wept and fainted, men swore and stamped, but did not weep. Men sat sprawled in any position, women demurely crossed their ankles. Men had jobs and made money and took over all that was rough, dangerous, and likely to sully their women—being voted as the sex better fitted to cope with all dirt except the fluff under the bed and the grime behind little boys' ears.

But to-day groups of little girls and boys of kindergarten age face each other with the same stance, the same gleam in their eyes, the same readiness to fight or to avoid fighting.

Both sexes are told not to fight, and then boys are watched very anxiously, girls almost as anxiously, to see if they show signs of being quitters, of not being able to take it. At this age, the little girl appears to be given by her upbringing greater resources than her brother. Her relationships to her father are both less exacting and more immediately rewarding than are her brother's relationships to his mother. We know from other cultures that the mother who bows her head before the lordly maleness of her four-year-old son encourages his assurance as a male, and—to the degree that she serves as a model for her small daughter—instils into the daughter negative attitudes towards the female rôle. But in America, the little girl is flattered and spoiled by an indulgent, non-disciplinary father, and emerges very sure of herself indeed. Her mother's rôle is one of demandingness towards husband and son. This is not a rôle which need make a little girl feel that she is—by her very sex—condemned to a weak or an inferior rôle. Her brother is told to "be nice to his sister," and the sister is never told to polish his boots or wait upon him because he is a model of her future lord and master.

The plot that Wolfenstein and Leites have identified in the American movies of the middle forties comes out clearly. Boys expect their fathers to be either on their side, or else they are wicked—and may be completely defeated without guilt later in life. Girls expect their fathers, and later their husbands, to require a lot of working on; no victory is a final one, but must be re-enacted the next day. Boys see their mothers, and so ultimately their wives, as the persons from whom they get the assurance that they are good. These assurances are as necessary as the bread and jam eaten in the kitchen on a cold winter afternoon, but they are bought at a price, at the price of eschewing all the pleasure of irresponsibility, untidiness, undirected libidinal behaviour—in brief, by giving up going fishing. Meanwhile in the six-to-twelve age-group, some of the old cross-sex hostilities still survive. Boys find that the only way of differentiating themselves from girls whose tastes and behaviour are virtually identical is to have nothing to do with them. The boys' gang of the American small town at the beginning of the century had as a basis a contempt for girls who couldn't do anything that was any fun and just sat around and played silly games. The boys' gang of the forties is a desperate defensive measure against being sissies—which, loosely interpreted, means being like girls. But the girls are also busy not being sissies, roller-skating, coasting, skiing, exercising their long legs, which they no longer need keep demurely crossed. And for them the best way not to be a sissy—that is, not to behave like a boy behaving like a girl—is of course to keep on associating with boys. A generation ago, little girls had daintily set tea-tables to protect against rough boys who might break their dolls and trample their tea-sets—and mothers reared in an earlier era still give little girls tea-tables and suggest that it would be much nicer to have birthday-parties without the boys. But as sex models filter down to younger children through the behaviour of adolescents, through the increasing number of mothers who were themselves brought up not to be sissies, there is less acceptance on the part of the little girls of the dolls' tea-party at which boys as rough intruders give them practice in behaviour that would once have been called a flutter in the dovecotes. No one, least of all the men whom they will later attract and marry, wants fluttering females who blush and simper and haven't any "line." Characteristically, blushing is disappearing in its old form, in which children blushed when asked to perform before adults, and girls and women blushed when asked to do anything that was regarded as appropriate for boys and men only. "Look at her, she's blushing," becomes a way of saying—in mixed company—that she is actively enjoying some bit of flirtatious exhibitionism. "Something I'd do when I'm feeling pretty happy and confident," comments one twenty-year-old.

So we have a series of changes taking place as boys and girls are brought up more and more alike, playing the same games, efficient and competent in the use of their bodies. The break-down of the boys' and girls' gangs into a two-sex dating pattern is occurring earlier and earlier. "Last year," say the harassed teachers, "it was the seventh grade, this year it's started in the sixth." For the old institutionalized hostilities of broken dolls and pulled braids, girls' tears and boyish pranks, the new pre-puberty dating pattern is being substituted, doubtfully with less hostility, but with the hostility very differently phrased. During the very age when most of our comparative material suggests that boys are least ready to engage in sex activity in which they have to take the initiative, they are being drawn into a life that mimics the sex activities of late adolescence.

XIV

PRE-COURTSHIP BEHAVIOUR AND

ADULT SEX DEMANDS

THE DATING BEHAVIOUR OF AMERICAN ADOLESCENTS THAT IS held up in movies and radio serials, in advertisements that include recipes for correct behaviour, in *Your Manners Are Showing*, is of course middle-class behaviour. The corner boys, the boys who leave school in the seventh grade at fourteen, rural boys who leave school early to work on the farm, still tend to gang together until they are ready for complete sex activity. They continue to regard women as primarily there for their physical gratification before and outside of marriage, to bear their children, cook their meals, and sleep with them after marriage. Their habits, and the habits of the girls whom they will later pursue, and perhaps marry, are very different from the stylized dating pattern presented in popular art. But just as clothes are becoming stylized in so many prices that the poorest working-girl has a dress of cut, if not of make, like that of the much richer girl, so the styles set by the middle class spread. They inform the day-dreams and minister to the discontents of the groups who do not share in them. There are fewer first-generation immigrants among the lower economic groups who insist on chaperonage for their daughters until marriage, and more cheap hotels at which dances can be held that ape the elaborate affairs of the groups who make the society columns. The continued mechanization of such activities as "coming out," the shift of parties from homes in which there are no longer servants to hotels where gate-crashers are so likely that devices once limited to the tough Saturday-night dance in a mining town will now occur in almost the best circles, branding the couple who have once obtained admission—all these narrow the gap between the social styles of the underprivileged and the social styles of the privileged. This does not mean that all the nuances are not still there, that the girl who paid $100 for her dress cannot accurately gauge the dress of the girl across the aisle in the movie as having cost $14.78. But they are both in the same movie theatre, sitting in the same-priced seats, and a drawing of their silhouettes would betray no difference. The most élite may shy away from the word "date," but they weep as hard when they sit alone on a Saturday night. So it is not that we are getting less snobbish, or insisting less on class lines, but simply that the differentiations among the classes are getting smaller all the time. Factory girl, society girl, daughter of a sharecropper who can borrow the copy of *Life* she cannot afford to buy, all react to the dress that is described as "date bait"—one shudders over the phrase—"that we wouldn't use," and the other two ruefully compare the prospects in clothes and the behaviour of possible escorts next Saturday night. But the image sinks deep into their minds, to play a different rôle there, of course, from the rôle it plays in the life of the girl who lives completely the part that is described in the picture.

With the establishment of dating in a group of junior-high-school boys and girls,[1] the old battles for father's approval and favours, for mother's approval and favours, the old need for reassurance, crop up again, needs that were fostered in the early years when both parents worried as to whether their children were going to amount to something. In many of the societies I have described earlier in this book children are permitted a long surcease from sexual competition while they live in one-sex children's groups, slowly ripening into adults. It is perhaps very significant that a most conspicuous division is found between groups of small boys and girls in those societies where the final relationship between men and women is most specifically sexual, Samoa and Bali, and least cast in terms of assertiveness, aggression, rivalry, and the like. Parental love and parental withdrawal of love have not been organized around their children's developing assertiveness and aggressiveness, but have instead been attuned to their bodies, bodies seen as bodies of boys and girls who will later be men and women, sexed as men and women. From this demand on their sexuality, far too great to be manageable for boys, and too early to be socially safe for girls, the children withdraw, to wait until they are old enough to re-enter the picture, and find lovers for themselves on the model they have learned from their parents.

But American parents are not primarily concerned with relationships to their children as members of one sex or the other, little creatures with bodies who are responding to the touch of their parents' hands or the light in their parents' eyes. Primarily they are concerned with their children as persons, as little potential bundles of high achievement, who must be given the very best chance, the best education, the best habit-training, for success in life. Life is a race that both boys and girls must run clear-eyed, sweet-breathed, well-bathed, with their multiplication tables in their heads, and feet that come down accurately on the mark. It is a race they must enter as soon as possible, telephoning at four, handling money, exercising and exhibiting competence in adult patterns.

In other societies growing-up is a somewhat frightening business to the child who thinks of it as taking on the bodily rôle of an adult, to the boy who must become a lover of a grown woman and the father of children, to the girl who is to become a lover and a mother. As the small girl inspects her diminutive body, or the boy his embryonic genitals, they know that they must wait, give up the play of being Mother's boy and Father's girl—which can never be anything but an unsatisfactory, one-sided game—and wait, wait for ten years or so, until they are old enough for such things. On the whole, the more specifically sexual the adult relationship is going to be—which can include of course a view of marriage that insists on great sexual avoidance without substituting any other content—the more the children brought up to see adulthood in terms of such specific sexuality seem to need a period of withdrawal, to grow in peace, undisturbed by demands that they cannot meet. It is probably correct to discuss latency, the period between childhood sexuality focussed on the parent and the stirring of adolescent sex awareness, as a specialized phenomenon of *sexual* maturation, which can be muted or enhanced, depending upon the social arrangements.

But in America, with the greater emphasis of the parents on children as achieving personalities, lightly differentiated in behaviour and expected character structure by their sex, lightly anchored to the model of the same-sex parent, there is less and less place for latency. Growing-up does not mean to the American boy taking on the responsibilities and the trials of full sexual behaviour. Growing-up means wearing long pants like his elder brother, driving a car, earning money, having a job, being his own boss, and taking a girl to the movies. A little petting, certainly, a lot of petting maybe with the kind of girl whom nobody would take out for anything else, but no one expects the imitations of adult behaviour that are involved in dating to have results, either in a lifelong union or in pregnancy. Instead it is just part of the competitive game in which boys and girls demonstrate their popularity by being seen with popular members of the other sex.[2] Success with the girls, if you wear the right hat or bathe with the right soap, is part of the personality of the young man who will sooner or later be called into the head office and told he has been appointed to that coveted junior-executive job. But just as the personnel manager will be glad to know that the young employee is a good date, he will frown upon the same-aged youth who has a reputation for active premarital sex relations. The love and success for which both boys and girls work and dream, groom their hair, clean their finger nails, study the etiquette books, save up their pocket-money and earnings, has extremely little to do with sex, or with the body.

The game is described as dating; boys take out girls, girls have to be asked, boys have to ask, both must dress correctly according to the adolescent styles of the moment, the date must be conducted in some way so that it can be known to the rest of the group—otherwise it doesn't count. The long association of courtship and costume through the ages rather obscures the issue here. Because dating and dressing are so closely associated, the assumption is that it is courtship. But men have worn war-paint to impress their enemies or their male comrades, and women have done battle against their own sex in pearls and ostrich-feathers, before now. The clothes, the flowers, the dancing, are all part of the game, but they are to be equated neither with courtship nor with behaviour that is primarily sexual, although the pattern of dating does in the end have a profound effect on the later relationships of men and women in America.

That dating is primarily a competitive game in which publicly affirmed popularity is the prize can be illustrated by considering the behaviour of those who do not date, but withdraw, sometimes quite early in adolescence, to "going steady." For here we find two groups: young people whose stirring sexuality has been genuinely aroused so that they may be said to be "in love" with each other, and who find the game of dating meaningless because they prefer each other's company; and young people who, without being in love, depend on each other for protection, the unpopular girl and the unpopular boy, concealing their failure in the popularity game by pretending to prefer each other. Outside the dating group are much larger peripheral groups: girls and boys who are so physically immature and dysplastic that they feel disqualified for this game where mimic physical readiness for sex is expected; girls and boys who lack the money and the clothes; girls and boys who have such a deep interest in something else that it protects them from wanting to spend their time in a game that is to them irrelevant. But for those who are allowed to play, the deep fear of deviance—natural offspring of our hurriedly assembled and slightly learned cultural patterns—keeps them in the game, demonstrating that they are successful in the way in which their adolescent social world, and every magazine they pick up, and their parents' expectation, decrees that they shall be.

But what effect on the actual sex behaviour of Americans does the dating pattern have? In the first place, it defines the relationship between a male and a female as situational. You "have a date," you "go out with a date," you "groan because there isn't a decent date in town." A situation defined as containing a girl—or boy—of the right social background, the right degree of popularity, a little higher than your own, is what one sighs for, or boasts about. Now superficially this may not look very different from the "girl in a punt" of English undergraduate day-dreams, or the "girl and a full moon" recurrent in romantic song. But the boy who longs for a date is not longing for a girl. He is longing to be in a situation, mainly public, where he will be seen by others to have a girl, and the right kind of girl, who dresses well and pays attention. He takes her out as he takes out his new car, but more impersonally, because the car is his for good but the girl is his only for the evening. This long practice in longing for and getting satisfaction from situations that are in themselves quite contentless will stand the American in good stead later, as he adapts to the demands of a new job, or learns to forget the companions on the old job because they are no longer part of the group to which he is expected to respond with continuous stylized warmth.[3] During the last war English observers were confused by the apparent contradiction between the American soldiers' emphasis on the buddy, so grievously exemplified in the break-downs that followed a buddy's death, and the results of detailed inquiry that showed how transitory these buddy relationships were. It was found that men actually accepted their buddies as derivative from their outfit, and from accidents of association, rather than because of any special personality characteristics capable of ripening into real friendship. But the buddy, like the date, is a function of a situation within which behaviour is defined. Nor does this mean that a date that goes badly cannot cause much heart-ache, for obligations to those with whom one finds oneself situationally paired are felt as very important by American young people. Letting your date down is not any the less heinous because you have never met him or her before. In fact it is worse, because he or she is more helpless, less able to relate your behaviour to some regular and forgivable idiosyncrasy, and so take it *impersonally*.

Patterns of behaviour learned during dating not only prepare American boys and girls for a situational approach to personal relationships, but they are significant because this is the first occasion in the life of Americans since the blue or pink ribbon on the rattle or the baby-carriage cover in which the emotional counterpart of sex membership has been positively emphasized. The fear that the boy will be a sissy is, of course, always present. But in many societies, breast-fed babies whose mothers react to their boys with a direct realization that the boy is of the opposite sex, the girl of their own sex, the primary learning about sex rôle comes very early, and remains indisputable through life. Such learning is in a deeply emotional situation, and the feeding situation is a prototype of the adult sex relationship that is to come later, a prototype not only in complementary design, but also in emotional tone. As the mother is teasing, permissive, provocative, yielding, passionately changeable, so later will the wife or lover be, and so later will the husband or lover want his wife to be. But in the American pattern, the treatment of both children as persons, and the intervention of things—bottles, cribs, clothes—between the bodies of the parents and the bodies of the children, all serve to mute this original learning. Where sex differences are emphasized, the emphasis is upon assertion and aggression rather than upon repression of physical feeling. Instead of the situation in which children's sex membership is very conspicuous at four and then held in steady abeyance until puberty, we have the situation of muted childhood sexuality and sense of one's own sex, followed by a high development of play-acting in early puberty, instigated neither by an upsurge of glandular activity nor by memories of childhood's bodily delights, but instead by the demands of the dating game. So children are drawn into the dating game not by their bodies, but by their assertiveness, their desire to achieve, to succeed, to be popular. Yet the game is cast in highly sexual terms; breasts and legs are emphasized for girls, all sorts of trappings of maleness are emphasized for boys. An accentuation of one's sex membership is phrased as a counter in the game, and sex becomes a secondary thing, a way of getting what one wants, of arriving where one wants to get.

The girl learns that both in the office and on the dance-floor, the more attractive she makes herself, the better chance she has for the next promotion or the right marriage. And she learns that attractiveness is something that can be worked at, on which judgment and money and skill can be used. A girl has no excuse for relaxing in despair because initially she lacks a good figure or the right-shaped eye-brows. Proper diet or a carefully cut girdle will correct the one, proper cosmetics the other. In one of the famous charm schools, at graduation a "before" picture of each graduate, overweight, dowdy, badly dressed, is thrown on the screen, and then the "after" girl herself, slim, svelte, perfectly dressed and made-up, pushes back the black-velvet curtain. And the applause goes not to the most beautiful, but to the girl who has shown the greatest improvement. The boy who refuses to take out a girl who doesn't keep her stocking seams straight is making the same point in reverse. He ap-plauds and rewards and is proud of the girl who pays at-tention, who keeps herself well groomed, who shows that she has made an effort to be the kind of girl that he is proud to take out. And male looks are coming more and more into the same category; his hair, his teeth, his grooming, the right hat and the right suit, all show that he is paying attention—to promotion, to the customer or the prospect or the client, and to his desirability as a date. Viewed from the standpoint of another culture, or even from a recent visit to one's own un-conscious, this all gives a picture of a people, especially a youth group, who are tremendously preoccupied with sex, whose only interest in life is love, and whose definition of love is purely physical. Yet this seems to me to be an enormous misstatement. Rather, this continuous emphasis on the sex-ually relevant physical appearance is an outcome of using a heterosexual game as the prototype for success and popularity in adolescence.

The dating pattern affects adult sex relations in still another way. As a culture, we have given up chaperonage. We permit and even encourage situations in which young people can indulge in any sort of sex behaviour that they elect. At the same time we have not relaxed one whit our disapproval of the girl who becomes pregnant, nor simplified the problems of the unmarried mother who must face what to do about her child. We disapprove of abortion, and adequate and available birth-control information is almost impossible to obtain because of the conflict in attitudes between Protestants and Roman Catholics on the ethical issues involved. We bring girls up to be free and easy and unafraid, without the protections given by shyness and fear to girls of many other societies. We bring our boys up to be just as free and easy, used to girls, demanding towards girls. We actually place our young people in a virtually intolerable situation, giving them the entire setting for behaviour for which we then punish them whenever it occurs. The curious adjustment that American culture has made to this anomalous situation is petting, a variety of sexual practices that will not result in pregnancy. Technical virginity has become steadily less important, but the prohibition of extra-marital pregnancy remains. Petting is the answer to the dilemma. But petting has emotional effects of its own; it requires a very special sort of adjustment in both male and female. The first rule of petting is the need for keeping complete control of just how far the physical behaviour is to go; one sweeping impulse, one acted-out desire for complete possession or complete surrender, and the game is lost, and lost ignobly. The controls on this dangerous game that is so like a ski-slide, yet which must never be treated as a ski-slide, are placed in the hands of the girl. The boy is expected to ask for as much as possible, the girl to yield as little as possible.

A date can be a success on which there is no petting at all, but merely a battle of wits, of verbal parrying, while the boy convinces the girl that he is so popular that he has the courage to ask for anything, and the girl convinces the boy that she is so popular that she has to give nothing. If physical attraction is strong, then, when petting does occur, the boy expects the girl to keep it within bounds. The girl expects the boy to permit her to keep it within bounds.

From this game, played over and over again, sometimes for ten years or so before marriage, arises the later picture of married life in America, in which it is the wife who sets the pattern of sex relations. From it comes the inability of many American women to make complete sexual surrenders, which foreigners find so confusing and frustrating, and from it also come the various compensations, the use of alcohol to induce a lowering of control, and the popular myths of the invincible, irresistible lover. Even before the girl has matured enough to respond to the cautions of her own body, she has been faced with the need for being the conscience for two, and at the same time playing gaily, deftly, a game that is never finished and at which she may always lose. It is small wonder that films and magazine stories of love glorify the impulse, never to be indulged, of complete surrender.

For the boy, the pattern is just as coercive. He learns to value the situation in which he is checked, to devalue the situation with the bad girl, the girl of whom he is only desirous for immediate physical satisfaction, and to value as the genuinely rewarding situation the relationship to a woman who can always say No, and who says it frequently. Analysts of contemporary films have emphasized the growing importance of the image of the good-bad girl, the girl who is attractively cast as possibly bad and in the end turns out to be good.[4] But this same trend was previsioned in the couplet of the early twenties, "Won't somebody give me some good advice, On how to be naughty and still be nice?"

In a sense the answer has been found and is embodied in our adolescent culture. The number of pregnancies in high schools and colleges to-day does not seem to be appreciably greater—when considered in relation to the change in number and types of student—than it was twenty-five years ago, when chaperones and early hours still existed. Faced with the demand that they play this dangerous and exacting game, young people play it bravely, heads up; a surprising number take the good from the situation, the fact that boy and girl are partners together in keeping their heads above water. This partnership, in which each must rely on the help, the understanding, the good-sportsmanship, of the other, is the basis of modern American marriage, the young marriages that have survived, it would almost seem by a miracle, through the trials of war-camps, life with relatives, inflation, too-early parenthood, war neuroses, isolation in strange communities. The partnership behaviour that the two learned when each had to play with sex, and to a degree defeat it, holds them together, and they might be quite happy if discrepant norms for sex happiness had not simultaneously been added to the demands that American culture makes on each individual to be happy.

During the dating period, there is the imperative that one ought to be able to play with sex all the time, and win. The younger the boy and girl when they learn to play this game of partially incomplete, highly controlled indulgence of impulse, the more perfectly they can learn it. There are fewer chances of the break-through of deep emotion, to confuse the learning process. But then comes marriage, with a different imperative. Now both man and woman must have a "happy sex life," defined not with the symmetry of dating days in which the girl and boy, in the same dangerous situation, joined hands to win together, but in which a happy sex life is defined differently for the man and for the woman. For the man, the demon to be avoided at all costs is lack of potency, defined in a number of quantitative ways—frequency, time, interval before rearousal, accuracy in judging the strength of his own impulse. There is an implicit assumption for males that if one copulates one is happy. The sort of sex life that was once placed outside marriage, in the red-light district of the nineties, has to a degree been imported into it. Now, as then, the man is not schooled in any elaborations; technique, even if learned, is to a degree learned unwillingly and despised. But during the period when the split was closing between the good woman—whom one married and respected, and did not expect to take liberties with —and the bad woman—to whom one repaired for physical relief and whose allure was regarded merely as an aid to rapid sexual desire—the new patterns of dating and petting were developing. A tremendous clamour arose in the literature in England and America about women's need for and right to the same sort of sexual satisfaction that men have.

This clamour was heavily disguised as an exploration of the female psyche, which revealed that women were as much in need of sexual pleasure as men. The white-bearded, saintly-faced men who wrote and worked to get acceptance for this point of view certainly felt like Santa Clauses dispensing blessings and largess where there had been dearth and deprivation before. The news spread, and about the time of World War I this emphasis coincided with the loosening of sex controls and the entrance of women in greater and greater numbers into industry. Good women became women who should enjoy sex, and enjoy it in a way that is definitely analogous to male enjoyment. Now this is not an untenable way of viewing sex behaviour. Both in France and in Samoa, happy sex relationships are postulated on the male's taking pride and pleasure in gratifying the female, in inducing in her a climax behaviour comparable to his own. In neither Samoa nor France is simple copulation expected to produce such results. We might possibly have shifted from the Puritan position in which good women took no pleasure in sex, and bad women took no pleasure in anything else, to a philosophy and a practice in sex in which men learned a variety of ways of evoking climactic behaviour in women. But a second influence—almost as strong as the first—entered the scene. This was the doctrine that women should have climaxes just like men, and they should get them not by learned responsiveness, but from the simple act of copulation. If they did not, they were voted as frigid by a psychiatry in which a European male version of sex differences was very influential. Yet there seems no reason to believe that climactic responses to simple copulation are "natural" to all women, or even to any large proportion of women.

So we now have a very complicated set of standards of sex adjustment that have been developing side by side with the change in adolescent sex behaviour, but are not very well integrated with it. During adolescence, the male learns to let his direct potency be checked by a girl who learns not to be moved beyond the point of control. Then in marriage they are faced with the demand that he be simply and directly potent, and that she experience climactic satisfaction from his simple, unelaborated potency. Returns to the procedures of petting are suspect as regressive on both their parts. The husband resents interference with the display of his potency, now an index of his successful masculinity. The wife feels inadequate if she insists on substitute gratifications, and if she is not swept away—after years of learning not to be swept away. Yet the complete total relaxation of feminine surrender, as distinguished from specific orgasmic behaviour, is hardly available to women who have had to live through years of bridling their every impulse to yield and surrender.

These discrepancies between the demands that are made on very young boys and girls to act out and yet control a whole series of heterosexual activities, and the later standards that cause so many marriages to fail to supply what amounts to an impossible demand for sexual happiness, are not surprising. Success in marital sexual happiness now becomes a duty like every other success-demand in America. American culture has grown up so fast, and been compounded from so many sources, that the presence of contradictions such as are found even in much older and more integrated cultures is to be expected. But it does seem important to realize that the more successfully young adolescents deal with the difficult problems of freedom and demanded dating, the less prepared they are to meet the particular criteria for sex adjustment in marriage.

XV

SEX AND ACHIEVEMENT

THERE HAS LONG BEEN A HABIT IN WESTERN CIVILIZATION OF speaking as if it were possible for men to have a picture of womanhood to which women reluctantly conformed, and for women to make demands on men to which men adjusted even more reluctantly. This has been an accurate picture of the way in which we have structured our society, with women as keepers of the house who insist that men wipe their feet on the door-mat, and men as keepers of women in the house who insist that their wives should stay modestly within-doors. There have been a thousand varieties of these demands, from the way a tea-cup was balanced to the prohibition on a wife's smoking or on daughter's cutting her hair. From one point of view they provided a pleasant tension on which drawing-room etiquette could be based, or by way of which a man could proclaim his natural masculine desire to be free and dirty and careless and unpunctual *if* his wife had not insisted that he be home every night promptly for dinner. The picture can be obsessively elaborated, and girls attempting to plan their own lives may stop every other moment to say, "But men don't like women who . . ." However, it is one thing to recognize these phrasings as cultural devices which maintain a working equilibrium between male and female rôles, but quite another thing to take them seriously and talk about a "man-made" world, or to say, as Emily James Putnam does in the introduction to *The Lady*, "Where he put her, there she stays," [1] and thus deny the far more fundamental fact that both men and women share the same images of what makes a marriageable or an unmarriageable woman, a good husband, a fascinating lover whom any woman would be a fool to marry, or a born old bachelor. The phrases "a man's man" or "a woman's woman" do not mean a basic disagreement between men and women about which type of man gets on better with men than with women, but a basic agreement between men and women about each kind of man or woman. When a man and a woman get into an argument about some solid, plodding, devoted young woman, and the woman says, "But she'll make some man a very good wife," and the man says "I don't believe any man will want to marry her," there is no real conflict between them. The dissenting man means the same thing as the woman speaker by the words "good wife," only he is saying, "But who wants that kind of a good wife?" In the last century, when the upper-class and middle-class worlds were so neatly protected against bad women who wore bright colours and were filled with allure, this did not mean that good women thought bad women were unalluring. The man who, exhausted by the demands of a wife who had taken permanently to a sofa after the birth of her first child, sought out a glittering lady in a large plumed hat, and his wife who lay on the sofa and imagined the lady in the hat, both agreed that she was alluring, and both also agreed that it was both natural and wrong for the husband to be allured and both natural and right for his wife to resent it. So both father and mother, brother and sister, neighbour and preacher and teacher, future mother-in-law, possible mistress, local Don Juan, and village wiseacre, as well as the comics, the radio, the films, build together the images of the different kinds of men and women who will be loved, valued, hated, and ignored by their own sex, the opposite sex, or both.

So every hesitancy in a woman and every bit of bluster in a man are not to be laid to some male conspiracy to keep women in their place, any more than every bit of blundering shyness in a man or of conceited demandingness in a woman is to be laid to some female conspiracy to dominate men. Different cultures have styled the relationships between men and women differently. When they have styled the rôles so that they fitted well together, so that law and custom, ideal and practical possibilities, were reasonably close together, the men and the women who lived within that society have been fortunate. But to the degree that there have been discrepancies in the two rôles, to the degree that a style of beauty that was unobtainable by most people, or a style of bravery or initiative, modesty and responsiveness, was insisted upon although the culture had inadequate devices for developing such initiative or such responsiveness, then both men and women suffer. The suffering of either sex—of the male who is unable, because of the way in which he was reared, to take the strong initiating or patriarchal rôle that is still demanded of him, or of the female who has been given too much freedom of movement as a child to stay placidly within the house as an adult—this suffering, this discrepancy, this sense of failure in an enjoined rôle, is the point of leverage for social change. One has only to follow the fortunes of the demand for equal political rights for women from one country to another to note how contrasting are the responses from women in different countries, and how slight the overt relationship between low position of women and the eager demands for women's rights. Unfortunately we do not have as good comparative material on attempts to change the status of men—parallel movements such as the abolition of alimony, controversies as to whether family subsidies are to be paid to fathers or mothers, arguments over community-property laws. Attempts to free men from responsibilities and limitations that no longer appear reasonable or just are not neatly summed up under a men's-rights movement, or considered by international subcommissions on the legal status of men. Yet detailed analysis of any of these legal reforms would show quite clearly that there is a continuous movement also to free men from limitations that are out of line with the contemporary calendar. Breach-of-promise cases are a silly excrescence in a world in which women do half the proposing, and alienation-of-affection cases between two men, which assume that the woman is a gently pliant lily, ring just as false. Alimony for a young childless woman with an education equal to that of her husband, who must postpone his next marriage to support her, is coming to seem glaringly unfair. But the historical trend that listed women among the abused minorities, and which was a natural outcome of the sorts of inspection of legal and social abuses that went with our transformation from a society of status, where rights were inherent, to a society of contract, in which rights have to be established, lingers on to obscure the issue and gives apparent point to the contention that this is a man-made world in which women have always been abused and must always fight for their rights.

It takes considerable effort on the part of both men and women to reorient ourselves to thinking—when we think basically—that this is a world made not by men alone, in which women are unwilling and helpless dupes and fools or else powerful schemers hiding their power under their ruffled petticoats, but a world made by mankind for human beings of both sexes. In this world male and female rôles have sometimes been styled well and sometimes badly; sometimes the men have an easier time while the women have recourse to soothsayers, day-dreams, autoerotic devices, gigolos, somatic diseases, and downright insanity. Sometimes it is the women whose rôle has been cast in terms so close to the realities of their fate that they present a picture of relative placidity while the men pursue phantoms. But there seems little doubt that the relative attainability of either rôle has its effect on both men and women. Women who seem placid while the men seem erratic and bewitched pay a price for the discrepancies in the men's rôle; men who appear far more favoured and more free than their women-folk have not yet reached the level of self-realization that would have been theirs had their wives and mothers also had rôles that they could attain and enjoy.

Literature in the United States at present is raucous and angry on this whole question of the relationship between men and women. We have had a spate of books that claim women are being masculinized, to their ill, to men's ill, to everybody's ill, and another spate, or sometimes the same spate, of books that insist that men are being feminized. When one follows the shrill insistencies of books like *Modern Woman: The Lost Sex*, which end by attacking men as well as women, one realizes that we are passing through a period of discrepancies in sex rôles which are so conspicuous that efforts to disguise the price that both sexes pay are increasingly unsuccessful. Only if we perpetuate the habit of speaking about "the position of women" in a vacuum will we fail to recognize that where one sex suffers, the other sex suffers also. As surely as we believe that the present troublesome problems of sex adjustment are due to the position of women alone, we commit ourselves to a long series of false moves as we attempt to push women out of the home, into the home, out of the home, adding mounting confusion to the difficulties born of a changing world-climate of opinion, a shifting technology, and an increasing rate and violence of cultural change.

It has been fashionable in the last few years to call America a matriarchy, and thus do considerable violence to a useful anthropological concept. A matriarchal society is one in which some if not all of the legal powers relating to the ordering and governing of the family—power over property, over inheritance, over marriage, over the house— are lodged in women rather than in men. So we may speak of matrilineal societies, in which a man inherits his name, his land, and his position, or any one of these from his mother's brother, through his mother. This may not mean a great deal of power for women, although it is a system in which women are sufficiently favoured so that polygamy, for instance, does not work well within it. Or we may speak of a matrilocal society, in which house and land are owned by women and pass from mother to daughter, and husbands move in and move out. This system is even less compatible with polygamy, or with the exercise of very much authority by the husband-fathers, who live under their mother-in-law's roof. Then there are a variety of modifications, in which a woman is returned to be buried on her own kin's land, or in which ties through the mother play an important but different rôle than do ties through the father, or where, as in Samoa, the sister's son retains a veto in the councils of his mother's family. There are very rare systems, such as that of the Iroquois Indians, where political power is in women's hands, since the women elders nominated the holders of titles who also wielded political powers.

When contemporary American society is viewed against such sets of arrangements, it is obvious that the word "matriarchy" not only is not descriptive, but actually obscures the basic issues.[2] In the United States women take their husband's names and the children bear their fathers' names. Women are expected to live where their husbands elect to live, and refusal to do so is tantamount to desertion. Men are liable for the support of their wives and children, and women are not liable for the support of their husbands, nor are brothers liable for the support of their sisters. The basic legal assumption is that a woman as a minor is dependent upon her father, and thereafter upon her husband. In our legal forms we are a patrinominal, patrilineal, patrilocal, and legally, for the most part, a patriarchal society. The circumstance that American fathers don't conform to some folk-lore concept of a patriarch with a long beard and ten children is not relevant. Both men and women are reared within this explicit paternally oriented framework. There are laws against a man's beating his wife, but other concepts have to be invoked when his wife beats him. The female is defined by usage as helpless, in need of protection, especially of support. We are also, of course, a monogamous society in which every form of polygamy, even the most casual, is frowned upon.

This is the framework of the family we have inherited from Europe, but it was brought to this country under exceptional conditions. The power of the father over the son was sapped by the weakening of the property sanction, and the infinite possibilities in the new country for leaving home. The power of the husband over the wife was altered more subtly. In frontier days, women were few, and sheer competition made it necessary for the man to woo differently than in countries in which he had been able to pick and choose among a dozen girls, each with a dowry thrown in, or at least to relax in self-assurance as some dozen mothers threw their daughters at his head. The dowry disappeared and women were wooed for themselves. The valuation placed on female qualities shifted. Meekness, home-abidingness, timorous clinging to the saddle of a husband as he rode away for a two-mile journey, were all very well in the Old World. But an American frontier woman might have to keep a lonely farm going all by herself for weeks, disciplining the half-grown children, succouring the passing stranger, even fending off the Indians. Strong women, women with character and determination, in fact women with guts, became more and more acceptable. The stereo-type of the old maid shifted from the British picture of the manlike spinster who had a tom cat and preferred her nephews to the mild little woman who kept female cats and preferred her nieces. Along with this demand for women who have strength of character and the ability to manage money and affairs, there went no parallel premium on women's looking masculine. A woman was still expected to have womanly qualities, still to be attractive, in fact she was expected to be increasingly attractive as she came to be chosen in marriage for her dowryless self alone. Mar-riages of choice, phrased as marriages of love, laid increas-ing demands on both men and women to please the opposite sex openly.

In the hurly-burly of settling a new continent, many tasks were delegated to women in addition to running the farm and disciplining the children and keeping off the Indians while their husbands were away. As rough little frontier settlements assumed the appearance of a real village, the cleaning-up process, closing down the gambling-hell or the saloon, was thought of as coinciding with the arrival of one or more good women. The finer things of life—moral and aesthetic values—were delegated to women in a new and more active form; America was not Europe, where women had been expected to do more praying than the men but not to take any responsibility outside the home. The woman crusader who flouted the dictates of feminine decorum to campaign for the right has been a familiar part of our history since the early days of Anne Hutchinson, and is recognized by both men and women as a valid part of our culture. It is permitted to men to hope that their own wives may not receive the call to reform the world, but this is a hope of the same order as that permitted to a religious mother who still somehow—while she instructs her little son in his prayers—hopes he will be chosen to be a sea-captain and not a priest. An ideal arrangement of ethical behaviour in the United States would leave good works, those so-necessary good works, to widows and spinsters, thus keeping these two supernumerary classes of women happily occupied in a way that is socially useful. It has been interesting to notice the changes in attitudes towards Mrs. Roosevelt and towards her vigorous, untiring interest in social welfare. As the wife of the President, she was attacked and condemned by men who would be the first to raise their hats in tribute to the long line of noble American women who campaigned, for instance, against slavery. This resentment, however, notably decreased after President Roosevelt's death, when her continued vigorous championing of the right set a pattern for widows rather than wives.

The spinster champion of the right, of education, village improvement, social legislation, freedom for oppressed minorities, has gradually been stereotyped in those occupations in which women are professionally engaged in good works, particularly education and social work. These are both fields that men enter on peril of accusations of effeminacy, unless they enter in an administrative or a financial rôle. "Where," asks the Englishman who is prominent in social welfare, "are your men? We see their names on the letter-heads of organizations, but when we go to international conferences, we meet almost entirely women." "Our men—oh, they are the chairmen of boards, they determine the financial policy of our agencies, but they leave the practice to women. They are too busy to go to conferences."

In such a historical development as this, it is of course impossible to speak of cause and effect. We must speak rather of an endless spiralling process, in which good women were the immediate occasion of some reform, reform became thought of as women's field, this attracted women into it and further styled the field as feminine, and so kept men out. Between the two world wars there was a marked decrease in the willingness of women to enter those fields which had been ear-marked as fields of "service"; that is, fields in which the bad pay and heavy work were supposed to be ignored because they gave an opportunity to exercise womanly qualities of caring for the young, the sick, the unfortunate, and the helpless. This whole trend towards the professionalization of service fields means a shift from an occupation to which one gives oneself—as a woman still does in marriage and motherhood—to an occupation to which one gives definite hours and specified and limited duties. It is evident that this ideal for American women is passing as a rôle both for the woman who expects to marry and for the spinster seeking a way of life. This whole shift is part of the assimilation of female ideal and male ideal to each other. Boys and girls sitting at the same desks, studying the same lessons, and absorbing the same standards alike learn that the two most respectable criteria for choosing one's life-work are that the work should have chances for advancement and that it should be "interesting." Even social workers, every hour of whose working day must, if they are to do their chosen tasks, be devoted to warm helpfulness, will defend their choice of a career because it is interesting, or one in which women can do well. Only with many apologies do they now admit to a simple desire to help human beings.

Meanwhile, during this period of history when styles in

women were shifting and changing, a style in men was also being built up. The man had to make a living, he had to deal with the harsh realities of the competitive world, hack and slash at forests and cut corners in a world in which any man could be President. The average American town gave him no education in understanding or enjoying the arts, and conventional aesthetic expressions were closed to him, and regarded as womanish. To this day, the choice of music or painting or poetry as a serious occupation is suspect for an American male. Men demonstrated their maleness in the practical world of business, of farming (where the women were kept indoors while the men even did the milking), and of politics (the down-to-earth, corrupt kind as compared with the milk-and-water reform variety). As our transitional culture made more simplified values inevitable in order that immigrants from many lands could communicate with one another, so competition increased for these simple signs of success—money, the things that money could buy, power over persons and over things.[3] The harsh realities of a competitive world where each man's pace is determined by the pace of his rival, and the race is never ended, hit men earlier than they hit women. The rapidly expanding economy that brought more amenities to the lives of women made more demands on the lives of men. Finally we arrive at the stereotypes of to-day, the tired husband who just wants to sit at home with his shirt-collar open and the wife who wants to be taken out, the mother who sees too much of the children and is forever importuning the father to see more of them, while the husband himself feels that if he had a chance he would go fishing. To receive recognition—from both men and women —a man in America should be, first of all, a success in his business; he should advance, make money, go up fast, and if possible he should also be likable, attractive, and well groomed, a good mixer, well informed, good at the leisure-time activities of his class, should provide well for his home, keep his car in good condition, be attentive enough to his wife so that he doesn't give other women an opportunity to catch his interest. A woman to receive equal recognition should be intelligent, attractive, know how to make the best of herself in dress and manner, be successful in attracting and keeping first several men, finally one, run her home and family efficiently so that her husband stays devoted and her children all surmount the nutritional, psychological, and ethical hazards of maturation, and are successful too; and she should have time for "outside things," whether they be church, grange, community activities, or Junior League. A woman who has time only for her own home is likely to be stigmatized either as "having too much to do," which means either that she is incompetent, or as having a husband doesn't make as much as he should, or that the couple have been shiftless and had too many children.

But success in their rôles rather than the specific qualities of the rôles is what is emphasized. Both the successful man and the successful woman will be liked by both sexes, rewarded for their reaffirmation that it is possible for human beings to be what Mother said you must be if you wanted her to love you. It is possible for the public-opinion interviewer to ferret out a great deal of envy among Americans.[4] They find people who listen to programs like "Information Please" in order to hear "college-educated people fail." But this envy, like the detraction of the well-known personality that fills the tabloids whenever some scandal gives opportunity, is still a small component compared with the very wide-spread pleasure Americans take in some one who is really successful, whether it be shown at the testamentary dinner to the departing executive who is taking a better job, or at the block-party for the only family that got into the new housing project. For with the carefully prepared formula that maternal care has placed in its bottle the American child drinks in the admonition to succeed, to be the right weight, to learn to walk at the right time, to go up grade by grade in school, with good marks, to make the team, to make the sorority or clique, to be the one to be chosen by others for success. For the father who disciplined a child who was conceived of as filled with Satan and in need of many beatings, and the mother who succoured and comforted the child and taught him how to avoid the beatings, we now have the mother almost alone, not curbing the child's innate wickedness, but yearningly searching for signs that he will make the grade, make good, fail to fail.

This training, which is now so similar for boys and girls, has very different impacts upon them. For the boy, it has two important effects. He is trained by women to be a male, which involves no identification of the self with the mother-teacher.[5] He is to be a boy by doing the things Mother says, but doing them in a manly way. After all, boys grow by eating the right food, they get good marks by studying—in fact by obeying Mother's admonitions—but also they must be manly, they must not be sissies, they must stand up for themselves. All fighting must be defensive, and yet it is being a sissy not to be able to fight, so situations must be arranged that will satisfy the mothers of both little males that each is fighting in self-defense, obeying the highest standards and learning how not to be a sissy at the same time. Only from older brothers and the older brothers of companions does the little boy get any straight-out tutelage in how to be a boy. It was notable how enormously juvenile delinquency increased during the last war when the older boys were withdrawn from the family. But the older brother is himself straining to meet the adult rôle that his mother and the world have defined for him, and the small boy who tags along imitates and follows some one whose eyes are on future things, a job, a car, a raise.

In enclaves where the newly arrived or the very unsuccessful are hemmed in in slum areas this sequence of social development is distorted.[6] The older boys are unable to take their fathers' failures as clues to a remote pattern of male success as reinterpreted by the mothers. They become gang leaders, in turn effectively short-circuiting the development of their younger brothers in the society. This asocial gang-life of boys provides a basis for the adult criminal world in America. It high-lights the normal American development, in which a mother who understands the American world can point to a father who, while not a good enough model for the boy merely to imitate, is nevertheless on the right road—whom the boy himself will surpass. In this pattern, older boys, their faces turned not back towards an admiring juvenile audience but forward towards a welcoming, possibly applauding adult world, permit younger boys to tag along and learn—as long as they don't make any trouble. The eyes of the whole family, the whole neighbourhood, face ahead, and every male in the group is merely an indication of where and how males should advance.

No one represents a permanent place on the ladder. In peace-time the small boy's heroes, whether his own father keeps a grocery store or is the president of a bank, are policemen, firemen, flyers, cow-boys, and baseball-players, men who act out in their real life rôles the springing active motor impulses of the small boy's body. His mother alternates between letting him jump on the sofa because the books say children shouldn't be restricted and telling him not to break things. And in her voice, in the voice of the radio announcer who introduces his favourite radio program, in the teacher's voice at school, in the voices of every one around him, the little boy who wants to be a policeman or a baseball-player hears that he will grow up to accept some responsible money-making rôle. He learns that if he wants to argue for choosing the police force or professional base-ball, he will have to argue not that this is what he wants to do, but that it is something in which he can make good and make money and advance. He learns that unless he has a job and a car and a wife and kids, he will never be able to respect himself—because his own self-approval, like his mother's now, will be withdrawn, leaving him lonely and unsatisfied. Life is a job at which he can succeed if he tries. All desirable qualities can be acquired if he pays attention to his looks, his skills, his relations to people. And he also learns that the reward of success is love and approval, light in his mother's eyes, bread and jam and an ice-box with no rules about raiding it, relief and pleasure in his father's eyes. Here is no mother who thrills to his war-whoop in an Indian suit—although she bought him an Indian suit because children should have some imaginative play, or because all the other children have them—but rather she thrills to his first good grades, his first earned money. Here is no father whose awareness of his own masculinity makes him feel his small masculine son as a threat and a challenge. The father has long since become a parent, and the success of his son is part of his success as a proper husband and father. He is often, in fact, over-anxious and over-protective towards his son. So, even in wealthy middle-class suburbs, little American boys still have paper routes, and Chief Justices and presidents of companies take those paper routes when their sons are ill in bed so that the boys will not default in their business obligations. In fact, the rewards are so great for displaying to admiring and helpful parents those qualities of initiative, independence, and assertiveness in the workaday world that will ensure success later that even though there is fear of failure, the American child grows up to be exceedingly optimistic, exceedingly responsive to praise, recognition, and acclaim from others. Failure is stylized as a temporary set-back, obstacles are made to be overcome, only a sissy takes defeat as anything but a stimulus to trying harder.

"The difficult we do at once, the impossible takes a little longer."

The chief trap for the boy in this pattern of maturation lies in the conditional nature of the whole process. On the one hand he can always win applause by taking the next step, moving from the third team to the second team, from the position of the worst in the class to the position of the next to the worst, by gaining a pound or growing an inch; the applause is hearty and ungrudging from parents who feel they owe their children every chance to succeed and have a right to take their success as a full repayment for parental sacrifice. On the other hand, none of this accept-ance and this applause is final. If the next step up is not taken, then the approval becomes only a remembered happi-ness, now withdrawn, which must be worked for again. Mother loves you *if* you succeed; Father is grinning and proud if you succeed, something a little ruefully comforting when you fail. But at no time in childhood, often at no time in one's whole life, is it possible to arrive, to win love and praise that are not strictly contemporary and condi-tional and which can never be taken away from one. This is the background of those American attitudes—failure to admit immigrants, ungenerous state laws about welfare settlement for indigent families—that contrast so sharply with American willingness to help others, to give freely of time and goods and services. It is not that Americans learn, as some peoples do, that the supply of goods is limited and so one man's gain is another man's loss. They rather learn that the number of prizes in the race, the number of A's in the class, are more limited than is the number of contestants. If there are more contestants, the endless race for the A's, for the prizes, becomes that much harder. It is not that the boy learns interest in defeating others, but that he fervently hopes he can beat enough others to be counted a success; the others are incidental, not so much rivals to be worsted as entrants to be outdistanced. His upbringing permits him no admitted glee in open battle, and later, in a competitive world that demands harsh and sometimes savage competition, he takes little pleasure in the game itself. He accepts the behest that he must continue and continue and continue to succeed, to advance, to keep his place among others. The methods he has to use are just part of it, to be laid aside in a compensatory good-fellowship that is often mixed right into the distasteful competitive relationships. In those relationships between men when the competition can be laid aside altogether, a delicious game of pretended aggression can be played endlessly, with thrust and counter-thrust, harmless and healing.

But the rôle of sisters and girls and wives is a very complex one in this world in which the boy's whole springing masculinity is diverted into the game of success. Because it is the mother's and not the father's voice that gives the principal early approval and disapproval, the nagging voice of conscience is feminine in both sexes—that voice which says, "You are not being the success you *ought* to be." The man who feels he is failing is a man who is angry with women, and angry with those values for which women stand—social values, social-security legislation, "sentimental schoolmarmish goodness." And it is not only the man who is failing who finds himself angry with women, but also the man who is paying too high a price for his success, and so reiterates over and over how hard he works, how self-made he is, how the modern world is making it too soft for people. The American who is successful without feeling he has paid too high a price will be at ease with himself and his conscience, and give generously to the Community Chest or the union relief fund, send food to starving Europeans, vote for social legislation, even sit on a board to see that his wife's pet charity gets what it needs. But at any moment this easy good nature may shift to an angry assertiveness against the "do-gooders," those who have set his feet on a path he cannot bear, that path which in ruthless competitiveness seems a long way from the task of maintaining a hospital, or raising the salaries of school-teachers, to which he is now asked to give help. Any great yielding to the demands of civic virtue is suspect; a man to be a man must go out to prove he is a man, and then, and only then, can he leave a fortune to the orphans' home. The American ideal career is the poor boy who learned his prayers at his mother's knee, worked his way up against fearful odds, used without womanish softness and without enjoyment the methods appropriate to such a battle, and in the end, a millionaire, leaves his money—not to his children to ruin their characters by denying them a gradient on which at least some sort of success is possible, but—to good works, giving to the town or to the nation schools, libraries, art galleries, and orphan asylums. These are the things his mother told him that he ought to respect while he himself puts his whole effort into being a success. Good women made him what he is, and in the end they get the proceeds for their own ends, and in between he worked hard being the man they told him he ought to want to be. So as the mother's love has become more and more conditional upon success, the mother and the school-teacher have tended to merge in the child's mind, with the teacher taking on some of the aspects of the bad mother that were once given to the stepmother in the fairy-tales of another age.

The sister in America has a very special rôle in the life of the American boy, geared as he is to succeed on a scale in which he is measured by his age and size against others of like age and size, and rewarded by women rather than by men. The sister becomes a double rival as she grows faster than he, does her lessons more dutifully, gets into fewer scrapes, learns the woman-taught lessons more easily. Characteristically, the sister in America is the big sister, whose side the parents always take, who is so slick she always wins, who gets away with murder—that is, gets the same rewards with less effort—and the day-dream sister is the little sister, over whom one can win without effort.[7] The habit of American mothers of egging their children on by invidious or challenging comparisons is at its most aggravated in the case of sister, girl-cousin, girl next door. The boy is taught both that he ought to be able to beat her record, as he is a boy, and that it is fair to compare their achievements on the same scale at the same age, because they both ride bicycles or sleep alone on the third floor, or are in the fast-moving section of the fourth grade. They are treated as alike whenever it suits the rest of the world, and as unlike whenever that provides a better goad. If a boy cries, he is scolded more than a girl who doesn't cry; when she outstrips him, he is told it is even worse than if he had been outstripped by a boy, and yet she may be almost twice his size and he has also been told not to hit her because she is a girl. Side by side they sit in the nursery to be compared on table-manners, side by side in school to be compared on neatness and punctuality as well as reading and writing and arithmetic. She sits and challenges him, and beats him at least half the time and often more than half, until high school provides the blessed relief of science and shop, where girls aren't encouraged to succeed any longer. And as he sits and is beaten—at least half the time —he learns both that girls can do most of the things that boys can do for which rewards are meted out and that it is intolerable that they should, because it has been made humiliating.

This is expressed in later life in the relatively high accessibility of most occupations to women, but also in the bitter fight that is put up, even in those fields where women are the best trained, as in some government services, against giving women jobs that carry high salaries or administrative powers over people—the two most usual ways in which men demonstrate their success. Many societies have educated their male children on the simple device of teaching them not to be women, but there is an inevitable loss in such an education, for it teaches a man to fear that he will lose what he has, and to be forever somewhat haunted by this fear. But when in addition to learning that at all costs he must not be a girl, he is continually forced to compete with girls at the very age when girls mature faster than boys, and on women-set tasks to which girls take more easily, a sharper ambivalence is established. American men have to use at least part of their sense of masculine self-esteem as men on beating women, in terms of money and status. And American women agree with them and tend to despise a man who is outdistanced by a woman. When American women do rise to positions of power and status, they have great difficulty in treating their male subordinates with any decent sensitivity—for aren't they failures to be there?—and shrink with horror from making more money than their husbands to the extent that they wish to feel feminine, or throw their success in their husband's faces to the extent that their own cross-sexual competitiveness has been developed. So we end up with the contradictory picture of a society that appears to throw its doors wide open to women, but translates her every step towards success as having been damaging—to her own chances of marriage, and to the men whom she passes on the road.

It is just in the middle class, and among those who aspire to middle-class position, that this antagonism waxes strongest, because the middle-class skills are those in which it is easy for women to excel and where men find themselves most fenced in, any rampant masculinity denied and fettered in the interest of saving and postponement of indulgence in impulse. Middle-class mothers, educated and still at home, have a great deal of time to give to moulding their growing children, giving and withholding love as the children display the proper attitudes. And middle-class virtues —saving, thrift, punctuality, foresight, hard work, control of present impulse, respect for the opinion of others, conformity to a code of manners—are virtues that can be learned. Those skills in which the body plays a rôle and in which it is easier for men to attain superiority, such as hunting, riding, or fighting, are absent from the middle-class list. Middle-class virtues learned out of reciprocal relationships between mother and child are patterned originally in the gastro-intestinal tract, taking in, keeping, ordered giving out, in which the male child has all the complication of sorting out the control imposed on elimination from the need to keep somewhat available his impulsive masculinity. The female, although her special feminine characteristics are not evoked, has a lesser problem as she learns to observe the rules of time and place. So all through an American boy's childhood he has to compete, at home and at school, with girls who have an edge in almost all the activities for which reward is given, as one is, for example, rewarded for standing up for oneself but not for fighting. Athletics with their close relationship to bodily strength and vulnerability remains almost the only field from which female competition is barred, and they provide through life a thrilling escape, if only in the pages of a newspaper, for American boys and men. And escape is needed from a game in which all the dice are loaded and yet one must not lose—on penalty of losing love and so self-esteem.

Meanwhile, what is the position of the girl whose easy and successful competition with her brother is assured by the conditions of home and the school system? Seen through male eyes, she is big sister who has it easy, who always gets the breaks. Instead of being told that she mustn't do things because she is a girl, that she must cross her legs and lower her eyes and sit on a cushion and sew a fine seam,

she is told that she must learn the same things as a boy.
The boy is told that he ought to be ashamed to be beaten
by a girl, and outworn symbols of sheer male physical
superiority are invoked for such routine tasks as remembering to brush one's teeth or do one's lessons. The male's age-
old feeling that to be sexually successful he must be strong
is invoked in the interest of activities that have lost their
immediate relevance. But at the same time the girl is told
that she ought to be doing better than her brother, not
because she will be humiliated if she fails, but because it
is easier for girls to be good. This paradox of boy-girl competition was summed up in Whittier's "In School Days,"
one of the first poems to celebrate the pleasures and the
penalties of co-education, which tells the story of the girl
who worsted the boy in spelling: [8]

> "I'm sorry that I spelt the word:
> I·hate to go above you,
> Because,"—the brown eyes lower fell,—
> "Because, you see, I love you!"

And it is significant that the poet—a male—while writing so
sweetly and wistfully about her, moralizing so nicely on
how her attitude contrasts with most people's—

> He lived to learn, in life's hard school,
> How few who pass above him
> Lament their triumph and his loss,
> Like her,—because they love him.—

also very deftly and definitely kills the lady off:

> Dear girl! the grasses on her grave
> Have forty years been growing!

Just so the New Guinea native tells the story of the woman
who hands to men the symbols by which they can compensate themselves for their inferiority to her, and then adds
that they had better kill her. Love on such terms is unbear-

able. So there is built into the girl in America a conflict of another order. She too must do her lessons and obey her mother, or she will lose her mother's love, her teacher's approval, and the rewards that are accorded to the success-ful. She too likes bread generously spread with jam and an ice-box that is always open. These are hers, almost for the asking. "For all little girls," reads the sign in a New York candy-shop window, "and for *good* little boys." Hers, by natural right, but at what a price! If she learns the rules well, if she gets good marks, wins scholarships, gets the cub reporter's job, by so much she has done an unforgiv-able thing, in her own eyes and in the eyes of all of those around her. Each step forward in work as a successful American regardless of sex means a step back as a woman, and also, inferentially, a step back imposed on some male. For maleness in America is not absolutely defined, it has to be kept and re-earned every day, and one essential ele-ment in the definition is beating women in every game that both sexes play, in every activity in which both sexes engage.

To the extent that the little girl shares the attitudes of Whittier's dead heroine, she rejects the dilemma. True, she may have to spell the word now, in the third grade, for failure is too bitter for her small, success-oriented soul to bear. But later she will shift the field and get out of the unfair competition, go away from the game of loaded dice, and be a success in a different field, as a wife and a mother. The desperate need for success remains; it is not as strong as for the boy, because for the girl success is demanded only as it is demanded of all human beings, and not with a threat that if she does not succeed she will not be regarded as a true female. Boys are unsexed by failure; girls, if they are also pretty, may be more desirable if they need a male Galahad to help them with their lessons. But this is becom-ing steadily less true. Subtly the demand for the same kind of character structure for men and for women is spreading throughout the country. In a 1946 *Fortune* poll, men were asked which of three girls equally good-looking a man would prefer to marry: a girl who had never held a job, a girl who had held a job and been moderately successful at it, or a girl who had held a job and been extremely successful.[9] The preferences ran: 33.8 per cent for the moderately successful, 21.5 per cent for the extremely successful, and only 16.2 per cent for the girl who had never held a job. The *moderately* successful are still preferred, but with this preference goes increasing pressure on a girl to work before marriage, perhaps to work until the first child comes, and to "begin doing something," if it is only volunteer work or vigorously pursuing a hobby, as soon as her children are in school. Men want their wives both to reassure them by being less successful than they are and to gratify their competitive aspirations, vicariously, by "being successful." It is probably safe to say that the introspective distance between the words "moderately" and "extremely" means "at some one else's expense by playing in another league" as against "beating me at my own game," with the over-all emphasis on success gradually winning out. A girl who has never held a job is becoming increasingly suspect. Maybe she couldn't get a job; maybe if she had tried she would have been a failure, and who wants a wife, however personally pliant and reassuring, who might have been a failure? It is interesting also that in the female replies, 42.2 per cent of the women thought men would prefer a moderately successful girl, only 12.1 per cent thought a man would prefer the girl who had never held a job, and only 17.4 per cent thought they would prefer the exceedingly successful. The *Fortune* commentators go on to say:

"Evidently men are not as afraid of capable girls as women think they are. This is especially true of poor men, of whom 25% think that the extremely successful girl would make the most desirable wife. Poor women also give an unusually high vote for the extremely successful girl (24.7%), while women in the upper middle class give her very little backing, only 12.3%." And note that it is in the upper middle class that girls are treated most like boys in their education, compete with men most directly during childhood, and experience most directly the pressures I have been discussing.

So throughout her education and her development of vocational expectancy, the girl is faced with the dilemma that she must display enough of her abilities to be considered successful, but not too successful; enough ability to get and keep a job, but without the sort of commitment that will make her either too successful or unwilling to give up the job entirely for marriage and motherhood. "Two steps forward and one step back" is the dance-call she must obey. Or take the consequences. And what are the consequences? Failure to marry? If that were all, it might not be so serious. There are more women than men in the world, and societies have found it very possible to stylize vows of celibacy and poverty and still give women dignified lives. The nun who offers her potential wifehood and motherhood to God on behalf of all mankind, and who substitutes prayer and care for the children of God for the creation of particular children, can feel herself a part of God's plan, fulfilling the duty of human beings to "cherish and protect the lives of men and the life of the world." [10] In the crowded bus or cars of the subway, where men now let women stand with children in their arms—because women make money, don't they?—seats are still given to Sisters of Charity and Mercy.

But the woman in the United States who chooses a career instead of marriage is accorded no such satisfying and accredited place in the world. The same feeling that makes Americans, so often generous almost without parallel in the world, vote against the entrance of a few thousand homeless orphans, plus the feeling that any success in a woman calls men's manliness into account, defeats the possibility of her rôle's being fully rewarding. If she succeeds in a profession like school-teaching, men either desert it altogether, or are driven to such appalling expedients as rules that women are incapable of teaching second-year American history, so that the very enactment of the defensive measure further lowers them in their own eyes. No one, neither the men themselves nor the women with whom they compete successfully, thinks it is a good thing for an inadequate man to get the job of principal of a school over the heads of five better-equipped women. Neither sex is made happy by the situation, neither the women, able, conscientious, and hard-working, who may be 80 per cent of the contestants, nor the men who may constitute the other 20 per cent, a large proportion of whom suspect that the real reason for the promotion was just because "they wanted a man."

Perhaps this situation in which able women see themselves perpetually passed over in favour of a man after spending their lives in a "service" profession, a profession in which the womanly virtues of detailed imagination and patience with children are very heavily called for, is one important reason why women are leaving these professions for factory work and business, where they cannot be passed over so easily. And here they can use other weapons. For where the weapons of the school-teacher and the social worker are the weapons of mother's voice and the persistent demand that men be good, the weapons of the woman in business in the United States may include those of the woman who uses her sex to attain her ambitious ends. Ilka Chase's *In Bed We Cry* is a tragedy of just this situation, of the menace that the successful business woman is to herself and to the man she loves.[11] The little girl who hears the call of success more sharply than the call of her future wifehood and maternity hears a call to competitive action in which no holds are barred. Her brother has been better schooled than she has been for this expected behaviour in a competitive world. Fair play, no bullying, do not throw your weight around, are part of the ethics both she and he learned on the playing-fields, but here the pretence that all boys are stronger than all girls was kept up. Some of her very drive for success may come from this comparison, this statement that boys should always outdistance girls; some of her drive may come from doors barred to her because "women always leave and get married," some from a sneer from a brother or a father that "girls have no heads for figures." However this may be, she has been defined as weaker, and there are no rules in American life for the good behaviour of under-dogs. To the extent that American women—most American women—follow the rules of fair play and give-and-take and no alimony, they do so because they think of themselves as strong human beings, human like the men of whom they re-fuse to take an advantage. But to the woman who makes a success in a man's field, good behaviour is almost impossible, because her whole society has defined it so. A woman who succeeds better than a man—and in a man's field there is no other practical alternative to beating a certain number of men—has done something hostile and destructive. To the ex-tent that as a woman she has beauty or attractiveness of any sort, her behaviour is that much more destructive. The man-nish woman, the ugly woman, may be treated as a man in disguise, and so forgiven her successes. But for the success of a feminine woman there are no alibis; the more feminine she is, the less can she be forgiven. This does not mean that every woman who enters business or fields where she is in an extreme minority is hostile and destructive. But it does mean that any woman who in the course of her childhood had an extra amount of destructiveness developed and re-pressed is in psychological danger when she is placed in a rôle that is so destructively defined. To the woman whose maternal attitudes are highly developed, the position may be wholly intolerable.

So brother and sister, boy and girl, educated together, learn what each wishes from and what each can give to the other. The girl learns to discipline and mute an ambition that her society continually stimulates, as all girls working in white-collar jobs are said to have "careers," and careers are glamorous, while most men with similar skills merely have jobs. And we have the situation that looks so strange on the surface, that as more and more women work, women seem on the whole less interested in the battle that permits them to succeed professionally. A half-century ago the eyes of the specially able girl who went to college faced ahead towards a profession, towards a career. The idea of marriage was often pushed aside as a handicap. To-day, the girl of the same ability is usually willing to admit that she wants to marry, and seems more willing to sacrifice her career to marriage than to sacrifice a chance for marriage to her career. Because it is now more and more accepted that girls should work until they marry—and if one is unlucky, this means all one's life—girls work hard at acquiring skills and professions. If they have brains and ability, sheer virtuosity plus the need to succeed may lead them to become engrossed in their work, but seldom so engrossed that the desire for marriage is blocked out.

Nor will society to-day treat the woman who is not chosen with the simple pity accorded the wallflower of a century ago. Less kindly verdicts—"She must be neurotic," "She doesn't pay attention," "She hasn't made the most of her chances"—come all too easily to the lips of the young unmarried woman when she speaks of the older one. Success for a woman means success in finding and keeping a husband. This is much more true than it was a generation ago, when men were still supposed to do the seeking, and some women found their new freedom outside the home so intoxicating that they could abandon themselves to their work. Nor is this surprising in a world where the unmarried man is also looked upon as a failure in human relations, a queer bird who, in spite of all of the girls there are to marry, never succeeded in finding one, some one who is just too lazy, too do-less, to make an effort. But the more successful a man is in his job, the more certain every one is that he will make a desirable husband; the more successful a woman is, the more most people are afraid she may not be a successful wife. The *Fortune* survey summarized the reasons people gave why men should prefer extremely successful girls—their greater efficiency and understanding of money and their ability to help their husbands, and it adds: "Very few look upon her intelligence as an asset, and practically none say that she would be easier to get along with." The well-worn phrase "even the best cooks are men" should be foot-noted by a recognition that American men are not reared to enjoy being the husbands of successful chefs.

XVI

EACH FAMILY IN A HOME

OF ITS OWN

THE BELIEF THAT EVERY FAMILY SHOULD HAVE A HOME OF ITS own seems like a truism to which almost every American would assent without further thought. Most Americans also accept the fact that we have a housing shortage as the consequences of a failure to build in the thirties and during World War II, and of discrepancies between housing costs and wages that should somehow be reconciled. But it is important to realize that the word "family" has come to mean fewer and fewer people, the number of families has steadily increased, and so the need for housing units as distinguished from living-space has also increased by leaps and bounds. Although Southern Senators may occasionally argue against some piece of legislation for women, claiming that women's place is in the home, most legislators yield, at least nominally, to the question, "Whose home?" Women's place in the United States is no longer in the home, and her exclusion from a right that has been hers in most societies is part of our belief that every family should have its own home—

with only one woman in it. Furthermore, each family should consist only of a husband, a wife, and minor children.

All other forms of living are seen as having great disadvantages. A mother-son combination is classified as bad for the son, and a failure to break the silver cord; it will spoil his life. A father-daughter household is not as disapproved, but if the girl appears marriageable, then the father may be condemned and the daughter urged to bestir herself. Brother-and-sister households, such a common refuge of the genteel poor in other ages, are also frowned upon, even where one is widowed and has children. Somebody will be said to be sacrificed to somebody else in such an arrangement. Unmarried children who are self-supporting shouldn't be clinging to the home; they should get out and get married and start homes of their own. Nor should the elderly parents of married children live in their children's homes, certainly not if they are both alive to be "company for each other," and not unless absolutely necessary when only one survives. The rigorousness of the American belief that in-laws, especially mothers-in-law, are ruinous to marriages takes little account of the loneliness of elderly people. We respect them when they "make their own lives," without, however, any social arrangements that make it possible for them to do so. The two exceptions to the insistence on the inferiority, and indeed genuine undesirability, of any other form of living-arrangement than the biological family with young or no children, are the cases of two unmarried women living together and of the divorced or widowed woman with some children who returns to the home of some relative, often an unmarried sister, or a father.* The proper attitude

* In 1947 one family in ten did not maintain a separate home. Of these, 2,500,000 were married couples with or without children; that is, individuals who are culturally entitled to feel that their happiness is as seriously endangered as their health would be during a famine. Three-quarters of a million were parent-child groups (nearly all mother-and-child groups).[1]

towards a woman with children to support whose husband is dead, or who is divorced, is to hope that she will marry again, and that the present living-arrangement is merely temporary. Children need a man in the home to bring them up, and are to be pitied if they haven't got a father. Grandfathers and uncles are not thought of as really good substitutes. As for the households in which two unmarried women live together, they are still regarded with a tolerance that includes some of the last century's pity and absolution from blame of the woman who did not marry, but this is markedly decreasing. Young women to-day who work and share a household have to draw heavily on the housing situation or considerations of economy to justify their continuing such an arrangement. There will be doubts, perhaps fears, that at least the chances of marriage, for one if not both, are being compromised by the arrangement. Group living for men is only really tolerated in college dormitories, in armies, and in work-camps, highly patterned situations where either men are assumed to be too young to marry or their wives cannot accompany them. Men who keep house together have to fend off very heavy social doubts as to their heterosexuality. The ethics that informs all these various social disapprovals, which is expressed in private upbraiding of the one who is assumed to be selfish and attempts to rouse the one who is assumed to be suffering, is the firm American belief that one of the most heinous sins is to limit other people's emotional freedom to live the good life. As the good life is defined as marriage, obviously any living-arrangement is wrong that may make any marriageable individual forgo marriage, and to benefit from such an arrangement is selfish and exploitive.

All of these attitudes and preferences add up to a world in which one should either be married, with a home of one's own, or live alone, eating in restaurants, reading all night in bed, seeing the same movies twice, dependent upon endless daily plans and initiative for companionship. Against such a background it is not surprising that Americans see one of the principal values in marriage as companionship, for we are a gregarious people, needing the presence of others to give us a full sense of ourselves. Nowhere in childhood or youth is there any training or any practice in self-sufficient isolation. Everything that a child does quietly by itself is suspect. "He is so quiet he must be up to mischief." Day-dreaming is frowned upon. People who would rather stay at home with a good book than go out with friends get poor scores on personality quizzes. Even simple sensuous pleasures, such as reading in the bath-tub on Sunday morning, are regarded as pretty self-indulgent and antisocial. Most time spent alone could be spent better if spent with others, and time and money are valuables that ought to be spent in the best way possible. The child goes from a home in which the whole family share a living-room to a school in which he studies and plays in groups, through an adolescence in which any night when he doesn't have to study he feels left out if he hasn't a date, to an adulthood in which any break in ready companionship is felt as almost unbearable. In his empty room he turns on the radio as soon as he enters, to dispel the silence. "Silence," says a generation brought up to study in groups with a radio blaring over their heads, "is embarrassing." Which is another way of saying that when one is left alone with oneself, the question "What have you done to deserve being alone?" is almost inevitable, for children who are watched if they seek isolation are also as punishment sent out of the room or to bed.

> And if you doubt what things I say,
> Suppose you make the test;
> Suppose when you've been bad someday
> And up to bed are sent away
>   From mother and the rest—
> Suppose you ask, "Who has been bad?"

And then you'll hear what's true;
For the wind will moan in its ruefullest tone:
"Yooooooooo!
"Yooooooooo!
"Yooooooooo!" [2]

Self-sought loneliness and involuntary loneliness are both unattractive and suspect. The more popular and loved one is,
the more sought-after, the more selfish it becomes to sit at
home with a good book, and so make at least one other person involuntarily unhappy. Good-sportsmanship, which has
shifted much of its meaning in America from its traditional
English content, includes never refusing to do something
labelled as fun if one or more other people ask you to, on
such grounds as being tired, fed-up, or even needing to
study, or write letters, or mend one's stockings. Critics of
Americans' need for the reassurance of other people's company often neglect to stress that in a culture like ours universally acknowledged needs also imply universal duties,
and that if every one is defined as lonely when he is alone,
then it is obviously every one's duty to be with some one
else. So children have to have "some one to play with," adolescents have to have dates, and adults have to marry and
have a home of their own.

Assured companionship and parenthood thus become the
two socially desirable values that cannot be obtained outside marriage. Almost every other human need that has historically been met in the home can now be met outside it:
restaurants serve food; comics, movies, and radio provide
amusement, news, and gossip; there are laundries and dry-
cleaners and places that mend one's socks and store one's
winter coat, wash one's hair and manicure one's nails and
shine one's shoes. For sex satisfaction it is no longer necessary to choose between marriage and prostitution; for most
of those without religious scruples sex is available on a
friendly and amateur basis and without responsibility. The

automobile has made it even unnecessary for one of a pair of temporary sex partners to have an apartment. Entertaining can be done in a hotel or at a club. When one is sick, one goes to a hospital, and when one dies, one can be buried quite professionally from an undertaking establishment. A telephone service will answer one's telephone, and a shopping service do one's shopping. The old needs of food, shelter, sex, and recreation are all efficiently met outside the home—and yet more people are married to-day than ever before in the country's recorded history.

Marriage is a state towards which young Americans are propelled, and within which American women, educated to be energetic and active, try to live out the desires that have been both encouraged and muffled in them as children. Although there are other cultures in which women dominate the home more, America is conspicuous for the extent to which women have set the style of the home. This may be referred to a variety of background events: to the way in which the realm of the aesthetic was left to women during pioneer days, to the emphasis on work for every one which meant that men were too tired to spend much of their effort on the home; and, very importantly, to the division of labour among non-English-speaking immigrants. When immigrants came to this country, the husband set to work to make a living, the wife to find out how to live, and this division between making a living and a way of life, one as man's field, the other as woman's, has been intensified. Our patterns of urban life, with its highly developed transportation systems which mean that fewer and fewer men ever come home to lunch, are also one of the supporting factors in the situation. As more schools are consolidated and the distance from home is increased, and as school-lunches develop, the home with school-age children is deserted all day long, while Mother is free to study the magazines and rearrange the living-room or her knowledge of world peace or the community's school system, in between answering the telephone, waiting for the laundry-man, and doing the next errand.

So it falls to the lot of women to design the way of life of the family, consulting her husband on major issues only, simply because that is her job. Into it, during the early days of marriage and motherhood she pours all the energy that comes from a healthy well-fed active childhood. If she has had a good education and is trained for some outside work, or even possibly for a career, even more if she was successful before marriage, there is likely to be an extra bit of emphasis in the way she manages her home and her children, in her insistence on what a good mother and what a good wife she is. Sometimes she can even say frankly: "Yes, I know my child is old enough to go to school alone, but I still take her. After all, that is my justification for staying home." More often, without any articulate comment on her doubt as to whether home-making really is a full-time job, she simply puts more effort into her complex day. Here the same standards apply that apply to her husband: like him, she also must succeed, must make good, must meet higher and higher standards.

When we analyze the task of home-making in the United States to-day, in the home that is celebrated in the pages of the women's magazines and assumed in the carefully unspecific radio serials, we find some very curious contradictions. The well-equipped home—towards which all the advertisements are pointed—is a home in which everything can be done more quickly and more effortlessly, clothes get white in no time, irons press almost without your noticing it, the extra attachment on the vacuum cleaner will even brush the backs of your books, the new silver-polish keeps your silver looking like new. In fact, the American woman, and the American woman's husband, who does not escape the advertisements even if he misses the radio serials, are told how fortunate, modern, and leisurely she can be—if she simply equips her house properly. There really seems to have been a period—back in the twenties, when domestic servants were still relatively available—when a married woman who had a goodly supply of gadgets, and at least one servant, did get quite a little time to play bridge. Her image lingers on in the avid comments of professional women over fifty who still see the home-maker as having a wicked amount of leisure—especially when contrasted with the life led by the woman who must both work and discharge all the duties of the home-maker, as so many American women do, not by choice but by necessity. There was a time also when in the first fine flush of laundries and bakeries, milk deliveries and canned goods, ready-made clothes and dry-cleaning, it did look as if American life was being enormously simplified. A vacuum cleaner was a great addition to a home that kept the standards of a carpet-sweeper and a broom, laundries were a godsend to a household whose routine of sheet-changing was geared to the old-fashioned wash-tub, and bakeries to homes in which the making of bread had dominated one whole day. But just as our new medical palliatives are creating new vulnerabilities and new disease states, so the new equipment has led not to more leisure, more time to play with the baby, more time to curl up and read by an open fire, or to help with the PTA, but has merely combined with other trends in making the life of the American home-maker not easier, but more exacting. Most urban-living women do not realize that, as the Bryn Mawr report shows, housekeeping activities consumed 60.55 hours a week in a typical farm family, 78.35 in urban households in cities under 100,-000, and 80.57 in households in cities of over 100,000.[3] This was in pre-war days, and in a world that has been moving steadily towards a forty-hour week on the job.

Perhaps the most significant word in family relationships that has been invented for a very long time is the word "sitter"—the extra person who must come into the family and sit whenever the two parents go out of it together. The modern wife and mother lives alone, with a husband who comes home in the evening, and children, who as little children are on her hands twenty-four hours out of twenty-four, in a house that she is expected to run with the efficiency of a factory—for hasn't she a washing-machine and a vacuum cleaner?—and from which a great number of the compensations that once went with being a home-maker have been removed. Except in rural areas, she no longer produces, in the sense of preserving and pickling and canning. She has no orgies of house-cleaning twice a year. She doesn't give the sort of party where she is admired because of the heaps of food that she has ostentatiously prepared, but instead she is admired just in proportion to the way she "looks as if it had taken her no time at all." As our factories move towards the ideal of eliminating human labour, our home ideals have paralleled them; the successful home-maker to-day should always look as if she had neither done any work nor would have to do any; she should produce a finished effect effortlessly, even if she has to spend all day Saturday rehearsing the way in which she will serve an effortless Sunday-morning breakfast. The creativity that is expected of her is a creativity of management of an assembly-line, not of materials lovingly fashioned into food and clothes for children. She shops, she markets, she chooses, she transports, she integrates, she co-ordinates, she fits little bits of time together so as "to get through the week," and her proudest boast often has to be "It was a good week. Nothing went wrong."

The average young American woman is very cheerful over these tasks. They are a drain on her nervous energy rather than on her physical strength, time-consuming rather than back-breaking; in her incredibly clean and polished home, her kitchen where the handle of the egg-beater matches the step-ladder in colour, she moves lightly, producing the miracle dishes that will make her husband and children happy and strong. Two things mar her happiness, however: the fear that even though she never has any time, she is not perhaps doing a full-time job, and the fact that although she, like her brother, was taught that the right to choose a job is every American's sacred right, she doesn't feel that she chose this one. She chose wifehood and motherhood, but she did not necessarily choose to "keep house." That, in the phrasing of contemporary America, is thrust upon her because she is a woman; it is not a full status to be proudly chosen, but a duty that one cannot avoid and still find happiness in marriage. Women who have jobs ask her what she is doing and she says, "Nothing," or, "Just keeping house." Eighty hours a week of work, a sitter perhaps one evening a week, great loneliness as she rushes through the work that no other woman now shares, with an eye on the children as they play, hurrying so as to look "fresh and rested" when her husband comes home.

As we have narrowed the home, excluded from it the grandmother, the unmarried sister, the unmarried daughter, and—as part of the same process of repudiating any sharing of a home with another adult—the domestic servant has vanished, we have multiplied the number of homes in which the whole life of the family has to be integrated each day, meals cooked, lunches packed, children bathed, doors locked, dogs walked, cats put out, food ordered, washing-machines set in motion, flowers sent to the sick, birthday-cakes baked, pocket-money sorted, mechanical refrigerators defrosted. Where one large pot of coffee once served a household of ten or twelve, there are three or four small pots to be made and watched and washed and polished. Each home has been reduced to the bare essentials—to barer essentials than most primitive people would consider possible. Only one woman's hands to feed the baby, answer the telephone, turn off the gas under the pot that is boiling over, soothe the older child who has broken a toy, and open both doors at once. She is a nutritionist, a child psychologist, an engineer, a production manager, an expert buyer, all in one. Her husband sees her as free to plan her own time, and envies her; she sees him as having regular hours, and envies him. To the degree to which they also see each other as the same kind of people, with the same tastes and the same preferences, each is to a degree dissatisfied and inclined to be impatient with the other's discontent.

It is not new in history that men and women have misunderstood each other's rôles or envied each other, but the significant aspect of the American scene is that there is a discrepancy between the way we bring up boys and girls—each to choose both a job and a marriage partner—and then stylize housekeeping as a price the girl pays without stylizing the job as the price the boy pays. Men are trained to want a job in a mill, or a mine, on a farm, in an office, on a newspaper, or on a ship as a sign of their maleness, their success, and to want a wife and children to crown that success; but women to-day are not given the same clear career-line—to want an apartment, or a semi-detached house, or a farm-house, or a walk-up, or some other kind of home, as their job. The American woman wants a husband, yes, children, yes, a home of her own—yes indeed, it's intolerable to live with other people! But housekeeping—she isn't sure she wouldn't rather "do something" after she gets married. A great proportion of men would like a different job—to have at least better pay, or higher status, or different working-conditions—but they are not asked to face the seeming discrepancy between being reared for a choice and reared to think that success matters, and also that love matters and that every one should marry, and yet not be able to feel that the mate one chooses and the job one does after marriage are independent. It is as if a man were to make a set of plans for his life—to be an accountant, or a lawyer, or a pilot—and then have to add, "Unless of course, I marry." "Why?" you ask. "Because then I'll have to be a farmer. It's better for the children, you know."

It is not that we have found any good substitute for the association between home-making and motherhood. Good nurseries and schools can put children into good settings for many hours a day, settings that are often better than the small family where two bitter little rivals may otherwise spend hours quarrelling and traumatizing each other. Freezers and frozen-food services and pressure cookers make it possible to prepare meals without long hours beside a watched pot. Hospitals do care for the very ill. But the task of integrating the lives of little children, even with the help of nursery-schools, kindergartens, and play-grounds, remains a full-time charge on some woman's time. If one woman leaves the home to work, part time or full time, another woman must replace her unless the children are to suffer. The nursery-school is no answer for the child with a cold, or the child who has been exposed to some contagious disease that it has not contracted. American women have become steadily more independent, more enterprising, more efficient, less willing to be merely part of some on-going operation, more insistent that when they do paid work, they work on a strictly professional basis, with part of their personality only, and that when they keep house they must be completely in control. But the price of this autonomy has risen also. It is almost as if the pioneer dream, which led Europeans of all sorts of backgrounds to become the independent American farmer, who could turn his hand to anything—and which survives to-day in the perennial nostalgia for a chicken-farm, or a business where one is one's own boss—had been transferred to the women, who live it out in their homes, but without the full pleasure of feeling that this is the job as well as the husband, the routine as well as the children, that they chose.

The intensity with which the American woman with children tends to her task of home-making includes innumerable excursions out of the home, as consumer, as transportation officer of the family, as responsible citizen who must protect the environment in which her children grow up by working for better schools, better play-grounds, better public-health regulations. To the old puritan vigour of the pioneer woman is now added a recognition that the modern isolated home, just because it is so isolated, is also terribly dependent upon the community. The functions that no one woman in a home by herself can possibly discharge must somehow be organized in the community around her, and even so, mothers cannot get sick. When they do, there are no adequate ordinary social ways of meeting this major emergency in the lives of their children. But however actively a married woman with small children takes responsibility for community work, still her life is centred in, her time filled by, her home, but principally by the children. She may importune her husband to take her out, she may complain loudly of the loneliness and the boredom of housework, but she does not complain that she has nothing to do.

It is all the harder for the mother of adolescent children when the break comes, when the children leave home for school or jobs and her task is over. Every social pressure to which she is subjected tells her that she should not spoil her children's lives, that she should let them lead their own lives, that she should make them independent and self-sufficient. Yet the more faithfully she obeys these injunctions, the more she is working herself out of a job. Some day, while she is still a young woman, she will have to face a breakfast-table with only one face across it, her husband's, and she will be alone, quite alone, in a home of their own. She is out of a job; her main justification, the work for which she "gave up everything," is gone, and yet there are still two, possibly three, meals a day to get, the door to be answered, the house to be cleaned. But there are only dishes for two and floors do not need to be polished so often when there are no chil-

dren's feet to track them up. She isn't completely out of a
job, but she is on the shelf, kicked upstairs, given one of
those placebos by which large organizations whose employees have tenure try to disguise from the employee who
is still too young to be retired the fact that he ought to be.
This domestic crisis is of course much more difficult if it
occurs at and is reinforced by the hormonal instability and
emotional fears that surround the menopause, and combine
unjustified fear of the loss of physical desire with the necessary recognition of the end of reproductivity.[4] For married
American women who have had children, the fear of loss of
attractiveness and the fear of becoming emotionally unstable outweigh worries about the end of reproductivity, for
they have had the one or two or three children that validate
their marriages and, at least consciously, do not want more.

Meanwhile the father has been facing difficulties of his
own. His rôle in the maturation of his children, especially
in the maturation of his son, is to be the friendly ally of the
boy, to help him cut free from his mother's apron-strings.
To the extent that he sympathizes with and facilitates his
son's growing desires for a job and a girl, he is a good father.
He must pooh-pooh the mother's anxieties, back the boy up
in minor escapades, be fraternally understanding. But to the
extent that he does this he runs several risks. He relives,
at least in imagination, his own budding freedom as a young
adult, the freedom that he traded in so young, so willingly,
for the continuous unremitting work that has kept his marriage going. Remembering, he may begin to feel that he has
never really lived, that he settled down too early. This feeling may be all the stronger if it comes at a time when he
realizes that further advancement in job or profession is
unlikely. As long as the gradient of his life was rising, he
was spurred on by the great rewards that Americans find in
success. But now it will rise no further, he will instead in
many cases have to work simply to hold his place, a dispirit-

ing thought. Helping his son escape from his mother further identifies his wife for him as one from whom he has, after all, never properly escaped himself into the pleasant by-ways of irresponsible dalliance. Seeing his wife through his son's eyes, and through the eyes of his son's friends, he discovers a new impatience with her, as the representative of finished, self-satisfied achievement. Here he is, only in middle age, and his life is over—no new love, no new fields to conquer, only emptiness ahead. So while he is not out of a job—indeed he may often be at the height of his work-strength—the very nature of the life-cycle in America is such that he feels like an old man. He may have to fight very hard to resist the impulse to break away from it all, and he may develop serious health disturbances and die prematurely.

Superficially, the problem that faces the middle-aged couple in the home of their own is that the mother's main life-task is done while she is strong and well, and she must now find some other channel for her energies and still keep her life adjusted to the habits and needs of a husband who has lived terribly closely with her in that little self-contained home, while that husband's life-task is still going full tilt. But because of the great emphasis on Youth, because Youth is the period to which both sexes look back and age holds so few rewards, both face a deeper crisis of disappointment. This crisis may be further intensified if there are deaths of aged parents to be faced, with all the complications of the disposition of a surviving parent, long months of illness, sales of houses and furniture, all of which exacerbate the conflict about growing older. Every step of this process is made more acute by the insistence that each married couple should be self-sufficient, because many such couples have forgotten how. Yet they cannot look forward to combined homes with their married children, or with their widowed or unmarried siblings. Deeply dependent upon each other in every way, they have often become so just to the extent that the marriage is a good marriage. They have become so much like a single person that, like most individuals in America, they feel the need of others to complete themselves, to reassure them that they are good, to rid them of the self-searching that comes from being left alone and the self-reproach that attends condemning others to aloneness.

There are emerging solutions to this crisis when the children leave home. Some couples attempt a last child, for which there are even affectionate slang phrases—"little post-script," "little frost blossom"—that change the tone of the old folk-phrase "change-of-life baby." To have such a child is one way of facing the extent to which the woman's life in that home, and the marriage itself, has centred on the children. The most familiar solution is for women to make much of the independence for which they have openly yearned during the time they were tied down and go in for some active voluntary work, or even go back to the work they did before they were married. But in this event they face new hazards, especially if they have lived successfully through the instabilities of the menopause. Free of their major previous responsibilities, with twenty good years ahead of them, such women may start out on a gradient that rises steeply as they become involved in community activities or the delights of a job from which they have had a long vacation. And as it is the gradient that matters so much in America, their enthusiastic new spurt may contrast sharply with their husbands' unhappy acceptance of a plateau. A daughter's marriage and permitted absorption in grandchildren may mute the wife's energetic attitude towards her new activities, but that involves a severe problem for the husband who has to face the fact that he is a grandfather. In a country that gives so few rewards to age, who wants to be a grandfather? The woman of his unlicenced day-dreams is still a slim girl in her teens, now younger than his married daughter, who with each step that she takes towards maturity puts him more definitely out of the running.

Increasingly, the more aware middle-aged couples are treating this period seriously, assaying their personal as well as their material resources, and directing their plans not towards some dim and unhoped-for retirement, but towards the next twenty years. To the extent that both are able to re-plan their lives together, they make of the crisis a step forward rather than a step back. It is probable that society will recognize this period as a period in which professional counselling is needed as much as in adolescence. For each married couple alone in a home of their own is exposed to pressures and difficulties unknown in differently organized societies. And expressive of the shifting cycle of responsibility, the young married sons and daughters sit in their own small homes and try to decide what to do about Father and Mother. This is a question that is not answered by their all taking a house together, but by finding the parents something they can be interested in. Ideally, they will readjust their lives, live independently of their children except for grave emergencies, act as sitters, which means they go in as their children go out, and finally retire to a cottage in Florida, where their children piously hope they will have a lot of friends of their own age.

XVII

CAN MARRIAGE BE FOR LIFE?

THE AMERICAN MARRIAGE IDEAL IS ONE OF THE MOST CON-
spicuous examples of our insistence on hitching our wagons
to a star.* It is one of the most difficult marriage forms that
the human race has ever attempted, and the casualties are
surprisingly few, considering the complexities of the task.
But the ideal is so high, and the difficulties so many, that it
is definitely an area of American life in which a very rigorous
re-examination of the relationship between ideals and practice is called for.

In the American marriage ideal, choice by both partners
is not only approved but demanded. Life is easier if parents
approve, but neither the law nor social expectation demands
that they should. Young people who let their parents inter-
fere with their marriages are regarded as either emotionally
immature or trapped by bribes that parents with money and
influence can pay. But the ideal girl and the ideal boy choose
and marry each other in spite of all obstacles. They may

* See Appendix II.

have been school-mates all their lives. This is a familiar
sentimental theme, "When you wrote on my slate, 'I love
you, Joe,' when we were a couple of kids," or the opposite
picture of male initiative, "I've loved you since you were a
baby, since you used to crawl on the floor." They may have
been members of the same high-school gang, dated together,
and then finally realized that they were made for one another. They may have met on a train, on a boat, in an accident, at a fire, in a shipwreck, standing in line at the Grand
Central Station, on a blind date, or by mail. "On Sunday, May
2, 1943, I got my first letter from her. I was in Albuquerque,
New Mexico, and on Saturday, June 3, 1944, we were married in St. Louis, Missouri." Their acquaintance may have
been launched into certainty by discovering that the brother
of one and the uncle of the other had both played, at different times, on the football team of a small Middle Western
college. But whether it is sitting side by side in the fourth
grade while he dips her pigtails in the ink, or riding home on
the same street-car line, or eyes that meet in a service club
during a war, or the excitement that springs up between a
man and the girl his room-mate invited to the spring prom—
all of this is the special lucky chance which brings the two
together that each may choose the other. Same school, same
town, same railroad wreck, have the same functional position in a romantic structure which disregards all of those
realities of time and place, of common habits and common
social background, on which marriage has usually been
based. All the parents' compensatory efforts to keep their
children in groups with their own kind of people, own religion, own class, own race, can be partly interpreted as precautions against this romantic ideal of choosing some one
for themselves alone, reinforced, fortunately for the stability
of American marriage, by the American fear of getting out
of one's own class, or at least out of the class that one wants
to belong to. Not only the parents, but the young people

seeking a mate, do a good part of their seeking in approved quarters where the chance that brings true-lovers together can only operate on an approved invitation list. But counter-pointed against this caution we find the recurrent theme in popular art of the boy or the girl met under circumstances that make them seem unavailable, only to discover in the end that in addition to all the personal qualities that make them lovable, they also are not really kitchen knaves or hat-check girls, but have been to the right schools and known the right people, or conversely, were poor boys or girls them-selves who have just risen to success, and really understand. Very small primitive societies often phrase marriage as choice, but the choice is among some eight to ten girls, most of whom, usually all, the boy has known all his life, or if they are sought in the next village, all of whom at least come from a completely similar background. But in the United States, theoretically only the major racial divisions limit choice, so that several million boys and girls are potential mates if they meet and fall in love. This falling-in-love may happen anywhere, and for men at any time from the kinder-garten to old age; for women it is regarded as dangerous, and leading to more trouble than happiness, to fall in love after their children reach adolescence and after they stop pretending that they are thirty-five.

Nor is this falling-in-love seen as patterned on the past and as reinstating an age-old way of life shared by their an-cestors, one of whom died in the bed in which they were born. "I want a girl just like the girl who married dear old Dad," and the converse, "Oh, if Mother hadn't married Daddy, Daddy might have married me," are songs about parent-child relationships rather than any recognition that the future will repeat the past. The girl of a man's dream will neither dress like his mother nor look like his mother; she may speak with a very different accent, cook different food, manage her house differently in every respect, and she will be expected to disagree with both his mother and hers on most of the details of living. The choice of one's life, one's fate, comes out of the future, either unrelated to or definitely contradictory of the past. A first sign of assimilation of the foreign-born is the marriage out of the group, reinforced by the fact that it is easier for parents who see their children turning away from every Old World custom to blame a mixed marriage than to accept the defection of two young people of the same background. A recent popular novel, *White Fawn*, a paper edition, sums up the whole position.[1] A girl of Boston blue blood meets under most unconventional circumstances—he runs over her dog—a promising young doctor of very simple Irish parentage. Both are presented as loving their families, and all the advisers in the case declare the marriage impossible, as both families live in Boston, and he has set his heart on success in spite of Boston's socially closed doors. Then comes the solution: not in Boston, never in Boston, but in some other city far away, in Seattle, they can "begin life over again." He has an education as good as hers, Seattle will be new to both of them, and any manners that he may have which fit another social level will quickly drop away under the tutelage of a wife who loves him enough to leave everything for him. Love wins, democracy wins; the honest pride of the Boston Irish, the faithfulness to the essentials of caste phrased in moral individualistic terms, are both vindicated, and a new growing American city gets a fine young doctor and a family on which it can depend. In this story there is a sub-theme of the girl's mother's flirtation with a younger man who is tied to a sick wife. The mother nobly "lets him go" as soon as his wife dies and he is free to marry. So while the absolute overriding importance of love as between the marriageable is insisted upon, love that cannot be expressed in marriage must be given up. The mother, although still young and charming and given to pretty négligées, is rewarded for her own self-denying life with a stern older husband by her joy in her daughter's solution. Thousands of marriages that, while not as dramatic, contain just as difficult background contrasts take place every year in America, and will take place even more frequently as young women become almost as foot-loose as young men.

Romantic love when the choice is among only ten possible girls, all of similar backgrounds and appropriate domestic skills, can safely follow the dictates of physical attraction. The nestling of a curl on the neck, a way of glancing from under the eyelids, a little trill of laughter in the girl, or in the boy a certain swing of the shoulders, a certain shyness or boldness of the eyes, can be used to distinguish one young farmer or one young fisherman from another. Such delicious qualities are not as safe guides when one is choosing a mate from a million otherwise unidentified people. Yet it remains the ideal for men, and only a little less the ideal for women. While the cautious may say, "I want to find out more about him before I fall for him," "I fell for him before I knew how to spell his name" remains the more romantic ideal and frequent enough practice. During the period when a marriage is regarded as successful and happy, it will be the incautious type of behaviour that will be dwelt on as proving that the marriage is based on real love. When her daughter repeats the same incautious gesture, the mother cannot repudiate the romantic story that has been told so often, unless she wishes at the same time to tell her daughter the ways in which her marriage has disappointed her in order to warn the daughter against the same lack of caution.

It has been pointed out that a frequent theme of modern movies is the "good-bad" girl, the girl who, met under compromising circumstances, turns out to be nevertheless a good, marriageable girl.[2] Such an unconventional, anonymous meeting with a girl of suitable class and religion is the ideal solution of the American marriage dilemma, in which in order to prove love you must disregard every practical consideration in making a marital choice, but to have a happy marriage the mates should be as much alike as possible.

For here comes the other side of the romantic picture, the acceptance of women on a very close to equality status, and the hope of that companionship and understanding which comes from similar tastes, politics, athletic skills, choice of friends, and even, according to one style in predicting marriage success, the same amount of introversion or of self-confidence. There is less and less sense that the strong should marry the weak, that an intelligent man is better off with a frivolous wife (though he may prefer a non-intellectual one), that quantitative differences in education between husband and wife are a good thing. And since education is so similar for boys and girls, this means a premium on similarity. "Give-and-take in marriage" is one of our ideals. Simple contrasts, such as contrasts in height or colouring, may add piquancy; there is an insistence that the wife accept home-making as her status in order to settle at least one point of differentiation. But actual personality differentiation between the sexes is devalued. So the dilemma that is solved so neatly in film and novel is not solved so easily in real life. A man must find a girl who is the identical twin of himself in every aspect of background, religion, education, and experience, under circumstances which will convince both that each chose the other from among millions of competitors for something intrinsic and independent of all these considerations. Young people exclaim over the pretty girl or the football hero who instead of venturing forth to new pastures marries the boy or the girl next door, and put them down as frightened and lacking in what it takes; they expect no good to come of it. Wiser heads shake over the chances for happiness when there are great differences in class and education, and expect no good to come of that.

As individual choice is expected to be the one criterion for planning a marriage, so also individual choice and the price of the marriage license and ceremony are all that is required for any two unmarried people who are of age (subject to some racial bars in some states) to marry each other. A few states demand a doctor's examination; sometimes the couple is required to wait three days. But nothing else is required. There is no insistence that the man have a job or prove that he can make a living. There is no requirement that the girl have a single skill necessary for home-making. She may never have boiled an egg or held a baby in her arms, or even done her own hair or washed her own stockings. Not only is parental assent not required, but there is no invocation of any representatives of the past of either man or girl, who might introduce such considerations as the six months that one of the two has spent in sanitarium, mental institution, or prison. Alone, without a single record of the other's past, and without a single socially required guarantee of the future, the two are permitted to contract a state to which emotionally, as well as legally, they are theoretically bound for life. It is only during wars and in big cities that such marriages are very frequent, but the fact that they can occur high-lights the form of our marriage, the lack of protection that we give young people who attempt to act out completely the social expectation that they themselves are adequate to judge their own life-partners, and need neither help nor advice.

Nor are the newly married conceived of as needing material help. In fact the employer who pays a married man a better wage than an unmarried one is often thought of as having found a clever way of underpaying his unmarried employees. We also find condemnation of the department-store that prefers unmarried girls who live cheaply at home with their parents and will accept low wages. Both are thought of as exploitive. A firm may prefer married employees because they are steadier, or refuse to employ married women because they have too many personal home problems, but in that case the personnel policy is protecting the firm, not the married men and women. Unions, fighting for seniority privileges, override the needs of the married, even to putting women with young children on graveyard shifts. The world in which the newly married couple have to fend for themselves does nothing about them, and if pregnancy is apparent, the young wife will find that househunting suddenly becomes much more difficult, and that there are large blocks of apartments in which children are not wanted.

Nor are parents expected to do anything for them materially. A wedding is something that an indulgent father or a social-minded mother either "gives the daughter" or perhaps insists on against the young people's will. Friends may give showers, but here again this depends upon the exigencies of time and place. No dowry, no bride-price, no settlement on the wife, no wagon loaded with feather-beds and copper kettles, no cow whose calf will feed the new baby, no plot of ground, no newly built tent, no peasant cot in which the old people now take a back seat, no four-poster bed, no fine linen, are essential to the new marriage. This does not mean of course that many fathers do not give their daughters or their sons substantial gifts, even houses and cars, at marriage, but this is extra, it is not expected. Parents are not chided if they fail to provide for their children, and the children are a little apologetic about any such gifts— for young people ought to stand on their own feet. So strong is this feeling about independence that wealthy parents who plan to leave all their money to their children let the young people struggle along in poverty for years when their needs are greatest rather than give them help that would be bad for their characters. The fear of falling back upon father or father-in-law is always there to goad the young couple into renewed efforts, because maturity is never won finally in the United States, but is dependent upon the ability to support oneself.*

So without benefit of the careful sanctions and help with which many other societies have surrounded their new marriages, each young couple starts off life alone. They start to "make a life together." Ideally, they alone choose where they will live, what their style of life will be, whether their money will go for a car or a little place in the country, a living-room set or a bedroom set, a lamp or a radio. To the extent that their parents set the style in which they live, the parents are felt as interfering, which is one reason why it is so very difficult to be the children of upper-class parents in the United States, who have preserved a sense that they should be allowed to manage their children's way of life because it reflects on the family name. But the prevailing American ideal makes it more appropriate for children to remonstrate with their parents over their way of living than for parents to remonstrate with their children. This independence of parental interference is of course accompanied by the most meticulous attention either to the style of the clique to which they belong, or hope to belong, or to some image of such a clique derived from the magazines and the department-store windows. The choice that is exercised is often within very narrow limits, even when it seems to have the enormous individuality of a modern Christmas-card with a picture of your own dog or your own baby on it. But whether to furnish a house in a style that is modern or period or mixed, or whether to have a white or a mahogany radio,

---

* This same fear of loss of hard-won maturity can be found in American attitudes towards Great Britain, with the recurrent political appeal of preserving our freedom from British interference and political capital being made of the danger to Chicago, as in the thirties, of domination by King George.

a Ford or a Chevrolet, live in the city or become a commuter
—these are all felt as genuine choices, and choices that a
married couple increasingly make together. It is no question of the bride's fitting into the relentless domination of a
mother-in-law, or the husband's either imposing his own
style of life or accepting that of his wife. Although the consumption skills of the wife are more crucial to the class position of a family, the ideal is that the husband be in agreement with the choices; the details he leaves to her. Together
they plan when the first baby is to come—unless they belong
to a faith which feels these are matters which should be left
to God; they name it, and plan its future. Here again, all
the details of discipline and training are left to the wife,
but the husband is supposed to take an interest. It is no
longer a question of a patriarchal bread-winner who asserts
his right to rule his own home, but rather of a wife who complains that a husband who doesn't participate in that home
is not living up to his rôle.

To the extent that their backgrounds are similar, they can
stylize their minor disagreements as part of the pattern of
marriage and quarrel happily for twenty-five years over
whether they want to keep a dog or a cat, go to the seaside
or the mountains, go out or stay in, because the issues will
all be minor ones within an agreed-upon frame. But where
class and region, nationality and religious difference, are
present, the small decision, expected to be merely the next
stitch in the firmly knitted new life, may instead unravel the
whole mesh. The smallest decision—whether to eat a hastily
assembled meal in the kitchen or to put the breakfast food
on the table in one of the trade boxes that children have
learned from the radio to like; whether to turn out the light
on the wedding-night or send a telegram instead of writing
a letter—any one of these may suddenly make them see each
other as worlds apart, not because the personality for which
each chose the other is not there, but because the unrealized,

unallowed-for differences in background are deeper than either bargained for.

The sexual ideal with which young people come to marriage, always one to which men are expected to give only lip-service, is that of chastity for both. The man who can say to a girl that she is the first is still valued by American girls almost as much as the man values being his wife's first lover. Until the era of petting, all the husband's premarital experience had to be ignored, and if possible pushed out of the wife's consciousness. Now each is condemned to wondering how far the other has gone, with whom, under what circumstances. The various conventions of frankness that are growing up are an overlay on the old concealment based on a prevalent but repudiated double standard, but they are still an overlay. For the old requirement of real virginity in the bride and a decent reticence in the groom—which included a taboo on displaying any skill as a lover—there is being substituted a determination to start with a "clean slate." Starting with a clean slate often means making a clean breast of all one's past sex experience, but this is also a very effective way of making sure that it contributes nothing to the new marriage. Instead of offering each other the relaxation, the capacity to pause and listen a little to the beating of another heart because the sound of one's own quickened heart-beat has ceased to be so astonishing, the attempt is made to offer the new marriage, which is to be "for keeps," an *as if* position in which none of the past is relevant.

This ability to block out the past, to enter each new situation, be it job or love-affair, with the kind of innocence that it seems to Europeans could only be acquired by amnesia from a blow on the head is a peculiarly American characteristic, bred of the need to be both poised for flight and firmly rooted in the immediate landscape.[3] Oriented outward, towards time and place and the actual concrete realities of life, we develop a capacity to respond quickly, learn and use first names, take the woes and joys of the man at the next desk or the woman across the aisle in a train as our own. Nostalgia for the past is out of place among a people who must always be moving, to a better job, a better house, a new way of life. To the immigrant from Poland to New Jersey or from Massachusetts to Iowa or from Illinois to California, nostalgia for the past way of life is an acute threat to good adjustment in the new environment. To the children of immigrants, there is a new danger, that they may absorb not the direct nostalgia for Poland or Massachusetts, but the parents' sense of unreality, of repudiated roots, of rootlessness. This too must be fended off, and it can be fended off by taking the present reality as the only reality and yet keeping one eye always on the future, which may be different. So Americans do not find it shocking to say to three different girls in a year, "You are the only girl I have ever loved," because the girl who came before is defined as unloved by the very fact that another is loved now. Past loves, past experiences, are named over to be by that very act eliminated. Each lover brings to marriage a conviction that this is the real thing, the only reality for either one. If it fails, then it is not the real thing, but the next experience may be. So each job, each home, each friend, and each lover can be eagerly accepted, optimistically, whole-heartedly, and no failure along the way finally disproves—for the healthy—the possibility of a later success.

Greater sex experimentation has not therefore contributed as much as it sometimes does to an easier sex relationship in marriage. Facility remains as a suspect reminder that the slate cannot be wiped clean after all, and past failures consciously repudiated are still there as a carking anxiety. The exaggerated over-concern with the other that is the American version of good interpersonal relations, in which each worries for fear the other will worry, puts an extraordinary strain on sex behaviour, and especially dampens spontaneity. The more women realize what sex satisfaction can mean to men, the more they worry for fear their husbands are not getting it, and the more men worry as to whether or not their wives are unsatisfied, the less able either one of a pair is to respond simply and immediately to the other. And American culture offers very little middle ground between continuous relatedness to other people's wishes, desires, hopes, thoughts, feelings, and a complete indifference to anything except one's own desires. This possibility that once an active concern for others is repudiated as too difficult, nothing will remain except a licensed self-indulgence runs through American sex behaviour, and makes marriage, all-exacting marriage, seem the only alternative to sheer rampant, meaningless exploitation of another's personality. Affairs that do not lead to marriage are seen as exploitive; sometimes both partners are exploiting each other, so the moral stigma of hurting another person is removed, but even so the general expectation is that anything but a final and difficult commitment is in the end unrewarding.

This hope for a complete commitment fits very well with our traditional marriage form, in which Church and State combine to insist that all marriages are for life, and that no marriage can be broken without branding the one who breaks it as a failure, if not a criminal and an enemy of society. All the poetry, the phraseology, the expectation of marriage that would last "until death us do part," has survived long after most states have adopted laws permitting cheap and quick divorces. The pressure for divorce is easy enough to understand on many counts. The emphasis on choice carried to its final limits means in marriage, as it does at every other point in American life, that no choice is irrevocable. All persons should be allowed to move if they don't like their present home, change jobs as often as they can get another, change schools, change friends, change political parties, change religious affiliations. With freedom to choose goes the right to change one's mind. If past mistakes are to be reparable in every other field of human relations, why should marriage be the one exception? If their choice of each other was what made a marriage a "real marriage," then once either makes another choice, its reality is gone. The spouse who clings to such a marriage is committing one of the worst acts in the American list of sins, limiting the freedom of another person, exploiting and taking advantage of some one else's past, dead impulse, freezing a past mistake into a present prison. The more modern psychology and modern literature emphasize the importance of impulse gratification, the tighter every spouse is caught in the obligation not to limit the impulse gratification of the other person. In every triangle, where two are married, three are trapped just because the man or woman who is desired by two others is free to choose between them. Because he and she can get a divorce if they really love the third person, not getting a divorce becomes a hostile act for the one who loves both, while failing to give a divorce on the part of the partially rejected spouse is limiting the freedom of two other people. Ethical dilemmas that do not arise in countries where Church and State not only advocate and teach, but enforce, marriage for life are recurrent, inexorably associated with the degree of freedom that exists in the United States.

So an ethics that is peculiarly American has arisen in the United States, to support a marriage-and-divorce code of great contradictoriness. Young people are still encouraged to marry as if they could count on marriage's being for life, and at the same time they are absorbing a knowledge of the great frequency of divorce and the ethics that may later enjoin divorce upon them. There has been much inveighing from the pulpit and the bench which assumes that all those who get divorces are selfish, self-indulgent creatures. But as long as divorce was limited to the selfish and the self-indulgent, there were very few divorces, and it was safe to encourage young people to think of divorce as something that could happen to other people, but not to them. Divorce has now been so absorbed into our ethics that husbands or wives lie sleepless and torn, wondering, "Ought I to get a divorce? Would she be happier with somebody else? Would he develop more with somebody else? Am I spoiling his life? Am I spoiling her life? Isn't it wrong to stay with some one out of mere loyalty? What will happen to the children if this goes on? Isn't it bad for the children to live in a home with this much friction?" Not only the possibility that any marriage except the marriage where *both* partners are deeply committed to some religious orthodoxy may end in divorce, but the phrasing of divorce as something that at least one of the partners in an imperfect marriage *ought* to get, is permeating the whole country, altering our expectations, making marriage many times more difficult.

It is difficult on two counts: because the expectation of permanency is still great enough to brand every impermanence as a failure, if not a sin, and also because to all the other insecurities of American life insecurity about marriage is added. In the United States, where all status is relative, where all jobs can be lost, where men are judged by how much they continue to advance, sometimes a little by how far they have advanced, but never simply by where they are —here marriage in former generations offered one refuge from this eternal uncertainty, this endless incitement to anxious effort. Whether a man succeeded or failed, his wife was there, and whether a woman was an invalid, a failure at housekeeping, an incompetent mother, or a paragon, her husband was there—in most cases, in enough cases to reassure every healthy person that here was one harbour in which his ship could ride at anchor where the winds of success and failure blew less harshly. It was safe to be romantic when there was no real danger that new romances could tempt you away.

When I should be her lover forever and a day,
And she my faithful sweetheart till the golden hair was gray;
And we should be so happy that when either's lips were dumb
They would not smile in Heaven till the other's kiss had come.[4]

These were verses that could be appropriately written into a poem about one's wife entitled "That Old Sweetheart of Mine." The romance need not be scrutinized too carefully where there was no other choice; after the altar it was never again put to the test.

But to-day, with the growing recognition that divorce may come to any marriage, no matter how devoted, how conscientious, how much in love each spouse originally was, a marriage is something that has to be worked at each day. As the husband has to face the possibility of losing his job, so also the wife has to face the possibility of losing hers, of finding herself companionless, out of the job she chose, often with small children to care for alone. Both husband and wife face the need to re-choose each other, to reassert and re-establish the never permanent claim of one upon the other's choice. The wife in curl-papers is replaced by a wife who puts on lip-stick before she wakes her husband, and the husband with a wandering eye finds that his eye wanders less happily because at any moment it may light on some one whom he will choose instead of his wife. As it is her obligation to make herself continuingly desirable, so it is his obligation not to put himself in positions where other women may become desirable to him. This means never going out in mixed company without his wife. It means that all casual flirtations take on a menacing quality that Europeans newly come to America find it very difficult to understand. Where there is freedom to divorce, there is less free-

dom for either casual relationships or passionate extra-
marital love of any sort.

Yet the implied expectation of permanency, still based of
course on statistics—for frequent as divorces are in some age-
groups, most marriages are still permanent marriages—not
only does not protect the new marriage, it actually compromises it. For American behaviour in marriage, the behaviour that young people have learned in their own homes,
from their own and their friends' parents, is behaviour that
depends on the finality of marriage. Quarrelling, sulking,
neglectfulness, stubbornness, could be indulged very differently within a frame that could not be broken. But now over
every quarrel hang the questions: "Do you want a divorce?
Do I want a divorce? Does she want a divorce? Will that be
the end of this? Is that where we are going?"

There is no reason why we cannot develop manners and
customs appropriate to the greater fragility of marriage in
the United States; they are very badly needed. For it seems
unlikely that the other solution, tightening up on divorce
laws, is likely to occur. Once freedom of divorce has become
part of our ethics, as it has for many segments of the United
States, simply going back becomes a genuinely retrogres-
sive step. The very reasons that made divorce necessary, the
enormous heterogeneity of our population and the great
chances of maladjustment under our system of free marital
choice, would remain. Rather the more likely development
would seem to be forward to a new pattern of behaviour
that fits the new conditions. And there are signs that such a
new pattern of behaviour is developing.

In a pattern for marriage which accepts the fact that
marriage *may* be for life, *can* be for life, but also may not
be, it is possible to set to work to find ways of establishing
that permanence which is most congruent with bringing up
children, who are defined as immature until the early twenties. Although it is possible to argue and bring together much

evidence that children are more damaged when they live in an unhappy home, resonant with the spoken and unspoken resentments of at least one parent, than when they live in a better relationship with just one parent, it is not possible at present to claim that children are better-off in a broken than in a whole home. One of the most important learnings for every human child is how to be a full member of its own sex and at the same time fully related to the opposite sex. This is not an easy learning, it requires the continuing presence of a father and a mother to give it reality. If the child is to know how to hold a baby in its arms, it must be held, and if it is to know how a member of the opposite sex holds a child, it must be held by both parents. It must watch both parents meet its springing impulse, watch both parents discipline and mould their own impulses so that the child is protected, and at adolescence be set free by both parents to go out into the world. Ideally, both parents will be there to bless and define the marriage, and to help their grown children assume the parental rôle by the way in which they take their grandparenthood. This is the way in which human lives have been given full stature, and as yet we know no better way.

We do know, however, that this continuity is of a different order in a changing society than it is in a stable one, and in a heterogeneous society than it is in a homogeneous one. In a changing society like ours the models can never be so perfect, and they must be far less detailed. Daughters do not learn to make the bread that mother used to make; at best they learn to enjoy feeding their families, with different food, differently prepared. The picture of how one will look and feel, act and think, at seventy cannot be filled in by concrete details of Grandmother's gold-rimmed spectacles and Grandfather's tapping cane. At best something of the vigour with which they set out on journeys at eighty, or the placidity with which they sit in the sun and remember the hymns they sang in childhood, may become part of the child's faith in the life that he will live. There is need of developing forms of education, forms that supplement the particularness of the single family, that will make it possible for the child to learn ways of feeling and acting which can be used in a world yet unborn, a world that the imagination of the elders is powerless to anticipate. The world will be the poorer if children learn patterns of behaviour so concrete and particular that twenty years later, as adults, they must wander homeless in nostalgia for a lost way of life. We now know a great deal about how to do this, how a nursery-school can translate and broaden the child's own home experience and make the experience of each child available to the others, how parental precepts can shift from the sureness of "Never eat on the street," "Never ring a door-bell more than three times," "Never accept a present from a man that you can't use up at once or return," to a different kind of teaching which includes the recognition that eating must always be disciplined to make it possible for people to enjoy eating in each other's company, that social fictions are useful and worth respecting, and that relations between the sexes need some kind of patterning to protect those who participate in them. But it is a complicated thing to learn how to transmit a pattern in such a way that the next generation may have its protection without making that protection a prison, may have its delicate discriminations without the inability to make new discriminations, may in fact neither simply repeat nor complete it, but develop a new pattern of their own. The casualties are bound to be greater than in those old traditional societies where five generations played hide-and-seek under the same apple-tree, were born and died in the same high bed.

One of the particular characteristics of a changing society is the possibility of deferred maturity, of later and later shifts in the lives of the most complex, the most flexible individuals. In very simple societies children have completed their acceptance of themselves and their rôles in life by the time they are six or seven, and then must simply wait for physical maturity to assume a complete rôle. But in most societies, adolescence is a period of re-examination, and possible re-orientation of the self towards the expressed goals of society. In cultures like ours, there may be a second or a third adolescence, and the most complex, the most sensitive, may die still questing, still capable of change, starting like Franz Boas at seventy-seven to re-read the folk-lore of the world in the light of new theoretical developments. No one who values civilization and realizes how men have woven the fabric of their lives from their own imaginations as they played over the memory of the past, the experience of the present, and the hope of the future, can count this postponed maturity, this possibility of recurrent adolescent crises and change of life-plan, as anything but gain.

But a world in which people may reorient their whole lives at forty or fifty is a world in which marriage for life becomes much more difficult. Each spouse is given the right to and the means for growth. Either may discover a hidden talent and begin to develop it, or repudiate a paralyzing neurotic trend and begin anew. Ever since women have been educated, marriages have been endangered by the possible development or failure to develop of both husbands and wives. "He outgrew her," or less common but with increasing frequency, "She outgrew him." In a society where mobility is enjoined on every citizen and each man should die a long distance from the class he comes from—or devote his life to preventing downward movement, the only recourse left to the upper class—the danger that spouses will get out of step is very great. To all the other exorbitant requirements for a perfect mate, chosen from all the world yet in all things like the self, or complementary on a trivial basis, must be added "capacity to grow." Arapesh parents

perform anxious little magical tricks to keep the girl who
grows too fast smaller than her young husband, lest the marriage be ruined by the disparity. But American lovers have
neither divinatory methods nor precautionary magic to ensure them that they will grow and change in step. Only the
recognition of the problem itself can help to solve it, to
make young people pause in their choices as they evaluate
whether he or she will make a life companion, add to their
other criteria "capacity to grow at something like the same
rate." And they need to be able to treat failures to grow as
tragedies, but not as personal betrayals. Some day a discovered and intractable discrepancy in rate of growth may
seem a really legitimate reason for divorce, and one that
both couples can accept as simply as do those peoples who
accept childlessness as a reason for ending a marriage. Once
there is recognition that change in rate of growth is simply
a function of living in a complex modern world, then the
marriage that is developing a dangerous discrepancy may
be given professional help, just as the childless may seek the
advice of the sterility clinic. And as in the sterility clinic,
some of those who seek for help can and some cannot be
helped. But the whole way of looking at life will be changed.
For thousands of years men and women have blamed ghosts
and demons, witches and elves and the sorcery of the next
tribe, and most of all each other's inferiority or malice, for
childlessness. But to-day it is possible to seek expert help
from physiologist or psychiatrist, and the needless tragedies
can be averted, and those which cannot be averted can be
accepted gently by both. For just as there is no good marriage in which each does not wholly choose it, so there is no
good divorce that is not chosen by both partners. Among the
Negrito people of the Philippines, where vigorous little
men and women obey their chief implicitly in a society that
seems rather like the childhood of the world, when both
partners agree on a divorce it is granted at once; there

simply is no marriage. The acceptance of a religious faith that includes the ideal and the promise of indissoluble marriage carries with it dignity for man. But a civil marriage that marries any pair who choose each other and can show no legal impediment, and then will not permit them to choose to end that choice, is a travesty of all the values of human dignity. There are at best something like 71,000,000 church members in the United States, and many of these are no longer guaranteed by their faith that they will be able to stay married for life. For the other 61,000,000 a pattern must be found that will make it possible for them to treat divorce when it does occur with dignity and regret, and so make it possible for each married pair to work openly to keep and keep on keeping their marriages safe.

There are signs that a vigorous younger generation are doing just that. They are learning to handle the unprecedented and contradictory premarital freedom that they have been accorded by society so that they know the rules and can keep them. They are learning to guard their expectancies of falling in love so that the chance-met girl in the railroad station who becomes one's fate will stay more in the movies, where she belongs, and less in real life, where she is more likely to be a disappointment. They are developing new patterns of learning to know each other, to replace the outmoded long engagement, with its stylizations that now seem artificial and lacking in sincerity. For the old theory that a girl would somehow become "awakened after marriage," and the later compensatory demand for trial marriages, new methods of getting acquainted and demonstrating confidence are being worked out. These include more stages of partial commitment, the slow involvement of more friends in the possible marriage, provision for more retreats with unimpaired dignity for each partner. They are making more realistic demands on the personality of the future partner, partly under a sobering recognition of how many marriages in the war generation have gone to pieces under pressures of absence, housing, and so on, revealing a lack of what it takes to stay married in the United States to-day.* Meanwhile the society as a whole is becoming more conscious of the terrific strains that have been placed on marriages, and of the need for a variety of new measures, pre-marriage counselling, marriage counselling, nursery-schools, housekeeping services, and so on, to reduce the strain on each young couple asked to build single-handed a whole way of life in a world in which neither they, nor any one else, have ever lived. For the careful protective care that kinship groups and tribal elders, family councils and parents, once gave young people, wider social institutions that will serve the same function in a new fashion are springing into being, slowly, and against great resistance, but surely.

Meanwhile, young married people seem to be, if anything, more anxious to have children than they have been in our immediate past. Children are regarded neither as an inescapable part of life nor as a penalty of marriage, but as a value that can be consciously sought and worked for, a value that makes life worth living. The demand for symmetry between husband and wife is of course being felt here, the demand that each share in the choice made, in the planning for the children, and in the enjoyment and care of the children. As working-hours are cut down and a free Saturday becomes an American institution, many of the evils of the household that lived in a suburb for the children's sake, and so Father never got home in time to see the children, and was too tired on Sunday, can be overcome. Two free days out of seven provide enough leeway so that even very tired, overstrained men can first relax, loosen their belts and kick off their shoes, and when rested, be ready to start something sizable with the children. The definition of chil-

---

* Postwar divorces in 1945 were one for every three marriages, and will probably, according to William F. Ogburn, drop to one for every five or six.[5]

divorce
RATE

dren as joy rather than as duty is spreading rapidly, though with all the hazards that a duty-ridden people will then ask, "Am I enjoying my children enough?" and "Are my children really enjoying me?"

But whatever the possibilities for anxiety, marriage that is a responsible, chosen, and joyous way of life seems a more possible goal for the descendants of Puritans than the mere unhappy reaction to a loss of orthodoxy in which duty to some unnamed entity pathetically and inappropriately replaces a duty to God. To the extent that all marriage and all parenthood become more responsible, the religiously orthodox will also be safer, less threatened by the disintegrating standards of a society where so many live without even missing religion.

But if such responsible new patterns are to develop, then it is crucial that in theory, and in practice, the fact that divorce may come to any marriage—except where the religion of both partners forbids it—must be faced. The stigma of failure and of sin must be removed, the indignities of divorce laws that demand either accusation or collusion must be done away with. Social practices must be developed so that the end of a marriage is announced, soberly, responsibly, just as the beginning of a marriage is published to the world. This means a sort of coming-to-terms with sorrow that Americans have been finding difficult to practice in regard to death as well as divorce. We jubilate over birth and dance at weddings, but more and more hustle the dead off the scene without ceremony, without an opportunity for young and old to realize that death is as much a fact of life as is birth. A world in which one really says, "Let the dead bury the dead," is an ugly world in which corpses lie rotting on the streets and the living have to flee for their lives. A dead marriage is sad, a marriage that is broken by death is also infinitely sad (in 1947 of every 100 families, 12 were broken, 9 by widowhood, 1 by divorce and 2 by separation). Both are part of life. If we recognize that we live in a society where marriage is terminable, and in some cases should be terminable, we can then give every newly married pair, and every old married pair, a chance to recognize the hazards they face, and to make genuine efforts to survive them. Marriage was once a harbour from which some marriages set sail safely, some lay in it and rotted, some were simply wrecked on the shore. It is now a voyage in the open sea, with no harbour at any point, and each partner is committed to vigilance and deep concern if the ship is to sail at all. Each form of marriage can be dignified and rewarding, if men choose to make it so.

As long as divorce is something disgraceful, for which however no one is punished, something to be hidden and yet something available to any one, we may expect an increasing number of irresponsible marriages in which one or both partners simply say, "Oh well, if it doesn't work, we'll get a divorce." From such an attitude, many divorces are the expected crop. But if young people can say instead, "Knowing every hazard, we will work to keep our marriage," then the number of irresponsible marriages and irresponsible divorces may begin to fall. But society must recognize and honour those who try again, recognize the belief in marriage so well summed up in the movie title *This Time, for Keeps*.

XVIII

TO BOTH THEIR OWN

WE HAVE SEEN HOW CHILDREN OF EACH SEX LEARN, FROM their own bodies and the way in which others respond to their bodies, that they are male and female. And we have seen that each sex position can be stated as the surer one, with the other sex a pallid or compensatory or imperfect version of the other. We have seen that the girl may feel herself an incomplete person and spend her life trying to imitate male achievements, and that equally the boy may feel himself incomplete and spend his life in symbolic and far-fetched imitations of the girl's maternity. Each sex may be distorted by the presence of the other sex, or it may be given a fuller sense of sex membership. Either solution is possible, neither is inevitable. If parents define one child as less complete, less potentially gifted, with less right to be free, less claim to love and protection, or less a source of pride to themselves than the other, the child of that sex will, in many cases, feel envy. If society defines each sex as having inalienable and valuable qualities of its own but does not relate those qualities to the reproductive differences between the sexes, then each sex may be proud and strong, but some of the values that come from sex contrast will be lacking. If women are defined without reference to their maternity, men may find that their own masculinity seems inadequate, because its continuance into paternity will also lose definition. And if men are defined in terms of paternity rather than as lovers, women will find that their own capacities of wifehood have been muted in favour of their capacities for motherhood.

Externally at some given period of history and in some set of social arrangements it may often look as if one sex gained and the other lost, but such gains and losses must in the end be temporary. To the extent that women are denied the right to use their minds, their sons suffer as well as their daughters. An over-emphasis on the importance of virility will in the end make the lives of men as instrumental as an over-emphasis on their merely reproductive functions makes the lives of women. If our analysis is deep enough and our time-perspective long enough, if we hold in mind all the various possibilities that other cultures hint at or fully embody, it is possible to say that to the extent that either sex is disadvantaged, the whole culture is poorer, and the sex that, superficially, inherits the earth, inherits only a very partial legacy. The more whole the culture, the more whole each member, each man, each woman, each child will be. Each sex is shaped from birth by the presence and the behaviour of both sexes, and each sex is dependent upon both. The myths that conjure up islands of women who live all alone without men always contain, and rightly, some flaw in the picture. A one-sex world would be an imperfect world, for it would be a world without a future. Only a denial of life itself makes it possible to deny the interdependence of the sexes. Once that interdependence is recognized and traced in minute detail to the infant's first experience of the contrast between the extra roughness of a shaven cheek and a deeper voice and his mother's softer skin and higher voice, any program which claims that the wholeness of one sex can be advanced without considering the other is automatically disallowed. Isolated consideration of the position of women becomes as essentially one-sided as the isolated consideration of the position of men. We must think instead of how to live in a two-sex world so that each sex will benefit at every point from each expression of the presence of two sexes.

To insist on building a world in which both sexes benefit does not mean that we gloss over or deny the differential vulnerability of either sex, the learnings that are harder for boys, the learnings that are harder for girls, the periods of greater physical vulnerability for one sex than the other. This does not mean that we deny that when both sexes are cared for more by the mother than by the father, the learnings will be different as the boy accepts a first-beloved person who is unlike himself and the girl one who is like herself, as each lives out its first warm contacts with the world with eager little mouths that for one will remain a prototype of adult relationships, but for the other will be reversed. Nor does it mean that we fail to recognize the period when the little girl's sex membership is so much less explicit than the little boy's that while he is proudly, exhibitionistically sure of his masculinity, she has to ignore what seems like a deficiency in herself in favour of a promised future maternity. It means recognizing that training to control elimination, to plan, to respond, to inhibit, appropriately, in terms of time and place, has a different impact on the boy and on the girl. It does mean that we also recognize that as both children seize on the behaviour of grown men and women to give them clues as to what their future rôles will be, the conspicuousness of pregnancy to which the girl can look forward overshadows the paternal rôle that is so much harder for a small boy's imagination to follow through. As the girl is left vulnerable to any cultural arrangements that seem to deny her some freedom—the right to use her mind or her body in some way that is permitted to a boy—so the boy is left vulnerable to cultural arrangements that spur him on to efforts that may be beyond his strength, if achievement is defined as necessary to validate an otherwise imperfect maleness.

Giving each sex its due, a full recognition of its special vulnerabilities and needs for protection, means looking beyond the superficial resemblances during the period of later childhood, when both boys and girls, each having laid many of the problems of sex adjustment aside, seem so eager to learn, and so able to learn the same things. Paced too closely together, with a school system that closes its eyes to the speed with which the girls are outdistancing the boys in height, and the greater ease that girls have in learning certain kinds of lessons, both boys and girls may be injured during this period, the boy given a fear of the superiority of the girl, the girl given a fear of being superior to the boy. Each fear is deeply detrimental to the full development of each sex later, but it operates differently, making the boy angry and grudging about achievement in women, making the girl frightened and deprecatory about her own gifts. At puberty, there is again a difference. The girl's attainment of puberty is definite and clear. Only cultural arrangements which insist that chronological age is more important than maturity, or which fail to recognize that late maturation is as normal as early, can make the girl as doubtful of herself and of her full sex membership as is the boy as he responds to the less sure, less definite signs of his own puberty.

As young adults ready for a full sex relationship, both boy and girl are limited by the irrevocability of a full sex experience for a woman as compared with that of a man. This irrevocability of the severed hymen often stays the man's spontaneity as greatly as it does the girl's. Then in the full sex relationship there is again a shift. The man may live over again phantasies of re-entering his mother's body, but the woman must accept her obligation to herself, the willingness to become a body in which new life is sheltered. However, once she has borne a child, her full sex membership, her ability to conceive and carry and bear another human being, is assured and can never be taken away from her. The male who has impregnated a female is given no such full assurance; his paternity remains to the end inferential, his full sex membership has to be referred again and again to continual potency rather than to past paternity. And with advancing years, the woman faces a moment when giving up her productive maternity will occur as irrevocably and unmistakably as the beginning was once signalled at menarche. But the male's loss of his potential paternity, like the diminution of his potency, is gradual, indefinite, reversible. It has neither the quality of a single devastating event, which is the way women often experience the menopause, nor the possibility of a peaceful acceptance of a consummated step in life, which is also possible to women. He keeps the rewards and the psychological hazards that go with a less punctuated ageing process.

Our tendency at present is to minimize all these differences in learning, in rhythm, in type and timing of rewards, and at most to try to obliterate particular differences that are seen as handicaps on one sex. If boys are harder to train, train them harder; if girls grow faster than boys, separate them, so the boys won't be damaged; if women have a little less strength than men, invent machines so that they can still do the same work. But every adjustment that minimizes a difference, a vulnerability, in one sex, a differential strength in the other, diminishes their possibility of complementing each other, and corresponds—symbolically—to sealing off the constructive receptivity of the female and the vigorous outgoing constructive activity of the male, muting them both in the end to a duller version of human life, in which each is denied the fullness of humanity that each might have had. Guard each sex in its vulnerable moments we must, protect and cherish them through the crises that at some times are so much harder for one sex than for the other. But as we guard, we may also keep the differences. Simply compensating for differences is in the end a form of denial.

But if each sex is to realize sex membership fully, each boy and each girl must also feel as a whole human being. We are human beings first, and while sex membership very quickly overrides race feeling, so that boys of a race that assumes itself superior will express themselves as more willing to be males of the "inferior" race than to be females in their own, people do not similarly choose not to be human. The most boldly swaggering male would be staggered by the choice of keeping his masculinity at the price of becoming a lion or a stag, the most deeply maternal female would not elect to be turned into a ewe or a doe rather than lose her femininity. Humanity at any price, but please God, a human being of my own sex, fully, sums up the approach that men and women make in every culture in the world. We may bring them up to wish they had been born a member of the other sex, and so impair forever their full and happy functioning, but even so they would not barter away their humanity. Yet we have seen how damaging to full sex membership can be some of the conventions by which each society has differentiated the sexes. Every known society creates and maintains artificial occupational divisions and personality expectations for each sex that limit the humanity of the other sex. One form that these distinctions take is to deny the range of difference among the members of one sex, and so insist that all men should be taller than all women, so that any man who is shorter than any woman is less a man. This is the simplest form of a damaging conventionalization. But there are a thousand others, rooted in our failure to recognize the great variety of human beings who are now mingled and mated in one great mélange that includes temperamental contrasts as great as if the rabbit mated with the lion and sheep with leopards. Characteristic after characteristic in which the differences within a sex are so great that there is enormous overlapping are artificially assigned as masculine or feminine. Hairiness may be repudiated by both sexes and men forced to shave their beards and women to shave their legs and armpits; hairiness may be a proof of maleness, so that women shave their heads and men wear false curls. Shaving takes time, the male who has no beard feels unmanned, the woman who has three hairs between her breasts may be taken for a witch, and even so adjustment to such stereotypes does relatively much less harm than when personality differences are assigned in the same way. If initiative is limited to one sex, especially in sex relationships themselves, a great number of marriages will be distorted and often destroyed, to the extent that the one to whose sex initiative is forbidden is the one of that particular pair who is able to initiate, and so either refrains from the relationship or conceals and manipulates and falsifies it. As with initiative, so with responsiveness. Each sex is capable of taking certain kinds and certain types of initiative, and some individuals in each sex in relation to some individuals of the other sex, at certain times, in certain places, should, if they are to act as whole individuals, be initiating regardless of their sex, or be responsive regardless of their sex. If the stereotypes forbid this, it is hazardous for each to do so. We may go up the scale from simple physical differences through complementary definitions that overstress the rôle of sex difference and extend it inappropriately to other aspects of life, to stereotypes of such complex activities as those involved in the formal use of the intellect, in the arts, in government, and in religion.

In all these complex achievements of civilization, those activities which are mankind's glory, and upon which depends our hope of survival in this world that we have built, there has been this tendency to make artificial distinctions that limit an activity to one sex, and by denying the actual potentialities of human beings limit not only both men and women, but also equally the development of the activity itself. Singing may be taken as a very simple example. There are societies in which nobody sings in anything but a flat, rhythmic, dull chant. Significantly enough, Manus, which is built on the duller similarities of men and women, is such a society. There are societies in which women sing, and men sing falsetto. There have probably been societies in which men sang and only women who could sing alto were allowed to sing. There are societies that wished to achieve the full beauty of a chorus which spanned the possibilities of the human voice, but in linking religion and music together also wished to ban women, as unsuited for an active rôle in the church, from the choir. Boys' voices provide an apparently good substitute. So also do eunuchs, and so in the end we may have music modelled on a perfect orchestration of men and women's voices, but at the price of the exclusion of women and the castration of men.

Throughout history, the more complex activities have been defined and re-defined, now as male, now as female, now as neither, sometimes as drawing equally on the gifts of both sexes, sometimes as drawing differentially on both sexes. When an activity to which each could have contributed—and probably all complex activities belong in this class—is limited to one sex, a rich differentiated quality is lost from the activity itself. Once a complex activity is defined as belonging to one sex, the entrance of the other sex into it is made difficult and compromising. There is no heavy taboo in Bali against a woman if she wishes, or a man if he wishes, practising the special arts of the other sex. But painting in Bali has been a male art. When a gifted little adolescent girl in the village of Batoean, where there were already some sixty young men experimenting with the modern innovation of painting on paper, tried a new way of painting—by setting down what she saw rather than painting conventional stylized representations of the world—the boy artists derided and discouraged her until she gave up and made poor imitations of their style. The very difference in sex that made it possible for her to see a little differently, and so make an innovation, also made her so vulnerable that her innovation could be destroyed. Conversely, the entrance of one sex into the activities of the other if the other has less prestige may be simply destructive. In ancient Samoa, the women made lovely bark-cloth, pressing out the fluctuating, beautifully soft lines against mats on which the pattern was sewed in coconut-leaf riblets. When iron tools were introduced, the men, because men were defined as the carvers, learned to carve wooden pattern-boards that were stronger and easier to work with than the old fragile mats. But the designs, made for an art for which they had no feeling, suffered, became stiff and dull, and even the women's attempt to get some freedom back into the designs by painting imitations rather than using the boards failed.

In religion we find the same gamut. Religious experience and religious leadership may be permitted to one sex alone, and the periodic outbreak of vision in the wrong sex may be penalized. A woman may be branded as a witch, a man as an invert. The whole picture may become so confused between real gift and social definition of sex rôle that we get the final institutionalized patterns that confuse sex inversion, transvestitism, and religious functions, as among some Siberian tribes. It is always possible for society to deny to one sex that which both sexes are able to do; no human gift is strong enough to flower fully in a person who is threatened with loss of sex membership. The insistence on limit-

ing a two-sex potentiality to one sex results in the terrible
tragedies of wrong definition of one's own sex in the man
who becomes a homosexual because of the way in which society defines his desire to paint or to dance, or in the woman
who becomes a homosexual because she likes to ride horses,
or use a slide-rule. If the interest the other sex takes in a
one-sex activity is strong enough, then the intruders may
win, as men have been largely driven from teaching in the
schools of the United States. Or even more peculiar things
may happen. In some particular place and time a developing medical practice may include obstetrics within the
proper sphere of the doctor. Those male physicians who have
had the strongest interest in the reproductive capacities of
women may gravitate initially towards obstetrics and pedi-
atrics. So also may females whose interest in medicine has
been defined as male. There may come to be a group of
practitioners that includes males who have been very
strongly influenced by their conceptions of what a female
rôle is, and females who are strongly repelled by their conceptions of the limitations of the female rôle. Together they
may shape medical practice into strange forms in which the
women who might make a contribution from a first-hand
knowledge of femininity are silent, and the men are left
freer to follow their phantasies than they would have been
had there been no women among them. Such a development may sometimes finally include a determination to in-
doctrinate women in "natural child-birth," in fact to return to them the simple power of bearing their own children, which in the course of a most devoted but one-sided
development of medicine has practically been taken away
from them.

I have elaborated this particular example in some detail,
because no matter with what goodwill we may embark on a
program of actually rearing both men and women to make
their full and special contributions in all the complex proc-

esses of civilization—medicine and law, education and religion, the arts and sciences—the task will be very difficult.
Where an occupation or an art is defined as feminine, the
males who are attracted to it are either already in some way
injured or may be injured if they try to practise it. If simple
social definition does not set them to doubting their manhood, the very feminine rules and procedures of the occupation itself may so befuddle and exasperate them that they
inevitably do not do different and good work, but similar
and worse work, than the women who are already there.
When an occupation is defined as masculine, the women
who first enter it will be similarly handicapped.[1] They may
have entered it out of a simple drive to act like a male, to
compete with males, to prove that they are as good as males.
Such a drive, compensatory and derivative rather than
primary, will blur their vision and make clumsy fingers that
should be deft as they try to act out the behaviour of the
other sex, deemed so desirable. Or if they enter the occupation not out of any desire to compete with men, but out of
simple primary motivations, of curiosity or a desire to create or to participate in some activity that is fascinating in
itself, they too, like the men who enter occupations in which
women have set the style, will find themselves handicapped
at every turn by a style that has been completely set by the
other sex. As the member of another culture fumbles and
stumbles in a different land, with hand stretched out for a
door-knob that is not there, a foot raised for a step that is
missing, an appetite that rises insistently at an hour when
there is no food, and an ear trained to wake to sounds that
are never heard in these strange streets, so the immigrant
coming into an occupation that has been the sole preserve
of the other sex will stumble and fumble and do less than
is in him or her to do. How can such an immigrant compete
with those whose upbringing fits them to find their way, effortlessly, gracefully, with never a false step or a wasted

motion? Whether it be the arts or the sciences, the whole pattern of thought, the whole symbolic system within which the novice must work, facilitates every step taken by the expected sex, obstructs every step taken by the unexpected sex. These same one-sex patterns also restrict the sex that practises them the longer they are practised by one sex alone, and not made new by the interwoven imaginations of both. It may even be that one of the explanations which lie behind the decline of great periods of civilized activity, when philosophies fail, arts decline, and religions lose their vigour, may be found to be a too rigid adherence to the insights and the gifts of one sex. The higher the development of some faculty of creativeness that has been defined as rigidly male or rigidly female, the more the personality of the practitioner is split, and the deeper the danger that the personal life of mating and parenthood, which must be keyed to the presence of the other sex, may be divorced from the creative life of thought and action. This may in turn result in a secondary solution, such as the split in Greek society between the uneducated wife and the sophisticated mistress; it may push a large part of society towards celibacy or homosexuality, simply because a heterosexual relationship involves unbearable complications. The deeper the commitment to a creative activity becomes, be it government or science, industry or the arts, religion or exploration, the more the participating individuals will seek wholeness in it, and the more they will be vulnerable if the activity itself is one that only partially expresses our full two-sexed humanity.

There is likewise the very simple consideration that when we have no indication that intelligence is limited to one sex, any occupational restriction that prevents gifted women from exercising their gifts leaves them, and also the world that is sorely in need of every gift, the poorer. I have not put this consideration first, because there is still the possibility that the world might lose more by sacrificing sex differentiation than it would lose by limiting the exercise of that intelligence to certain ways of life. It is of very doubtful value to enlist the gifts of women if bringing women into fields that have been defined as male frightens the men, unsexes the women, muffles and distorts the contribution the women could make, either because their presence excludes men from the occupation or because it changes the quality of the men who enter it. There is slight gain if the struggle the intruders have to go through limits any primary feminine contribution they could make. It can be cogently argued that the profession of education—which should be by both sexes for both sexes—has lost as much if not more than it has gained as men departed not only from the primary grades, where the special gifts of women were badly needed, but from the higher grades, where boys have suffered because taught only by women. Men teachers took refuge in the universities, where they jealously guard their departments against the entrance of any woman into fields where women's insights are needed. Such sequence can well make one pause, and suggest that the cure is often worse than the disease.

This is more likely to be so whenever women's abilities are seen quantitatively in relation to men's.[2] The phrasing is then that there are many women who are as bright or brighter, as strong or stronger, as good or better organizers, than men. Crusades based on the rights of women to enter any field are likely to recoil upon themselves. The entrance of women is defined as competitive, and this is dangerous, whether the competition be expressed in the Soviet woman railroad engineer's plaint that women are allowed to run only engines on freight trains, or in the devastating antagonisms that are likely to occur in America, where it is so hard to forgive any person who wins in the same race, although so easy to acclaim success in races one has not entered. Almost every excursion of American women into fields that women had never, or at least not for many epochs, entered has been phrased in just these competitive terms. How dangerous it is can be measured in many ways: by the big poster advertisements on the Pacific coast in the spring of 1948, which advertised bread with a girl wielding the bat and the boy behind her holding the catcher's mit; by the "Here's How" in the New York subway, in which a text that describes the wedding-ring as a sign of subjection is illustrated by a *male* in evening-dress putting a ring on his *own* third finger. It is folly to ignore the signs which warn us that the present terms on which women are lured by their own curiosities and drives developed under the same educational system as boys, or forced by social conditions that deny homes and children to many women—a fourth of American women reach the menopause having borne no children [3] —are bad for both men and women. We have to count very carefully what gains there are, what possibilities there are of drawing rapidly enough upon the sensitivities of both men and women to right the balance and still go on.

There will be very great temptations in America to right the balance rudely, to tighten the lines against the continued entrance of women into these new fields, rather than to change the nature of that entrance. To the extent that we do go backwards we lose an opportunity to make the social inventions that will make it possible for women to contribute as much to civilization as they now contribute to the continuance of the race. As matters now stand and have stood through history, we have drawn on the gifts of men in both ways, and on the gifts of women almost entirely in one way. From each sex, society has asked that they so live that others may be born, that they cherish their masculinity and femininity, discipline it to the demands of parenthood, and leave new lives behind them when they die. This has meant that men had to be willing to choose, win, and keep women as lovers, protect and provide for them as husbands, and protect and provide for their children as fathers. It has meant that women have had to be willing to accept men as lovers, live with them as wives, and conceive, bear, feed, and cherish their children. Any society disappears which fails to make these demands on its members and to receive this much from them.

But from men, society has also asked and received something more than this. For thousands of generations men have been asked to do something more than be good lovers and husbands and fathers, even with all that that involved of husbandry and organization and protection against attack. They have been asked to develop and elaborate, each in terms of his own ability, the structure within which the children are reared, to build higher towers, or wider roads, to dream new dreams and see new visions, to penetrate ever farther into the secrets of nature, to learn new ways of making life more human and more rewarding. And within the whole adventure there has been a silent subtle division of labour, which had its roots perhaps in a period of history when the creativeness of bearing children outweighted in splendour every act that men performed, however they danced and pantomimed their pretence that the novices were really their children after all. In this division of labour, there was the assumption that bearing children is enough for the women, and in the rest of the task all the elaborations belong to men. This assumption becomes the less tenable the more men succeed in those elaborations which they have taken on themselves. As a civilization becomes complex, human life is defined in individual terms as well as in the service of the race, and the great structures of law and government, religion and art and science, become something highly valued for themselves. Practised by men, they become indicators of masculine humanity, and men take great pride in these achievements. To the extent that women are barred from them, women become less human. An illiterate woman is no less human than an illiterate man. As long as few men write and most men cannot, a woman may suffer no loss in her sense of herself. But when writing becomes almost universal—access to books, increased precision of thought, possibilities of communication—then if women cannot learn to write because they are women, they lose in stature, and the whole subtle process begins by which the wholeness of both sexes is undermined. When the women's sense of loss of participation is compensated for by other forms of power, by the iron will of the mother-in-law who has been the docile, home-bound wife—as in China and Japan—then the equilibrating pattern may take the form of covert distortions of human relationships that may persist over centuries. When women's sense of impaired participation in society is expressed directly, in rebellion against the restrictions that it has placed on her, we may find instead the sort of freedom for women that occurred just before the break-down of the Roman Empire, or in the goals of the women's movement of the last century. But whatever the compensatory adjustment within the society, women's belief in their own power to contribute directly to human culture will be subtly and deeply impaired, and men's isolation, either covertly threatened or openly attacked, in a world that they have built alone will increase.

If we once accept the premise that we can build a better world by using the different gifts of each sex, we shall have two kinds of freedom, freedom to use untapped gifts of each sex, and freedom to admit freely and cultivate in each sex their special superiorities. We may well find that there are certain fields, such as the physical sciences, mathematics, and instrumental music, in which men by virtue of their sex, as well as by virtue of their qualities as specially gifted human beings, will always have that razor-edge of extra gift which makes all the difference, and that while women may easily follow where men lead, men will always make the new discoveries. We may equally well find that women, through the learning involved in maternity, which once experienced can be taught more easily to all women, even childless women, than to men, have a special superiority in those human sciences which involve that type of understanding which until it is analyzed is called intuition. If intuition is based, as it seems to be, upon an ability to recognize difference from the self rather than upon one to project the self in building a construct or a hypothesis, it may well be that the greatest intuitive gifts will be found among women. Just as for endless ages men's mathematical gifts were neglected and people counted one, two, two and one, and a dog, or were limited to counting on the fingers of their hands, so women's intuitive gifts have lain fallow, uncultivated, uncivilized.

Once it is possible to say it is as important to take women's gifts and make them available to both men and women, in transmittable form, as it was to take men's gifts and make the civilization built upon them available to both men and women, we shall have enriched our society. And we shall be ready to synthesize both kinds of gifts in the sciences, which are now sadly lop-sided with their far greater knowledge of how to destroy than of how to construct, far better equipped to analyze the world of matter into which man can project his intelligence than the world of human relations, which requires the socialized use of intuition. The mother who must learn that the infant who was but an hour ago a part of her body is now a different individual, with its own hungers and its own needs, and that if she listens to her own body to interpret the child, the child will die, is schooled in an irreplaceable school. As she learns to attend to that different individual, she develops a special way of thinking and feeling about human beings. We can leave these special learnings at the present level, or convert them into a more elaborate part of our civilization. Already the men and women who are working together in the human sciences are finding the greatly increased understanding that comes from the way in which their insights complement each other. We are learning that we pay different prices for our insights: for instance, to understand the way a culture socializes children a man must return in imagination to childhood, but a woman has also another and different path, to learn to understand the mothers of these children. Yet both are necessary, and the skill of one sex gives only a partial answer. We can build a whole society only by using both the gifts special to each sex and those shared by both sexes—by using the gifts of the whole of humanity.

Every step away from a tangled situation, in which moves and counter-moves have been made over centuries, is a painful step, itself inevitably imperfect. Here is a vicious circle to which it is not possible to assign either a beginning or an end, in which men's over-estimation of women's rôles, or women's over-estimation of men's rôles, leads one sex or the other to arrogate, to neglect, or even to relinquish part of our so dearly won humanity. Those who would break the circle are themselves a product of it, express some of its defects in their every gesture, may be only strong enough to challenge it, not able actually to break it. Yet once identified, once analyzed, it should be possible to create a climate of opinion in which others, a little less the product of the dark past because they have been reared with a light in their hand that can shine backwards as well as forwards, may in turn take the next step. Only by recognizing that each change in human society must be made by those who carry in every cell of their bodies the very reason why the change is necessary can we school our hearts to the patience to build truly and well, recognizing that it is not only the price, but also the glory, of our humanity that civilization must be built by human beings.

NOTES TO CHAPTERS

NOTES TO CHAPTERS

PART ONE

CHAPTER I

From "Discourse with the Heart," by Léonie Adams:

"Heart, that have loved, nor known it holy part,
(Truth is, live hearts must love as lips shall breathe)
By this shall lift with sanctifying art
Your act of life, who live but to bequeath:
As lips that countless, graceless times have fed,
Save themselves hungry, and bite blessèd bread."

From her *Those Not Elect, McBride,* New York,
1925, p. 12.

CHAPTER II

Mead, Margaret, "Anthropological Data on the Problem of Instinct," *Psychosomatic Medicine,* Vol. IV

(1942), pp. 396-97 (Symposium—Second Colloquia on Pschodynamics and Experimental Medicine).

2 Armstrong, W. E., *Rossel Island,* Cambridge University Press, 1928, p. 100.

3 Demetracopoulou, Dorothy, review of Durham, M. E., *Laws and Customs of the Balkans, American Anthropologist,* N. S. Vol. 32 (1930), p. 670.

4 For those who are interested in the way in which such results are used in formulating hypotheses that may be tested out with primitive materials, a description of a further step may be illuminating.

Once we have made such studies, arranged the odd jumble of nonsense syllables into a phonetic pattern and a grammar, ordered into a kinship system the words that children call after adults, the terms by which people describe each other at different times and in different contexts, and learned the meaning of such phrases as "he's a chicken-hawk," "but we never took the skull," and "his neck was fast," at last we must bring it all home and set it down. How do we use it? Perhaps a brief sketch of the way my own mind would work in answer to a question may help. Suppose some one interested in the psychology of child development or religion asks me: "Can you say anything on the relationship between people staying young and beliefs about immortality?" First, I rapidly run through in my head whole areas of primitive society, reviving in my mind the knowledge that American Indians are on the whole very little interested in immortality, and the personalized dead play a slight rôle. Perhaps I repeat the phrase, "we spring up like the grass in the morning and in the evening are cut down," which I have come to use to characterize Plains Indians' attitude towards death. At the same time a dozen concrete and special images will run through my mind of Indians preaching to the fish to come and be caught, and then throwing their bones back to be reincarnated; the spirits of the dead—a whole pantheon from the other world, but not one's dead grandfather or grandmother—coming to dance in masks at the pueblo of Zuni; the Omaha belief that twins are all reincarnated. Small significant bits from the work of hundreds of ethnologists give immediacy to the problem. Then my mind will turn to another part of the world, perhaps searching for a category as I go. That is, I may say, "And in Indonesia . . ." and begin to let my mind range over the attitudes towards ancestors, or I may say, "Yes, and let's bring such matters as ancestor worship and reincarnation into the picture." If reincarnation seems relevant, I may think over the cultures known to have a belief in reincarnation, and may then add, "Of course it will be interesting to see what is the relationship between who you are when you are born and who you will be when you die." This may lead to comparing Eskimo and Balinese; among both peoples infants are treated as having prophetic powers at birth, and in both of them children learn complex skills early. I may add a question here, "Is the relationship between learning and a theory of birth and immortality perhaps a key point?" and then compare the Balinese position—in which the individual is reincarnated over and over in the same family, so that the life-cycle lacks real climax, but merely completes one of an endless set of circles between this world and the other—and the Manus position, where human beings are originally built from material from fathers' and mothers' bodies, reach their full powers at maturity, survive a little as strong ghosts immediately after death and then dribble off into lower and lower levels of sea-slugs and slime. Then I may say: "The Balinese believe you can learn at any age—the very young and the old learn with

great relative effortlessness, beauty lasts into old age—
while among the Manus, people are finished at forty.
Perhaps we may suggest that there is a relationship
here which it would be worth while to explore further." From there I may go on to consider whether I
know any instances of a group who believe in reincarnation but also have a sharply marked decline in vigour
during the life-span—thus looking for negative instances
to disprove my developing hypothesis. At the same
time, I will be running over in my mind what we know
about learning at different ages in different cultures,
holding at one level what we know about learning itself
—kinds of learning, rote learning, learning by reward,
learning by punishment, learning by avoiding punishment—and at another level, concrete materials, motion
pictures of a carver learning to carve, material on the
ages at which boys can become apprentices to skilled
craftsmen, etc. Or I may turn back to two ethnological
categories, like "belief in reincarnation" and "life-cycle,"
in which case it would be possible to go up to Yale
University and pull out a card catalogue in which material on a great many societies has been arranged in
such categories, so that it is possible to see how the two
things fit together. Or I may come out with a whole
set of questions that I want to look up in special books:
"Did that comparative study of the way members of
two African tribes learned a new story have anything
in it about age of learning?" "It would be a good idea
to go back over that Jemez manuscript which described
the way women past the menopause regarded themselves as just beginning to learn how really to enjoy
sex," etc.

This is one way of using comparative material. It is
a process of starting an exploratory bit of thought; using
the known comparative materials on the world; form-

ing preliminary hypotheses as one goes, and testing them out, tentatively, by memory; and finally pinning down some hypothesis that seems fruitful, and capable of testing, perhaps by the existing literature, perhaps by undertaking new field-work. It may lead back not into primitive material, but on into the psychological laboratory or the clinic. Each individual anthropologist uses the comparative method differently, but the essence of the method remains the same. (See Bateson, Gregory, "Experiments in Thinking about Observed Ethnological Material," *Philosophy of Science*, Vol. 8 (1941), pp. 53-68.)

PART TWO

The material in this section is almost entirely drawn from my own field-work or from the work of my field collaborators. Complete bibliographies of these published materials on these seven cultures will be found in Appendix II. In these notes I shall give only an occasional reference that I think may especially interest the reader, or give proper recognition for some point.

CHAPTER III

1 Bender, Lauretta, and Montague, Allison, "Psychotherapy through Art in a Negro Child," *College Art Journal*, Vol. VII (1947), pp. 12-17.

2 These concepts were originally developed by Gregory Bateson on the basis of Iatmul material. See especially his "Culture Contact and Schizmogenesis," *Man*, Vol. XXXV (1935), pp. 178-83; *Naven*, Cambridge University Press, 1936; "Some Systematic Approaches to the Study of Culture and Personality," *Character and Personality*, Vol. XL (1942), pp. 76-84; "Morale and Na-

tional Character," in *Civilian Morale,* ed. by Goodwin Watson, Houghton Mifflin, Boston, 1942, pp. 71-91.

3   In this use of the term "reciprocal" I have departed somewhat from the use of the word as defined in Bateson's article "Morale and National Character" (*loc. cit.*). Using the Manus as the type culture, I am defining reciprocal behaviour as behaviour in which things, commodities, or ideas are involved in an interchange between two individuals or groups. Let us take an act sequence: A hits B, B hits A, when A is a father and B a child. This may be seen as *complementary* if the father's blow is given and received in a quite different spirit than the child's return blow; i.e. the father's chastising, the child's pettish or weakly retributive. It may be seen as *symmetrical* if the emphasis is that father and child face each other and, with similar attitudes towards each, hit each other. It may be seen as reciprocal if the relative strength or weakness, chastising, succouring, comparability or incomparability of parent and child, are ignored in favour of a phrasing which emphasizes that a *blow* is given and a *blow* received. A blow given and a *present* given back if it was the blow and the present which formed the core of the sequence, as seen.

As Gregory Bateson has emphasized, it is the way in which a behaviour sequence is seen by the participants that makes it possible to distinguish these various types for purposes of further analysis.

4   I did not begin to work seriously with the zones of the body until I went to the Arapesh in 1931. While I was generally familiar with Freud's basic work on the subject, I had not seen how it might be applied in the field until I read Géza Róheim's first field report, "Psychoanalysis of Primitive Culture Types," *International*

Journal of Psychoanalysis, Vol. XIII (1932), Pts. 1-2 (Róheim Australasian Research Number).

I then sent home for abstracts of K. Abraham's work. After I became acquainted with Erik Homburger Erikson's systematic handling of these ideas, they became an integral part of my theoretical equipment. Part of the presentation of *Balinese Character* is organized around them, especially Plates 38-44. It was while developing this presentation that Gregory Bateson systematically related Erikson's zonal chart to the categories of *complementary* behaviour. For an intermediate version of the chart, see Mead, Margaret, "Research on Primitive Children," in *Manual of Child Psychology,* ed. by Leonard Carmichael, Wiley, New York, 1946, pp. 670-72.

5   Bateson, Gregory, "Social Planning and the Concept of 'Deutero-Learning,'" in *Science, Philosophy, and Religion, Second Symposium* (Conference on Science, Philosophy, and Religion), New York, 1942, pp. 81-97. This article outlines the general approach to learning used in this book.

6   These are described in detail in Bateson, Gregory, *Naven,* Cambridge University Press, 1936.

CHAPTER V

1   Field, Eugene, "To a Usurper," *Poems of Childhood,* Scribner, New York, 1904, p. 80.

2   Mead, Margaret, "Age Patterning and Personality Development," *American Journal of Orthopsychiatry,* Vol. XVII (1947), pp. 231-40; Bateson, Gregory, and Mead, Margaret, *Balinese Character,* Plate 74; Mead, Margaret, "The Family in the Future," in *Beyond Victory,* ed. by Ruth Nanda Anshen, Harcourt, Brace, New York, 1943, pp. 66-87.

3   Bateson, Gregory, "Sex and Culture," *Annals of the New York Academy of Science,* Vol. 47 (1947), pp. 603-64.

CHAPTER VI

1   Devereux, George, "Institutionalized Homosexuality of the Mohave Indians," *Human Biology,* Vol. 9 (1937), pp. 498-527.

2   Greulich, William Walter, and Thoms, Herbert, with collaboration of Ruth Christian Twaddle, "A Study of Pelvic Type and Its Relationship to Body Build in White Women," *Journal of American Medical Association,* Vol. 112 (1939), pp. 485-93.

3   Our obligations in the choice of hypotheses about mankind are deep and binding. As scientists pledged to a search for the best hypotheses, we have certain clear obligations. As members of human society in the year 1948, we also have clear obligations to explore actively those hypotheses which would seem to open up the most important next fields of research. Hypotheses of constitutional type are two-edged swords. To the degree that they emphasize that there may be deep and inalienable differences between individuals, they lend themselves to dangerous extensions to racial groups. It is so very easy to identify a certain type of human being and confuse that type with some localized group, such as northern Europeans, and because type A is tall and lean as an individual type, to attribute his characteristics to some people who as a group happen to be taller and leaner than some other group. The next step to such fallacious reasoning is a recrudescence of racism of a new sort, with all the usual attendant dangers of racism, when the direction of order at this period in history seems far better served by emphasizing man's modifiable rather than his unmodifiable characteristics. The student of constitutional types has

only to make two errors—to confuse the cultural institution of the behaviour congruent with a particular
type with the innate temperament and confuse relative
physique within a group with relative position within
the human race—and we have been landed in a very
parlous state of inadmissible racism. In fact this danger
is so great that in a choice of research lines, the pursuit
of the implications of constitutional differences must
be undertaken with an extra sense of responsibility.

CHAPTER VII

1   Rahman, Lincoln, Richardson, Henry B., and Ripley,
    Herbert S., "Anorexia Nervosa with Psychiatric Ob-
    servations," *Psychosomatic Medicine*, Vol. 1 (1939), pp.
    335-65.

PART THREE

In this section I have used anthropological observations to
illuminate general problems of the family, inter-relationships between the sexes, problems of fertility and sterility,
heterosexuality and homosexuality, against a background of
recent research in endocrinology, comparative psychology,
human physiology and development. My method of work
has been to rely heavily on discussions with individuals in
each field whose approach I knew and trusted, reading such
individual studies as they recommended to me as especially
pertinent. I shall not attempt here to present a systematic
bibliography; I do not propose to survey these fields, nor
am I equipped to do so. In preparing this book, I tried to
ask selected scientists questions in such a way that I would
be led to materials which contradicted or illuminated the
problems on which I was working. I am personally indebted
to Lawrence K. Frank and his wide orientation in the literature and to Earl T. Engle, William Greulich, Gregory Bateson, and Evelyn Hutchinson, and to the published work of

Kingsley Noble, Frank Beach, A. Maslow, R. Carpenter, S. Zuckerman, and T. C. Schneirla.

CHAPTER VIII

1 Mead, Margaret, *Sex and Temperament in Three Primitive Societies,* William Morrow, New York, 1935 (Reprinted in *—From the South Seas,* William Morrow, New York, 1939), p. 94.

2 Miner, Horace, *St. Denis, A French-Canadian Parish,* University of Chicago Press, 1939, p. 5.

CHAPTER IX

1 I owe my recognition of this important distinction and its social implications to Zuckerman, Solly, *Functional Affinities of Man, Monkeys, and Apes,* Harcourt, Brace, 1933.

2 For a summary of some of these contrasts see Mead, Margaret, "Contrasts and Comparisons from Primitive Society," *Annals of the American Academy of Political and Social Science,* Vol. 160 (1932), pp. 22-28.

3 This was done by women members of the Areois society in ancient Tahiti and by certain women in Natchez Indian society who could thus raise their rank.

4 Seligman, B. Z., "Incest and Descent, Their Influence on Social Organization," *Journal of the Royal Anthropological Institute of Great Britain and Ireland,* Vol. LIX (1929), pp. 231-72; Fortune, Reo, "Incest," in *Encyclopedia of the Social Sciences,* ed. by Edwin R. A. Seligman and Alvin Johnson, Macmillan, New York, 1932, Vol. 7, pp. 620-22.

CHAPTER X

1 Benedek, Therese, and Rubenstein, B., "Correlations between Ovarian Activity and Psychodynamic Proc-

esses: I. The Ovulative Phase; II. The Menstrual Phase," *Psychosomatic Medicine,* Vol. 1 (1939), p. 245 ff., p. 461 ff.

2 This hypothesis of adolescent sterility was advanced to me by Earl Engle, and I went over my Samoan data in a first attempt to check it. Ashley Montague has been continually interested in the problem (see "Adolescent Sterility," *Quarterly Review of Biology,* Vol. 14 (1939), pp. 13-34, 192-219). My comments here are made in full awareness of the hypotheses about the mutually sterilizing effects of semen from several males, but I do not consider this a hypothesis that checks with the facts from primitive society.

3 Compare with the ancient Jewish regulations that a man who shows little aptitude for thought should only sleep with his wife once a week and save what energies he has for becoming more meditative, but the scholar should sleep with his wife every night so as to leave his mind free for his studies. Such constructs as these may be said to describe another type of potency, a piece of learned behaviour, no longer automatic, but so well integrated with the whole of the character structure that it may work reliably and well (*Babylonian Talmud: Seder Nashin,* Vol. I, "Tractate Kethuboth," English translation, Soncino Press, London, 1936, Chapter V, pp. 369, 372).

4 McGraw, Myrtle B., *Growth: A Study of Johnny and Jimmy,* Appleton-Century, New York, 1935.

5 Gesell, Arnold, *Wolf Child and Human Child,* Harper, New York, 1941.

6 Davis, Clara M., "Self-Selection of Food by Children," *American Journal of Nursing,* Vol. 35 (1935), pp. 403-10.

7 Richter, C. P., Holt, L. E., Jr., and Barelare, B., Jr., "Nutritional Requirements for Normal Growth and Re-

production in Rats Studied by the Self-Selection Method," *American Journal of Physiology,* Vol. 122 (1938), pp. 734-44.

8 Young, Paul T., "Appetite, Palatability and Feeding Habit: A Critical Review," *Psychology Bulletin,* Vol. 45 (1948), pp. 289-320.

9 Beach, Frank A., *Hormones and Behavior,* with a foreword by Earl T. Engle, Paul B. Hoeber, New York, 1948.

10 See Mead, Margaret, "Table showing length of time since puberty, periodicity, amount of pain during menses, masturbation, homosexual experience, heterosexual experience, and residence or non-residence in pastor's household," *Coming of Age in Samoa,* William Morrow, New York, 1928, Appendix V, Table I, p. 285.

11 Frank, L. K., Hutchinson, G. E., Livingston, W. K., McCulloch, W. S., and Wiener, N., "Teleological Mechanisms," *Annals of the New York Academy of Sciences,* Vol. 50 (1948), pp. 178-278, especially Livingston, W. K., "The Vicious Circle in Causalgia," pp. 247-58.

CHAPTER XI

1 Mead, Margaret, "The Concept of Culture and the Psychosomatic Approach," *Psychiatry,* Vol. 10 (1947), pp. 57-76; Booth, Gotthard C., "Variety in Personality and Its Relation to Health," *Review of Religion,* New York (May 1946), pp. 385-412; Wolff, Harold G., "Protective Reaction Patterns and Disease," *Annals of Internal Medicine,* Vol. 27 (1947), pp. 944-69.

2 In Dr. Kinsey's book *Sexual Behavior in the Human Male* (Kinsey, Alfred C., Pomeroy, Wardell B., and Martin, Clyde E., Saunders, Philadelphia, 1948), the discussion assumes such a simple relationship between man and his impulses. Dr. Kinsey takes as his unit of behaviour what he calls an "outlet," the immediate resolu-

tion of tumescence, and regards all contexts in which this occurs as comparable.

3   Suggested to me by Ernst Kris.

PART FOUR

CHAPTER XII

1   For discussions of the systematic question in the analysis of heterogeneous and changing societies, see Mead, Margaret, "Educative Effects of Social Environment as Disclosed by Studies of Primitive Societies," in *Environment and Education* (symposium), University of Chicago Press, 1942, pp. 48-61 (Supplementary Educational Monographs, No. 54; Human Development Series, Vol. I); "The Concept of Culture and the Psychosomatic Approach," *Psychiatry*, Vol. 10 (1947), pp. 57-76; and "Implications of Culture Change for Personality Development," *American Journal of Orthopsychiatry*, Vol. XVII (1947), pp. 633-46; Bateson, Gregory, "Character Formation and Diachronic Theory," *Social Structure: Studies Presented to A. R. Radcliffe-Brown*, ed. by Meyer Fortes, to be published by Clarendon Press.

2   Frenkel-Brunswick, Else, and Nevitt, Sanford R., "Some Personality Factors in Anti-Semitism," *Journal of Psychology*, Vol. 20 (1945), pp. 271-91.

CHAPTER XIII

1   "Women in America," Part I, *Fortune* Survey (October 1946) p. 10.

CHAPTER XIV

1   For earlier analyses of dating see: Mead, Margaret, "What Is a Date?" *Transatlantic*, Vol. 10 (1944), pp.

54, 57-60; Gorer, Geoffrey, *The American People*, Norton, New York, 1948, Chapter IV, pp. 106-32.

2   Some of my most valuable detailed material on American dating behaviour of the early '40's I owe to the unpublished observations of Ray Birdwhistel.

3   For discussions of the need for this type of adaptability in American character, see: Erikson, Erik H., "Ego Development and Historical Change," in *The Psychoanalytic Study of the Child*, Vol. II (1946), ed. by Anna Freud and others, International Universities Press, New York, copyright 1947, pp. 359-96; Mead, Margaret, "Trends in Personal Life," *New Republic*, Vol. 115 (1946), pp. 346-48; Gorer, Geoffrey, *The American People*, Norton, New York, 1948.

4   Leites, Nathan, and Wolfenstein, Martha, "An Analysis of Themes and Plots," *Annals of the American Academy of Political and Social Science*, Vol. 254 (1947), pp. 41-48.

CHAPTER XV

1   From the preface of *The Lady* by Emily James Putnam, Sturgis and Walton, New York, 1910.

2   Mead, Margaret, "On the Institutionalized Rôle of Women and Character Formation," *Zeitschrift für Sozialforschung*, Vol. 5 (1936), pp. 69-75.

3   For discussions of the relationship between culture contact and competitiveness due to single scales of value, see: Mead, Margaret, "Interpretive Statement," in *Cooperation and Competition among Primitive Peoples*, ed. by Margaret Mead, McGraw-Hill, New York, 1937, pp. 458-511; and "Brothers and Sisters and Success," in *And Keep Your Powder Dry*, William Morrow, New York, 1943, Chapter VII, pp. 99-114; Bateson, Gregory, "Bali: The Value System of a Steady State," in *Social Structure: Studies Presented to A. R. Radcliffe-Brown*, ed. by Meyer Fortes, to be published by Clarendon

Press, London; and "The Pattern of an Armaments Race, Part 1: An Anthropological Approach," *Bulletin of the Atomic Scientists,* Vol. 2 (1946), pp. 10-11; "Part 2: An Analysis of Nationalism," Vol. 2, pp. 26-28; Frank, Lawrence K., "The Cost of Competition," in *Society Is the Patient,* Rutgers University Press, 1948, pp. 21-36.

4 Herzog, Herta, "Why People Like the *Professor Quiz* Program," in *Radio and the Printed Page,* ed. by Paul Lazarsfeld, Duell, Sloan & Pearce, New York, 1941.

5 For discussions of this point, see: Mead, Margaret, "The Chip on the Shoulder," in *And Keep Your Powder Dry,* William Morrow, New York, 1943, Chapter IX, pp. 138-57; Gorer, Geoffrey, *The American People,* Norton, New York, 1948, Chapter II, pp. 50-69.

6 I owe an understanding of this point to applying the analytical device called "end linkage" (Bateson, Gregory, "Morale and National Character," in *Civilian Morale,* ed. by Goodwin Watson, Houghton Mifflin, Boston, 1942, pp. 71-91) to the material presented in Tannenbaum, Frank, *Crime and the Community,* Ginn, Boston, 1936.

7 The series of cartoons called "Big Sister," which ran for so many years in American newspapers, summed up one side of this picture, and "little-sister" festivals of Boys' Clubs in lower New York give the compensatory counterpoint.

8 From *Collected Poetical Works of John Greenleaf Whittier,* ed. by Horace E. Scudder, Houghton, Mifflin, Cambridge, 1894, p. 407.

9 "Women in America," Part I, *Fortune* Survey (October 1946), p. 8.

10 From the *New York Times* (March 18, 1946, p. 1) report of an address by Cardinal Spellman to graduating medical students, Georgetown University, March 17.

11   Chase, Ilka, *In Bed We Cry*, Doubleday, New York, 1943.

CHAPTER XVI

1   From *Working Papers of the National Conference on Family Life*, Vol. 1 (1948), p. 1.
2   From Eugene Field's "The Night Wind," in *Poems of Childhood*, Scribner, New York, 1904, p. 112.
3   Quoted and discussed by Ethel Goldwater, "Woman's Place," *Commentary* (December 1947), pp. 578-85.
4   Benedek, Therese, "Climacterium: A Developmental Phase," to be published in *Psychoanalytic Quarterly*.

CHAPTER XVII

1   Prouty, Olive Higgins, *White Fawn*, Houghton Mifflin, Boston, 1931.
2   Wolfenstein, Martha, and Leites, Nathan. See note 4, Chapter XIV.
3   Erikson, Erik H. See note 3, Chapter XIV.
4   From "An Old Sweetheart of Mine," in *The Complete Works of James Whitcomb Riley*, collected and edited by Edmund Henry Eitel, Bobbs-Merrill, Indianapolis, 1913, Vol. I, pp. 68-72.
5   Ogburn, W. F., "Who Will Be Who in 1980," *New York Times Magazine*, May 30, 1948, p. 23.

CHAPTER XVIII

1   Mead, Margaret, "Cultural Aspects of Women's Vocational Problems in Post World War II," *Journal of Consulting Psychology*, Vol. 10 (1946), pp. 23-28.
2   The best summary of this approach to sex differences may be found in Seward, Georgene H., *Sex and the Social Order*, McGraw-Hill, New York and London, 1946.
3   Ogburn, W. F. See note 5 for Chapter XVII.

APPENDIX I

IN THE FOLLOWING NOTES I HAVE ATTEMPTED TO PROVIDE some brief orientation for the reader on where the various peoples are, what sort of knowledge exists about them, and when and under what auspices my own work was done; also to provide bibliographical materials. Each culture presented different problems. In Samoa I worked alone; there had been much work done before, and more has been done since. There were a dictionary and a grammar, and English could be used to learn the language. In Manus we had to analyze the language, using pidgin English as the interpreting language, and this was true also of Arapesh, Mundugumor, and Tchambuli, and of Mr Bateson's original work in Iatmul, which I was able to use as a background. Balinese has been extensively analyzed, but with the help of an English-speaking linguistic assistant we found it more satisfactory to make a new analysis along the lines used with totally unknown languages. In all cases the language was learned.

a base was established in a native village, and one village was intensively followed and studied.

Detailed discussions of field-methods may be found in appendices and introductions to my various publications, especially *The Mountain Arapesh*, II, "Supernaturalism" (see below, section C); pp. 259-65, Appendix II, of *Coming of Age in Samoa;* Appendix I of *Growing Up in New Guinea;* and four papers: "More Comprehensive Field Methods," *American Anthropologist*, Vol. 35 (1933), pp. 1-15; "Native Languages as Field Work Tools," *American Anthropologist*, Vol. 41 (1939), pp. 189-205; "Living with the Natives of Melanesia," *Natural History*, Vol. 31 (1931), pp. 62-74; "Anthropological Data on the Problem of Instinct," *Psychosomatic Medicine*, Vol. IV, October 1942.

A general discussion of the Sepik Aitape district in which Arapesh, Mundugumor, Tchambuli, and Iatmul are located will be found on pp. 153-66 of *The Mountain Arapesh*, 1, "An Importing Culture," Vol. XXXVI, Pt. III, 1933. The research methods used in Bali and Iatmul, which represent a considerable advance over earlier methods, are discussed in my article, "Researches in Bali, 1936-39: I. On the Concept of Plot in Culture, II. Methods of Research in Bali and New Guinea," *Transactions of the New York Academy of Sciences*, Series 2, Vol. 2 (1939), pp. 24-31.

THE SEVEN PACIFIC CULTURES

In the following sections I will present in as compact a style as possible the ethnographic outlines of the seven cultures on which I have drawn in the preceding pages. I am using technical vocabulary because any other method of presentation takes up too much space. These appendices are designed for the student and for the general reader who is interested in such matters as population size, nature of the terrain, date when the people were studied, etc. I have arranged them in the order in which I studied them, and have appended a bibliography of all of my own publications, the publications of my collaborators, and significant publications that have followed my work in these various fields. Major bibliographies of earlier work will be found in my publications.

A. SAMOA

MY MATERIAL WAS GATHERED DURING A NINE-MONTH FIELD-trip in 1925-26 as a Fellow in the Biological Sciences of the National Research Council, on a research project designated as the study of the adolescent girl.

The Samoan Islands, with a population in 1926 of 40,229, are peopled by a Polynesian group, a people with light-brown skins and wavy black hair who speak a Polynesian language. The islands were Christianized in the first half of the nineteenth century, and were administratively divided between a League of Nations Mandate under New Zealand called Western Samoa, which comprised the islands of Upolu and Savaii, and American Samoa, which was governed by the United States Navy. Warfare, the taking of trophy heads, capital punishment administered either by heads of families or by village councils, infanticide, polygamy, and the public taking of the tokens of virginity had been abolished. The people were literate in the Samoan language, written in a European orthography, and taught by Samoan missionaries, while both governments provided some formal schooling in English. Copra was the principal export-crop, in return for which the people bought cloth, which had replaced bark-cloth and mat clothing except for ceremonial purposes, and mosquito netting, which had replaced bark-cloth mosquito nets. Kerosene lamps and kerosene, soap, starch, iron knives, and buckets had been introduced. Paper and pen and ink, as well as pencils, were used to keep records and for voluminous correspondence among the islands. Taxes were paid from the copra proceeds, and

a very small number of Samoans worked for money. Alienation of land was forbidden, so that neither plantations nor
foreign traders flourished. The level of medical care was
high under adequate Navy staffing. The Naval Station was
maintained by about two hundred persons, and every three
weeks a steamer called on the run both to and from San
Francisco and Sydney. The church was a part of every village and was the seat of a school. The pastor's family was
maintained by the community and shared in ceremonial
honours. A mild form of Congregationalism (London Missionary Society) was the prevailing religion, with Roman
Catholic missions and schools on Tutuila and a small Mor-
mon mission.

All of my detailed work was done in the remote island of
the Manua group, principally in the village of Taū on the
island of Taū, and the comments which follow refer only to
that group, although most of the pattern of the family is
constant for the whole area. However, different experiences
with Europeans in the larger islands, especially near Upolu,
which has had a European population for a long time, have
undoubtedly introduced some differences in the pattern
other than those which can be referred to aboriginal conditions.

The Samoans lived in autonomous villages, held together
within the form of ceremonial relationship in which the men
holding the highest titles from each village were combined
in a formal seating-plan called the Great Fono. Each village
had a large supply of titles held in family lines and subject
to co-operative disposition by the family members, with advice and occasional interference from the village council,
which consisted of all the heads of families. Each title was
classified as either a chiefly title or a talking-chief title, and
the functions of these two groups were complementary. The
form of the village council was duplicated in a group of
wives, one of young and untitled men, and one of girls and

the wives of untitled men, and these four groups divided the communal activities of the village. Each village had one or more high chiefs who had the right to bestow a special title, *taupou,* on a girl of his household, and one, *manaia,* on a youth. Each household, which was presided over by a titled man, consisted of an extended family within which work was divided by age and status, the head of the family deciding who should garden, who fish, how much mat-weaving should be planned, etc., and the proceeds were all handled as family property. Biological families rarely lived alone, and discipline was centered in the *matai* (title of head of household) rather than in the biological father. Individuals preserved claims on the land of both family lines, as far as residence was concerned, and exercised a veto in the councils of the mother's family. The kinship system was of a simple bilateral type, with a strong brother-and-sister taboo. Rank was closely associated with title, the sons of chiefs being classified with untitled men.

The Samoans lived in round unwalled and oval houses, with high thatched roofs, and pebble floors on which mats were spread for sleeping or sitting. Their food consisted of taro, yams, bread-fruit, bananas, coconuts, supplemented by fish, shell-fish, pork, and fowls. It was cooked in family or village earth ovens and served on fresh leaves. They had no pottery. The ceremonial drink was a non-intoxicant made from the root of *Piper methysticum.* Clothes consisted of a short sarong—called a lavalava, now made of cloth—a cloth blouse for women on most occasions, and shirts for men when attending church. Some of the young men were still tattooed, but tattooing had been forbidden on Manua for two generations. Both sexes went barefoot. They slept on mats, but with the addition of hard kapok pillows, and under modern mosquito nets. European utensils and cutlery had been introduced, but only for the occasional service of a European-like meal to visiting officials. The houses of the chief and of the pastor also contained a table and a chair or so for visitors; otherwise all life was conducted on the floor.

Each household was sufficient for everyday needs, but certain men specialized in fishing, and the fish were then exchanged in a gift-giving context among related households. House-building and canoe-building were also specialized crafts, for which elaborate payments were made. There was no trade, but elaborate affinal exchanges, with mats and bark-cloth constituting the contribution from the female side, and foods, wooden bowls, canoes, etc., the male contribution. There was also continuous small informal borrowing. Households participated in village levies of work and contributions to village feasts, often phrased as *rite de passage* for members of the chiefly household. The pattern of relationship within the household had been generalized into the social organization, so that the whole village acted as the blood-kin of the chief, and the talking chiefs, as a body, exercised powers comparable to those exercised by the female descent line within a lineage. Lineage prerogatives included titles, land, house-site, and sometimes specific privileges attached to one of the titles.

Samoa was outstanding among Polynesian groups for the emphasis upon social organization rather than upon supernaturalism, and for the importance of secular sanctions. "In the old days, we had two gods, Tangaloa and the Village, but the greatest of these was the Village." The local village community remained the centre and source of all authority and power; the superstructure of titles on the one hand, and of great gods and lineage gods on the other, was much more lightly regarded. Oratory and dancing were well developed, but decorative arts, with the exception of the design rubbed and painted on the bark-cloth, slightly patterned mats, and a few clubs, were undeveloped. Literature also was undeveloped. Warfare was stylized as part of the inter-relationship between villages that were ceremonial rivals, and occasioned few casualties. Hostility between individuals was expressed covertly in the form of gossip and political machinations rather than open clashes. The society represented an economy of plenty, a flexible and workable form of social organization into which individuals fitted in terms of age, sex, and status, a set of expectations of the individual that most individuals were able to meet, and a definition of the desirable life—in terms of personal rewards, food, shelter, sex, pleasure, status, and security, which it was also able to provide. The most serious diseases were framboesia and conjunctivitis, both of which yield to modern medication, and today the rate of population increase is the highest in the world. Up to World War II, and possibly even through it—of which we have as yet no good records— the Samoans represented one of the most successful and untraumatic adjustments to culture change of which we have any record. This successful adjustment may be attributed in part to the flexibility of the culture, to the economic protection that prevented the alienation of land and the introduction of European economic competitive values, to the happy congruence between the pattern of English Congregationalism and Samoan social organization, and to an equally fortunate counterpoint between the Samoan system of rank and status and that of the United States Navy.

PUBLICATIONS ON SAMOA

Mead, Margaret, *Coming of Age in Samoa* (description of family life and psychological development), William Morrow, New York, 1928 (reprinted in *—From the South Seas*, William Morrow, New York, 1939)

English editions: Jonathan Cape, London, 1929; Penguin Books, London, 1943

Spanish edition: *Adolescencia y Cultura en Samoa*, trans. by Elena Dukelski Yoffe, Editorial Abril, Buenos Aires, 1945

Mead, Margaret, "A Lapse of Animism among a Primitive People," *Psyche*, Vol. 9 (1928), pp. 72-77

—— "Samoan Children at Work and at Play," *Natural History*, Vol. 28 (1928), pp. 626-36

—— "The Role of the Individual in Samoan Culture," *Journal of the Royal Anthropological Institute*, Vol. 58 (1928), pp. 481-95

—— "Americanization in Samoa," *American Mercury*, Vol. 16 (1929), pp. 264-70

—— *Social Organization of Manua* (formal theoretical and descriptive treatment), *Bernice P. Bishop Museum Bulletin* 76, Honolulu, 1930

—— "Two South Sea Educational Experiments and Their American Implications," *University of Pennsylvania Bulletin*, Vol. 31 (1931), pp. 493-97

—— "The Samoans" (a short account that combines social structure and personality structure), in *Cooperation and Competition among Primitive Peoples*, ed. by Margaret Mead, McGraw-Hill, New York, 1937; Chap. IX, pp. 282-312

LANGUAGE

Steubel, Otto, *Samoanische Texte, Veröffentlichungen aus dem Königlichen Museum für Völkerkunde*, Vol. 4, Pt. 2-4, Berlin, 1896

Pratt, George, *Grammar and Dictionary of the Samoan Language*, 4th ed., London Missionary Society, Malua, Samoa, 1911

The Bible has been translated into Samoan by the London Missionary Society.

PHYSICAL ANTHROPOLOGY

Sullivan, Louis R., *A Contribution to Samoan Somatology*, *Bernice P. Bishop Museum Memoirs*, Vol. 8, pp. 81-98, Honolulu, 1921

—— *Marquesan Somatology, with Comparative Notes on Samoa*

and Tonga, Bernice P. Bishop Museum Memoirs, Vol. 9, pp. 141-249, Honolulu, 1923

CULTURE CONTACT

Keesing, Felix M., *Modern Samoa: Its Government and Changing Life,* Stanford University Press, 1934
—— *The South Seas in the Modern World,* John Day, New York, 1941 (Institute of Pacific Relations, International Research Series)

PSYCHOLOGY

Cook, P. H., "The Application of the Rorschach Test to a Samoan Group," *Rorschach Research Exchange,* Vol. 6 (1942), pp. 51-60
Rowe, Newton A., *Samoa under the Sailing Gods,* Putnam, New York, 1930
Copp, J. D., *Autobiography of a Modern Samoan Boy,* to be published by Beacon Press

POPULATION

Durand, John D., *The Population of Western Samoa, Reports on the Population of Trust Territories* No. 1, United Nations Department of Social Affairs, Population Division, Lake Success, New York, January 17, 1948

LITERATURE

Stevenson, Robert Louis, *Vailima Letters,* Stone & Kimball, Chicago, 1895
—— *In the South Seas,* Scribner, New York, 1896
Fraser, John, "Some Folk-songs and Myths from Samoa," *Journal and Proceedings of the Royal Society of New South Wales:* Vol. 24 (1890), pp. 195-217; Vol. 25 (1891), pp. 70-86, 96-121, 121-46, 241-86; Vol. 26 (1892), pp. 264-301
—— "Some Folk-songs and Myths from Samoa," *Journal of the Polynesian Society:* Vol. 5 (1896), pp. 171-83; Vol. 6 (1897), pp. 19-36, 67-76, 107-22; Vol. 7 (1898), pp. 15-29

MATERIAL CULTURE

Te Rangi Hiroa (P. H. Buck), *Samoan Material Culture, Bernice P. Bishop Museum Bulletin* 75, Honolulu, 1930

B. THE MANUS PEOPLE OF THE ADMIRALTY ISLANDS

IN 1928, WHEN THESE STUDIES WERE MADE, THE MANUS PEOPLE were a group of about 2000 living in eleven autonomous villages along the south coast of the Great Admiralty Island, the central island of the Admiralty Archipelago, an island group located between 1° 50′ and 3° 10′ South latitude and between longitudes 146° and 148° East. It forms "the north-westerly germination of the long curved chain of large islands and groups of islands, which stretching roughly N.E. and S.W. is composed of New Ireland, Solomons and New Hebrides groups." [1]

The people are light-brown in color, tall and well built, with the frizzly hair of the Melanesian, and speak a Melanesian language. Their villages are built in lagoons adjacent to their fishing-grounds, and with the exception of the village of Mbuke, which makes pottery, and a few sago-grounds won in war from the land people of the Great Admiralty, they depend upon fishing and trading for their entire livelihood. Wood for house-building, bast for fish-lines, utensils and tools, are all traded from the other peoples of the Admiralties, the transportation of trade articles in Manus deep-sea-going canoes being an important item in what they have to offer other peoples. They had an elaborate currency of dogs' teeth and shell money, and in spite of their peripheral position, with no land except small built-up platforms and occasional precipitous little islands, were a dominant, wealthy people, preferring trade to war, but competent warriors when they did engage in war. Their houses

[1] Quoted from the naturalist aboard H.M.S. *Challenger*, by R. F. Fortune, p. lv of "Manus Religion" (see below).

were filled with wooden objects, large slit gongs, carved platform-beds, and scores of beautifully made pots, traded from other peoples, and they depended upon daily routine fishing and monthly large fishing activities to obtain carbohydrate foods.

Political life in the village was organized around a complex system of affinal exchanges in which imperishable valuables were exchanged against food, pots, grass skirts, etc., thus providing a continual stimulus to economic effort. This effort was further reinforced by a religious system under which each household was stimulated and chastised, and protected against the ghosts of other households, by a protective ghost of a recently dead male. Men were organized in working constellations of financial leaders and dependent followers, with a fair number of independents who merely fished and fed their own families. There was no chieftainship, although there were remnants of rank, and no village council of any sort. The strong moral code, enjoining industry and sexual control where Manus women were concerned, and enforced by a belief that all sickness was a ghostly punishment for economic or sexual sin, kept the community integrated and active, with occasional breakaways of individuals who joined other communities.

The Admiralties came under European control as part of German colonization, and passed to an Australian Mandate after World War I. At the time I studied them they had not yet been missionized, but had decided that they would ultimately—after the present most ambitious economic leaders had given the biggest inter-village economic exchange possible for a man to give—become Roman Catholics, and substitute the seal of the confessional for their present exacting system of open confession, at the same time learning to write and to keep accounts. Many Manus had served in the native constabulary, even in German times, and most adolescent boys who had not yet been away to work spoke pidgin English. Iron was commonly used, beads supplemented shell-money, sail-cloth had replaced mat sails, cloth cloaks for women, on whom elaborate avoidances were enjoined, had replaced mats, cotton cloth the men's G-strings of bark-cloth. But the Manus drew on the resources of European civilization skilfully and prudently. They had kept such practices as making fire with a fire plough, regarding matches as an unnecessary expense. In working for Europeans they showed high intelligence, ability to handle machinery, and the type of character structure that fitted particularly well into the police-force—an occupational choice that was interrupted by their participation in the famous strike of native labour in Rabaul in 1929, the strike itself being organized by the police, who were predominantly Manus.

They present the curious anomaly of a small group of people at Stone Age level without monotheism, without any political forms more complex than kin groupings held together by affinal ties and exchanges, who have developed a form of character structure that in its puritanism, its capacity to postpone pleasure for economic gain, its industriousness, its capacity to exploit other individuals for profit, and its high free level of intelligence—including great ease with machinery—is curiously like the character structure associated with the rise of Protestantism and modern capitalism in western Europe.

The Admiralties were captured by the Japanese in World War II, and recaptured by United States-Australian forces. A large United States Naval Air Station was built at Lorengau. The islands are now under the new trusteeship government that includes the former Mandated Territory of New Guinea and the former Papua.

Field-work was conducted by Dr. R. F. Fortune and myself during a six-month period in 1928-29, when I held a Fellowship from the Social Science Research Council. This was my first culture in which pidgin English had to be used as the intermediate language, so that pidgin had to be learned from a Manus-speaking schoolboy with an understanding, although hardly any speaking knowledge, of English at the same time we were working on the Manus language.

PUBLICATIONS ON THE MANUS OF THE ADMIRALTY ISLANDS

Mead, Margaret, "The Manus of the Admiralty Islands" (short general summary), in *Cooperation and Competition among Primitive Peoples,* ed. by Margaret Mead, McGraw-Hill, New York, 1937; Chap. VII, pp. 210-39

—— *Growing Up in New Guinea* (discussion of child-rearing and character development), William Morrow, New York, 1930 (reprinted in —*From the South Seas,* William Morrow, New York, 1939)

English editions: George Routledge, London, 1931; Penguin Books, London, 1942

—— *Kinship in the Admiralty Islands* (detailed study of the kinship organization), American Museum of Natural History *Anthropological Papers* (Vol. 34, Pt. II), 1934

Fortune, Reo F., *Manus Religion* (detailed study of the religion with verbatim accounts of the way in which the religious sanctions work), American Philosophical Society, Philadelphia, 1935

EARLY EXPLORATION

Parkinson, Richard H., *Dreissig Jahre in der Südsee,* Strecker und Schröder, Stuttgart, 1907

LANGUAGE

Meier, P. Josef, "*Mythen und Sagen der Admiralitätinsulaner,*" *Anthropos;* Vol. 2 (1907), pp. 646-67, 933-41; Vol. 3 (1908), pp. 193-206, 651-71; Vol. 4 (1909), pp. 354-74

See also: Fortune, Reo F., "Manus Religion," *Oceania,* Vol. 2 (1931), pp. 74-108

Mead, Margaret, "An Investigation of the Thought of Primitive
    Children with Special Reference to Animism," *Journal of the
    Royal Anthropological Institute*, Vol. 62 (1932), pp. 173-90
—— "Two South Sea Educational Experiments and Their Amer-
    ican Implications," *University of Pennsylvania Bulletin*, Vol.
    31 (1931), pp. 493-97
Spitz, René A., *"Frühkindliches Erleben und der Erwachsenen-
    kultur bei dem Primitiven; Bemerkungen zu Margaret Mead
    'Growing Up in New Guinea,'"* Imago, Vol. 21 (1935), pp.
    367-87

POPULAR ILLUSTRATED ARTICLES

Mead, Margaret, "Melanesian Middlemen," *Natural History*,
    Vol. 30 (1930), pp. 115-30
—— "Living with the Natives of Melanesia," *Natural History*,
    Vol. 31 (1931), pp. 62-74
—— "Water Babies of the South Seas," *Parents' Magazine*, Vol.
    5 (1930), pp. 20-21
—— "Savage Masters of the South Seas," *Safety Education*,
    Vol. 10 (1931), pp. 226-30

C. THE ARAPESH

THE ARAPESH ARE A PAPUAN-SPEAKING PEOPLE, BROWN-
skinned and frizzly-haired, who occupy a wedge-shaped
piece of territory on the northwest coast of New Guinea,
reaching from the Pacific coast over the triple range of the
Prince Alexander Mountains, down into the plains that form
the watershed of the Sepik River. The borders of the territory are indeterminate, the people have no name for the
whole group, and the word "Arapesh" was coined by the
anthropologist from the native word for human beings. The
people live in three different environments: on the beach,
where they fish and trade with the adjacent islands; in the
mountains, where they eke out a very precarious livelihood
with hunting, gardening, and sago-working; and on the
plains, where they are in active contact with head-hunting

peoples, and have large yam gardens. Their number has been estimated as between 8000 and 9000. The Mountain Arapesh were studied intensively by Dr. R. F. Fortune and myself during seven months in 1931, and by Dr. Fortune on a return visit in 1936.

The Mountain Arapesh lived in tiny hamlets, the largest of which was a base for some 85 people, with scattered gardens and garden huts. The hamlets, theoretically belonging to one patrilineal line, were held together by a loose allegiance to a named locality, which occasionally became involved in boundary disputes or disputes over women. There was no form of political organization, but a loose government by older men who had made many feasts and by the members of the organized men's cult, which could impose a sanction against social offenders. Work patterns, gardening, hunting, and house-building, involved a great deal of helping of one person by another, responding or initiating some piece of group-work. Food was very scarce, feasting rare, and actual hunger always a possibility.

The people lived between the intimidation by the more vigorous Plains Arapesh, who demanded, on threat of sorcery, hospitality and economic blackmail, and the Beach traders, from whom they obtained elaborate festivals, and objects of adornment and amusement. The organization of economic activity sufficient to appease the Plains and make the desirable importations from the Beach and maintain a minimum of local ceremonial life taxed their energies to the utmost.

Kinship organization was patrilineal, residence prevailingly patrilocal, but ties through the mother played an important rôle. Houses were built both on piles and on the ground; women's clothing consisted of two aprons of bast and men's of a narrow bark-cloth G-string. Affinal exchanges were nominal in character. The major moral sanction was a system, supported by taboos and sanctioned by *marsalais—*

spirits of rain living in localized spots, where the ghosts of the dead also gathered—that separated growth, and all the processes connected with growth and life, from active sexuality, aggression, and death.

Bows and arrows, spears, pots, net bags, stone tools, were all imported, although very simple imitations were sometimes made. The Mountain Arapesh had an attitude of extreme humility towards their own craftsmanship or artistry, and made only the most rudimentary attempts to copy the more elaborate artistic work of their neighbours.

As part of the old Mandated Territory of New Guinea, recruiting began in this area after World War I, and in 1931 all adolescent boys expected to go away to work. From European culture they had taken knives, adzes, beads, matches, razor-blades, and a small amount of cloth, worn by the men as loin-cloths and by women when dancing. They are in the area that was occupied by the Japanese in World War II, and were exposed to fighting between the Japanese and the United States-Australian forces. Gold was discovered in the Plains about a day inland from the village of Alitoa where we worked, and this had meant considerably greater contact even before World War II.

PUBLICATIONS ON THE ARAPESH OF NEW GUINEA

Mead, Margaret, "The Arapesh of New Guinea" (short summary), in *Cooperation and Competition among Primitive Peoples*, ed. by Margaret Mead, McGraw-Hill, New York, 1937; Chap I, pp. 20-50

CHILD-REARING AND CHARACTER STRUCTURE

Mead, Margaret, "The Mountain-Dwelling Arapesh," Pt. One of *Sex and Temperament in Three Primitive Societies*, William Morrow, New York, 1935 (reprinted in *—From the South Seas*, William Morrow, New York, 1939), pp. 3-161
English edition: George Routledge, London, 1935

Spanish edition: *Sexo y Temperamento,* trans. by Ines
Malinow, Editorial Abril, Buenos Aires, 1947
Swedish edition: *Kvinnligt, Manligt, Mänskligt,* trans. by
Gulli Högbom, Tidens Förlag, Stockholm, 1948
Fortune, Reo F., "Arapesh Maternity," *Nature,* Vol. 152 (1943),
p. 164

SOCIAL ORGANIZATION, ECONOMICS, MATERIAL CULTURE, DETAILS OF
EVENTS IN EVERYDAY LIFE

Mead, Margaret, *The Mountain Arapesh,* American Museum of
Natural History, *Anthropological Papers,* New York: I. "An
Importing Culture," Vol. 36 (1938), Pt. 3, pp. 139-349; II.
"Supernaturalism," Vol. 37 (1940), Pt. 3, pp. 317-451; III.
"Socio-Economic Life; IV. Diary of Events in Alitoa," Vol.
40 (1947); Pt. 3, pp. 163-419; V. "The Record of Unabelin"
(with Rorschachs), in press

LANGUAGE AND FOLKLORE

Fortune, Reo F., "Arapesh," *American Ethnological Society Publications,* Vol. 49 (1942), New York

WARFARE

Fortune, Reo F., "Arapesh Warfare," *American Anthropologist,*
Vol. 41 (1940), pp. 22-41
——"The Rules of Relationship Behaviour in One Variety of
Primitive Warfare," *Man,* Vol. 47 (1947), pp. 108-10
Mead, Margaret, "The Marsalai Cult among the Arapesh,"
Oceania, Vol. 4 (1933), pp. 37-53

POPULAR ILLUSTRATED ARTICLES

Mead, Margaret, "Where Magic Rules and Men Are Gods,"
New York Times Magazine, June 25, 1933, pp. 8-9
——"Where Sorcerers Call the Tune," *Asia,* Vol. 34 (1934), pp.
232-35

Mead, Margaret, "Tamberans and Tumbuans in New Guinea," *Natural History*, Vol. 34, pp. 234-36

———"How the Papuan Plans His Dinner," *Natural History*, Vol. 34 (1934), pp. 377-88

D. THE MUNDUGUMOR OF NEW GUINEA

THE MUNDUGUMOR PEOPLE, SOME THOUSAND IN NUMBER, speak a Papuan language that bears some marks of having been simplified by having been a trade language. They live in two hamlet clusters, four on one side and two on the other of the swiftly flowing Yuat River, which joins the south bank of the Sepik River at Yuarimo. Dr. Fortune and I worked among them for three and a half months in the autumn of 1932. At this time, although not missionized, and only so recently under government control that children of ten and eleven had been cannibals, they presented the picture of a broken culture. Ceremonials were infrequent; a large number of men were away at work, only a few of the first group of recruits to go away had come home.

The Mundugumor were interwoven by kinship and exchange relationship among lineages of alternating sex called ropes, so that a man belonged to his mother's father's rope, a woman to her father's mother's rope. A system of exceedingly difficult arranged marriages between the rope grandchildren of cross-cousins was maintained as a fiction only, and the dominant men in the community had large polygamous households, partly recruited from the miserable, ill-fed intimidated people of the grass-lands between rivers, who had provided head-hunting and cannibal-feast victims also, and continued to provide baskets, pots, sleeping-baskets, etc., for the dominant Mundugumor. Each village had been alternatively involved in alliances and warfare with other Mundugumor villages and with neighbouring villages. Head-hunting, with elaborate treaties, alliance systems of hostages and spies, and ceremonials honoured more in the breach, had been the principal occupation of the men, who were so divided by the social-organization arrangements that each man's hand was against each other man's, except for temporary alliances or truces during ceremonies. The men did a little hunting and trading, and quite a good deal of carving and painting and ornamenting of wooden figures, having developed a distinctive artistic style. The women did the rest of the work, assisted by young boys, working sago, fishing, climbing coconut-trees, moving with a free, aggressive sureness through a violent, dangerous world.

The Mundugumor live in the Sepik District of the old Mandated Territory and were missionized at some time between 1933 and 1938, when I had an opportunity to see again my principal informant, Omblean of Kenakatem, the village in which we made our headquarters. In the division of labour in the field, I worked principally on child behaviour and material culture. There are no other published studies of the area.

PUBLICATIONS ON THE MUNDUGUMOR OF NEW GUINEA

CHILD-REARING AND CHARACTER STRUCTURE

Mead, Margaret, "The River-Dwelling Mundugumor," Pt. Two of *Sex and Temperament in Three Primitive Societies,* William Morrow, New York, 1935 (reprinted in —*From the South Seas,* William Morrow, New York, 1939), pp. 164-233 (For other editions, see page 409.)

MATERIAL CULTURE AND ART

Mead, Margaret, *The Mountain Arapesh:* I. "An Importing Culture," American Museum of Natural History, *Anthropological Papers,* Vol. 36, Pt. 3, pp. 139-349, New York, 1938 (illustrated)
——— "Tamberans and Tumbuans in New Guinea," *Natural History,* Vol. 34 (1934), pp. 234-36 (illustrated)

E. THE IATMUL OF NEW GUINEA

THE IATMUL PEOPLE OF THE MIDDLE SEPIK REPRESENT ONE OF the most noteworthy cultures of New Guinea. Their villages occupy country on both banks of the river from about 150 to about 250 miles from the mouth of the river. They speak a complex Papuan language, which also has a simplified form used as a trade jargon by neighbouring tribes. Their magnificent villages, with great pile dwelling-houses and impressive men's houses, were part of each year under water. Canoes built for warfare were beautifully decorated. An elaborate system of patrilineal clans, balanced by great attention to matrilineal ties, three different forms of marriage, and several types of age-grading and moiety systems, resulted in a rich and complex form of social organization. The separate villages were loosely inter-related by a complicated cosmological and totemic system of names and by theories of origin that trace one village back to another. But there was no central political organization, and even in the villages, the largest of which has 500 people, an uneasy form of order was maintained only by pitting sub-groups against each other. Head-hunting and an enormous number of ceremonials formed a framework within which all the men's activities were carried on. Economically, the people were rich, depending on large supplies of sago, and fishing done by the women in artificial ditches. There was some gardening. Although some villages traded with the bush-people, in markets, and for special commodities like pots, stone axes, and ochre, the Iatmul were on the whole self-sufficient, practising a rich range of crafts and arts—basketry, carving, bark-painting, modelling on skulls, etc.

Our knowledge of the culture is based on four field trips by Gregory Bateson: 1929, a short expedition up the river for collecting and reconnaissance; 1930, six months in the village of Mindimbit; 1932-33, in Kankanamun and Palim bei; and an eight-month stay in 1938 in Tambumum on which I accompanied him, studied the children, and co-operated in collecting photographic records to provide comparative materials for Bali. I have drawn extensively upon Mr. Bateson's wide knowledge of Iatmul culture, but all specific materials on children come from this Tambunum field-trip, and are related to the differentiations of Tambunum culture from the up-river Iatmul culture on which the study of transvestitism in *Naven* (see below) is based.

Publications on the Iatmul of New Guinea

Bateson, Gregory, "Social Structure of the Iatmul People of the Sepik River," Pts. I-III: *Oceania*, Vol. II (1932), pp. 245-91, 401-53

—— "Music in New Guinea," *Eagle*, Vol. 48 (1935), Cambridge, Eng., pp. 158-70

—— "Culture Contact and Schismogenesis," *Man*, Vol. 35 (1935), pp. 178-83

—— *Naven: A Survey of the Problems Suggested by a Composite Picture of the Culture of a New Guinea Tribe Drawn from Three Points of View*, Cambridge University Press, 1936

Mead, Margaret, "Public Opinion Mechanisms among Primitive Peoples," *Public Opinion Quarterly*, Vol. 1 (1937), pp. 5-16

—— "Character Formation in Two South Seas Societies," *Transactions of the 66th Annual Meeting of the American Neurological Association*, 1940, pp. 99-103

—— "Conflict of Cultures in America," *Proceedings of the 54th Annual Convention of the Middle States Association of Colleges and Secondary Schools*, 1940, pp. 1-19

—— "Administrative Contributions to Democratic Character Formation at the Adolescent Level," *Journal of the Association of Deans of Women*, Vol. 4 (1941), pp. 51-57

—— "The Family in the Future," in *Beyond Victory*, ed. by Ruth Nanda Anshen, Harcourt, Brace, New York, 1943

—— "Research on Primitive Children," in *Manual of Child Psy-*

chology, ed. by Leonard Carmichael, John Wiley, New York, 1946, pp. 667-706

Mead, Margaret, "Age Patterning in Personality Development," *American Journal of Orthopsychiatry,* Vol. 17 (1947), pp. 231-40

F. THE TCHAMBULI

THE TCHAMBULI PEOPLE ARE A SMALL TRIBE—ONLY 500 IN ALL —who live on the edge of the Tchambuli lake, under the Tchambuli mountain. Two water-ways connect the lake with the Sepik River about 180 miles from its mouth. They speak a difficult Papuan language, which is not understood by the people around them, whose languages they have to learn. At the time that Dr. Fortune and I studied them, in 1933, they had been under control by the government of the Mandated Territory of New Guinea some seven or eight years, and just previously they had fled their ancestral territory, in fear of the warlike Iatmuls, and gone in three separate groups to live with bush-people. Now, under the Pax Britannica and with iron tools, they were involved in a cultural renaissance, building a series of elaborately decorated men's houses along the shore, and great family dwelling-houses inland. They had a few gardens, but depended mainly on fishing and on trading for other food in periodic markets. The women were industrious makers of mats, baskets, rain-capes, mosquito baskets; the men spent most of their time carving, painting, and preparing elaborate theatrical displays. Each of the three hamlets was divided into patrilineal clan groups; the clans were knit together by marriage into the mother's brother's group and clans or parts of clans were arranged into various sorts of cross-cutting moieties. Interest in the arts and in ceremonial was greater than that in warfare, and head-hunting victims were either bought or were criminals from the next hamlet. Along the edge of the polished black surface of the lake, the elaborately decorated, posturing people conducted a sort of perpetual ballet, the women going out to fish with great pink water-lilies stuck in their arm-bands.

The planned division of labour in field-work was the same as in Mundugumor, and the only publications on the Tchambuli are Part III of my *Sex and Temperament,* and the sections on material culture and the arts cited here.

G. BALI

THE PEOPLE OF BALI CONTRAST STRONGLY WITH ALL OF THE other peoples discussed in this book. They are not a primitive people, but Indonesians speaking a Malay language who for many hundreds of years have been exposed to the high cultures of Southeast Asia and China. Almost a million people on their tiny island—only 2905 square miles in size—east of Java, they have lived in a society that in many ways resembled the Middle Ages in Europe, or did so until Netherlands rule was instituted at the beginning of this century. The country was divided into small kingdoms, in which rulers of Kesatria caste presided loosely over a Brahman priesthood, and exacted mild tribute from a prevailing casteless peasant population who lived in villages each of which had a perfectly organized self-sufficient social structure, which regulated land-tenure, irrigation, and all types of social organization except those few which reigning princes had abrogated to themselves. Hinduism had penetrated the religious structure deeply, but there were also many traces of old Buddhism. Caste, believed to have been brought in from Java when the Hindu Javanese fled the spread of Mohammedanism, sat rather lightly in Bali, where it was possible for high-caste men to marry low-caste women and yet bequeath some caste to their children.

The economic structure was based on a combination of communally and feudally administered agriculture, in which rice was the chief crop, and a system of markets in which the craft products of individuals and groups, and foods, were bought and sold for money, copper Chinese cash. Houses were relatively small but beautifully built and fitted together, and temples consisted mainly of terraced open courts and small shrines, in which Hindu gods and pre-Hindu gods were worshipped in accordance with a calendar of great complexity. Priests and scribes knew how to write in an ancient script on pages cut from palm-leaves. Iron, gold, and silver were worked, and elaborate textiles, including double-tied dyed textiles, were woven.

The arts, especially music, dancing, and the theatre, were enormously developed, and a great part of the time of a people whose remote dreamlike behaviour included a great capacity for almost endless untiring activity was spent in preparing for one dramatic ceremonial after another. Gambling, centring around cock-fighting, was highly developed, but drinking, in spite of the availability of intoxicating liquors, was rare. Trance, divination, and calendrical ritual all played important parts in the religious life, which embraced every facet of Balinese living, from the small offerings made after each meal to ceremonies given by princes costing hundreds of thousands of guilders. In spite of the conspicuous differences between prince and peasant, between Brahman priest and local village-temple officiant, between the crude Mountain craftsman and the Plains artisan, in its ceremonial and its symbolism a great part of Balinese life was available to every Balinese. So although we find extreme and detailed differences between one part of Bali and another, or between the formal behaviour of different castes, or between different priestly sects, the character structure seems to be extremely homogeneous, with little difference between the villages whose inhabitants never go into trance and those where almost everybody goes into trance.

Study of such a complex society is of necessity a very different task from the recording, at most by two people, of the culture of some small just-discovered and already disappearing primitive culture. In the two years, 1936-38, and a return visit in 1939, in which Gregory Bateson and I worked there, in close association with Jane Belo, who had spent several years there earlier; indebted to the special insights of Colin McPhee, who was studying the music, the late Walter Spies, who had devoted several years to an intensive personal exploration of all the arts, and Katherine Mershon, who specialized on dance and religious behaviour—in that time we still could only sample, in small intensive ways, aspects of the culture, following groups of children, or a special set of trance dancers, or a group of young artists, or the calendar of a particular village, with written records and still and ciné records also. There is of course a great literature on Bali, both technical and popular. Netherlands scholars have studied the law, and constructed archaeological sequences from a detailed study of archaeological remains. I shall present here only a bibliography of our own work, and such work of our collaborators as we have ourselves drawn on during its preparation.

PUBLICATIONS ON BALI

CHARACTER STRUCTURE AND SYMBOLIC SYSTEM

Bateson, Gregory, and Mead, Margaret, *Balinese Character: A Photographic Analysis*, New York Academy of Sciences Special Publication, 1942 (100 plates)

Abel, Theodora M., "Free Designs of Limited Scope as a Personality Index," *Character and Personality*, Vol. 7 (1938), pp. 50-62

Bateson, Gregory, "The Frustration-Aggression Hypothesis," *Psychological Review*, Vol. 48 (1941), pp. 350-55

—— "Bali: The Value System of a Steady State," in *Social Struc-*

ture: Studies Presented to A. R. Radcliffe-Brown, ed. by Meyer Fortes, to be published by Clarendon Press

Belo, Jane, "The Balinese Temper," *Character and Personality*, Vol. 4 (1935), pp. 120-46

―――― "Bali: Rangda and Barong," *American Ethnological Society Monograph* No. 16, to be published in February 1949

Mead, Margaret, "Researches in Bali, 1936-39," *Transactions of the New York Academy of Sciences*, Ser. II, Vol. 2 (1939), pp. 1-4

―――― "Public Opinion Mechanisms among Primitive Peoples," *Public Opinion Quarterly*, Vol. I (1937), pp. 5-16

―――― "Character Formation in Two South Seas Societies," *Transactions of the 66th Annual Meeting of the American Neurological Association* (1940), pp. 99-103

―――― "Administrative Contributions to Democratic Character Formation at the Adolescent Level," *Journal of the National Association of Deans of Women*, Vol. 4 (1941), pp. 51-57 (reprinted in *Personality in Nature, Society, and Culture*, ed. by Clyde Kluckhohn and Henry A. Murray, Knopf, New York, 1948; Pt. III, Chap. 37, pp. 523-30)

―――― "Conflict of Cultures in America," *Proceedings of the 54th Annual Convention of the Middle States Association of Colleges and Secondary Schools*, 1940

―――― "Educative Effects of Social Environment as Disclosed by Studies of Primitive Societies," in *Symposium on Environment and Education* (E. W. Burgess, W. L. Warner, Franz Alexander, Margaret Mead), *Supplementary Educational Monographs* (University of Chicago) No. 54 (1942), pp. 48-61

―――― "Research on Primitive Children," in *Handbook of Child Psychology*, ed. by Leonard Carmichael, John Wiley, New York, 1946, pp. 667-706

―――― "The Family in the Future," in *Beyond Victory*, ed. by Ruth Nanda Ashen, Harcourt, Brace, New York, 1943, pp. 66-87

―――― "Age Patterning in Personality Development," *American Journal of Orthopsychiatry*, Vol. 17 (1947), pp. 231-40

SOCIAL ORGANIZATION AND RELIGION

Bateson, Gregory, "An Old Temple and a New Myth," *Djawa*, Vol. 17 (1937), pp. 1-18

Belo, Jane, "A Study of Customs Pertaining to Twins in Bali," *Tijdschrift voor Ind. Taal-, Land-, en Volkenkunde*, Vol. 75 (1935), pp. 483-549

—— "A Study of a Balinese Family," *American Anthropologist*, Vol. 38 (1936), pp. 12-31

THE ARTS

Bateson, Gregory, Bali: The Human Problem of Reoccupation; Supplementary Material on the Exhibit, Museum of Modern Art, New York, 1942 (mimeographed)

—— (with Claire Holt), "Form and Function of the Dance in Bali," in *The Function of Dance in Human Society, a Seminar Directed by Franciska Boas*, Boas School, New York, 1944, pp. 46-52

Belo, Jane, "Balinese Children's Drawings," *Djawa*, Vol. 17 (1937), pp. 1-13

Holt, Claire, *"Les danses de Bali,"* Archives internationales de la danse, Pt. I (April 15, 1935), pp. 51-53; Pt. II (July 15, 1935), pp. 84-86

—— *"Théâtre et danses aux Indes Néerlandaises,"* Catalogue et Commentaires, XIIIᵉ Exposition des Archives Internationales de la Danse (1939), Maisonneuve, Paris, 1939

—— Analytical Catalogue of Collection of Balinese Carvings in the American Museum of Natural History, New York (unpublished)

McPhee, Colin, "The 'Absolute' Music of Bali," *Modern Music*, Vol. 12 (1935), p. 165

—— "The Balinese Wanjang Koelit and Its Music," *Djawa*, Vol. 16 (1936), p. 1

—— "Angkloeng Music in Bali," *Djawa*, Vol. 17 (1937)

—— "Children and Music in Bali," *Djawa*, Vol. 18 (1938), pp. 1-14

McPhee, Colin, "Figuration in Balinese Music," *Peabody Bulletin,* May 1940

―― *A House in Bali,* John Day, New York, 1947

―― "Dance in Bali," *Dance Index,* to be published in January 1949

―― "Five-Tone Music of Bali," *Musical Quarterly,* to be published in April 1949

―― Recording: Music of Bali; six Balinese compositions arranged for two pianos and performed by Benjamin Britten and Colin McPhee, G. Schirmer, New York

―― Published Music: Balinese Ceremonial Music―Pemungkah, Gambangan, Tabuh Telu; transcribed for two pianos, G. Schirmer, New York

Mead, Margaret, "Strolling Players in the Mountains of Bali," *Natural History,* Vol. 43 (1939), pp. 17-26

―― "The Arts in Bali," *Yale Review,* Vol. 30 (1940), pp. 335-47

―― "Community Drama, Bali and America," *American Scholar,* Vol. 2 (1941-42), pp. 79-88

Zoete, Beryl de, and Spies, Walter, *Dance and Drama in Bali* (preface by Arthur Waley), Harper, New York and London, 1939

APPENDIX II

THE ETHICS OF INSIGHT-GIVING

THE SOCIAL SCIENTIST, WORKING WITH AN EMERGING AWARE-
ness that if pursued will surely alter the shape of our world,
carries a heavy load of obligation. When the social scientist
says understanding will make men freer to shape their own
destiny, he claims not only that understanding itself is a
good, but also that he can offer some of that understanding,
or at least the way to attain it. There are those who will
argue that greater understanding is always destructive, that
once man loses his innocence—that is, his capacity to ignore
the unconscious and unacknowledged parts of his personality, which have played an unrecognized rôle in his actions—then also he loses what limited capacity he had for
good behaviour. Those of us who believe in awareness, who
believe that only by a greater understanding of man himself can we build a world in which human beings can realize more of their potentialities and live in greater harmony

one with another, are committed to the opposite position. Our contention is that man has already lost the particular forms of innocence that were possible in a pre-scientific age, and that now, his innocence shattered, he must go forward still further or accept the penalties of either an ostrich-like sentimentality or a cynicism in which power and immediate satisfactions are alternative solutions. We believe that it is possible to attain a new innocence; that is, a new wholeness in which Christ's admonition, "Let not thy left hand know what thy right hand doeth," can again mean wholeness and integration, but on another level.[1]

No social scientist who has been closely in touch with the uses of social science in World War II, or even studied closely the ways in which propaganda and indoctrination methods were used after World War I, can doubt that awareness and understanding can be used destructively as well as constructively, that social science in itself carries no guarantee of good to mankind, any more than theoretical physics does. Pursued without responsibility, either may lead to evil as easily as to good, though it be the rotting of a social structure rather than the obliteration of a ten-mile area of a modern city. Most social scientists who entered the psychological-warfare departments of their various countries, or participated in operations involving the improvement of rela-

[1] Matt. 6:3. I wrote this paragraph using the quotation from the Sermon on the Mount in the sense in which I had learned to interpret it; that is, that when one acted, one should act as a whole person, not calculating the gains to be obtained from a generous action. But I soon found that most of those who read the manuscript or were questioned about the meaning of the quotation did not interpret it that way. Almost every one thought it was a description of evil behaviour, hypocritical, scheming at worst, or in modern psychiatric terms schizoid. Most people did not know who had said it. I was also interested to discover that the interpretation of evil dissociation rather than innocent spontaneity had been prevalent in the Middle Ages. (See especially Combe, Jacques, "La Mort de l'Avare," in Jerome Bosch, Libraire Rimbali, Paris, 1946, No. 42.) However, I have decided to keep the figure, as it high-lights so well our present confusion about the inter-relationships between increasing degrees of insight and the possibility of innocence at higher levels of awareness.

tionship between allies, or the raising of domestic morale, did on the whole take the position that the job in a war was to defeat the enemy, maintain good relations with allies, and keep domestic morale high. The ethics of the various operations by which these ends were accomplished had to be worked out on the job,[2] on intervention committees, in intelligence services, in counter-intelligence services, in war relocation centers, in prisoner-of-war interrogations, attached to joint headquarters, in planning agencies that intercepted letters or planned anti-rumor campaigns. Even the first evaluations are not all in yet; many of those who played an active part have not yet spelled out their separate learnings. But none of those who during the war applied social-science skills doubt that there is a problem here which must be faced.

As we go on working in this uneasy peace-time, we have the task of making clearer to ourselves and to the world an ethics of insight, an ethics to guide those who are beginning to apply social science consciously and responsibly. One aspect of the discussion is focussed on whether it is right to provide any concrete knowledge in a form that can easily be

[2] Mead, Margaret, "On Behalf of the Sciences," in Symposium "Toward an Honorable World," *Wilson College Bulletin*, Vol. III (1940), pp. 19-29; *Idem*, "The Comparative Study of Cultures and the Purposive Cultivation of Democratic Values," and Bateson, Gregory, comments ("Social Planning and the Concept of 'Deutero-Learning'"), both in *Science, Philosophy and Religion: Second Symposium, Conference on Science, Philosophy and Religion*, New York, 1942, pp. 56-69, 81-97 respectively (papers delivered in September 1941); Bateson, Gregory, and Mead, Margaret, "Principles of Morale Building," *Journal of Educational Sociology*, Vol. 15 (1941), pp. 206-20; Mead, Margaret, "Are Democracy and Social Science Compatible Each with Each?" in *And Keep Your Powder Dry*, William Morrow, New York, 1942; Chap. XI, pp. 176-92; *Idem*, "Reaching the Last Woman down the Road," *Journal of Home Economics*, Vol. 34 (1942), pp. 710-13; Bateson, Gregory, "The Science of Decency," *Philosophy of Science*, Vol. 10 (1943), pp. 140-42—a reply to Dr. Langmuir; *Idem*, "The Pattern of an Armaments Race," Part 1: "An Anthropological Approach"; Pt. 2: "An Analysis of Nationalism," *Bulletin of the Atomic Scientists*, Vol. 2 (1946), pp. 10-11, 26-28—presented in discussion of inter-cultural implications of atomic discoveries.

used by those who cannot be held responsible for the way in which they use it. If one analyzes a contemporary culture —either one's own, that of an ally, of an uneasy friend, or of a possible or a declared enemy—that analysis, to the extent that it is accurate, may be used either for good or for evil. This is quite a different thing from the technical description of the culture of the Mundugumor, who sixteen years ago were a vanishing and disintegrating group of people on the banks of an obscure river in New Guinea. Only by taking such remote ethnological knowledge, stating it very abstractly, and then translating it back again into a concrete contemporary situation, can it be used for any practical purposes whatever. Political propagandists, subversive plotters, advertising men cunningly promoting one brand at the expense of another brand, agents of a foreign power attempting to promote cleavages within another country or to obtain unwilling co-operation from an ally—these cannot use this material without further knowledge. Applied anthropology depends not only upon the knowledge of a set of abstractions brought out of the primitive laboratory, but upon a concrete, specific knowledge of the situation to be changed.[3] Without a knowledge of American, Russian, German, French, Chinese, English, Japanese culture, the most careful studies of Eskimo and Hottentot, Arapesh and Cheyenne, remain on the whole quite innocuous. Once however the same analyses are made of contemporary cultures, new possibilities of exploitation enter in, new possibilities of manipulation, of corruption, of destruction. This is a risk

[3] For a concrete example of the handling of such abstractions, see Bateson, Gregory, "Morale and National Character," in "Civilian Morale," ed. by Goodwin Watson, *Second Yearbook of the Society for the Psychological Study of Social Issues,* Houghton Mifflin, New York, 1942, pp. 71-91; and the further application of these abstractions to problems of Anglo-American relations as described in Mead, Margaret, "A Case History in Cross-National Communications," in *The Communication of Ideas,* ed. by Lyman Bryson, Institute for Religious and Social Studies, New York, 1948; Chap. XIII, pp. 209-29.

that must be faced frankly. The more we know about ourselves and the other peoples of the world, the more harm
we can do, as well as the more good. Only if one believes in
awareness, believes that the truth will make men free, is one
justified in attempting to find and disseminate such knowledge.

Those of us who are deeply concerned about the relationship between our social-science skills and our world are trying to solve the problem in various ways. As applied anthropologists we so far limit ourselves to very simple ethical demands upon each other. We insist that the applied anthropologist must take into account the relationship between
ends and means, must think as far and as long ahead as he
can, must take the good of the whole into account, and must
be faithful to the idea of an emergent dynamic equilibrium
in society that leaves the future free. Beyond these imperatives, simple, incomplete, but difficult enough in all conscience, each must submit his methods to the test of his
own ethical standards.[4]

There is a second aspect of the problem summed up in the
saying "A little learning is a dangerous thing." Anything
that any of us can say about contemporary cultures is only
a very little. It is partial, inadequately formulated, incomplete—as is all science, especially in its beginnings, and always so in periods of new growth. But very few of those who
have followed the history of medicine, from the first tre-
panning operation to the modern transplantation of the
cornea, would agree that we should have abandoned medicine because at each stage in history first attempts at opera-
ations have been unsuccessful. A little learning, if it is the
first learning, is the way in which men move on to new

[4] The Committee on Ethics of the Society for Applied Anthropology has
been working since May 1946, and the Committee's report was adopted in
substance at the Philadelphia meeting, May 30, 1948. It is now being prepared for publication.

knowledge, and it can be regarded as dangerous only when practitioner or patient overestimates it. The apothecary did the best he could, and he did not need to be legislated out of the tasks of diagnosis and treatment because of his little learning until there were medical schools in which more learning could be obtained. And then it was not the layman using first-aid who had to be legislated against and controlled, but the apothecary, and later the nurse. A little learning can be a dangerous thing when used by those who share only part of a growing tradition. The apothecary and the nurse, who have access to drugs and methods they have not fully learned to understand, and yet can command faith from those who know less than they, must be controlled and limited in what they are allowed to do. But if men had said the best surgeon, using his skill to the limits of his experience, might not try a new operation, or that a new drug developed under the best protective experimentation that man knew could never be given—then medicine could never have developed. The danger lies always in the practitioner who overestimates his actual knowledge rather than courageously and humbly, knowing that he does not know, takes, with the patient's full knowledge and consent, that patient's life in his hands. The danger lies in the patient who overestimates the physician's skill, and trusts him even where the physician himself has said, "This is a place for faith but not for trust." Responsible behaviour on the part of those who use the methods of science in any way that affects the lives of their fellow-men consists in recognizing, as fully as they themselves are able, the meaning of what they do. Nor does it stop there. It consists in communicating to others this same knowledge of the relationship of new knowledge to their lives and the lives of their children. There is no ivory tower except one in which the scientist seals himself up, and promises that the results of his research will never be communicated in any form to any other human being. Learning is not dangerous because there is only a little of it, but it is dangerous not to know just how little there is. The anthropologist working in society is often faced, both in the United States and in Britain, first with complete scepticism, and then, if accepted at all, with an equally complete and irrational trust. His obligation is to establish in his own mind and that of others what—at a given period of anthropological development—he knows, what he can hope to know, and what may be the consequences of such knowledge.

In connection with the section of this book which deals with American culture, I have spelled out as explicitly as I can, and in terms of American culture, both the hazards and the safeguards that I feel are involved in this particular discussion. Cultural knowledge, because of its special relationship to our particular national habits of self-criticism, has dangers in America that it does not have in other cultures, who have their own different vulnerabilities to increased self-awareness.

We in America have always believed in hitching our wagon to a star. We disagree about the way the wagon should be built and about the immediate path that it should follow, but we have little doubt that as long as there is a star to be seen in the sky, we cannot as Americans hitch our wagon lower. To aim at less than the best is not a possible course. We have many ways of limiting our definition of the best, of closing our eyes to the state of the rope, of unhitching the wagon for a joy-ride, but with our first breath of that air which the new-comers from Europe say makes children so fresh we draw in a belief that the star should be there.

But a society that hitches its wagon to a star, which commits itself to living always with an unattainable ideal, so that the ideals of yesterday, once attained, become nothing but most imperfect approximations of the ideals of tomorrow, is also committed to many other things—to styles in prophecy and rebellion, to casualties for whole segments of the population who are sacrificed to a fiction, and casualties to individuals who are betrayed by ideals they were unable to bear or to live with, to the continued onslaught of the impatient utopian revolutionary and of the nostalgic reactionary, neither of whom can any longer stand the tension. In such a society, where so many inevitably hold different views of the good, and different views of how to solve the problems that arise when wagons are hitched to stars, all who speak are rightly subjected to scrutiny, and each who speaks is a part of the whole. There are the prophets who warn that the vision of the star is getting dim, or that a particular star has fallen and another one must be found. These are the finders of new stars. There are those who find intolerable the distance between the wagon lumbering along in the half-frozen ruts of a spring thaw and say: "Enough of this slow pilgrimage that will never end. Let's cut the rope free of the star, free of the endlessly moving and unattainable ideal that is only a fraud, and hitch our rope to some firm—and absolutely realizable—past or future point, and then go there fast." These are those who think that one can establish, by fiat or revolution, a Utopia on earth. There are those who say: "Look at the impossible distance between your wagon and your star. Accept the fact that you can never reach it; cut the rope and be done with it, and let's take life as we find it. Let's have a joy-ride, a straw-ride. You've only one life to live." All these points of view are articulate in American life; each fears the other, each fears that the other will coerce the country, and so himself, into a path he does not wish to take. It is of the nature of our kind of civilization that all these points of view should be here. It is the problem of our kind of civilization to find ways in which all can contribute to the whole.

One way of solving this problem is to shift attention from the exact *nature* of the star or the lamentable *pace* of the wagon, to the relationship between them, that is, to the *tautness of the rope*.[5] The rope must be taut enough so that those who know there is a star can lend their eyes to the earth-bound and the night-blind, and so that those who fear the star will fall will lose their fear and go on. The rope must not be so taut that it tips the wagon on to its back wheels and further impedes its progress, so that those who are worried about the pace of the wagon are tempted to say: "Let's accept an ideal obtainable in time and on this earth, and let us get it by quick methods." Or, feeling as if there were no movement at all: "Let's just cut the rope." When one thinks of the tautness of the rope it does not mean that one questions the importance of the star, nor that one questions the importance of the pace of the wagon, either. One simply says: "I accept the nature of my culture as one framework of civilization, and the one within which I am best fitted to work, and I accept the responsibility for actively cherishing it. I accept the importance of the Jeremiahs, but also the danger that if there are too many Jeremiahs, the people will simply despair and not repent. I accept the importance of Amos and Hosea, but also the danger that if too much emphasis is laid on men's failure to live up to their ideals, people will be tempted to take short cuts, some into the future-oriented Utopia, which is the theme of the communist idealist, some into the over-simplified acceptance of power as an ultimate good, which is the theme of the fascist idealist. Finally, I accept the importance of the people who speak for simple joy, who say, 'But I want to live now, in my own lifetime,' because they keep both the prophets and the Utopians from ruthlessly sacrificing all of this life for a future life, or sacrificing those who are alive now that others just like

[5] The particular obligation of the social scientist to attend to the relationship between inculcated ideals and their practical realization was first brought home to me in a lecture by Ruth Benedict in Baltimore during World War II.

them may some day live better." Accepting all of these, one asks: What needs to be done?

Keeping the rope at a right degree of tautness means being continually alert lest our ideals get too far out of line with our practice. It means being ever watchful for areas where this occurs, and searching for the surest way of reducing the tension. In Chapter XVII, "Can Marriage Be for Life?" I have discussed in detail one of those areas where, because our marriage ideal includes an explicit guarantee that marriage can be for life—a guarantee that contemporary society no longer supports—we are condemning thousands of marriages to death that might otherwise be saved. Similarly, in the present ideals we set up for women, we insist that women should be full, choosing human beings and then define the choice that most of them make—home-making for a husband and children—as somehow no proper choice at all. In our education of boys we demand simultaneously a high level of defensive aggressiveness and a belief that to start a fight is wrong.[6] As we have built our culture, always oriented towards the future, always oriented to a pattern made up of details each one of which, if attained, must be condemned as not good enough, we have more and more committed ourselves to a need for a continuing, aware watchfulness over these very patterns and those who must live them.

I myself unequivocally accept as a task to which I can bend all my efforts the task of keeping that rope taut and not too taut, strong but not heavy. I personally accept the culture within which I live and move and have my particular being as a way of life within which it is possible to work towards the welfare of all mankind in all places on the face of the earth. I accept the prophets who lament our blurred and imperfect vision, I accept the right of the rev-

[6] Mead, Margaret, *And Keep Your Powder Dry*, William Morrow, New York, 1942; Chap. IX, "The Chip on the Shoulder," pp. 138-57.

olutionist to challenge and to break a society that cannot keep itself whole enough to stand against him. I accept the indomitable will to live of those who, bruised by demands greater than they can bear, demand joy, however slight and cheap, rather than sink into apathy and despair. I accept the vision of the saint, but I preserve the right to point out that the priests sometimes, instead of preserving the vision of saints, construct ways of life that make men sinners. And I accept also those who say: "I will have none of it, it is not my way—not mine to change nor mine to accept. Mine is another country—not of this age, not of this earth."

> And let his enemies gibe but let them say,
> That he would throw this continent away
> And seek another country,
> As he would do.[7]

For no culture has yet been created by the loving imaginations of men that has an equal place for every temperament,[8] or a store of blessings that outweight the traumas which some of those in each culture will inevitably suffer. I also accept the responsibility of defending such freedom against all who would destroy it.[9]

In accepting as part of the world within which I can live and keep my soul those who in one way or another have found it unlivable, I run peculiar risks of being misunderstood, and so also do all of us who work with this particular evolutionary faith. And it is absolutely essential that we be understood in order to make sure that the case can be

[7] Last lines of John Crowe Ransom's "Persistent Explorer," in *Two Gentlemen in Bonds*, Alfred Knopf, New York, 1927.

[8] My systematic understanding of the problem of deviance I owe to Ruth Benedict, who lectured on the subject for many years before the publication of *Patterns of Culture* in 1934.

[9] This is not to be interpreted as cultural relativism in the sense that any set of values is as "good" as any other. Once one has asked the question "Good for what?" different values may be seen as better or worse or merely different ways of attaining a given good.

judged on its true merits and not on some unwitting but nevertheless destructive falsification. Those who feel that this country is a morass of sin and wickedness, of licentious forgetfulness of God, where men live only for the day, forgetful both of their souls and of their fellow-men, will find it hard to believe that I both agree with many of their denunciations and yet disagree about the means they would employ to set matters right. I am shocked at the present handling of death in this country, but I do not think it can be righted by a simple call to repentance. Nor do I believe that the next step is a positive move by the ministerial association to take the business back from the undertakers. Rather, I describe carefully our loss of sensitivity to the spiritual implications of death, and relate this to the type of change that is going on in our society. And Reinhold Niebuhr mistakes my meaning and says that I believe in modern undertaking rites.[10] For how can one speak without denunciation unless one is wholly on the side of the Devil? Those who have set up their vision of an earthly Utopia, progressive or reactionary, as a blue-print to be fought for and won will recognize me quite accurately as being on the other side. With my concept of what makes our culture I recognize their right to challenge, even while I make every effort to strengthen our society so that they cannot break it—because I believe in a society that permits such challenges. Those others who have abandoned the struggle to look at stars, and who sit behind curtained windows hoping that drink or food or sex or money will bring them the happiness that too much star-talk in their childhood has

[10] In 1945, I contributed an article entitled "How Religion Has Fared in the Melting Pot" to a series on *Religion in the Post War World*, ed. by Willard Sperry, Harvard University Press. In reviewing this series in the *New York Times*, Dr. Niebuhr so thoroughly mistook my meaning that he accused me of advocating the trends in the culture that I was describing with regret (*New York Times: Book Review Section*, Sept. 2, 1945). Dr. Niebuhr very generously wrote correcting his misinterpretation when it was drawn to his attention (*New York Times*, Sept. 30, 1945).

put beyond their reach, will stir in their chairs restlessly, if they read at all, and wish this book was a radio so that they could turn to another station. My voice will inevitably have in it echoes of those very voices which drove them to the self-proclaimed search for personal happiness that they now pursue. They will be frightened lest I win them again, afraid that they are being got at, seduced with the false promise that if you are good, life will be meaningful, although they feel that every joy and every zest are being crushed out of their vigorous, sensuous love of life. Finally, some of those who would "throw this continent away," as far as they themselves are concerned—not traitors but eternal exiles in their own country—may feel particularly betrayed. This will be especially so if they have read my own or other anthropologists' accounts of other, far-away, quite different cultures, and sensed in those descriptions that there could have been ways of life in which they would not have been strangers, but at home. Then we seemed to be on their side, as we described, with every faithfulness we could muster, the way another people quite different from ourselves had structured the world. And now, now we betray them when we speak, with the same faithfulness to each value, of how we ourselves, as a whole people, have structured the world. Because however much they may repudiate this way of life in which they were born, regarding it as perhaps designed for others but not for themselves, some part of it is in their hearts. The very language is after all the language that their mothers spoke, and their mothers gave them at least the clear humanity that made rejection seem a possible and a dignified choice. And so they will say that it is right to describe other cultures, and attempt to reproduce faithfully the set of values that are embodied in other peoples, but if one does it for America, it is manipulative.

All of us, men, women and children, prophet and revolutionary, hedonist, cynic, and the disinherited, those who care about the tautness of the rope, steel our hearts against manipulation in different ways. Before we accept it within the borders of our own domain we must rename it as the will of God, or of the party, or as a natural drive that cannot be rejected. We fight it to the death when it comes from outside. But those of us who, recognizing the values of a democratic society, are wholly committed to a society that can grow and change, and within which other men will be left free to make new choices, are not only committed to resist manipulation, but are also committed not to manipulate. This is a difficult and an ever changing problem. It is not solved by declaring one's purposes openly, for those who partially share them will find them manipulative. It is not solved by rigorously refusing all efforts directed towards individuals and working only with cultural processes—though this is essential.[11] It is not solved by retaining a sense of humility and relative powerlessness as one works with cultural processes—though this is important.[12] Neither is it solved by naming that against which one fights, for naming any enemy as even the Devil himself gets one strange bedfellows and corrupts the clarity of one's position. It is not solved by linking oneself with wholeness, with wholeness for the world, because those who are not themselves whole may feel that the very statement of wholeness is itself an unfair seduction. Nor is it solved by outlining one's methods by saying: "See, you too can follow the pattern if you will only look. See, it is there in that child's toy on the floor, in the cartoon in the paper in your hand, in

[11] These were the points which I thought most important when I wrote the chapter "Are Democracy and Social Science Compatible Each with Each?" in *And Keep Your Powder Dry*, William Morrow, New York, 1942, pp. 176-92.

[12] Mead, Margaret, "Human Differences and World Order," in *World Order: Its Intellectual and Cultural Foundations*, ed. by F. Ernest Johnson, Institute for Religious Studies, New York, 1945; Chap. IV, pp. 40-51.

that last announcement over the radio, in the head-line being cried in the street." For then those who feel that they have been personally trapped by life will feel that this too is another plot, that the toy must have been put there to prove the point, the radio announcer was bribed, the head-line is a fake.[13]

The whole dilemma of knowledge and freedom can be solved, I believe, only by a climate of opinion in which those who work and those with whom they work, those who write and those who read, those who teach and those who are taught, those who cure and those who come for curing, learn to share together the belief that increased knowledge can indeed make men free, that one can fashion one's culture closer

[13] A careful warning against this situation was editorially deleted in spite of my very strong protest from an article on group-work (Mead, Margaret, "Group Living as a Part of Intergroup Education Workshops," *Journal of Educational Sociology*, Vol. 18 (1945), pp. 526-34):

"One further problem of leadership may be suggested. If the group are to trust the group experience, not seek for individual help from the leaders, but learn to place their reliance in thinking things through together, it is necessary for some member of the leadership team to weave together many apparently disparate items—an incident which occurs one day, a story an informant tells another day, a confusion which spoilt some point in the discussion, a sudden outburst of disagreement which at the time seemed inexplicable. These have to be picked up, the connection between them demonstrated, and thus a double purpose is served, learning is accelerated and the continuity of emotion is used constructively. . . . But there is one danger in this procedure. The more perfectly each opportunity is seized, the better the inter-relationship between a confusing incident on Monday, and a sudden slip of the tongue on Tuesday, is articulated, the more coherent the group behavior is likely to appear. Most of the members of an intercultural school are totally unused to regarding life systematically, to seeing cultural, group or individual behavior as embodying regularities which may be perceived and acted upon. Under these circumstances, those individuals among them who have the greatest anxieties to cover up their own discrepant emotions, may become frightened and begin to accuse the leaders of domination. Although it is the inexorability of the processes which the leader has been demonstrating which is really feared and resented, it is probable that the issue will be stated in more familiar terms, as a failure to 'follow the accepted practices of adult education,' for instance. It is doubtful whether treatment of such antagonisms on the symptomatic level, that is, appointing a committee or suggesting a discussion when that is what is asked for, is of very much use in such situations."

to the image of all human hearts, however different, without manipulation, without the power that kills, without the loss of innocence that deprives us of spontaneity. I furthermore believe that the social scientist who works alone or does the behest of only a single segment of his society—whether revolutionary, reactionary, reformer, government bureau or national organization, scientific discipline or propagandist cult—runs the risk of working destructively unless his premises are understood by all the others.[14] The others, those whom his work affects directly and those whose lives may be influenced by it fifty years from now, need not agree either with his methods or with his goals. But all whom his work affects need to understand the nature of his guiding belief. In my own case, the belief is that truth seen as the understanding of living people on this earth to-day can make those living people freer, and so better, human beings.

Put simply, the social scientist who believes in such a relationship between knowledge and freedom and the good life can work constructively only in a society that understands this position. It is not the efforts of some one with whose methods or goals one disagrees that do harm; the harm is done when those methods and those goals are misunderstood. Catholic and Protestant physicians have worked co-operatively within the medical profession, both committed to the Hippocratic oath, yet each referring to a different religious belief the terrible recurrent need for choice in childbirth between the life of the mother and the life of the child. As long as each understands the other, and believes in the relationship between the religious ethics and the medical ethics—in the sincerity of the Catholic insistence that you cannot take a life to save a life, even though this means *letting* the mother die, and in the sincerity of the Protestant

[14] Mead, Margaret, "Contemporary Anthropology" (abstract of a lecture delivered before the Royal Anthropological Institute, London, Oct. 5, 1943), *Man,* Vol. 45 (1944), pp. 48-49.

insistence that a life that has been partly lived must take precedence over a life that has not begun—the ethics of the whole society remains undamaged. But if Protestants fail to see the relationship of the Catholic belief to the central faith of the physicians' responsibility for life and interpret it instead as a move to make more Catholics, or the Catholics, in comparable misunderstanding, believe that the Protestants elect to *kill* the child, then the possibility of sound ethical co-operation between Catholics and Protestants is seriously endangered. A recognition of the essential difference between disagreeing with a position but respecting it because its basic premises are understood—although rejected—and rejecting it because it is not understood at all, thus provides some guidance to the way in which we use our emerging cultural understanding. With those who advocate murder there is no possibility of any compromise.

It is because I believe that enough of the American people are committed to the importance of freedom that comes by knowledge and understanding rather than from coercion, fixed authority, or final revelation, that I feel that it is justifiable in this country to use methods themselves keyed to such a belief. I also recognize that it is necessary that those who do not believe in this kind of open-ended freedom, but think some other solution is better for mankind, should understand the relationship between my approach and theirs. If they call this approach wrong for the right reasons, then a world in which understanding is being invoked is still a safe world for all those who live in it. Burning witches where witch and witch-hunters agree that witches are in league with the Devil makes a coherent world, in which the next generation retains a choice as to whether to be witches or not. It is when the gentle and the good, who love God after their fashion, are betrayed into burning as witches those who are not witches at all, but merely love God in another way, that the whole ethics of a culture is in danger. Within the group where one works, one has an equal obligation to make clear one's premises to those who agree and to those who disagree with one's goals and one's methods.

In Appendix III, I discuss some selected aspects of the rôles of men and women in our American culture.

The reader finds very little in my discussions about the deviations within our society that make it possible to speak of society itself as a patient. I do not plan to discuss the cultural meaning of prostitution and promiscuous homosexuality, venereal disease, acute alcoholism, and sex crimes. These all occur, and their form and frequency are indices of the maladjustment that exists in the United States, as in every modern society. They are symptoms of the state of society, just as the phobias and compulsions of the patient are symptoms. They are systematically related to the culture, and if I were giving a complete account of any primitive society, I would include a description of all the deviations. But although it may be fairly said, as Lawrence Frank has said, that "society is the patient," individual Americans reading a book about American society are not themselves patients voluntarily come to a consulting-room, where as they are treated they are also protected against insights that crowd too fast upon them. Just because the aberrations of the maladjusted are systematically related to the best behaviour of the well adjusted, discussion of these aspects of the culture may have undesirable effects in given contexts. If the reader is ever forced or manoeuvred into a recognition that a healthy trend in his own personality, the development of which he owes to his culture, is closely related to some behaviour that he does and must reject, then he may take little good from an analysis of the main trends in his culture. The healthy who owe their health to having successfully rejected solutions that would have made them unhealthy or dangerously deviant simply push the discussion away. Or they may act, for a few minutes, like the physician who after reading Freud went and rode on a bus-top and solemnly examined himself as to the nature of his homosexual feelings toward the other male passengers. He concluded he had none, and came down to attack vigorously Freud's insights, a process that retards rather than facilitates the growth of therapy. Possibly the particular conflicts that result in so many alcoholics are present in almost every American, but the non-alcoholic cannot afford to be too closely reminded of this, and for those whose cultural adjustment is precarious, such a discussion may even be dangerous. While no cultural exposition of why some Americans drink, or commit crimes, is likely to lead to the symptoms themselves, it may make it necessary for many to strengthen their moral defenses unnecessarily. And this in turn may mean that these particular readers, jeopardized in their own adjustment by a recognition that "there but for the grace of God go I," may, instead of holding out their hands in mercy, start on a destructive crusade against those whose strength has been less than their own. Most crusades have depended on mobilizing just such tendencies, but the responsible social scientist will pause before unleashing such activities.

Society is the patient. Those who have been in some way hurt or distorted give us many invaluable insights into what is wrong with it. But to cure society, we need also individuals who can use their strength in altering those cultural processes which lead towards disease. I believe that those people are able to use their strength better whose own cultural integration is left intact, at the same time that they are given a new insight into how the main regularities in culture look to a comparative anthropologist. The psychiatrist at a cocktail-party may see symptoms in his friends that disturb him, but he schools himself not to mention them unless one of them enters his consulting-room as a patient. Similarly, the anthropologist who looks at a modern society may see symptoms that are deeply disturbing, and indeed this may be a principal drive towards work. But I believe that such analysis should be reserved for the specialized work of competent professional groups with well-developed ethics of responsibility. When one writes in a way that is easily accessible to all interested citizens, I believe one should put oneself in those readers' place, and not force them either to accept or to reject interpretations the implications of which they would not have chosen to hear had they been fully aware of them.[15] We have certainly not reached a stage in social awareness when ordinarily functioning men and women can afford to carry about with them a knowledge of the cultural psychodynamics that unites them with psychopath and criminal, or those whose inability to bear the strains of the culture has driven them to alcoholism or illness as a defence against them. At the very moment of our acceptance of the fact of our common humanity and our responsibility as citizens to improve a world in which such casualties occur, we must also, at least as the world is organized to-day, push away such detailed knowledge. The problem of accepting an awareness of our conscious behaviour—the behaviour that Mother labelled good, and for which the teacher gave a prize, the behaviour for which we pray and work and ceaselessly struggle—is quite difficult enough.

[15] This is one of the most serious criticisms that can be levelled at the way in which the Kinsey report was permitted to become a best-seller. The sudden removal of a previously guaranteed reticence has left many young people singularly defenceless in just those areas where their desire to conform was protected by a lack of knowledge of the extent of non-conformity. See Mead, Margaret, "An Anthropologist Looks at the Report," in *Problems of Sexual Behavior: Proceedings of a Symposium on the First Published Report of a Series of Studies of Sex Phenomena by Prof. Alfred C. Kinsey, Wardell B. Pomeroy, and Clyde E. Martin*, American Social Hygiene Association, New York, 1948, pp. 58-69.

APPENDIX III

SOURCES AND EXPERIENCE IN OUR
AMERICAN CULTURE

ANTHROPOLOGISTS HAVE TRADITIONALLY GONE TO OTHER CUL-
tures to exercise their objectivity, and we have as yet a very
slightly developed ethics or rationale concerning the use of
anthropological training in looking at a culture of which
one is also a fully functioning member. Emotion, choice,
moral preferences, inevitably enter in to colour the comment
of an anthropologist on a contemporary culture, either his
own or one within which he has lived as a member of that
society. When an attempt is made to present the analysis in
very cool analytical terms, without obvious or articulate sub-
ject-weighting, as was done by Geoffrey Gorer in his recent
book, *The American People,* and as I have occasionally attempted to do, especially in "How Religion Has Fared in
the Melting Pot," [1] the reviews indicate that this often leads

[1] See below, page 462.

to misunderstanding. When one writes warmly or furiously, combining the ability to diagnose and analyze with the ability to be openly partisan, there are other dangers, which are discussed in Appendix II.

The best that can be done at present is to state very clearly the basis of what understanding one does possess, how it was obtained, from whom, for what purposes, and how conscious one is of the pitfalls. Perhaps the greatest annoyance the anthropologist has to face is from those who will grant his scientific right to analyze primitive cultures but who, either out of unwillingness to be classified with primitive peoples, which they feel is implied, or out of resistance to any sort of understanding, insist upon regarding any statement about our contemporary culture as a "brilliant intuitive insight"—a form of criticism that is also extended to books like Ruth Benedict's *The Chrysanthemum and the Sword*. This sort of criticism means that when two anthropologists using the same premises on the same data come independently to the same conclusion, or use with full knowledge a conclusion arrived at earlier by one of them, the public is hopelessly confused and wonders who got their insights from whom, a query that does not arise if two ethnologists agree that a given primitive people are patrilineal or practise transvestitism.

In a complex society one has both more and less material than one has in a primitive society. True, with a note-book and pencil I can get down a very large part of what a small non-literate group of people are able to carry in their memories. But I have no history, no written records, no moving pictures and comic strips and radio scripts, no opinion-polls and census-statistics and readers' guides, to supplement the knowledge that my collaborators and I can acquire in a few months of field-work. What we see and write down or photograph or transcribe is all we have. The homogeneity, the slow rate of change, the small population, the non-literacy, are all in our favour, and constitute a perfect laboratory for learning to see patterned regularity and for collecting contrasting materials on human learning. As a laboratory the primitive society is unsurpassed, and no research anthropologist would elect to work out theory in our own society as long as a suitable primitive society was available. On the other hand, applications of theory for the contemporary purposes of mankind include applications within our own society. For such applications, knowledge of our society of the same order—that is, analytical study of patterns, based on data collected by anthropological methods—is necessary. It is not yet possible to apply methods based on anthropological theory to societies on which our data are all based on the methods of collection and analysis used by other sciences, be they sociology, history, or psychology.

Therefore when we try to apply anthropological methods to contemporary cultures, we use the methods we have developed in primitive society. We study the behaviour of living people: what they say, how they act, what they eat, how they walk. We study the popular art, advertising, movies, films, radio, as well as the culturally localized versions of internationally shared fine arts. We use statistics and opinion-polls, census-reports and clinical records, to check our observations. The state of many of these hypotheses has been clearly outlined by Nathan Leites in "Psycho-Cultural Hypotheses about Political Acts." [2]

We necessarily work pretty much alone, which means that we use the methods one uses in the field, looking until one gets a regularity, then ceasing to record every instance of the regularity but watching continuously for exceptions, and following each observed exception through. It means that in order to say that a necktie is part of conventional male attire in the United States the anthropologist does not

[2] *World Politics*, Vol. I (1948), pp. 102-19.

count men in neckties, but having once observed the regular appearance of the necktie, he does notice carefully when, by whom, and under what circumstances neckties are not worn, jokes about neckties, suicides with neckties, girls who wear neckties, at what age little boys wear neckties, who can go without neckties, etc. Once one has identified a pattern, one carries with one a live awareness to any deviation from it, or any change within it, just as I sat in my house in Iatmul between two roads and as I worked watched the groups of people who went by. I did not stop to record each group, I did not even consciously name them over as they passed. But the minute there was a strange combination, a child with an adult who would not ordinarily care for it, two people who had not been on speaking terms, someone who was alleged to have gone on a trip or to be confined to the house by illness, I was on my feet, following up the clue. This is something which one normally does in one's own culture, unconsciously, all the time, and which is expressed in verdicts that there is "something wrong" in a friend's family, outside on the street, at the club, or in the office. The pattern of expected relationships, sounds, furniture arrangement, rate of laughing at a joke, time for meals, speed in answering the door-bell, are all there, and to them deviations are referred and judgments are made: "They've had bad news." "There must have been an accident." What every one does for ordinary social relationships between people and between people and things in his own environment, the anthropologist is trained to do, not merely in regard to social situations, but in regard to the whole culture. One's eye is alert to a change in the symbolism in advertising, to a new solution to a moral dilemma in a popular magazine-story, to the use of a word like "subjective" in a news-article in the *New York Times*, to the developing use of quotations in reporting ideologically divergent events, to new emphases in the displays for Mother's Day, or the appearance of candles in Easter decorations. The more articulate the hypotheses, the more systematic their formulation has been, the more such observations one can make in a day as one walks, reads, talks with people, sits in restaurants or subways or busses. And to the extent that one has learned to feel that observation of others is a friendly act, that it is pleasant to study others and pleasant to be studied, and that new insight carries new delight, this ceaseless, almost unconscious taking notes is as painless and rewarding an activity as watching for form and colour or the shape of face or a landscape is to a painter or a poet. It is analytical, but in a context so synthetic—because one is oneself wholly a part of the reality one is observing—that it carries with it none of the pain of dissection of something loved. Inevitably observations on such a complex pattern are backed by different amounts of data, but I have included no hypotheses in connection with which I have not weighed what relevant data there were available.

My own preparation for enjoying the rôle of cultural observer and analyst was exceptionally favourable. My grandmother was a sensitive and thoughtful teacher of little children, alert to every development in the child psychology of her day. She trained me not only to go out into the meadows and bring back a plant that she had described to me, but also to listen to the speech of my two younger sisters, to record it, and to understand it. My mother was one of the very early students of culture contact, and when I was still very small was completing her study of "Italian on the Land: A Study in Immigration" (*United States Bureau of Labor Bulletin,* 14:475-533, May 1907). I was weighed and measured as were the Italian children in the community in which we lived and in which my mother was making her study, and my first wedding was an Italian wedding, studied, appreciated, and enjoyed. As the household of a university professor anchored in an urban university,

we moved often, and each community was viewed critically
as to what it needed, how the schools could be improved,
etc. All of this I absorbed while I set myself to study changing patterns of run, sheepy, run or prisoner's base, to collect varieties of counting-out, or little-known folk-customs
like trade-lasts, behaviour when two people said the same
word, or when a couple walking hand in hand were parted
by a lamp-post or a tree. My cultural knowledge of and respect for social science were already developed and part
of me before, as a senior in college, I began to work under
Franz Boas and Ruth Benedict. For this reason, my observations on American culture go almost as far back as my ability
to use words. They have been sharpened and specialized
through the years, directed towards particular problems—
adolescence, teacher-training, nutrition, housing, community organization, psychosomatic formulations of disease,
conference organization, peculiarities of regional sub-cul-
tures, or efforts to establish communication with members
of other cultures. I have gained a great deal from working
closely on relevant problems with several social scientists
from other cultures: the late Kurt Lewin, Erik Homburger
Erikson, Gregory Bateson, Erwin Schuller, Nathan Leites.
The results of co-operative work with Geoffrey Gorer that
has extended over a twelve-year period have been published
in his *The American People* and my *And Keep Your Powder Dry,* and I have not attempted to indicate the details
of my indebtedness to his observations and analyses. During the last two years I have been fortunate in having many
industrious and perceptive students who have collected
and analyzed materials on comics, moving pictures, advertising, etc. directed towards amplifying some of our existing
hypotheses. And I have benefited by the massive studies
that teams of social scientists have made on aspects of American culture, especially *Middletown* and *Middletown in
Transition,* and the "Yankee City" series, the work of the

Chicago ecological school and of the Chicago Committee on Human Development.

As an illustration of the types of written sources that are available, I include here: 1. A bibliography of some significant work on American culture relevant to sex and to the family, which is not meant to be in any sense exhaustive but will suggest to the reader the sort of material that is available. In using such materials, it is my own practice to regard the Southeast and California as very deviant variants of American culture, and to include materials from these areas only after very careful scrutiny. 2. A list of the learning and working situations in the study or analysis or diagnosis, or attempted alteration, of American culture that I have worked in and through which I have had access to enormous varieties of unpublished material, case-histories, original questionnaire blanks, children's essays, collections of art-work, committee records, government reports, etc. 3. A list of my own publications on American culture. These do not, of course, make my present comments more reliable except as they do attest to persistent interest and attention. They do indicate chronology, and type of interest.

SOME MATERIALS ON AMERICAN CULTURE

Bateson, Gregory, "Morale and National Character," in *Civilian Morale, Second Yearbook of the Society for the Psychological Study of Social Issues*, ed. by Goodwin Watson, Houghton Mifflin, New York, 1942, pp. 71-91

Davis, Allison, and Dollard, John, *Children of Bondage*, American Council on Education, Washington, D.C., 1940

Davis, Allison, and Gardner, Burleigh and Mary, *Deep South*, University of Chicago Press, 1941

Dollard, John, *Caste and Class in a Southern Town*, Yale University Press, New Haven, 1937

Erikson, Erik H., "Ego Development and Historical Change," in *The Psychoanalytic Study of the Child*, ed. by Anna Freud et al., International Universities Press, New York, copyright 1947, Vol. 2, pp. 359-96

Gorer, Geoffrey, *The American People*, Norton, New York, 1948

Hicks, Granville, *Small Town*, Macmillan, New York, 1946

Hohman, L. B., and Schaffner, B., "The Sex Life of Unmarried Men," *American Journal of Sociology*, Vol. 52 (1947), pp. 501-07

Kinsey, Alfred C., Pomeroy, Wardell B., and Martin, Clyde E., *Sexual Behavior in the Human Male*, Saunders, Philadelphia, 1948

Kluckhohn, Clyde and Florence R., "American Culture: Generalized Orientations and Class Patterns," in *Conflicts of Power in Modern Culture* (1947 Symposium of Conference in Science, Philosophy and Religion), New York, 1947; Chap. IX, pp. 106-28

Lynd, Robert S. and Helen M., *Middletown*, Harcourt, Brace, New York, 1929

—— *Middletown in Transition*, Harcourt, Brace, New York, 1937

Myrdal, Gunnar, *The American Dilemma*, Harper, New York, 1941

Parsons, Talcott, "Certain Primary Sources and Patterns of Aggression in the Social Structure of the Western World," *Psychiatry*, Vol. 10 (1947), pp. 167-81

—— "Age and Sex in the Social Structure of the United States," *American Sociological Review*, Vol. 7 (1942), pp. 604-16

—— "The Kinship System of the Contemporary United States," *American Anthropologist*, Vol. 45 (1943), pp. 22-38

Powdermaker, Hortense, *After Freedom*, Viking Press, New York, 1939

Warner, William Lloyd, and Lunt, Paul, *The Social Life of a Modern Community*, Yale University Press, 1941 ("Yankee Town Series," Vol. 1)

—— *The Status System of a Modern Community*, Yale University Press, 1942 ("Yankee City Series," Vol. 2)

Warner, William Lloyd, and Strole, Leo, *The Social Systems of American Ethnic Groups*, Yale University Press, 1945 ("Yankee City Series," Vol. 3)

West, James, *Plainsville, U.S.A.*, Columbia University Press, New York, 1945

SITUATIONS INVOLVING LEARNING ABOUT OR ACCESS TO MATERIALS
ON AMERICAN CULTURE

1925-26—Field-work in American Samoa, involving work within a framework provided by the United States Navy

1939– —Teaching at Vassar College in child-development and in sociology, at New York University, Columbia University, and Teachers College, involving large numbers of student papers on their homes and experiences and attitudes, and analyses of selected aspects of American culture

1934—Hanover Seminar on Human Relations, intensive work with selected members of other disciplines on preparing a frame of reference and materials for American adolescents on the nature of culture, and particularly American culture

1934-35—Commission on the Study of Adolescence of the Progressive Education Association, involving reading and evaluating case-histories on adolescents from different environments

1940—Survey of the existing literature on psychosomatic medicine, including published case material and interpretations, mainly based on American patients

1942-45—Executive secretary and director of the research of the Committee on Food Habits of the National Research Council, 1942-45, which included a large number of qualitative attitude studies, travelling all over the United States, and working with local communities, a diagnostic study of six block plans that had developed in large cities, a study of the impact of Federal programs on small towns, and direction of detailed research on aspects of American attitudes towards nutrition (summarized with bibliography in *Bulletins* 108

460   MALE AND FEMALE

(1943) and 111 (1945) of the National Research Council:
The Problem of Changing Food Habits and *Manual for the
Study of Food Habits*)

1942-48—Lecturing to a great variety of American groups all over
the country, in which audience responses were carefully
attended to

1943—Lecturer and interpreter of American-British relations in
Britain under British Ministry of Information and American
Office of War Information in Britain

1945—Integration of the research in the Family Study, auspices
of New York Hospital and Community Service Society of
New York, on a multi-disciplinary approach to family-
oriented treatment of illness (Richardson, Henry B., *Patients Have Families*, Commonwealth Fund, New York, 1945)

MARGARET MEAD'S PUBLICATIONS ON AMERICAN CULTURE

1927—"Group Intelligence Tests and Linguistic Disability among
Italian Children," *School and Society,* Vol. 25, pp. 465-68

1928—*Coming of Age in Samoa* (see page 409), Chaps. XIII and
XIV, pp. 195-248

1929—"Broken Homes," *Nation,* Vol. 128, pp. 253-55

1930—*Growing Up in New Guinea* (see page 418), Chaps. XIII-
XVI, pp. 211-77

1931—"Standardized America vs. Romantic South Seas," *Scribner's
Magazine,* Vol. 90, pp. 486-91

1931—"The Meaning of Freedom in Education," *Progressive
Education,* Vol. 8, pp. 107-11

1935—"Sex and Achievement," *Forum,* Vol. 94, pp. 301-03

1936—"On the Institutionalized Rôle of Women and Character
Formation," *Zeitschrift für Sozialforschung,* Vol. V, pp. 69-75

1940—"Conflict of Cultures in America," *Proceedings of the 54th
Annual Convention of the Middle States Association of College and Secondary Schools and Affiliated Associations,* pp.
11-14

1941—"Administrative Contributions to Democratic Character

Formation at the Adolescent Level," *Journal of the Association of the Deans of Women,* Vol. 4, pp. 51-57

1941—(with Gregory Bateson) "Principles of Morale Building," *Journal of Educational Sociology,* Vol. 15, pp. 206-20

1941—"On Methods of Implementing a National Morale Program," *Applied Anthropology,* Vol. 1, pp. 20-24

1942—*And Keep Your Powder Dry,* William Morrow, New York
  English edition: *The American Character,* Penguin Books, London, 1944
  German edition: . . . *Und haltet euer Pulver trocken!* trans. by Josephine Ewers-Bumiller, Verlag Kurt Desch, München, 1946
  Italian edition: *Carattere degli Americani,* trans. by Lina Franchetti, Edizioni U, Firenze, 1946
  Austrian edition: . . . *Und halte dein Pulver trocken,* trans. by Augusta V. Bronner and Amadeus Grohmann, Phoenix Verlag, Wien, 1947

1942—"An Anthropologist Looks at the Teacher's Role," *Educational Method,* Vol. 21, pp. 219-23

1942—"Has the 'Middle Class' a Future?" *Survey Graphic,* Vol. 31, pp. 64-67, 95

1942—"Customs and Mores," *American Journal of Sociology,* Vol. 47, pp. 971-90

1943—"The Cultural Picture" (No. 1 in series of four papers, "The Modification of Pre-War Patterns," Pt. II of "Problems of a War Time Society"), *American Journal of Orthopsychiatry,* Vol. 13, pp. 596-99

1943—"Why We Americans Talk Big," *The Listener,* Vol. 30, p. 494 (British Broadcasting Co., London)

1943—"Can You Tell One American from Another?" *The Listener,* Vol. 30, p. 640

1944—*The American Troops and the British Community,* Hutchinson, London (pamphlet)

1944—"A GI View of Britain, *New York Times Magazine,* March 19, pp. 18-19, 34

1944—"Women's Social Position," *Journal of Educational Sociology*, Vol. 17, pp. 453-62

1944—"What Is a Date?" *Transatlantic*, No. 10, pp. 54, 57-60

1944—"It's Human Nature," *Education*, Vol. 65, pp. 228-38 (Murray Dyer and Margaret Mead program of series "Science at Work" of American School of the Air, Columbia Broadcasting System)

1945—"Wellesley School of Community Affairs," *Progressive Education*, Vol. 22, pp. 4-8

1945—"What's the Matter with the Family?" *Harper's Magazine*, Vol. 190, pp. 393-99

1945—"How Religion Has Fared in the Melting Pot," in *Religion and Our Racial Tensions*, Vol. III of *Religion in the Post-War World Series*, ed. by Willard Sperry, Harvard University Press; Chap. 4, pp. 61-81

1946—"The American People," in *The World's Peoples and How They Live*, Odhams Press, London, 1946, pp. 143-63

1946—"Cultural Aspects of Women's Vocational Problems in Post World War II," *Journal of Consulting Psychology*, Vol. 10, pp. 23-28

1946—"The Women in the War," in *While You Were Gone*, ed. by Jack Goodman, Simon and Schuster, New York, pp. 274-90

1946—"Trends in Personal Life," *New Republic*, Vol. 115, pp. pp. 346-48

1946—*"Pouvoirs de la femme: Quelques aspects du rôle des femmes aux Etats-Unis,"* *Esprit*, Paris, November, pp. 661-71

1946—"The Teacher's Place in America," *Journal of the American Association of University Women*, Vol. 40, pp. 3-5

1946—"What Women Want," *Fortune*, Vol. 34, pp. 172-75, 218, 220, 223-24

1947—"The Application of Anthropological Techniques to Cross-National Communication," *Transactions of the New York Academy of Sciences*, Ser. II, Vol. 9, pp. 133-52 (reprinted and expanded as "A Case History in Cross-National Communications," see below)

1947—"What Is Happening to the American Family?" *Journal of Social Casework*, Vol. 28, pp. 323-30

1947—(with Alex Bavelas) "The Dallas Convention and the Future of AAUW," *Journal of the American Association of University Women*, Vol. 41, pp. 23-26

1948—"Some Cultural Approaches to Communication Problems," in *The Communication of Ideas*, ed. by Lyman Bryson, Institute for Religious and Social Studies, New York, 1948; Chap. II, pp. 9-26

1948—"A Case History in Cross-National Communications," *ibid.*, Chap. XIII, pp. 209-29

1948—"The Contemporary American Family as an Anthropologist Sees It," *American Journal of Sociology*, Vol. 53, pp. 453-59

INDEX
of Personal Names

INDEX
of Subjects